Commentary on Husserl's *Ideas I*

Commentary on Husserl's *Ideas I*

Edited by
Andrea Staiti

DE GRUYTER

The hardcover edition of this book was published in 2015.

ISBN 978-3-11-043842-0
e-ISBN (PDF) 978-3-11-042909-1
e-ISBN (EPUB) 978-3-11-042912-1

Library of Congress Cataloging-in-Publication Data
A CIP catalog record for this book has been applied for at the Library of Congress.

Bibliographic information published by the Deutsche Nationalbibliothek
The Deutsche Nationalbibliothek lists this publication in the Deutsche Nationalbibliografie; detailed bibliographic data are available on the Internet at http://dnb.dnb.de.

© 2017 Walter de Gruyter GmbH, Berlin/Boston
Typesetting: Konrad Triltsch, Print und digitale Medien GmbH, Ochsenfurt
Printing and binding: CPI books GmbH, Leck
♾ Printed on acid-free paper
Printed in Germany

www.degruyter.com

Table of Contents

Essential bibliograpy–Husserl's *Ideen I* —— VII

Andrea Staiti
Introduction —— 1

John J. Drummond
"Who'd 'a thunk it?"
    Celebrating the centennial of Husserl's *Ideas I* —— 13

Claudio Majolino
***Individuum* and region of being: On the unifying principle of Husserl's "headless" ontology**
    Section I, chapter 1, *Fact and essence* —— 33

Robert Hanna
Transcendental normativity and the avatars of psychologism
    Section I, chapter 2, Naturalistic misconceptions —— 51

Andrea Staiti
The melody unheard: Husserl on the natural attitude and its discontinuation
    Section II, chapter 1, The thesis of the natural attitude and its suspension —— 69

Hanne Jacobs
From psychology to pure phenomenology
    Section II, chapter 2, Consciousness and natural actuality —— 95

Burt C. Hopkins
Phenomenologically pure, transcendental, and absolute consciousness
    Section II, chapter 3, The region of pure consciousness —— 119

Sebastian Luft
Laying bare the phenomenal field: The reductions as ways to pure consciousness
    Section II, chapter 4, The phenomenological reductions —— 133

James Dodd
Clarity, fiction, and description
  Section III, chapter 1, Methodological pre-considerations —— 159

Dan Zahavi
Phenomenology of reflection
  Section III, chapter 2, Universal structures of pure consciousness —— 177

Dermot Moran
Noetic moments, noematic correlates, and the stratified whole that is the *Erlebnis*
  Section III, chapter 3, Noesis and noema —— 195

Nicolas de Warren
Concepts without pedigree: The noema and neutrality modification
  Section III, chapter 4, On the problems of noetic-noematic structures —— 225

John J. Drummond
The Doctrine of the noema and the theory of reason
  Section IV, chapter 1, The noematic sense and the relation to the object —— 257

Daniel O. Dahlstrom
Reason and experience: The project of a phenomenology of reason
  Section IV, chapter 2, Phenomenology of reason —— 273

Sonja Rinofner-Kreidl
Husserl's analogical and teleological conception of reason
  Section IV, chapter 3, Levels of universality of the problems of a theory of reason —— 287

Appendix

Ben Martin
A Map of the noesis-noema correlation —— 329

Authors —— 337

Index —— 339

Essential bibliograpy—Husserl's *Ideen I*

German editions of *Ideen*

Husserl, Edmund (1913): „Ideen zu einer reinen Phänomenologie und phänomenologischen Philosophie". In: *Jahrbuch für Philosophie und phänomenologische Forschung* I, pp. 1–323.
Husserl, Edmund (1950): „Ideen zu einer reinen Phänomenologie und phänomenologischen Philosophie. Erstes Buch: Allgemeine Einführung in die reine Phänomenologie". In: *Husserliana*. Vol. III. The Hague: Nijhoff.
Husserl, Edumund (1976): „Ideen zu einer reinen Phänomenologie und phänomenologischen Philosophie. Erstes Buch: Allgemeine Einführung in die reine Phänomenologie". In: *Husserliana*. Vol. III/1. The Hague: Nijhoff.

English translations of *Ideen*

Husserl, Edmund (1931): *Ideas. General Introduction to Pure Phenomenology*. Translated by W. R. Boyce Gibson. London: Allen and Unwin.
Husserl, Edmund (1983): „Ideas Pertaining to a Pure Phenomenology and to a Phenomenological Philosophy. First Book: General Introduction to Pure Phenomenology". Translated by F. Kersten. In: *Collected Works*. Vol. II. The Hague: Nijhoff.
Husserl, Edmund (2014): *Ideas for a Pure Phenomenology and Phenomenological Philosophy*. Translated by D. Dahlstrom. Indianapolis: Hackett.

Translations of *Ideen* in other modern languages

(Chinese) Husserl, Edmund (1996): 纯粹现象学通论：纯粹现象学和现象学哲学的观念(第1卷). Beijing: 商务印书馆.
(French) Husserl, Edmund (1985): *Idées directrices pour une phénoménologie pure et une philosophie phénoménologique*. Paris: Gallimard.
(Italian) Husserl, Edmund (1965): *Idee per una fenomenologia pura e una filosofia fenomenologica. Libro primo: Introduzione generale alla fenomenologia pura*. Torino: Einaudi.
(Polish) Husserl, Edmund (1975): *Idee czystej fenomenologii i fenomenologicznej filozofii*. Tom 1. Warsaw: Wydawnictwo Naukowe PWN.
(Portuguese) Husserl, Edmund (2006): *Idéias para uma fenomenologia e para uma filosofìa fenomenológica: Introdução general à fenomenologia pura*. Aparecida, SP: Ideias & Letras.
(Romanian) Husserl, Edmund (2011): *Idei privitoare la o fenomenologie pură şi la o filozofie fenomenologică. Cartea întâi: Introducere generală în fenomenologia pură*. Bucharest: Humanitas.

(Russian) Husserl, Edmund (2008): Идеи к чистой феноменологии и феноменологической философии. Moscow: Academic Project.
(Spanish) Husserl, Edmund (2013): *Ideas relativas a una fenomenologìa pura y una filosofìa fenomenològica. Libro primero: Introducciòn general a la fenomenologìa pura.* Mexico: Instituto de investigaciones filosòficas/Fondo de cultura econòmica.

Monographs and edited volumes on *Ideen I*

Brainard, Marcus (2002): Belief and Its Neutralization. Husserl's System of Phenomenology in Ideas I. Albany: State University Of New York Press.
Grandjean, Antoine/Perreau, Laurent (Eds.) (2012): Husserl: La science des phénomènes. Paris: CNRS editions.
Embree, Lester/Nenon, Thomas (eds.) (2013), Husserl's Ideen. Dordrecht: Springer.
Kohák, Erazim (1978): Idea & experience: Edmund Husserl's project of phenomenology in Ideas I. Chicago: University of Chicago Press.
Lavigne, Jean-François (2009): Accéder au transcendental? Réduction et idéalisme transcendantal dans les Idées I de Husserl. Paris: Vrin.
Mancini, Roberto (2011): Visione e Verità: Un Viaggio Nella Fenomenologia Attraverso le Ideen I di Edmund Husserl. Assisi: Cittadella.
Ricœur, Paul (1996): A key to Husserl's Ideas I. Milwaukee: Marquette University Press.

Andrea Staiti
Introduction

In his essay *Structuralism in Modern Linguistics* Ernst Cassirer describes Husserl's early work against psychologism in the *Prolegomena zu einer reinen Logik* (1899) as having had "the effect of a great thunderstorm. It dispelled the clouds and clarified the whole intellectual atmosphere" (Cassirer 1945: 103). The same cannot be said for the first book of *Ideen*. If anything (and in keeping with Cassirer's meteorological metaphor), *Ideen* let the temperature in the intellectual atmosphere drop below the dew point and the clouds returned.

By the time *Ideen* appeared as the opening essay of the newly founded *Jahrbuch für Philosophie und phänomenologische Forschung* (1913), a certain equilibrium seemed to have been achieved in the demarcation of empirical and philosophical disciplines, partly thanks to Husserl's earlier work, as Cassirer recognizes. The view underlying such equilibrium was as follows: empirical disciplines work on various provinces of reality with the aid of various methodological devices (experimentation and induction for the natural sciences, description, deduction, and statistical projection for the human sciences)[1]; philosophical disciplines, on the contrary, do not have any direct purchase on empirical being, but only on issues of validity (*Geltung*) and justification. In this picture, conscious experience is the province of empirical psychology, while logic and the theory of knowledge (*Erkenntnistheorie*) are disciplines working in an *a priori* fashion on ideal objects and laws. On this model, accepted by virtually all Neo-Kantian philosophers of the time and rendered canonical by Husserl's *Prolegomena*, no claim about the empirical structure of human consciousness has a bearing on logic (or: the *a priori* structure of scientific theory), and, conversely, no claim about logic (or: the *a priori* structure of scientific theory) can function as a premise to determine how human consciousness actually works.

If the second volume of Husserl's *Logical Investigations* already entailed significant gestures toward a problematization of this dualistic view, *Ideen* seemed to disrupt it completely. First, in *Ideen* phenomenology is presented as a *new science*, and not simply as a new way of reflecting on the already existing sciences, as it would befit a philosophical discipline in accordance with the predominant Neo-Kantian model. In the introduction to *Ideen* Husserl claims that there is a

---

[1] On the deductive and statistical method of the human sciences see for instance Mill 1846: 547–549. My gratitude to Claudio Majolino for this reference.

field of research that has been hitherto overlooked and that phenomenology has uncovered for the first time. Furthermore, phenomenology is declared to be the fundamental science for philosophy (*Ideen* 3/3), that is, phenomenology is a discipline that carves out a new intellectual space, in which the traditional problems of philosophy can be posed in a new key and raised to an unprecedented level of scientific rigor. In this sense, *Ideen* is meant to actually carry out the research project originally presented in the famous Husserlian manifesto *Philosophy as a Rigorous Science,* published two years earlier (Husserl 1981). Last but not least, in *Ideen* phenomenology is introduced as an *eidetic* science, that is, one that does not study facts, but rather essences, on the basis of an operation labeled *Wesensschau* or eidetic intuition. Puzzlingly enough, however, Husserl defines the novel field of inquiry at issue with terms like 'consciousness' and 'experience', which, *pace* Husserl, does seem to lead the whole project back to the object-domain of psychology!

Unsurprisingly, commentators and reviewers raised a veritable welter of questions and critiques. How could phenomenology deal with consciousness and yet claim to have nothing to do with psychology (see Messer 1914)? How could Husserl argue that phenomenologists help themselves to the essential structures of consciousness without consulting the deliverances of empirical psychology (see Maier 1914)? How could Husserl use strongly realistic-sounding language in the characterization of the 'essences' grasped by phenomenology, and yet claim to remain uncommitted to any form of metaphysical Platonism (see Elsenhans 1915, pp. 240–250)? Moreover, how could a philosopher working in the Neo-Kantian age consider essential structures to be intuitively accessible rather than conceptually constructed (see Natorp 1917 and Rickert 1920, pp. 28–29)? And finally, how could Husserl, the most famous critic of psychologism, now argue that precisely a science of consciousness ought to deliver the ultimate foundations of philosophy (see Steinmann 1917)?

In addition to external criticism *Ideen* elicited a wave of internal criticism by the group of young phenomenologists who worked with Husserl in Göttingen and, famously, by Heidegger. As is well known, a cohort of young and brilliant philosophy students had moved to Göttingen after reading the *Logical Investigation*, attracted by what they considered a refreshing surge of realism in a time that they perceived as dominated by subjectivism and skeptical relativism. Many of them (including the Polish philosopher Roman Ingarden) were baffled upon reading what they considered their mentor's inexplicable turn to idealism in *Ideen*, where Husserl unabashedly declares that "an absolute reality is no more or less valid than a round square" (*Ideen* 102/120) and that an annihilation of the world would leave the being of consciousness intact (see *Ideen* 89/104). Heidegger, on his part, criticized the determination of the field of phenomenology in *Ideen* as an absolute region of pure being (see Heidegger 1985: § 11). In Heidegger's reconstruction, while the *Logical Investigations* brushed against the fundamental question of being through the discovery of so-called categorial intuition, *Ideen* is a step backward. According to Heidegger in *Ideen* Husserlian phenomenology re-positions itself within the horizon of modern metaphysics of presence, which construes being as being-present and therefore identifies consciousness as absolute self-presence and being in general. In so doing, the question about the being of consciousness (as a region of *being*) remains unaddressed. It is hard to underestimate the force of this criticism, whose influence on the reception of Husserl continues in the work of Jacques Derrida and other post-war continental philosophers.

On a brighter note, *Ideen* is the book that won to the cause of phenomenology an entire generation of French thinkers, including Jean-Paul Sartre, whose studies of the imagination are deeply indebted to Husserl's analysis of neutrality (see Sartre 2012), and Emmanuel Lévinas, whose first publication (and one of the very first essays on Husserl in French) was a review of *Ideen* (see Lévinas 1929 and De Warren 2010). While their reception was not free of criticism and it was largely influenced by the Heideggerian reading mentioned above, their interest in *Ideen* secured a prominent place for Husserl in the French philosophical community.

Finally, *Ideen* was the first book-length work by Husserl to be published in English translation (in 1931), thus giving a decisive, long-lasting imprint on the reception of phenomenology in the Anglophone world. Here *Ideen* came to prominence once again in the nineteen-eighties, when a group of American philosophers working in the analytic tradition (Dreyfus, Føllesdal, Smith, McIntyre) 'rediscovered' the concept of *noema* and endeavored to connect Husserlian phenomenology and Fregean semantics. While this endeavor proved fundamentally incorrect as an interpretation of Husserl, it had the merit to revive the philosophical debate on *Ideen* and it elicited a variety of responses by more specialized Husserlian scholars (Drummond, Mohanty, Sokolowski, Welton, Zahavi, to name but a few), who contributed a great deal to the clarification of the key notion of noema.

Today, a hundred years after its publication, *Ideen* remains a pivotal, yet enigmatic text, whose checkered reception history and intricate language make accurate and unbiased scholarly investigation especially necessary.

Husserl was fond of telling the anecdote that he wrote *Ideen* "freely and uninterruptedly, in a sort of trance" (Cairns 1976, p. 61)[2] in just six weeks. There is certainly some truth to the story. However, it has been amply demonstrated that *Ideen* condenses the research conducted over a decade in Husserl's manuscripts and lectures (see Schuhmann 1973, pp. 38–70). Following Karl Schuhmann's indication (Schuhmann 1973, p. 20) *Ideen* can be read as the effort to fulfill the task Husserl set for himself in a heartfelt personal note from 1906: "In the first place I mention the general problem which I must solve if I am able to call myself a philosopher. I mean: *A critique of reason*, a critique of logical and practical reason, of normative reason in general" (Husserl 1994, p. 493). The problem of reason thus haunts Husserl's relentless work in the following years and finds its first, albeit provisional, formulation precisely in the final sections of *Ideen*.

Unlike Kant's critique of reason, however, a *phenomenological* critique of reason (i.e., one committed to *Anschaulichkeit* and radical bracketing of extra-experiential assumptions) cannot take its bearings from the high-level phenomenon of judgment and articulate itself merely as an a priori *Erkenntnistheorie*. Judgment is but the theoretical culmination of a vast and complex array of low-level, but nonetheless rationally structured achievements in the life of subjectivity. Thus, as Husserl puts it in a later course of lectures, "a theory of knowledge without phenomenology of perception, recollection, imagination, and all the above mentioned acts of consciousness is nonsense" (Husserl 2002b, pp. 109–110). In this respect, it is particularly illuminating to learn that at first Husserl planned to publish in the first issue of the *Jahrbuch* an essay on the theory of judgment (see Schuhmann 1973, p. 39) and only changed his mind at the last minute, thereby announcing a change in title of the lecture course for the summer term of 1912: from *Urteilstheorie* to *Ausgewählte Grundprobleme der Phänomenologie*. The reason for this change, reported in the lecture manuscript, is illuminating and deserves full quotation:

> Subsequently I had some worries [*scil*. about publishing a work on the theory of judgment, AS]. Considering the inner entwinement of higher and lower configurations of consciousness [*Bewusstseinsgestaltungen*] and considering the fact that the moment of 'belief', of holding-for-actual [*Für-Wirklich-Haltung*] cuts across all levels of consciousness (including the lowest levels) and has to be clarified in each of these levels, if the key problem of the relation between belief and judgment has to be solved—considering all this, it is not possible to present a theory of judgment without presupposing advanced knowledge about certain general configurations of consciousness, which here I can only hint at with a few

---

[2] As Schuhmann 1973, p. 3 reports, Husserl told this anecdote also in letters to Arnold Metzger and Gustav Albrecht, and in conversations with the first English translator of *Ideen*, Boyce Gibson.

coarse titles such as: outer and inner perception, experiential and temporal consciousness, recollection, expectation, attention, grasp [*Erfassung*], explication, etc. The phenomenology of these configurations of consciousness, however, cannot at all be presupposed. With the exception of a few works written by my students, there is nothing serviceable on these matters in the existing literature. [...] Now, I presuppose nothing at all, and, accordingly, I change the title [*scil.* of these lectures, AS] into *Selected Basic Problems of Phenomenology* (Husserl in a lecture course from 1912, quoted in Schuhmann 1973, p. 41).

This decision makes perfect sense in light of the priority list Husserl developed six years earlier in the aforementioned personal notes, where the achievement of a theory of judgment is only ranked number four. Husserl's top priority was "a work on an *introduction to the critique of reason*, in particular theoretical reason" (Husserl 1994, p. 495). Arguably, Husserl's *Ideen* is precisely that work.

Husserl's *Ideen*, i.e., Husserl's introduction to the critique of reason, differs from Kant's idea of a critique of reason not only with respect to how such critique has to be conducted (that is: judgment loses its function as the guiding thread and is replaced by eidetic analyses of the various configurations of consciousness). In Husserl's hands, the very notion of reason undergoes a radical transformation. Husserl refuses to consider 'reason' a special faculty or a power that resides in the mind of specimens of *homo sapiens*. We do not have phenomenological access to 'minds' (whatever that is supposed to mean), let alone to special powers residing in them. All we have are concrete experiences (including their objective correlates) and the manifold ways in which experiences (including their objective correlates) relate to (or fail to relate to) and cohere with (or fail to cohere with) one another. The meaning of reason, then, has to be sought in the configurations that such intra-experiential relations take. 'Reason' for Husserl names a relation holding between certain acts of consciousness and their intuitive fulfillment (e.g. thinking that the cat is on the mat, and thereupon seeing the cat on the mat), such that 'rational consciousness' is nothing but consciousness that 'posits' (that is, that commits itself to believing that things are a certain way) only in the context of intuitive fulfillment (*Ideen* 271/318).[3] In this respect, Husserl's achievement in *Ideen* could be characterized as a thoroughgoing de-mentalization of reason.[4] As careful commentators have remarked, this move brings

---

3 For an excellent summary of the main aspects of Husserl's theory of reason see Michele Averchi's entry "*Vernunft*" in the *Husserl-Lexikon* (Averchi 2010).
4 Dominique Pradelle uses the phrase "de-subjectivization of the concept of reason" (Pradelle 2012, p. 254) to make essentially the same point. However, I find the phrase "de-mentalization" more fitting because Husserl's analysis of rational consciousness does not remove the subjectivity of reason, i.e., that fact that reason and unreason *qua* relations among conscious acts only

Husserl's theory of reason much closer to Ancient Greek and medieval *logos* than to early modern *ratiocinatio* (see Nenon 2009, p. 183).

In a genuine Aristotelian spirit, then, for Husserl reason is said in many ways, that is, reason takes on different forms and distinctive configurations depending on the ontological domain in which the rationally posited object (i.e. the object posited on the basis of an intuitively fulfilled intention) belongs.[5] Considering Husserl's suggested expansion of formal ontology so as to include the formal correlates of the activities of valuing and willing (whose a priori norms are treated in formal axiology and formal praxis)[6] (see *Ideen* 294/343), and the manifold material ontologies defined by various *Urgegenständlichkeiten*, such as "thing", "lived-experience", etc. (see *Ideen* 22/25 and Claudio Majolino's essay in this volume), a complete phenomenological critique of reason has to ramify in a variety of directions. As Thomas Nenon elegantly puts it: "The insight that there are multiple regions of objects means that reason, too, can and must take on multiple forms" (Nenon 2009, p. 194).

For precisely this reason, Husserl's *Ideen* was originally conceived as the opening act of a three-book systematic project. Drafts for the second and third book have been written around the same years as the first book. The original manuscripts were heavily edited and rearranged by Husserl's assistant Edith Stein, but Husserl never resolved to publish them. They are now available as *Ideen II* and *Ideen III* in volumes IV and V of *Husserliana*, respectively. Scholars at the Husserl Archive in Cologne have been working to pull out Husserl's original drafts from Stein's heavy-handed editing, and the *Urtexte* of *Ideen II* and

---

appear as such to a subject who is capable of taking a stand toward them. Husserl dispels *a certain way* of considering reason a subjective phenomenon, i.e., one that construes the subject as a self-enclosed reckoning machine separated from the world of things, as the word 'mind' implicitly suggests. In spite of the differing termini, Pradelle would probably agree on this point, since earlier in his essay he aptly distinguishes between "subjectivity" and "subjectivism" and argues that Husserl rejects only the latter (Pradelle 2012, p. 249).

5 Husserl is certainly Aristotelian 'in spirit', however, this should not be taken to mean that he is *literally* an Aristotelian. In a compelling paper Alfredo Ferrarin has recently challenged the interpretation of Husserl as an Aristotelian by highlighting several differences between Husserl and Aristotle (Ferrarin 2015, pp. 65–70). I take Husserl's Aristotelian spirit to be encapsulated by the following statement: the principles of the intelligibility of things do not stem from the unifying and ordering power of the mind but rather from the ontological specificity of the object-domains (regions) in which said things belong. For a more thorough discussion (and critique) of the Aristotelian reading of Husserl see Majolino 2006 and Majolino 2008.

6 As Sonja Rinofner-Kreidl shows in her contribution to this volume, this issue is actually complex, since it's unclear whether the correlates of axiological consciousness can be legitimately ascribed to the formal region or they should be considered as members of a material region, e.g. 'value'. For an informative discussion see Gérard 2004.

Ideen III are scheduled for publication in late 2015. In *Ideen II* Husserl's critique of reason addresses the material ontological domains of nature (further broken down into physical and psychophysical or animal nature) and *Geist*, whereas in *Ideas III* we find an outline of the philosophical result of the whole investigation, in that Husserl endeavors to determine the locus of phenomenology in relation to various empirical sciences and to the pre-scientific structures of reality.[7] Interestingly, the formal ontological side of the ramification of reason (i.e., the inclusion of the correlates of formal axiology and formal praxis in the formal region) remains unpursued and while Husserl in the following years continues to invoke the necessity to work out this side of the problematic of reason, this is a project he never developed beyond the preliminaries.

Despite the embeddedness of *Ideen* in a broader systematic project, however, it would be an overstatement to argue that it only makes sense in conjunction with the other two projected books. The insights achieved in *Ideen* are neither formal-ontological nor material-ontological (both material and formal ontologies are bracketed out by the *epoché*, as Husserl makes clear in *Ideen* 107–111/125–130). The essential structures of intentional object-relatedness and rationality unearthed in *Ideen can* be reinterpreted as material essences pertaining to a definite region of being (consciousness), but only *derivatively*, as it were. Considered *per se* these structures are *meta-regional*. They describe the very possibility of objectivity *qua* transcendence (i.e. as a dimension that can exert normative force on our thinking *while* still being accessible in thought), or what Nicolas De Warren aptly calls "the thinkability of the world" (De Warren 2009, p. 21), prior to its ramification in this or that material region, and certainly prior to its formalization in the domain of the formal region. Thus, in a well-defined sense, the meta-regional critique of reason carried out in the first book of *Ideen* is detachable from the infra-regional critiques of reason carried out in the second book, and whose specifically philosophical implications should have been spelled out in the third book.

According to a widely spread interpretation, the later Husserl repudiated the picture of phenomenology offered in *Ideen* and he turned to a more historical *cum* existential (and less ambitious) conception of the subject. If this were the case, then one might legitimately wonder whether toiling through the dense philosophical prose of *Ideen* is still worth the effort. In point of fact, however, Husserl never repudiated *Ideen*. Quite to the contrary, he continued to rely on the key

---

7 However, it is important to keep in mind that the text published as *Ideen III* was not written as a draft for the projected third book, but rather as a concluding section for the second book.

phenomenological insights achieved therein, such that his later work (so-called genetic phenomenology and the transcendental-historical narrative in *The Crisis of the European Sciences and Transcendental Phenomenology*) is bound to remain unintelligible for those with insufficient understanding of *Ideen*. This is not to gloss over the self-criticism Husserl constantly exercised on his earlier work. There are, indeed, critical remarks directed at *Ideen* from the nineteen-twenties onwards. However, if one scans through these remarks, it becomes apparent that Husserl's worries do not pertain to the *substance* of the book but only, so to speak, to its pedagogy, that is, to its effectiveness as an introduction to phenomenology. Thus, for instance, in his self-portrayal for a philosophical encyclopedia written in 1937 (less than one year before his death), Husserl still contends about *Ideen* that it is "the actual fundamental writing (*Grundschrift*) of constitutive phenomenology", where "this new science comes to a systematically grounded interpretation of its own distinctive meaning and of its function as first philosophy, as 'fundamental science of philosophy' in general" (Husserl 1989, p. 251).

By way of exemplification, let us briefly consider two short texts from Husserliana XXIX (Text 34: Husserl 1993, pp. 424–426) and Husserliana XXXIV (Appendix VII: Husserl 2002a, pp. 122–124), texts the editors chose to entitle (perhaps slightly overinterpreting their content): "Toward a critique of *Ideen*". In both texts Husserl deals with the difficult question concerning the way leading to transcendental phenomenology and he assesses the effectiveness of the path undertaken in his earlier work. A drawback he now sees in *Ideen* is the lack of a sufficiently developed "phenomenological psychology", that is, "a fully coherent psychology of the purely psychical (*seelisch*) interiority of the human being" (Husserl 2002a, p. 123). Such psychology, once developed, could serve as a basis for transcendental phenomenology. Starting off from phenomenological psychology, the change of attitude brought about by the transcendental reduction would not be perceived as a leap into an unknown territory, but rather as a reinterpretation of descriptive-eidetic results already secured in a psychological register. In this respect, the path undertaken in *Ideen* is somewhat odd in that the *epoché* is introduced abruptly, then temporarily set aside (chapters two and three in the second section are written from the standpoint of the natural attitude) and then reintroduced. All we have is, in Husserl's words, a "fragment" (*Bruchstück*) (Husserl 2002a, p. 124) of a fully developed phenomenological psychology. *Ideen* provides a "typical description (*Typik*) of the happenings (*Vorkommnisse*) of transcendental life" (Husserl 2002a, pp. 123–124), but the phenomenological description is not extended to include an analysis of the transcendental ego itself and of the world as the permanent correlate of its transcendental life. In other words, the perspective of genetic phenomenology in *Ideen* is missing.

The dissatisfaction Husserl voices in this short text is made even more explicit in a famous passage from the *Crisis of the European Sciences and Transcendental Phenomenology* and in the second short text mentioned above. Here is the passage from *Crisis:*

> I note in passing that the much shorter way to the transcendental epoché in my *Ideas toward a Pure Phenomenology and Phenomenological Philosophy* [...], has a great shortcoming: while it leads to the transcendental ego in one leap, as it were, it brings this ego into view as apparently empty of content, since there can be no preparatory explication; so one is at loss, at first, to know what has been gained by it, much less how, starting with this, a completely new sort of fundamental science, decisive for philosophy, has been attained. Hence also, the reception of my Ideas showed, it is all too easy right at the very beginning to fall back into the naïve-natural attitude—something that is very tempting in any case. (Husserl 1970, p. 155)

In the short text from 1937 Husserl provides a similar diagnosis with respect to his earlier book:

> In the *Ideen* I thought I could introduce the phenomenological reduction in one leap and in so doing lead the reader to the new working field of phenomenological philosophy, a field in which it is necessary to learn a new way of 'seeing', of 'experiencing' and correspondingly a new way of thinking [...]. In *Ideen* the point of departure was the 'natural concept of the world'. [...] We shall see that this life-world (taken in its total temporal breadth) is nothing but the historical world. Therefore it is palpable that a comprehensive systematic introduction to phenomenology begins and has to be carried out as a universal historical problem. If one introduces the *epoché* without the historical theme the problem of the lifeworld, viz., of universal history resurfaces. The introduction of *Ideen* does maintain its legitimacy, but now I consider the historical path more principled and more systematic (Husserl 1993, pp. 425–426).

Both texts express a reservation about introducing the *epoché* in one leap, that is, as the second text makes clear, without sufficiently setting the stage for its introduction. The 'preparatory explication' Husserl invokes has to be on the one hand a 'phenomenological psychology' (as explained above), and on the other a historical consideration that justifies the necessity to assume the transcendental-phenomenological attitude in order to put an end to the constant oscillations between skepticism and dogmatism, empiricism and rationalism, objectivism and idealism, etc. characterizing Western philosophical history.

Note that all these reservations do not pertain to the specific phenomenological analyses of *Ideen*, but only to its effectiveness as an introduction to phenomenology. It is telling, for instance, that in the short text from which the second quote above is taken Husserl actually begins his meditation with some remarks on the theory of neutrality modification developed in *Ideen* (§§ 109–112) and suggests to change the terminology into *as-if* (*Als-Ob*) modification (see Husserl 1993, pp. 424–425). This shows clearly that he still regards the insight into that particular modification of consciousness (achieved in *Ideen*) as valid, indeed, so valid as to deserve continuing attention and terminological refinement over twenty years later.

In sum, the take-home point of Husserl's later reappraisals of *Ideen* seems to be that the book does not work well (or at least not as well as Husserl originally thought) as an introduction to phenomenology. However, the phenomenological insights achieved in it are so crucial that they cannot be set aside or ignored. An *introduction* to phenomenology that bypasses or downplays *Ideen* would thus fail to be an introduction to *phenomenology*. It is in consideration of this point that the idea of a cooperative commentary on *Ideen* originally took shape. The present volume is meant to *enhance*, as it were, Husserl's text in order to make it work, if not well, then at least significantly better for introductory purposes. This commentary's ambition is to enable first-time readers of Husserl to tackle *Ideen* directly (that is: to go for the central insights of Husserlian phenomenology without having to first detour through one of the by now innumerable introductions and companions to phenomenology on the market), while still getting the necessary 'roadside guidance' in order to avoid the interpretative perils Husserl identifies in his later remarks. As such, this commentary is not meant to be read as a stand-alone collection of essays but to accompany the close, careful and (above all) patient reading of Husserl's *Ideen*, a masterpiece of twentieth century philosophy whose depth is recalcitrant to bullet point lists and the pyrotechnics of Power-Point slides characterizing much present-day philosophy, but still has a lot of valuable philosophical knowledge to offer in exchange for the appropriate amount of reading time.

Before concluding this introduction with some much-deserved acknowledgments, a few comments about the reference system are in order. The book uses the standard in-text author/date system throughout. The only exception is Husserl's *Ideen*, whose title is abbreviated and followed by the page number of the superb new translation by Daniel Dahlstrom (Hackett 2014) and the page number of the critical edition of *Ideen* in *Husserliana:* Vol. III/1 (Nijhoff 1976). So, for instance, *Ideen* 190/198 refers to page 190 in the Dahlstrom translation and page 198 in *Husserliana* III/1. In some cases, for more general references, the authors chose to indicate only the paragraph number; for example *Ideen* § 21 refers to paragraph 21. Unless otherwise indicated, all quotes from sources that are not available in English translation are the author's own translation. Quotes from sources available in English translation reference the page number of the English translation alone.

The essays included in this volume were originally presented during a three-day workshop on *Ideen* at Boston College on November 8th–10th 2013, held to commemorate the centennial of the book's publication. The workshop was made possible by a generous grant of the Institute for the Liberal Arts at Boston College, and by the additional funding received from the Philosophy Department, the Dean's Office and the Jesuit Institute at Boston College. I would like to thank Mary Crane, Arthur Madigan, David Quigley and Frank Kennedy for their constant support before, during, and after the event. A special word of thanks goes to Monetta Edwards at the Institute for the Liberal Arts for all the work she put into the organization of the workshop, which was flawless. Florian Spannagel helped me a great deal with the editing and formatting of the final manuscript. Last but not least, I am thankful to Michiel Klein-Swormink and Christopher Schirmer at De Gruyter for shepherding me wisely through the process of getting the volume published. The completion of the editorial work and the preparation of this introduction were made possible thanks to a research leave sponsored by the Alexander von Humboldt Stiftung.

Bibliography

Averchi, Michele (2010): "Vernunft". In: Gander, Hans-Helmuth (ed.), *Husserl Lexikon*. Darmstadt: WBG, pp. 298–300.
Cairns, Dorion (1976): *Conversations with Husserl and Fink*. The Hague: Nijhoff.
Cassirer, Ernst (1945): "Structuralism in Modern Linguistics". In: *Word* 1, pp. 97–120.
De Warren, Nicolas (2009): *The Promise of Time. Subjectivity in Transcendental Phenomenology*. Cambridge: Cambridge University Press.
De Warren, Nicolas (2010): "Emmanuel Lévinas and a Soliloquy of Light and Reason". In L. Embree/T. Nenon (Eds.), *Husserl's Ideen*. Dordrecht: Springer, pp. 265–282.
Elsenhans, Theodor (1915): "Phänomenologie, Psychologie, Erkenntnistheorie". In: *Kant Studien* 20, pp. 224–275.
Ferrarin, Alfredo (2015): "From the World to Philosophy, and Back". In: Bloechl, Jeffrey/De Warren, Nicolas (eds.), *Phenomenology in a New Key: Between Analysis and History. Essays in Honor of Richard Cobb-Stevens*. Dordrecht: Springer, pp. 63–92.
Gérard, Vincent (2004): "L'analogie entre l'éthique formelle et la logique formelle chez Husserl". In Centi, Beatrice/Gigliotti, Gianna (eds.), *Fenomenologia della ragion pratica: l'etica di Edmund Husserl*. Napoli: Bibliopolis, pp. 115–150.
Heidegger, Martin (1985) : *History of the Concept of Time. Prolegomena*. Bloomington : Indiana University Press
Husserl, Edmund (1970): *The Crisis of European Sciences and Transcendental Phenomenology. An Introduction to Phenomenological Philosophy*. Evanston: Northwestern University Press.

Husserl, Edumund (1976): "Ideen zu einer reinen Phänomenologie und phänomenologischen Philosophie. Erstes Buch: Allgemeine Einführung in die reine Phänomenologie". In: *Husserliana*. Vol. III/1. The Hague: Nijhoff.
Husserl, Edmund (1989): "Aufsätze und Vorträge (1922–1937)". In: *Husserliana*. Vol. XXVII. Dordrecht: Kluwer.
Husserl, Edmund (1993): "Die Krisis der Europäischen Wissenschaften und die transzendentale Phänomenologie: Ergänzungsband. Texte aus dem Nachlass 1934–1937". In *Husserliana*. Vol. XXIX. Dordrecht: Kluwer.
Husserl, Edmund (1994): "Early Writings in the Philosophy of Logic and Mathematics". In: *Collected Works*. Vol. V. Dordrecht: Kluwer.
Husserl, Edmund (2002a): "Zur phänomenologischen Reduktion. Texte aus dem Nachlass (1926–1935)". In: *Husserliana*. Vol. XXXIV. Dordrecht: Kluwer.
Husserl, Edmund (2002b): "Natur und Geist. Vorlesungen Sommersemester 1919". In: *Husserliana-Materialienbände*. Vol. IV. Dordrecht: Kluwer.
Husserl, Edmund (2014): *Ideas for a Pure Phenomenology and Phenomenological Philosophy*. Indianapolis: Hackett.
Lévinas, Emmanuel (1929): "Sur les 'Ideen' de M.E. Husserl". In: *Revue philosophique de la France et de l'Etranger* 107. No. 3–4, pp. 230–265.
Majolino, Claudio (2006): "Les 'essences' des recherches logiques". In: *Revue de métaphysique et de morale* 49. No. 1, pp. 89–112.
Majolino, Claudio (2008): "Husserl and the Vicissitudes of the Improper". In *The New Yearbook for Phenomenology and Phenomenological Philosophy* VIII, pp. 17–54.
Maier, Heinrich (1914): "Psychologie und Philosophie". In: Schuhmann, F. (ed.), *Bericht über den VI. Kongress für experimentelle Psychologie in Göttingen, vom 15.bis 18. April 1914)*. Leipzig: Johann Ambrosius Barth, pp. 93–99.
Messer, August (1914): "Husserls Phänomenologie in ihrem Verhältnis zur Psychologie (zweiter Aufsatz)". In: *Archiv für die gesamte Psychologie* 32, pp. 52–67.
Mill, John Stuart (1846): *A System of Logic, Ratiocinative and Inductive, Being a Connected View of the Principles of Evidence and the Methods of Scientific Investigation*. New York: Harper & Brothers.
Natorp, Paul (1917): "Husserls 'Ideen zu einer reinen Phänomenologie'." In: *Logos* 7, pp. 224–246.
Nenon, Thomas (2009): "Husserls antirationalistische Bestimmung der Vernunft". In: Pfeifer, Markus/Rapic, Smail (eds.), *Das Selbst und sein Anderes. Festschrift für Klaus Erich Kaehler*. Freiburg/Munich: Karl Alber, pp. 181–194.
Pradelle, Dominique (2012): "La doctrine phénoménologique de la raison: rationalités sans faculté rationelle". In: Grandjean, Antoine/Perreau, Laurent (eds.), *Husserl. Las science des phénomènes*. Paris: CNRS Editions, pp. 243–263.
Rickert, Heinrich (1920): *Die Philosophie des Lebens: Darstellung und Kritik der philosophischen Modeströmungen unserer Zeit*. Tübingen: Mohr Siebeck.
Sartre, Jean-Paul (2012): *The Imagination*. New York/London: Routledge.
Schuhmann, Karl (1973): *Die Dialektik der Phänomenologie II: Reine Phänomenologie und phänomenologische Philosophie. Historisch-analytische Monographie über Husserls "Ideen I"*. The Hague: Nijhoff.
Steinmann, Heinrich Gustav (1917): "Zur systematischen Stellung der Phänomenologie". In: *Archiv für die gesamte Psychologie* 36, pp. 391–422.

John J. Drummond
"Who'd 'a thunk it?"
Celebrating the centennial of Husserl's *Ideas I*

1.

The year 2013 marks the centennial of the publication of the first volume of Edmund Husserl's planned three-volume work *Ideas Pertaining to a Pure Phenomenology and to a Phenomenological Philosophy*[1]–a ghastly title, although it at least announces something of what is to come in the book. My title, by contrast, has the serious defect of telling you nothing at all about what I shall say in this paper. Instead, it expresses my more-than-mild surprise at the fact that we are celebrating this centennial at all. I say that because *Ideas I* was hardly well received in its own time. Indeed, many of the younger philosophers who formed the core of the Munich Circle and the Göttingen Philosophical Society and who had been attracted to phenomenology by what they saw as the ontological realism of Husserl's earlier *Logical Investigations* (1900–1901) broke with Husserl's version of phenomenology upon the publication of *Ideas I* because they believed that in it Husserl had lapsed into idealism.

Moreover, those philosophers, such as Martin Heidegger, Jean-Paul Sartre, and Maurice Merleau-Ponty, who developed in various ways phenomenological

---

[1] The first volume of the planned three-volume work was published in 1913 in Husserl's journal *Jahrbuch für Phänomenologie und phänomenologischen Forschung*. Identical editions were published in 1922 and 1928. It was first published in a critical edition in *Husserliana–Gesammelte Werke* in 1950 after having been edited by Walter Biemel. A revised critical edition, edited by Karl Schuhmann, appeared in 1976 (cf. Husserl 1976). It has been translated into English three times. The earliest translation was W. R. Boyce Gibson's, which appeared in 1931 (Husserl 1931). A translation by Fred Kersten appeared in 1983 (Husserl 1983), and one by Daniel Dahlstrom appeared in 2014 (Husserl 2014). The original plan was to follow *Ideas I* with a volume discussing the relations of phenomenology to the physical sciences of nature, to psychology and the human sciences, and, in another direction, to the foundations of the a priori sciences as a whole. The third volume was to discuss the idea of philosophy as a body of absolute knowledge. This plan was never realized. Instead the first part of the second volume dealing with the relation of phenomenology to the physical and human sciences became *Ideas II* (Husserl [1912–1928] 1952a), and the second part of the second volume concerned with the foundations of the a priori sciences as a whole became *Ideas III* (Husserl [1912–1928, 1952b). Neither volume was published during Husserl's lifetime.

accounts of experience more in line with Husserl's approach to philosophy, nevertheless distanced themselves from Husserl's avowedly transcendental version of phenomenology. Some of this distancing was undoubtedly overstatement designed to highlight the originality of the author's position, for it was originally Husserlian views that were developed by these authors. The tendency to discount the influence of one's predecessors–and sometimes simply to deny all but a negative influence–inaugurated what I take to be a series of patricides characteristic of what has come to be called "continental philosophy." From Heidegger to Derrida we find thinkers who incorporate many phenomenological ideas distancing themselves from Husserl and positioning their philosophies in opposition to his. Often this involved christening their philosophies with new names–"existentialism," "hermeneutics," "deconstruction," and so forth. These approaches were advertised as departures from phenomenology rather than as cooperative and constructive developments of it, and, to be fair, they were often viewed that way by more Husserlian phenomenologists themselves. Farther down the historical trail, post-phenomenological thinkers in the continental tradition often framed their thought in reaction to Husserl's transcendental phenomenology. All of this paints a picture of a phenomenological movement far from what Husserl had hoped–a community of like-minded scholars working on a common project to elucidate the intentional structures of our experience.

It is, however, not merely the at best ambiguous and at worst negative contemporary reception of *Ideas I* that motivates my surprise and wonder at this centennial celebration; it is also my own love-hate relationship with the work. What's not to like? Well, there are many things, but I shall mention only three. First, as the initial large-scale presentation of Husserl's transcendental thought it remains hesitant, tentative, and groping. Second, Husserl omits important themes he had already begun developing in his lecture courses and research notes–most notably, the themes of temporality and intersubjectivity, but also the details of his accounts of evaluative and volitional intentionality. This leads him to sidestep problems his research into these themes raises for some of the analyses he undertakes and some of the claims, both methodological and substantive, he makes in *Ideas I*. And it means that his phenomenology–even by the time he wrote *Ideas*–was already much more robust than is presented in the work itself. Third, the work is rife with ambiguities. In trying to distinguish phenomenology from what earlier philosophers have done, Husserl had to choose between using an inherited vocabulary in new ways and introducing a new, technical vocabulary. Husserl in many instances chose the latter course, but the technical terms he introduces are not as precisely defined and not as sufficiently disambiguated as they should be.

Having said that, I treasure the work nevertheless, and again I shall mention three reasons. First, what is undeniable in the historical reception of *Ideas* is the manner in which and the degree to which Husserl largely set the agenda for the development of philosophy in so-called continental philosophy. Second, *Ideas I* is in one sense the most comprehensive of Husserl's published works. It is the only work in which he presents the full range of his phenomenological project. Much of it remains a sketch, but important progress is made on many central issues. Third, it is in *Ideas I* that Husserl first develops his transcendental account of intentionality, which he calls the "main theme" (*Hauptthema*) of phenomenology (Husserl 2014, 168), an account that he, in turn, develops into a comprehensive theory of reason. And the unified theory of intentionality and reason is arguably the chief and unique contribution of *Ideas I*.

What is distinctive about the analysis of reason in *Ideas I* is that it encompasses the full breadth of theoretical, axiological, and practical reason. *Ideas I*, in brief, does the best job of all Husserl's works in indicating how transcendental philosophy underwrites a full-scale research program into the nature and structures of subjectivity as well as of the world disclosed in and by the cognitive, affective, and practical experiences of an intersubjective community of rational agents. Husserl's sense of the grounding relations between different kinds of experience allows for the formation of transcendental phenomenology as a unified, systematic philosophy without it turning into a quasi-Hegelian philosophical system.

Since *Ideas I* lays out the principles of these intentional structures and relations, it is not inappropriate to say that it is *the* central work in the development of Husserl's transcendental phenomenology. This by no means entails, however, that *Ideas I* is his *best* work. What it does mean is that there can be no reading of Husserl that does not take *Ideas I* into account or that fails to provide a unified interpretation of it. Nor can there be a reading of Husserl that fails to relate *Ideas I* both to the issues Husserl was treating elsewhere around the time he wrote this book and to his other works. But reading Husserl and reading *Ideas I* will not be my main theme today.

It is a historical fact that as philosophy came to be dominated by so-called analytic philosophy in the guise of logical positivism, phenomenology, at least in the United States, found a home in institutions that cared about questions of meaning and value, including Catholic institutions such as our host Boston College, my alma mater Georgetown, and my present employer Fordham. When I speak of meaning in this context, I do not simply mean propositional meaning but the kind of meaning that is at stake when we think that something *matters* to us, that it is important, of great value. Logical positivists thought that meaning was found only in scientific expressions that could be experimentally verified, and that questions about value, ethics, God, freedom, and about immortality were not genuinely philosophical questions. Phenomenology is the antithesis of this view; indeed, virtually the whole of the continental tradition follows Husserl in his rejection of naturalism. Analytic philosophy today, of course, is no longer characterized by this narrow–and self-defeating–positivism, and metaphysical and ethical issues are not only no longer relegated to the sphere of the meaningless but have returned to center stage.

What this suggests is that the distinction between so-called analytic philosophy and phenomenology–and, more broadly, so-called continental philosophy–is not, or at least need not be, what it once was. In the remainder of the paper I shall briefly discuss another central fact about *Ideas I* that more than justifies our celebration, namely, the continuing relevance and importance of phenomenology not only for the continental tradition which issued from it but for those philosophical sub-disciplines where phenomenology engages non-phenomenological strains of thought and advances philosophy as a whole. I shall sketch some of the ways in which phenomenology intersects and contributes to current debates in non-phenomenological circles. I shall develop this picture by considering debates about intentionality at some length, and then I shall mention briefly some other areas, but by no means all, where phenomenology contributes to current debates.

2.

Given Husserl's view of phenomenology as a descriptive science of consciousness, the most natural point of intersection between phenomenologists and the larger philosophical community is the philosophy of mind and, in particular, the problems of intentionality and consciousness (or self-awareness). Many of the debates regarding intentionality revolve around how to solve what appears to be a scandal for those who assert the thesis of intentionality. The scandal arises from what Bernard Bolzano calls "objectless presentations" (Bolzano 1837, p. 304) and from what David Woodruff Smith and Ronald McIntyre (1984, pp. 11–13) call the "existence-independence" of intentional relations. If, the argument goes, intentionality is a relation of directedness to an object, then intentionality must be a relation like no other. In ordinary, real relations the *relata* must exist in order for the relation to hold, but an intentional relation–an experience's directedness to an object–apparently holds even when one of the *relata* does not exist.

There are several ways that one might attempt to avert this scandal:

First, one could deny Brentano's claim that intentionality is the irreducible "mark of the mental" (Brentano [1874] 1995, p. 68) and explain the apparent intentionality of experience in physical terms. For those inclined to naturalism or physicalism, the scandal is thought to reveal what Quine (1960, p. 221) referred to as the "baselessness of intentional idioms and the emptiness of a science of intention".[2] This is the kind of move made by psychological behaviorism and by the more recent physicalist accounts of intentionality found in thinkers such as Jerry Fodor (1987) and Fred Dretske (1980). In the light of phenomenology's rejection of naturalism, I shall put aside this response to the scandal, although remarks below will give some indication of the kinds of arguments a phenomenologist–or even a non-reductive physicalist–might advance against naturalistic accounts of intentionality.

Second, one could claim that the intentional relation invariably holds between the experience and a special kind of object–the intentional object–that is ontologically distinct from the intended object. This is Brentano's own alternative. The intentional object is not the intended object, the worldly entity. It is instead the immanent object that intentionally 'exists-in' the experience itself (Brentano [1874] 1995, p. 68). It is, in other words, a special kind of psychological entity to which an existent worldly object might or might not correspond. Brentano's own students–Husserl, Kasimir Twardowski, and Alexius Meinong–all rejected this notion of an immanent objectivity on the grounds that it is a form of psychologism.

Third, in order to avoid psychologism, one could claim that since we sometimes intend objects that do not exist, the intentional object must be a special kind of object that is neither a psychological entity nor the intended, worldly object and that in some fashion mediates the relation between the experience and the intended, worldly object. This is the option that motivates the interpretations of Husserl's theory of intentionality offered by Dagfinn Føllesdal (1969) and Smith and McIntyre (1984). Føllesdal claims that the intentional content intrinsic to a particular mental event or state intending an object in a determinate manner is the instantiation of a meaning-species (Føllesdal 1969, p. 684) or, alternately, the token of something like a Peircean type (Føllesdal 1990, pp. 270–71). This claim is modeled on Husserl's account of expressions in the first of the *Logical Investigations* where Husserl argued that the real contents of the expressive experience instantiate an ideal meaning-species or semantic essence, and by virtue

---

[2] It is likely that Quine was less concerned with the reduction of accounts of intentional experience to physicalist explanations that the reduction of intensional logics to extensional logics or intensional contexts to extensional contexts.

of this instantiation of an intensional entity the act receives both its meaning and its reference to a worldly object, whether or not the referent exists. Smith and McIntyre, while also appealing to an intensional entity, differently relate it to the intended, worldly thing (Smith/McIntyre 1984, p. 80). Drawing upon the correlational, noesis-noema language of *Ideas I*, they argue that the intentional object, the noema or sense, is an abstract particular (Smith/McIntyre 1984, p. 123). The mental event or state *entertains* a sense, which sense *prescribes* a worldly thing or state of affairs (Smith/McIntyre 1984, p. 143). It is by virtue of the mediating sense that the intentional relation to the intended worldly thing, if it exists, is realized.

Both these interpretations are important alternatives in thinking about the scandal of intentionality and important interpretations of Husserl that have much in the texts to support them. I have argued elsewhere–and repeatedly– against these interpretations on both textual and philosophical grounds (see Drummond 1990; 1992; 2003; 2012). Let me say here only that neither interpretation can provide an adequate account of *intentional* relations. On both understandings it is the *intensional* entity which in the first instance refers us to the object, and the experience refers because it has an intensional entity as its intentional content. But this fails as an account of the *intentionality* of consciousness, for it transforms the fundamental datum of the intentionality of conscious experience into something no longer fundamental. It is, first and foremost, experiences that are intentional. The intensionality of sense flows from the intentionality of experiences directed to objects in a particular manner such that the sense (*Sinn*) of the object as grasped in that particular manner is transformed into the objective determination, i.e., the meaning (*Bedeutung*), of a physical entity (a set of marks or sounds) by some conventional rule establishing the connection between the object as presented in a certain way and the physical entity. Both Føllesdal's and Smith and McIntyre's interpretations stand this relation between intentions and intensions on its head.

Fourth, one could appeal to the notion of intension in another way. Discussions of intentionality in the analytic tradition can be traced back to Roderick Chisholm's pioneering work in his book *Perceiving: A Philosophical Study* (Chisholm 1957). Chisholm set his work explicitly in the Brentanian framework of the revival of intentionality, but he adopted a typically analytic methodology of getting at the structures of thought through the structures of language. Chisholm claims that our descriptions of psychological attitudes necessarily involve what he calls "intentional sentences." A sentence is intentional if and only if one of three conditions is satisfied. First, in the case of simple declarative sentences, the sentence is intentional if neither the existence nor the non-existence of the object of the psychological attitude is entailed by either the intentional sentence or its negation. Second, in the case of sentences where the object of the psychological attitude is named by a complete propositional clause, the sentence is intentional if neither the existence nor the non-existence of the state of affairs named by the propositional clause is entailed by the sentence or its negation. Third, a sentence is intentional if the substitution of a coextensive singular term for the object of the psychological attitude fails (Chisholm 1957, chap. 11).

Chisholm's view—and this can also be said of the views of Føllesdal and Smith and McIntyre—conceal the fact that intensionality and intentionality are two distinct notions with related but nevertheless separate paths of development. The medieval term *intentio* named the concept that is "before the mind" in thought. But this concept can be thought of in two ways: from the logical point of view, the concept is an abstraction, an abstract entity, and from the psychological point of view, the concept is a component of the state of mind. In Aquinas, for example, when I know an object, the form of that object is taken up into the mind; it informs the mind and is a component of the mind as knowing the object. That form, then, has an existence that is natural in the thing and intentional in the mind, and this pertains to the psychological view regarding concepts. The notion of *intentio* fell out of discussions of psychology, but persisted in logic. In particular, Leibniz reinterpreted the Port Royal logicians' distinction between the extension and comprehension of a term as one between the extension of a term (the set of beings to which the term refers) and the intension of the term (the logical content or meaning of the term). Crudely and hurriedly put, this Leibnizian distinction was then applied to languages or contexts within languages or to the logics which study those languages and contexts. This means that an extensional context came to be understood as one in which existential generalization and the substitutivity of co-referring terms apply, and an intensional context came to be understood as one in which those principles do not apply (cf. Crane 2001a, pp. 8–11). It is not difficult to see that in Chisholm the notion of an intensional context has been used to provide an account of the intentional sentences used in describing psychological attitudes. But this confuses the psychological and logical notions of *intentio*. It is inadequate to ground the definition of intentionality in the notion of an intensional context, for there are other intensional contexts, most notably modal contexts that are intensional but not intentional (Crane 2001a, pp. 12–13).

Fifth, one could claim, flying right in the face of the scandal, that the intentional and intended objects are not ontologically distinct at all. John Searle, for example, takes this view. Searle characterizes his view as a "non-ontological" approach to intentionality (Searle 1983, p. 16), since he is not concerned to bring intentional events and states under an ontological category. He is instead concerned to bring them, or rather their content, under appropriate logical categories. An intentional state, on Searle's view, combines an intentional or representational content and a psychological mode in a manner similar to a speech act's combining a propositional content and an illocutionary force (Searle 1983, p. 6). The intentional object is, for Searle, "just an object like any other" (Searle 1983, p. 16); it is just the intended, worldly thing–what the mental event or state is directed upon. To use Searle's example, "if Bill admires President Carter, then the intentional object of his admiration is President Carter, the actual man and not some shadowy intermediate entity between Bill and the man" (Searle 1983, p. 16–17). The intentional object of the mental event or state might not exist, but the mental event or state is still characterized by a representative or intentional content in a psychological mode. The fact that a mental event or state might be directed to a non-existent intentional object is no more puzzling for Searle than the fact that linguistic expressions fail to satisfy their conditions of satisfaction. There is no need to posit "an intermediate Meinongian entity or intentional object" (Searle 1983, p. 17) for mental events or states to be about. A mental event or state has an intentional content, but it is not *about* that content.

Sixth, one could claim that intentionality, while it appears to be a relation, is not actually a relation at all. Indeed, one could push Searle towards this position since it seems odd to claim that intentional objects are ordinary intended objects, that some intended objects do not exist, and that intentionality is a relation between mind and an ordinary, intended object. That would mean, at the least, that experiences intending non-existent objects have no intentional object at all, but are only an intentional content and a psychological mode. And if this is true for experiences intending non-existent objects, why would it not be true for all intentional experiences?

Tim Crane, who holds a view similar in some respects to Searle's, attacks Searle on this point. On Crane's view, Searle's claim that intentional objects are ordinary existing entities is absurd, since it entails that some ordinary existing entities do not exist (Crane 2001a, pp. 14–15; 2001b, p. 337). He illustrates the point with a trilemma (Crane 2001a, p. 23):

1. All thoughts are relations between thinkers and the things which they are about.
2. Relations entail the existence of their *relata*.
3. Some thoughts are about things which do not exist.

While any two of these propositions can be true at the same time, it is impossible for all three to be true together. Crane takes (3) to be obviously true, and while he considers arguments against (2), he rejects them. On this basis Crane concludes that "not all thoughts are relations between thinkers and the thing they are about" (Crane 2001a, p. 26).

Crane, like Føllesdal and Smith and McIntyre, rejects the identification of the intentional object with the intended, worldly entity. Crane, however, denies that we can articulate a substantial conception of an intentional object, i.e., a conception that identifies those general features or conditions that make something a particular kind of object, e.g., a material object or an abstract object (Crane 2001a, p. 15; 2001b, p. 341). He claims that intentional objects, by contrast, have no nature of their own (Crane 2001a, p. 16; 2001b, pp. 340, 342) and that we can have only a schematic conception of an intentional object (Crane 2001a, p. 15). A schematic conception does not require that all intentional objects have some feature(s) in common or satisfy some condition(s) in common. Instead a schematic conception simply identifies the *role* of an intentional object as the object of a directed mental event or state. This makes sense of the claim that an intentional object can not-exist, for while all instances of a substantial category of objects exist, this need not be true for instances of a schematic conception (Crane 2001a, p. 17). An intentional object, for Crane, is whatever is designated in the response to the question, what is that mental event or state about? To say that an intentional object does not exist is simply to say that the answer to the question has no referent (Crane 2001a, p. 25). An intentional object is not a real entity of the sort that can be a *relatum* in a relation.

Following Richard Cartwright (1960, p. 633), Crane distinguishes reference from aboutness, which, by contrast with reference, is not a real relation. It obtains even when the object does not exist. But this does not make it some kind of non-real or intentional relation; it is not a relation at all. When I say that mental event A is about O, "is about" operates as a dyadic predicate, but, as Crane notes, not every fact expressed by a polyadic predicate is a relation (Crane 2013, p. 9). The predicates "conspired to commit murder" and "are teammates" are clear examples of polyadic predicates that are not relational. The persons named as the logical subject of these predicates do not stand in a relation; they are jointly the compound subject of a polyadic predicate.

Crane postulates three kinds of intentional states: (i) propositional attitudes, (ii) relational intentional states, and (iii) object-directed, non-propositional, non-relational intentional states (Crane 2013, p. 90). A propositional attitude represents what the proposition *p* represents, but it does so without representing that *p* is the case (Crane 2013, p. 101); a relational intentional state occurs when the object of the state exists, for example, in a veridical perception; and an object-directed, non-propositional, non-relational intentional state occurs when a state not involving a proposition is directed to a non-existent object, for example, in thinking about the planet Vulcan. As long as the mental event or state has representational content, it will be directed to an intentional object whether or not that object exists. Representation is a basic notion, and an intentional object is what is represented by the mind. This is why the notions of intentionality and of intentional object are also, for Crane, basic notions (Crane 2013, p. 93).

Seventh (and finally!), there is another way in which one might continue to advance the claims both that intentionality *is* a relation and that the intentional and intended objects are *not* ontologically distinct. On this view, the intentional object just is the intended object but apprehended in an importantly different way, in the manner appropriate to philosophical reflection. I take it that this is both Husserl's view and the correct view.

We must disagree with Searle's and Crane's distinction between the intentional object and intentional content where the intentional content is thought to be an intrinsic part of the mental event or state. Husserl's phenomenological reduction–and anyone's consideration of an object just insofar as it is the object of experience–discloses the correlation between experience and its intended object just as intended (i.e., the intentional object). There is no content other than the sense that attaches to the intended object and that is disclosed and elucidated by a subject in a particular experience. Of course, in all cases–perceptions, judgments, beliefs, emotions, evaluations, desires, and so forth–the disclosed and elucidated sense necessarily involves some influence by the subject by virtue of the subject's experiential history, interests, commitments, and so forth. We should not, however, infer from the fact that the sense of the intended thing is *relative* to the subject of the experience in which the object is intended to the conclusion that the sense *belongs* to the intending experience itself (as a property or part). The intentional content is an aspect of the object rather than an intrinsic part of the mental event or state. But it is not quite extrinsic either, since it is an essential feature of the experience to be directed to an object.

Moreover, *contra* Føllesdal and Smith and McIntyre, there is no ontological distinction between two entities; there is instead an attitudinal difference introduced by our adoption of a reflective stance, a shift that brings about a focus on the sense of the intended object. The intended object reflected upon as having precisely this sense for the subject(s) of the mental event(s) or state(s) just is the intentional object. Crane, in fact, echoes this view, but to a different end, when he says, "The idea of an intentional object is a phenomenological idea […]. It is an idea which emerges in the process of reflecting on what mental life is like" (Crane 2001a, p. 17).

This is not to deny that experiences can be directed to non-existent objects–the fact that led Crane to conclude that "intentional states cannot, in general, be relations to their objects" (Crane 2004, p. 225). We can, however, understand the expression "in general" in two ways. On Crane's account, we cannot generalize from those experiences whose intentional objects do exist–and where, consequently, a real relation obtains between the thinker and the worldly entity that is the object of her thought–to an "in general" conclusion about intentional relationality. It is the universal scope of the resultant generalization that "intentional states are relations to their objects" that Crane denies. This is a distributive understanding of "in general" insofar as it is a claim about intentional events or states taken individually. The question at hand concerns whether individual experiences involve real relations to their intentional objects. The response is "not each one does," so intentionality is not "in general" a relation.

Contra Crane, we can understand "in general" to mean "as a whole"; we can understand "in general" collectively rather than distributively. On this understanding we can say that intentionality is a relation between mind "as a whole" and world. Every mental event or state "hooks onto the world," even though some mental events or states are directed at a particular object that does not exist. This recalls the sense of mind we find in Crane's view that "a minded creature is one which has a world" (Crane 2001a, p. 4) and in the conjunction of the first and third senses of the term "consciousness" in the fifth investigation (Husserl 2001, pp. 81–82; Husserl 1984, p. 356), a conjunction that yields the correlation "consciousness of the world." My claim is that the primary predication of intentionality is to mind "as a whole" rather than to particular mental events or states.

Minding as such is intentional. Minding as such transcends itself towards the world and relates itself to the existent world, and every instance of minding the world participates in this relation, albeit in different ways. Mind's self-transcending in relating itself to the world is an intentional relation that encompasses a real relation to the world. We must, however, avoid the fallacy of division and claim that every experience that makes up a mind relates itself to an existent entity in the world. Hence, *contra* Crane, I believe that intentionality is "in general" a relation to the world, although I agree with Crane that the intentional objects of some individual experiences exist while the intentional objects of other individual experiences do not.

I can here only sketch how this view addresses the problem of non-existent objects. Husserl claims that any single phase of experience or any single concrete experience has "inner horizons" that intentionally refer to other possible manifestations of the same object that can be generated in a continuing course of experience and "outer horizons" that refer to the "surroundings" (whether spatial, temporal, traditional, theoretical, and so forth) in which the object is displayed. The horizontal content forms part of the present experience's sense of the object.

The description of experiences intending non-existent objects appeals to the outer horizons of the experience in order to account for how the intention of the non-existent arises. Let us consider a case where error is involved. Suppose I (unknowingly) see a mirage. I see water ahead on the road and form the judgment, "There is water ahead on the road." The perception intends a non-existent puddle, and the judgment intends a non-existent state of affairs. My recognition that the judgment is incorrect depends upon my recognition that the presumed perceiving of the water is non-veridical or–better–that there is in fact no perception of water at all. The latter recognition depends upon my awareness that as I approach what I (mis)take to be water, the water gradually disappears from view. In an ordinary perception, however, we would expect the activity of approaching the object to motivate an enlargement of the perceived thing's appearance in the visual field. The disappearance of the water motivates instead the recognition that the perception is not genuinely a perception of water at all but is illusory. The appearance of the water can be partially explained by causal features of the environment in which the appearance occurs. But it is facts about the interplay of the experiencing, embodied subject and the world as experienced that reveal the non-existence of the intended object.

It is worth noting that perception encompasses a moment of belief in the existence of the perceived object. It is, in other words, part of the structure of perception that the intentional relation proper to a veridical perception encompasses a real relation between the perceiver and the perceived object. When the puddle on the road disappears from our visual field, we do not modify our perceptual sense of the object as we might when, in taking an article of clothing outdoors, we modify our sense of the clothing's color. Instead, we say that our experience was not perceptual at all; it was a different kind of experience–an illusion. While the puddle does not exist, the intentional relation involved in the illusory experience maintains a real relation to the world, albeit not the non-existent puddle. The complex perceptual sense 'water-on-the-road' underlying the judgment that there is water on the road unifies in a theme/background relation presentations of different things comprised by the intended state of affairs, things including both the water and the road, the latter of which is actual and belongs to the outer horizon of the presumptively seen water. Thereby reference to an existent within the world is achieved in the apparently objectless intention, an existent, however, which is other than the thematically intended thing and which is apprehended in a manner other than it actually exists, that is, as wet rather than dry.

In contrast with perception, other kinds of experience *require* that their objects be non-existent. I can, for example, hope that the Syrian civil war will end quickly. The Syrian war's ending is a non-existent state of affairs, and if it were not, hope would not be the appropriate emotion. Hope has an affective dimension that involves, at least, valuing some state of affairs, recognizing it as possible and desirable, and recognizing that it cannot be actualized solely through one's own power. Hope does not and cannot include a belief in the existence of that for which one hopes; otherwise, it would not be hope. Hope necessarily intends a non-existent object.

The intending of non-existent objects cannot be understood solely in terms of a psychological representational content but must include a reference to the outer horizons of that for which one hopes. We can, in other words, in the case of hope identify those factors in the course of an experiencing agent's experiences that motivate the hoping with its intentional content. The account of what motivates the hope must include some understanding of the world, an understanding that is compatible with thinking that that for which I hope is a real possibility. An "explanation" of the hope necessarily involves reference to the world as understood by myself and others. But this world that we understand is not a psychological or logical content other than the existent world itself.

In the case of fictional objects, whose intending involves exercises of the imagination, the sense of the fictional object presupposes and modifies an understanding of actual existents. To claim that Sherlock Holmes is more famous than any detective in the world, to use Crane's example, presupposes an awareness of how famous Sir Ian Blair–the former police commissioner of the Metropolitan Police Department of London–and a whole host of other detectives are. Even to imagine Pegasus as a mythological winged horse requires an acquaintance with actual horses and actual winged animals. The fictional object has its sense both in relation to and in contrast with the actual world; it presents a non-actualized possibility for the world.

The ideal presentation, too, is possible only insofar as we can construct a progression of actual and imagined cases of, say, a figure, a progression that approaches an ideal of exactness in, for example, the reproduction of angular or length relationships. The ideal presentation, in other words, has its foundation in the experience of the actual and imaginative variations thereof. It is ideal only in its union and contrast with that series of actualities and possibilities in the real world rather than in a fundamental separation from the real (Drummond 1995, pp. 34–41).

It is, then, not appeals to representational content that explain intending non-existent objects; it is appeals to the world as presented and to the ways in which the sense of the world motivates new experiences in the experiencing agent, whether those experiences are of existent or non-existent objects. The emphasis in phenomenology, in other words, is on the world as represented by an experiencing agent, on the world as an object of thought, rather than on the representational (representing) content as an aspect of a psychological experience.

This extended treatment of intentionality reveals something about the manner and the degree to which the analyses of intentionality found in *Ideas I* can and do engage central issues in contemporary philosophy that are approached from other, non-phenomenological philosophical perspectives. The phenomenological account fits right into a systematic range of alternative positions drawn from a broad range of philosophical perspectives. It can address these accounts, revealing both their weaknesses and its own strengths. To the extent that we believe that phenomenology has something to say to the larger philosophical world, we must do more to bring phenomenological analyses into such conversations with other approaches and other disciplines.

3.

1. In the space remaining to me, I want to point, more briefly, to some other areas in which such conversations are occurring or can occur. The first involves Husserl's notion of temporality and the notion of consciousness as self-awareness. Husserl's account of intentionality is at the same time an account of pre-reflective self-awareness. For example, in hearing a song, I am aware not only of the presently sounding note or notes, I am aware of the song as a whole. It is only in this way that I can, upon hearing the opening bars of a song and assuming I have heard the song before, immediately identify the song as a whole and anticipate what is to come as the song unfolds (and, indeed, recognize when a note is wrongly sung). This indicates both that the object of which I am aware has a temporal extent and that my experience too has a certain "stretch" to it such that I am aware in the present of notes of the song as presently sounding, as having elapsed, and as yet to come. I am also aware, however, of a beginning and end to my hearing the song. The song, say, intruded upon my thinking about what to write, and when the song ends or I "put it out of mind" and return to my writing, I am aware of a new experience. In hearing the song, I am aware, in other words, of my hearing as forming a temporally extended unity with its own position in the course of my experience. This reveals a double aspect to my self-awareness. I am aware of my occurrent experience as a temporal unity and I am aware of it as having its own temporal position in the flow of my experience.

On pain of infinite regress, the awareness of a temporally extended and unified experience cannot itself be temporally qualified; otherwise we need to account for our experience of this awareness as temporal. Hence, Husserl posits an experiencing consciousness that is not itself in time but which makes possible the awareness of both subjective and objective time. This consciousness, however, cannot simply be the awareness of the "now," for temporality would then simply be the accumulation of successive appearings of the "now." That would account only for the succession of consciousness and not our awareness of that succession. The occurrent phase of experience must be structured such that there is an intertwining of the consciousness of what has elapsed, the consciousness of what is now, and the consciousness of what is yet to come, without this consciousness being itself in time.

Husserl claims, therefore, that there must be a non-temporal consciousness that is the universal condition for the experience of both subjective and objective time. Husserl characterizes this non-temporal consciousness as the invariant, intentional *form* of a concrete consciousness that constitutes itself as a flow, i.e., that brings itself to appearance as temporal (Brough 1991, p. xix). And the self-awareness achieved by virtue of this form is the pre-reflective consciousness of *my* experiencing a world, of myself as a *subject* of experience (cf. Drummond 2006).

This view of self-awareness provides phenomenology with an important counter to many of the positions advanced in current debates about consciousness and self-awareness. The view engages and provides a basis for criticizing the following sorts of views: (1) those that limit self-awareness to a subsequent, reflective self-awareness (cf., e.g., Locke [1688] 1959); (2) higher-order thought (cf. Rosenthal 1986) and higher-order perception (cf. Armstrong, 1968) accounts of self-awareness; (3) accounts in which an unconscious experience is aware of an experience that is itself conscious (cf. Henrich 1971); (4) a dual-object, intrinsically reflexive account of self-awareness (cf. Brentano [1874] 1995; Kriegel 2003); and (5) accounts that view consciousness as a modality of experience (Smith 2004).

2. Another area in which phenomenology intersects non-phenomenological approaches is the philosophy of the emotions. This should not surprise since emotional experiences are especially good examples of experiences that are intentional and in which self-awareness and the first-person perspective characteristic of phenomenological reflection are especially vivid. There are broad areas of disagreement among phenomenologists about the intentional structures of the emotions, but one area of agreement is that intentional feelings and the emotions are thought to be disclosive of the value of things. There is, on the one hand, a position that we might call "phenomenological constructivism," found, for example, in Sartre ([1943] 1992) and Merleau-Ponty ([1945] 2012), that claims that values are created in exercises of freedom. This is not completely dissimilar from the kind of constructivism we find in someone like Christine

Korsgaard (1996), although Korsgaard offers a radically different account of normativity from those proffered by Sartre and Merleau-Ponty. There is also a kind of intuitionism that we find in Scheler ([1913–16] 1973) wherein values are directly encountered via the feelings, and this encounter is logically prior to and independent of the cognition of the bearer of the value. Finally, there are what we might call "blended" accounts in which the affective and cognitive dimensions are united, and this recalls both historical and contemporary views of the emotions as having cognitive content. These cognitivist phenomenological accounts, however, are "perceptual" in character, whereas many of the non-phenomenological accounts view the cognitive content of the emotions as beliefs or judgments (or quasi-judgments having a propositional content). The phenomenological positions are united, however, in rejecting the James-Lange view that the emotions are directed to bodily feelings or changes. This, for the phenomenologists, simply mischaracterizes the intentionality of the emotions.

Husserl, Heidegger, and Scheler all agree that our original, straightforward experience of things is already charged with affective and practical significance. Scheler, as we have already mentioned, believes that the affective sense is prior to the other moments. Heidegger, by contrast, thinks the affective and cognitive are equiprimordial, and he understands the cognitive dimension as a kind of practical cognition (Heidegger [1927] 2010). Husserl believes the cognitive act is foundational. He claims that the intentional feeling or emotive act in which I recognize the value of the thing is founded on an act that presents the object with its non-axiological properties (Husserl [1908–14] 1988, p. 252). Given, however, that he also believes the original experience is already a blend of cognitive, evaluative and practical moments, we best understand his claim about cognition as foundational as a claim about the logical relations between the cognitive (objectifying) sense and the affective sense (rather than a claim about acts). When the affective response is appropriate to the underlying non-axiological properties, the intentional feeling or emotion truthfully discloses the value of the thing (Drummond 2013).

We should be careful, however, to distinguish two senses in which the emotion may be appropriate. It may be that the case that the experience is *motivated* by the underlying non-axiological properties; hence, if someone possesses something that I lack and desire, experiencing envy would be an "appropriate" emotion to feel. This motivational appropriateness, however, does not entail that the axiological sense is justified or that it is morally correct to feel that emotion. It means only that there are motivating reasons to feel envy and that feeling it is intelligible in the light of the circumstances.

An emotion is appropriate in another sense when the axiological sense is *justified* by the underlying non-axiological features of the object. When the emotion is both appropriately motivated and justified, the emotion truthfully reveals the value of a thing or situation. Saying this, however, means that phenomenological discussions of the emotions relate not merely to non-phenomenological discussions in the philosophy of mind but to discussions of fitting-attitude and response-dependent theories of value.

3. It is correct, I believe, to maintain a separation between the emotive and the conative since not every emotion motivates desire and action. Nevertheless, many emotions–or, at least, emotional episodes–do incline us to action, and this inclination to action manifests itself as desire or aversion depending on the quality of the evaluation achieved in the emotional episode. However, it is not merely the case that the emotions can motivate desire and action. Husserl's notion of intentionality is itself teleological; empty intentions are ordered toward fulfillment. More importantly, the life of a rational agent is ordered toward a self-responsibility in which the agent accepts responsibility for her beliefs, her attitudes, and her actions. This self-responsibility is realized in the striving for evidence, for fulfillment, and it occurs in all the spheres of reason. This tendency toward self-responsibility creates a moral urgency at the center of Husserl's philosophy (Drummond 2010).

This teleological view also suggests a way to bring phenomenology into the conversation regarding normative ethical views in interesting ways. The teleological character of Husserl's view suggests a connection to virtue ethics, and there have been of late attempts in the literature to make this connection as well as to provide phenomenological accounts of individual virtues. At the same time, however, Husserl's emphasis on rationality, intersubjectivity, and empathy suggests a kind of universalizing approach to ethics more reminiscent of Kantian views, and there have been development along these lines as well (cf. Hermberg/Gyllenhammer 2013).

These last two discussions of the emotions and of ethics, brief as they are, connect the account of intentionality to Husserl's broad view of reason as comprising the theoretical, the axiological, and the practical. This account of reason, I have suggested, is the unique contribution of *Ideas I*, and the continuing development of views regarding the subject, the emotions, value, and ethics in phenomenologically inspired literature reveals perhaps the most important reason to celebrate the centennial of the publication of *Ideas I*. Its continuing influence is important not merely for Husserl studies, not merely for the development of phenomenology and not merely for the development of continental philosophy, but for the development of philosophy–full stop.

References

Armstrong, David Malet (1968): *A Materialist Theory of the Mind*. London: Routledge and Kegan Paul.
Bolzano, Bernard (1837): *Wissenschaftslehre. Versuch einer ausführlichen und größtenteils neuen Darstellung der Logik mit steter Rücksicht auf deren bisherige Bearbeiter, Band I*. Sulzbach: J.E. v. Seidel.
Brentano, Franz [1874] (1995): *Psychology from an Empirical Standpoint*. Trans. Rancurello, Antos C; Terrell, D.B.; and McAlister, Linda L., ed. McAlister, Linda L. New York: Humanities Press.
Brough, John B. (1991): "Translator's introduction". In: Husserl, Edmund: *On the Phenomenology of the Consciousness of Internal Time (1893–1917)*. Trans. John B. Brough. Dordrecht: Kluwer Academic Publishers.
Cartwright, Richard (1960): "Negative Existentials". In: *Journal of Philosophy* 57, pp. 629–639.
Chisholm, Roderick M. (1957): *Perceiving: A Philosophical Study*. Ithaca, N.Y.: Cornell University Press.
Crane, Tim (2001a): *Elements of Mind: An Introduction to the Philosophy of Mind*. Oxford: Oxford University Press.
Crane, Tim (2001b): "Intentional Objects". In: *Ratio* 14, pp. 336–349.
Crane, Tim (2004): "Summary of *Elements of Mind* and Replies to Critics." In: *Croatian Journal of Philosophy* 4, pp. 223–240.
Crane, Tim (2013): *The Objects of Thought*. Oxford: Oxford University Press.
Dretske, Fred I. (1980): "The Intentionality of Cognitive States". In: *Midwest Studies in Philosophy* 5, pp. 281–94.
Drummond, John J. (1990): *Husserlian Intentionality and Non-Foundational Realism: Noema and Object*. Dordrecht: Kluwer Academic Publishers.
Drummond, John J. (1992): "De-Ontologizing the Noema: An Abstract Consideration". In: Drummond, John J./Embree, Lester (Eds.): *Phenomenology of the Noema*. Dordrecht: Kluwer Academic Publishers, pp. 89–109.
Drummond, John J. (1995): "Synthesis, identity, and the a priori" In: *Recherches husserliennes* 4, pp. 27–51.
Drummond, John J. (2003): "The Structure of Intentionality". In: Welton, Donn (Ed.): *The New Husserl: A Critical Reader*. Bloomington: Indiana University Press, pp. 65–92.
Drummond, John J. (2006): "The Case(s) of (Self-)Awareness". In: Kriegel, Uriah/Williford, Kenneth (Eds.): *Self-Representational Approaches to Consciousness*. Cambridge, Mass.: The MIT Press, pp. 199–220.
Drummond, John J. (2010): "Self-Responsibility and Eudaimonia". In: Ierna, Carlo/Jacobs, Hanne/Mattens, Filip (Eds.): *Philosophy, Phenomenology, Sciences: Essays in Commemoration of Edmund Husserl*. Dordrecht: Springer, pp. 411–430.
Drummond, John J. (2012): "Intentionality without Representationalism". In: Zahavi, Dan (Ed.): *The Oxford Handbook of Contemporary Phenomenology*. Oxford: Oxford University Press, pp. 115–133.
Drummond, John J. (2013): "The Intentional Structure of Emotions". In: *Logical Analysis and the History of Philosophy/Philosophiegeschichte und logische Analyse* 16, pp. 244–263.

Fodor, Jerry A. (1987): *Psychosemantics: The Problem of Meaning in the Philosophy of Mind*. Cambridge, Mass.: The MIT Press.
Føllesdal, Dagfinn (1969): "Husserl's Notion of Noema". In: *The Journal of Philosophy* 66, pp. 680–87.
Føllesdal, Dagfinn (1990): "Noema and Meaning in Husserl" In: *Philosophy and Phenomenological Research* 50 (Supplement), pp. 263–271.
Heidegger, Martin [1927] (2010): *Being and Time*. Trans. Stambaugh, Joan/Schmidt, Denis J. Albany, N.Y.: State University of New York Press.
Henrich, Dieter (1971): "Self-Consciousness: A Critical Introduction to a Theory". In: *Man and World* 4, pp. 3–28.
Hermberg, Kevin/Gyllenhammer, Paul (Eds.) (2013): *Phenomenology and Virtue Ethics*. London and New York: Bloomsbury.
Husserl, Edmund (1931): *Ideas: General Introduction to Pure Phenomenology*. Trans. Gibson, W. R. Boyce. London, G. Allen & Unwin.
Husserl, Edmund [1912–1928] (1952a): "Ideen zu einer reinen Phänomenologie und phänomenologischen Philosophie. Zweites Buch: Phänomenologische Untersuchungen zur Konstitution." In: *Husserliana*. Vol. IV. The Hague: Martinus Nijhoff.
Husserl, Edmund [1912–1928] (1952b): "Ideen zu einer reinen Phänomenologie und phänomenologischen Philosophie. Drittes Buch: Die Phänomenologie und die Fundamente der Wissenschaften." In: *Husserliana*. Vol. V. The Hague: Martinus Nijhoff.
Husserl, Edmund [1913] (1976): "Ideen zu einer reinen Phänomenologie und phänomenologischen Philosophie. Erstes Buch: Allgemeine Einführung in die reine Phänomenologie." In: *Husserliana*. Vol. III/1. The Hague: Martinus Nijhoff.
Husserl, Edmund (1983): "Ideas Pertaining to a Pure Phenomenology and to a Phenomenological Philosophy: First Book: General Introduction to a Pure Phenomenology". Trans. F. Kersten. In: *Collected Works*. Vol. II. The Hague: Martinus Nijhoff.
Husserl, Edmund [1900–1901/1913] (1984): "Logische Untersuchungen. Zweiter Band: Untersuchungen zur Phänomenologie und Theorie der Erkenntnis". In: *Husserliana*. Vol. XIX. The Hague: Nijhoff.
Husserl, Edmund [1908–14] (1988): "Vorlesungen über Ethik und Wertlehre 1908–1914". In: *Husserliana*. Vol. XXVIII. Dordrecht: Kluwer.
Husserl, Edmund (2001): *Logical Investigations*. Vol. II. London/New York: Routledge.
Husserl, Edmund (2014): *Ideas for a Pure Phenomenology and Phenomenological Philosophy. First Book: General Introduction to Pure Phenomenology*. Trans. Daniel O. Dahlstrom. Indianapolis: Hackett Publishing Company.
Korsgaard, Christine (1996): *The Sources of Normativity*. Cambridge: Cambridge University Press.
Kriegel, Uriah (2003): "Consciousness As Sensory Quality and As Implicit Self-Awareness". In: *Phenomenology and the Cognitive Sciences* 2, pp. 1–26.
Locke, John [1688] (1959): *An Essay Concerning Human Understanding*. 2 vols. Mineola, N.Y.: Dover Publications.
Merleau-Ponty, Maurice [1945] (2012): *Phenomenology of Perception*. Trans. Landes, Donald A. New York: Routledge.
Quine, Willard Van Orman (1960): *Word and Object*. Cambridge, Mass.: The MIT Press.

Rosenthal, David M. (1986): "Two Concepts of Consciousness". In: *Philosophical Studies* 49, pp. 329–359.
Sartre, Jean-Paul [1943] (1992): *Being and Nothingness*. Trans. Barnes, Hazel E. New York: Washington Square Press.
Scheler, Max [1913–16] (1973): *Formalism in Ethics and Non-Formal Ethics of Values*. Trans. Frings, Manfred S./Funk, Roger L. Evanston, Ill.: Northwestern University Press.
Searle, John (1983): *Intentionality*. Cambridge: Cambridge University Press.
Smith, David Woodruff (2004): *Mind World: Essays in Phenomenology and Ontology*. Cambridge: Cambridge University Press.
Smith, David Woodruff and McIntyre, Ronald (1984): *Husserl and Intentionality. A Study of Mind, Meaning, and Language*. Dordrecht: D. Reidel.

Claudio Majolino
Individuum and region of being: On the unifying principle of Husserl's "headless" ontology

Section I, chapter 1, *Fact and essence*

The sign above Plato's *Academy* allegedly read: "Let no one ignorant of geometry enter herein". The sign put above the entrance of Husserl's "pure phenomenology and phenomenological philosophy" reads instead: "*Fact and Essence*–or: let no one ignorant of formal ontology enter herein". The legend of Plato's sign doesn't relate whether anyone was actually prevented from joining his school, let alone understanding his philosophy; but we *do* know for sure that Husserl's warning worked all too well–for a whole host of readers, in the last century, have definitively given up joining the club of the "descriptive scientists of transcendentally reduced pure *Erlebnisse*"[1] because of the abstruse ontological subtleties gathered in this opening chapter. As for the others, both friends and foes of *Ideas I* have mostly moved into transcendental phenomenology from a backward entrance, as it were. Most analytically inclined philosophers have found in *Fact and Essence* something like Husserl's answer to Quine's question "What is there?" and started drawing long lists of Husserl's purported "categories" of entities[2]; as for many of the continental bent, they couldn't find any answer to Heidegger's question of Being, and concluded that Husserl surreptitiously equates being with being an object[3]. In both cases, Husserl's sign has been either misunderstood or ignored.

Since the content of the first sixteen paragraphs of *Ideas I* is indeed extremely dense and technical, I would like to proceed as follows. While trying to spell out its main tenets as precisely as possible, I will end up claiming that, buried in the mass of formal ontological distinctions, this chapter lays out what is probably one of the most important concepts of Husserl's phenomenology, i.e. the concept of *Individuum*. A concept whose proper understanding may shed some new

---

[1] As is well known, Husserl defines phenomenology in § 75 of *Ideas I* as the "descriptive eidetic doctrine of transcendentally pure lived experiences as viewed in the phenomenological attitude." (*Ideen* 134/139)
[2] See for instance David W. Smith's attempt to draw a Husserlian list of categories of entities in Smith 2010.
[3] The most explicit version of Heidegger's claim can be found in the Zähringen seminar. See Heidegger 2003, pp. 64–84.

light on the actual intertwinement between Husserl's transcendental project, its formal ontological prolegomena and their metaphysical import.

1. Two accounts of individuality?

At least at first sight Husserl does not seem to use consistently the term "Individuum", for two different–although clearly not unrelated–accounts of individuality can be singled out in his work.

(1) In very general terms Husserl often characterizes, quite unsurprisingly, an individual as something having:

> (...) an actual identity with itself and difference from any other, an actual individual that is in itself and has its own difference with respect to everything else, even to something (*a priori* always possible) entirely similar to it. (Husserl 2001a, p. 330)

This first use of the term echoes almost literally Aquinas's quite traditional definition of individuality:"Individuum non est divisum in se, et a quolibet ente divisum"[4] and, as we learn in the 2nd *Logical Investigation*, it applies to both concrete independent objects (like physical bodies or *Erlebnisse*) and abstract non-independent object-moments (like sounds and colors, or act-quality and act-matter)[5].

(2) But in *Ideas I* there is also another, more complex and less usual, account of individuality–a formal ontological one:

> An essence that is dependent is called an *abstractum*; an essence that is absolutely independent is called a *concretum*. A "this-here" whose material essence is a *concretum* is called an *individuum* (*Ideen* 30/35, translation modified).

---

[4] See also Aquinas, *Summa Theologiæ*, I q. 29 a. 4 co.: "Individuum autem est quod est in se indistinctum, ab aliis vero distinctum". Varieties of such a definition can be found in Suarez ("Individuum est indivisum a se et divisum a quolibet") as well as in several scholastic texts (such as Suarez 1982). More generally, on the topic of individuation in medieval philosophy see Gracia 1984.

[5] In Husserl's examples, objects denoted by proper names such as "Hans" or "Berlin" (Husserl 2001c, p. 199), definite descriptions like "the greatest of German statesmen" (Husserl 2001b, p. 231) and indexical expressions having the form "*this x*" (Husserl 2001c, pp. 198–199) are dubbed as "individual objects" (*individuelle Gegenstände*). But this also holds whenever the argument of *x* is a non-indipendent *abstractum* like *this* (individual) lived experience (Husserl 2001b, p. 231) or *that* (individual) red moment (Husserl 2001b, p. 239). Husserl extensively deals with abstract particulars especially in the first chapter (*Die allgemeinen Gegenstände und das Allgemeinheitsbewußtsein*) of the 2nd *Logical Investigation* (Husserl 2001b, pp. 239–247).

Contrary to the first informal use, this second definition seems clearly to imply that, somehow, only *concreta* are, strictly speaking, individuals–disavowing *de jure* Husserl's *de facto* talk of "abstract individuals" (see also Husserl 2012, p. 106). But why should Husserl want "abstract individuals" not to be "individuals" in a formal ontological sense? How are these two accounts of individuality actually articulated? Besides, one should hasten to add that in the formal ontological definition of "individuum", the terms "concrete" and "abstract" do not refer to objects in general but to "essences" and more precisely to "material essences". Thus, in order to understand properly the second account we have to know first (1) what an *essence* is, (2) what a *material* essence is and (3) what it means for a material essence to be *concrete* or abstract. And there is more, for a new term appears here: the *"this-here"* (*Dies-da*)–a term that, following Husserl's informal talk of individuality in the *Logical Investigations* one might have been tempted to take, naively, as a synonym of "individual". In *Ideas I* the naïve concept of individuality seems instead to split into two different concepts: *Individuum* and *Dies-da* (the latter being somehow more elementary than the former, for it enters into its definition); and a *Dies-da* is what Husserl also calls–explicitly using an Aristotelian term of which we will have to measure all the importance–a *tode ti* (*Ideen* 29/34). But what is a *tode ti* then and how are *Individuum* and *tode ti* exactly related?

Before we try to respond to these questions a few remarks about their relevance are in order. The importance of such notions cannot be underestimated for at least two reasons. (1) After having introduced the formal-ontological definition of *Individuum*, Husserl claims that of all object categories, that of individuality is somehow unique:

> the *Individuum* is the primitive object [*Urgegenstand*] required from a purely logical point of view, the logically absolute, to which all logical "variations" refer back (*zurückweisen*) (*Ideen* 30/35).

Now, Husserl never employs the word *Urgegenstand* for the most general notion of its formal ontology, i. e. the *Etwas überhaupt*–he saves it for the *Individuum*. Understanding the concept of "individual" is thus identifying what Husserl takes to be as the *Urgegenstand*, the most fundamental concept of logic and ontology. (2) As for the second reason, it has to be stressed that, without a precise account of the *Urgegenständlichkeit* of the individual, there is little chance to understand properly Husserl's notion of "ontological region"–a concept too often conflated with that of higher material genus or *summum genus*. In fact, as Husserl clearly states in § 15, the notion of region can be "rigorously analytically" defined *only* by understanding the individual as "a *tode ti* whose material essence is a *concretum*". As Husserl puts it:

> With the concepts '*individuum*' and '*concretum*', the scientific-theoretical, fundamental concept of a *region* is also defined in a rigorously 'analytic' manner. Region is nothing other than the *entire, supreme generic unity belonging to a concretum*, i.e., the essentially united connection of the supreme genera that pertain to the lowest differences within the *concretum*. The eidetic scope of the region encompasses the ideal totality of concretely unified complexes of differences of these genera; the individual scope encompasses the ideal totality of possible individuals of such concrete essences (*Ideen* 31/36).

We will have to come back to this quote later. As for now, let us simply state–in a provocative way–that according to this passage, those who talk of Husserl's "ontological regions" without having spelled out what an "*Individuum*" is,–at least in "rigorously 'analytic' terms"–do not actually know what they are talking about.

A few remarks on the structure of *Form and Essence* now. As already pointed out, the formal-ontological definition of individuality appears only late in the chapter, after Husserl has previously explained what a material essence (§§ 10, 12, 13), a *tode ti* (§§ 11, 14) and a *concretum* (§ 15) are. And one could even suspect that the whole chain of formal-ontological distinctions introduced in the previous paragraphs is displayed only to set the stage for the final "rigorous" definition of "region" by means of the concept of "individual" (§ 16). But if the rigorous definition of "region" in terms of *Individuum* is the *terminus a quo* of the whole chapter, the *terminus ad quem*, introduced at very beginning of *Ideas I*, is precisely that of "individual object". Already in § 2, for instance, we learn that:

> An individual object is not merely something individual, a *This here!* a "once and only" object. Fashioned as such and such "in its very self," it has *its own specific constitution*, its stock of *essential* predicables that must pertain to it (as "the entity as it is in itself"), so that other, secondary, relative determinations can pertain to it (*Ideen* 11/12–13; translation modified by the author).

And a few lines before:

> Individual being of any kind is, speaking quite generally, "contingent". It is in a certain way; it could, in keeping with its essence, be otherwise (Ideen 10/12).

Thus, it seems that in *Fact and Essence* Husserl proceeds from a broad talk about "individual objects" and "individual being" (which are ontologically contingent: *zufällig*) to the strict formal-ontological concept of *Individuum* (which, on the contrary, will turn out to be the true *Urgegenstand* and will play, at the very end of the chapter, an ontologically fundamental role in defining what a "region" is). It is precisely this track that I will suggest following now.

2. From individual objects to "their" essences

What in the first paragraphs of *Fact and Essence* Husserl calls "individual object" appears, broadly speaking, as the correlate of any empirical intuition, be it perceptual or abstractive (*Ideen* 13/15): perceiving *a* thing or *a* sound, an *Erlebnis* or one of its moments, is *eo ipso* perceiving an *individual* thing or an *individual* sound, or an *individual Erlebnis*, etc. And this broad use of the term is consistent with both the general Aquinas-like definition of individuality and the doctrine of the 2nd *Logical Investigation*. But Husserl also adds a further element: perceiving an individual thing or an individual sound is always and necessarily perceiving something that is both a unique *Dies-da*–literally: a "once only" or a "one-timer" (*ein einmaliger*) (*Ideen* 11/12)–, and a bearer of "predicables": a *So-und-so beschaffen*.

One might wonder whether by employing the very specific term of "predicables" (*Prädikabilien*) Husserl hints to the difference between *praedicabilia*–i.e. the list of four *katēgoroumena* detailed in Aristotle's *Topics* (101 b 17–25: *proprium, genus, accident, definition*), later expanded and modified in Porphyry's *Isagoge*–and *praedicamenta*–i.e. the *katēgoriai*, spelled out in the *Categories* (and referring to predicates of things, not predicates of predicates), but I will leave the question open for the moment. As for now, let us simply insist on the following point: according to this preliminary characterization, an individual object is a *this-here* fashioned in *such-and-such* a way, i.e. having a specific constitution (*Eigenart*) and a stock (*Bestand*) of predicates or "predicables". Now, what is interesting in this preliminary distinction is that the categorial concepts used by Husserl to name these two "internal moments" (*innere Momente*) of any individual object (the *dies-da* and the *so-und-so*) are precisely the two concepts later required to define analytically the *Individuum:* i.e. *tode ti* and "*Wesen*". Both "*tode ti*" and "*Wesen*" are also names of formal ontological categories, namely of "essences of essences" (*Wesen des Wesens*) (Husserl 1976, p. 578). As for the *tode ti*, Husserl defines it as a "pure syntactically formless individual singularity" (*eine syntaktisch formlose individuelle Einzelheit*) (*Ideen* 29/33), whereas an essence is precisely the "conceptual content" (*begriffliche Inhalt*) (Husserl 2012, p. 149) determining a singular individual as being an individual of a very specific kind (*Eigenart*).

If this may sound confusing, there is a very instructive passage in the *Bernauer Manuscritps* where Husserl expands on the notion of *tode ti* and explicitly refers back to *Ideas I*:

> Each entity has its essence and existence, for which it is customary also to say: Being-thus and being-there (...). The essence, the What of the substrate is, on the one hand, a concrete and a specific essence, what is "repeatable" and repeated in different individuals with different substrates and possible singularizations of this specific essence; on the other hand, it is the *tode ti*. The *tode ti* is what singularizes individually the specific, i.e. the lower and not further differentiable species, the *principium individuationis* (Husserl 2001a, p. 299).

This can be illustrated as shown in Fig. 1.

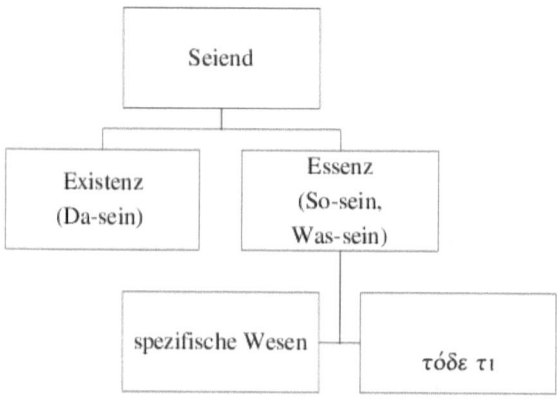

Fig. 1

Three points need to be stressed.

(1) With such an uncanny mishmash of terms (Greek, Latin, German) Husserl ultimately attempts to distinguish *a broad notion of essence* (named "Essenz", "Was sein" or "So-sein"), to which also belongs the *tode ti* (what singularizes the lowest species), from a narrower notion (called "*spezifische Wesen*") limited to the "predicables" that an individual object can have in common with any other individuals of the relevant kind. What is interesting, thus, is that according to the first broad notion, if we were to spell out the *Essenz* of any individual object whatsoever–such as it is intuitively given in the various forms of originally giving acts–we should say that it *includes* both its particularity (*Eigenart, spezifische Wesen*) and its singularity (*tode ti*). An individual object is therefore nothing but the substrate of an ultimately singularized essence. And, accordingly, an

empirical individual object is an actually existing (*daseiend*) ultimately singularized essence (*Ideen* 29/33). As in the best Scotist tradition, the *principium individuationis* belongs to the Form[6].

(2) This brings us the reference to the Aristotelian term *tode ti*. The term appears mainly in *Met. Z* 4 (1030a 19), when Aristotle refers to that feature of the ousia that is irreducible to the *ti estì*. While the demonstrative pronoun *tòde* has certainly a deictic function (like the *Dies* in Husserl's *Dies-da*) and may also formally be used to denote the subject of all possible predication (see *Z* 1, 1028a 15), in the complete formula *tode ti* the deictic *tòde* occurs as determined by the *ti*, namely as "something". This gets somehow lost in the English translation, for *tode ti* does not mean "this-here" but precisely "this-*something*". William of Moerbeke was well aware of this, for he translates *tode ti* precisely with *hoc aliquid*, "this-here that is a something". As in Aristotle, where the *ti* determines the extension of the *tòde*, in the Latin translation also used by Aquinas it is not the *hoc* that determines the *aliquid* but vice-versa. So for Aristotle *tode ti* is neither an indeterminate *this*, nor something merely determined by its deictic-bound spatial location (a *this-here*) but *a-determinate-this:* a substrate that is not *just* a substrate, but of which one can also say *what* it is and *how* is determined (*ypokeìmenon...rismènon*, Z1, 1028 a 27).

Now, Husserl's unexpected use of the *tode ti* is consistent with Aristotle's account in *Met. Z*. But *Ideas I* adds a further argument, an example to illustrate how a world of, say, "essence-less" *Dies-da*, of merely deictic *tòde*, as it were, would look like. A world whose objects would have only the categorial form of a bare singularity without being stable enough to carry any material determination would not be a world of individual objects as the one exemplified in our current experience. A "world" of "undetermined singularities", namely of *singularities whose determinations were constantly ever-changing and incapable of performing any individuation* would be a "non-world" (*Unwelt*) as the one described (although already with the vocabulary of constitution) by the example of the *Weltvernichtung* spelled out in § 49:

> It may be the case thereby that rough formations of unity would still come to be constituted to some extent–fleeting stopovers for intuitions that would be mere analogues of intuitions of a thing, since such analogues are entirely incapable of constituting sustained 'realities,' enduring unities that 'exist in themselves, whether they are perceived or not'. (*Ideen* 88/ 103–104; see Majolino 2010)

---

[6] This point is already suggested in Mohanty 1997, p. 7; 39. On Scotus's account of individuation see Ordinatio II, d. 3, p. 1, qq. 5–6, n. 188. See also Park 1988 and Park 1990.

So what *makes* an *individual object* out of a *tode ti* is precisely what makes one able to identify it and re-identify it as being the *same* individual and not *an*-other or even to conflate it with another, under certain circumstances, to be wrong about it, to correct our opinions etc..–namely the fact that the empty ontological form of the *ti* is materially complemented and fulfilled by some forms of "predicables". Thus, it is only as long as *being-something* is *being-something-of-some-kind* that there can be a world, stable enough to have the "behavior" of its individual denizens be captured by the laws of a science.

(3) But the text from the *Bernauer Manuscripts* also points out that the *Dies-da* (=*tode ti*) should not be conflated with the *Da-sein* (=existence) of the individual object, which does *not* belong to its *Essenz*. Of course, neither the *tode ti* nor the existence are "predicables"; however, while the existence does not determine *what* an individual is, the *tode ti* is precisely the name for the bearer of such an ultimate determination. The *tode ti* is in fact what singularizes the *infima species*: it is not a further predicate but *the non-predicative part of the essence of an individual object*. An individual object is ultimately nothing but a this-here fully determined by the sum-total of all and only its predicable features. For example, a this-here that has this-shade-of-red-here, this roundish-shape-here, but also these quantitative properties such as this mass-here, this momentum-here etc., and a whole host of ultimately determined quantities and qualities is a *physical individual*–something that can be given in sense perception. Or a this-here that has this-pitch-here and this-height here, and this-duration-here and this-loudness here, and this timbre-here is a *physical individual too*–although abstract, something that can be given in abstractive sense perception.

Now, all the internal moments of an individual object's *Wesensbestand* have not the same degree of generality. In Husserl's (Porphyrian-like) hierarchy of essences we have, right at the top, the highest genera, and down at the bottom the "lowest differences", also called "eidetic singularities", species that cannot be further specified but only carried by a *tode ti:*

> In this sense, in the purely logical domain of *meanings*, "meaning in general" is the highest genus, while each determinate form of proposition, each determinate form of a proposition-member is an eidetic singularity; proposition in general is a genus of what mediates [subordinate members]. So, too, *number* in general is a highest genus. Two, three, and so forth are its lowest differences or eidetic singularities. Examples of highest genera in the material sphere include the *thing* in general, *sensory quality, spatial shape, experience* [*Erlebnis*] in general; the essential components that belong to determinate things, determinate sensory qualities, spatial shapes, experiences [*Erlebnisse*] as such are eidetic singularities and thereby material singularities. (*Ideen* 26/30, translation modified).

This is illustrated in Fig. 2.

Section I, chapter 1 — 41

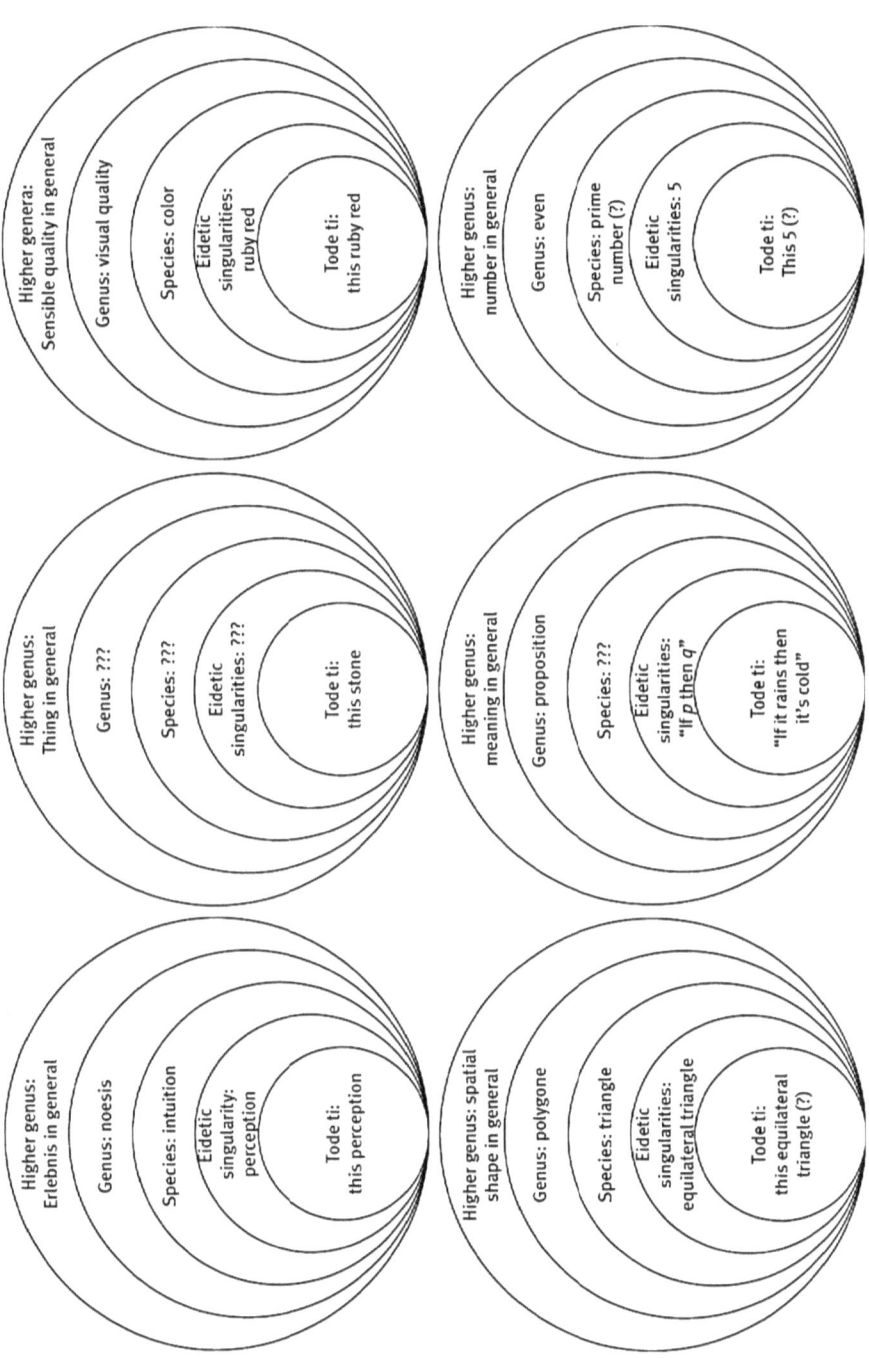

Fig. 2

One understands now why Husserl says that individual objects are *tode ti* having a *Wesensbestand* or a *Was*. In a way, each individual object is the singularization (*Vereinzelung*) of a lowest material difference (*eidetische Singularität*) or, to put it in slightly different terms, each individual object has its "own kind" (*Eigenart*) (*Ideen* 11/12)–its *hacceitas*, as it were. But since

> the eidetically singular *implies* (*impliziert*) all the universalities lying above it, universalities that, for their part, 'lie in one another' in a step-by-step fashion, the higher always in the lower (*Ideen* 26/31),

it can also *exemplify* essences of higher order. A *tode ti is* a singularization of an eidetic singularity, but it is only an example of the upper genera and species of which the eidetic singularity is the ultimate difference. This-particular-shade-of-red-here *is* "ruby red", but it is also an example among others of "red in general", "color" and ultimately "sensible quality".

It seems thus that Husserl's first, general, Aquinas-like, definition of individuality ("actual identity with itself and difference from any other") fits nicely with the characterization of what we have learned to call "individual objects", both concrete like a physical body (*Ding*) or a mental event (*Erlebnis*), and abstract like a sound (or a color) or an act quality. For it is precisely to the extent that an individual object is, as it were, a "*tode ti* with an *Eigenart*" that it can be "identical with itself and different from any other".

4. From essences to eide

Now that we know what the categorial structure (or *Essenz*) of all *individual objects* is (*tode ti+Wesen*), we are in a better position to understand what Husserl means by eidos and get some additional tools to avoid the usual conflation of eidos and *Wesen*.[7] In fact what Husserl calls "essence" is "at first" (*zunächst*) only the "What" (*Was*) of an individual object, the singularized essence which includes the *Dies-da* and the *So-und-so* empirically given in sense perception or in any of the relevant forms of originally giving intuitive acts having individuals as objects. In Husserl's words:

> 'Essence' *initially* designated what is to be found in the being that is proper to an individual itself as its *what* (*Ideen* 11/13).

---

[7] To my knowledge, the only scholar who consistently avoids this conflation is Rochus Sowa. See Sowa 2007.

Of course, such preliminary (*zunächst*) concept of "essence", that we have learned to call *Wesensbestand* or *Eigenart* or *So-und-so Beschaffenheit* etc., is *not* the eidos. When we perceive *this* or *that* object we always perceive *a fully determinate "this"* and, as a moment of the whole individual object as such, we also find as "already there" (*als Vorfindliche*) the stock of predicables determining its *So-sein*–or at least some of them. This concrete individual body is red and roundish, has a certain weight etc.; this abstract individual sound has its pitch, height and duration etc. And we perceive all these properties as long and insofar as we perceive the individual itself, for these are nothing but its "internal moments" (*innere Momente*). Now "essence" as a determination of a previously existing and empirically encountered individual object, differs from eidos because an eidos is not the essence-of-this-or-that-individual-object but a full-fledged "brand new object" (*ein neuartiger Gegenstand*) (*Ideen* 12/14). In a nutshell: the essence-*of* an (individual) object is called "*Was*" (or sometimes *So-sein*; or sometimes "*Wesen*" with scare quotes); the essence-*as an object* per se, is called eidos (or "*reines* Wesen"). Again, three remarks are now necessary.

(1) In order to switch from the simple intuition of the "*essence*"-*qua-Was* (embedded into an individual object) to the intuition of to the *pure-essence-qua- eidos* Husserl requires a further noetic step: the "*in-Idee-setzen* of the *Was*", i.e. the "ideation" (*Ideation*) or essential seeing proper (*Wesenserschauung, Wesenschauung, Wesensanschauung*):

> Each such 'what,' however, can be '*put into [the form of] an idea.*' *Experiential* or *individual intuition* can be transformed into an instance of *seeing the essence* (*ideation*)–a possibility that is itself to be understood, not as empirical, but as an essential possibility. What is intuited is then the corresponding *pure* essence or eidos, whether it be the highest category or a particularization of the latter, down to the full concretion (*Ideen* 11/13 translation modified).

Properly speaking, then, "being a highest genus", "being a genus", "being a species" or "being an eidetic singularity" are properties of *eide*, second order "predicables" (and, in a way, *praedicabilia* in the most proper sense), belonging to *pure* essences; whereas "being a spatial shape", "being a polygon", "being a triangle" and "being an equilateral triangle" are first-order predicables belonging to the *Wesensbestand* of individual objects. When one judges that "this is ruby red", the judgment refers to an individual object, namely a *tode ti* determined as being-ruby-red. This is what Husserl calls the subsumption (*Subsumption*) of an individual object under its essence (*Ideen* 28/32). "Subsumption" is the judgmental counterpart of the intuitive act of perception. But judging that "ruby red is a color" is already a case of *generalization* (*Generalisierung*), just as "colors are visual qualities" or "visual qualities are sensible qualities". Generalization is not a relation between individuals and essences, but between essences of different degree. Husserl calls such relation "subordination" (*Subordination*) of an essence under its higher species or a genus" (*Ideen* 28/32). And "subordination" is the judgmental counter part of the intuitive act of ideation.

(2) But *eide* as pure essences differ from essences as empirical determinations of individual objects, also for another reason. For *ideation*, although originally giving and intuitive, is nevertheless a founded act:

> It is certainly part of the distinctiveness of the intuition of an essence that a chief element of individual intuition, namely, the appearance or visibility of something individual, underlies the intuition of the essence, although it does so, to be sure, neither as an apprehension of what is individual nor, by any means, as a positing of [the individual] as an actuality. What is certain is that, as a consequence of this, one cannot have an intuition of an essence without being able to shift one's focus freely toward a 'corresponding' individual and form a consciousness of an example–just as, conversely, one cannot have an intuition of something individual without freely being able to form an idea of it and to focus within the idea on the corresponding essence that is exemplified in what is individually visible (Ideen 13–14/15).

Just as each essence singularized into an individual object can be seen as "posited into idea", each *eidos* can in turn be seen as exemplified (*exemplifiziert*) into an individual object. So if the *upward* movement, from individual object to *eidos* is called *ideation* (*Ideation*), the reciprocal *downward* movement from *eidos* to individual object is named *exemplification* (*Exemplifizierung*). However, the apparent symmetry suggested by the terms upward/downward is dispelled as soon as Husserl adds that although usually ideated from actual individual objects, *eide* can be *exemplified* by merely possible or fantasied individuals. And a fantasized individual object is *not* an individual object in the sense defined above, but a *quasi*-individual, for, by definition, it is never fully determined by its predicates (some of them being structurally left undetermined) (see for instance Husserl 1980, p. 302):

> The *eidos*, the *pure essence*, can be exemplified intuitively in instances of givenness in experience, in such instances in perception, memory, and so forth, but *also in those in mere fantasy* just as well (*Ideen* 14/16).

In other words, an *eidos* is a "*pure* essence" for at least two reasons: (*a*) because it is distinguished from the *singularized* "essence" of the *Was*; and (b) because it does not posit the existence of any actual individual, for pure essences can be eventually *exemplified* in both actual-perceptive individual and possible-fantasized quasi-individual objects: *eide* are "pure" in the first sense insofar as they hold as objects per se (and not as "mixed", as it were, with other object-moments within the *Was* of an individual object); but in the second sense, the talk of "pureness" has a very different meaning: *eide* are pure because they are a priori. They are not essences-of *this* or *that* existing individual object, but of all possible objects whose relevant predicates happen to be contingently (*zufällig*) exemplified *also* in *this* or *that* existing individual object. In that sense, if natural laws are true of "states of affairs posited as real for they bring together individual realities", this does not hold for eidetic sciences (*Ideen* 17/19 see also §§ 7–8).

5. From *eide* to regions

After having spelled out what an individual object is (§ 2); what "its" essence (§ 3) and what "an" *eidos* is (§ 4)–one last element is needed to understand Husserl's thesis that the "individual" is the *Urgegenstand*, as well as the "rigorous" definition of region it unfolds–i.e. the distinction concrete/abstract as applied not to objects in general (as in the 3rd *Logical Investigation*) but, more specifically, to *eide*.

According to § 15, if *eide* are dependent (or independent)–and thus abstract (or concrete) in the most "genuine" (*pregnant*) sense–it is because they "necessarily refer back to (or fail to refer back to) one another" (*notwendig zuückweisen; aufeinander gewiesen*). To put it differently, two *eide* are abstract (or concrete) if and only if they "are unthinkable without" (or fail to be unthinkable without) one another (*ohne einander nich denkbare*) (*Ideen* 29/34). Husserl's examples are very sparse but sufficiently clear. A sensible quality, say "color", is abstract because all its lower differences refer back to eidetic singularities belonging to the *eidos* "extension"; and the same holds for the *eidos* "substrate" that is necessarily related to the *eidos* "form" etc. (*Ideen* 30/35–36). Thus formal categorial essences in general–object in general, property, state of affairs, number, order, manifold, unity, identity, equality, part/whole, genus/species etc. (*Ideen* 27/32-3)-are abstract by definition, for they are all materially "empty" and in need to be complemented; hence, they "necessarily refer back to" or are "unthinkable without" other essences. And the same holds *stricto sensu* for all highest genera, genera and species as such.

By contrast, an essence is concrete if and only if it is fully determined and does not *necessarily* refer (*hinweisen*) to any other essence. As a result

> A concretum is quite obviously an eidetic singularity, since species and genera (expressions that in the usual way exclude the lowest differences) are in principle dependent. The *eidetic singularities* accordingly break down into *abstract* and *concrete* (Ideen 30/35).

Ruby-red is an abstract eidetic singularity and *"this-ruby-red"* is a fully determined *tode ti* whose material essence is nevertheless abstract, because it is "unthinkable without" or "necessarily refers to" a *tode ti* whose material essence belongs to the genus "spatial form". On the other hand, *"this-stone"*, fully provided with all the determinations of its *Was* (=eidetic singularity) is a *tode ti* whose material essence is a concretum, for its stock of predicables (*Bestand an Prädikabilien*) does not *need* to be complemented by anything else. In a sense, this-stone in its full concretion could be the only being in the world; and if there actually happen to be other things beyond this stone, this is a *fact*, not a matter of necessity—while the actual existence of *this-ruby-red* calls for at least the existence of another being, *an* extended surface like for instance *this-triangular(ish)shape*. It is precisely in this very specific sense that for Husserl, athough they are both, generally speaking, "individual objects", from an analytically rigorous point of view only *this-stone* is an *Individuum*, not *this-ruby-red*.

The consequences of this distinction are crucial for both Husserl's conception of ontology and his whole phenomenological project.

(1) To begin with, this implies that *eide* are related to each other in at least two ways. Vertically, as subordinated in the hierarchical order *highest genus/ genus/species/eidetic singularity*, and somehow horizontally, as united to form other *eide* belonging to different *highest genera*. The relationship between the *eidos* "red" and the *eidos* "green" is simply an *eidetic fact:* "red" and "green" are disjointed (*disjunkt*) species subordinated to the genus "color" and the highest genus "visual quality". As for the relationship between "red" and "color", or "color" and "visual quality", it is an *eidetic necessity*. But the relationship between "color" and "shape" is an *eidetic necessity of a different kind:* "color" and "shape" are not *subordinated* to a common *genus*, they *unite* to form another *eidos*, *heterogeneous* from both "sensible qualities" and "spatial shapes." In Husserl's words an *abstract* pure essence is an essence that "together with another, establishes the unity of one essence" (*ein Wesen [daß] mit einem anderen Einheit eines Wesens begründet*) (*Ideen* 30/35). Being-one as part of a genus, and being-one as part of another same-level although heterogeneous essence is not the same.

> Examples of concrete genera are 'real thing,' 'visual phantom' (a visual shape that appears and is filled out sensorily), "experience" [*Erlebnis*], and the like. By contrast, 'spatial shape,' 'visual quality,' and the like are examples of abstract genera (*Ideen* 31/36).

Spatial figure and visual qualities are higher genera, but they are also abstract in the sense that, *because of the mutual reference of their eidetic singularities*, their eidetic singularities *unite* into new *eide* belonging to the highest genus "visual phantasm (a visual shape that appears and is filled out sensorily)" ("*visuelle Phantom (sinnlich erfüllt erscheinende visuelle Gestalt)*") (*Ideen* 31/36). But as Husserl rightly points out "visual phantasm" is not a super-genus of which ruby-red would be a lower species, and this-ruby-red its singularization. "Visual phantasm" is an entirely different higher genus: a concrete higher genus, established by the unity of two heterogeneous highest genera, two essences brought to unity, neither of them being a "visual phantasm" all alone–only both together. "Vertically" *eide* are joined to each other either because they belong to a genus, in which case they now are "horizontally" united because their eidetic singularities are *either* individuals (visual phantasms, things, *Erlebnisse*), *or* because they are abstract parts of individuals (spatial figure, visual quality etc.).

(2) But there is more. Beyond the "unity of the highest genus" (=generic unity") and the "unity of abstract *eide* into new concrete *eide*" (=what we might call "mereologic unity" in the strict sense), Husserl needs a third kind of unity: the unity that brings together both abstract and concrete highest genera belonging to the same "region". *The unity of being.* And the time has come to finally turn back to the concluding, "rigorous", definition of region that closes *Fact and Essence.*

> Region is nothing other than the *entire, supreme generic unity belonging to a concretum*, i.e., the essentially united connection of the supreme genera that pertain to the lowest differences within the *concretum*. The eidetic scope of the region encompasses the ideal totality of concretely unified complexes of differences of these genera; the individual scope encompasses the ideal totality of possible individuals of such concrete essences (*Ideen* 31/36).

So a region is *not* a *highest genus*. A region is not a *genus* itself, but a *unity of highest genera:* the "entire superior unity of genera belonging to a concretum" (*die gesamte zu einem Konkretum gehörige oberste Gattungseinheit*); the "essentially united connection of the supreme genera that pertain to the lowest differences within the concretum" (*die wesenseinheitliche Verknüpfung der obersten Gattungen, die den nierdersten Differenzen innerhalb des Konkretums zugehören*; *Ideen* 31/36). What brings together essences like red and green is the subordination to the same higher genus: visual quality; what brings together essences like colors and shapes is their mutual reference as part of a concretum: the visual phantasm. But what–if anything–brings together, *abstracta* like colors and shapes, and *concreta* like visual phantasms and real things and eventually *Erlebnisse* into one single "ontological region," into *one* region of *being?*

Certainly not the fact that they are *objects*, for object is a formal-categorial concept, absolutely empty–and, as we have seen, absolutely abstract; thus incapable of forming a region. Husserl's response is striking: what unites a region of being is precisely the recourse to the *Urgegenständlichkeit* of one individual (*tode-ti* whose material essence is a concretum). Sometimes confused and quite often confusing, Husserl couldn't be more explicit on this point:

> If we transport ourselves into any eidetic science at all, for example, into the *ontology of nature*, then we find ourselves (this is, indeed, what is normal) not oriented toward essences as objects but instead toward objects of the essences that in our example are classified under the region of nature. We observe thereby, however, that '*object*' is a title for many different yet interrelated formations, for example, 'thing,' 'property,' 'relation,' 'state of affairs,' 'set,' 'order,' and so forth. These are obviously not equivalent to one another but instead *refer back (zurückweisen) respectively to one kind of object that has, so to speak, the prerogative of being the primordial kind of object* (auf eine Art Gegenständlichkeit die sozusagen die Vorzug der *Urgegenständlichkeit* hat), with respect to which all other [objects] present themselves to a certain extent merely as variants. In our example, the *thing itself* (over against the thingly property, relation, and so forth) naturally has this prerogative (*Ideen* 22/25; my emphasis).

Being becomes a region, many *highest genera* unite into one "*wesenseinheitliche Verknüpfung*", thanks to the back-reference of a distinctive manifold of *eide* (="essences as objects and not essences of objects", Husserl also says) to a paradigmatic individual, taken as *Urgegenstand*. Individuals are *Urgegenstände:* this is the stuff of which ontologies are made—the physicalistic ontology of Quine (whose individual *Urgegenstand* is the physical *Ding*), as well as the fundamental ontology of Heidegger (where the *Dasein* takes the leading role). *Husserl is not merely proposing an ontology here—he is showing how ontologies are made up.* As for "Nature," it becomes an "ontological region", i.e. its denizens are "together in being", because they are either *things*, or *properties of* things, or they are *somehow related to* things—i.e. they refer back (*zuruckweisen*) to "things" as *Urgegenstände*.

6. Headless ontologies and transcendental phenomenology

It is not clear whether the individuum whose material essence is a *concretum* of the kind "visual phantasm" could be used as the *Urgegenstand* to form a region of being—so that *Erlebnisse, Dinge* and *Phantome* would end up being three heterogeneous ontological regions. But I will leave the question aside. To conclude, I would simply like to point out that the term Husserl uses to establish the *non-generic* and *non-mereological* unity of an *ontological* region on the basis of the back-reference to a paradigmatic individual, i.e. *zurückweisen* should sound familiar for us. We have already encountered it in the context of Husserl's analysis of the non-independency of abstracta. But in this new context Husserl uses the term more loosely, for it now captures also that kind of unity of being that Aristotle's Γ2 (and Brentano in his dissertation) calls *"pros hen"*, i.e. unity related to a single focal meaning or "in relation to one." The unity of Husserl's ontology is therefore what is called a unity *"pros hen"*.[8] And, as far as we are concerned with Husserl' explicit *use of the term ontology*, nothing, really nothing seems to suggest that "being" is "being an object"; by contrast, everything–starting from Husserl's appropriation of the Aristotelian *tode ti*–clearly indicates that, ultimately (namely limiting oneself to the formal categories of the substrate, and abstracting from all syntactic cores) "to be" is to-be-an-individual or to-be-the-abstract-part-of-an-individual, or to-be-related-with-an-individual. For *Individual* is precisely the *Urgegenstand* out of which *Being* becomes a *region*–be it the region "thing", the region "consciousness" or, eventually, the region "phantasm". So when Heidegger says in the *History of the Concept of Time* that Husserl does not say anything about the meaning of "to be", he is utterly wrong. As wrong as all those analytic interpreters looking for Husserl's catalogue of what there is.

But there is also one last point I would like to stress, and it concerns Husserl's talk of *Ur-regionen:* world and consciousness. If "region" has to be taken rigorously, the same holds for *Ur-region*. New forms of unity are needed to bring together the ontology of nature, the ontology of psychophysical creatures like animals and the ontology of culture or *Geist* spelled out in *Ideas II* into one single *Ur-region* called "world". The point is that such new unity cannot be reached ontologically: it is neither generic, nor mereological, nor made out of the unique reference to an individual *Urgegenstand*. So Husserl will have finally to exit ontology, an ontology that remains ultimately and necessarily "headless", without highest genera nor *pros hen* unity, and conclude that the unity of the region world *is not* ontological–but *transcendental*. But I have to stop here. It should be readily apparent, however, that if one wants to enter into Husserl's transcendental phenomenology from the backyard, as it were–avoiding the main entrance of *Fact and essence*–one shouldn't be surprised then to find oneself, at one point, into a totally different place: a backyard belonging to an entirely different school.

---

[8] See Brentano 1862, pp. 144–148. On Husserl and Brentano with reference to Aristotle and the role of the *pròj ën*, see also Majolino 2008.

Bibliography

Brentano, Franz (1862), Von der mannigfachen Bedeutung des Seienden nach Aristoteles. Freiburg: Herder.
Gracia, Jorge J. E. (1984): *Introduction to the Problem of Individuation in the Early Middle Ages*. Munich/Washington DC: Philosophia Verlag and Catholic University of America Press.
Heidegger, Martin (2003): *Four Seminars* (transl. by A. Mitchell and F. Raffoul). Bloomington: Indiana University Press.
Husserl, Edmund (1976): "Ideen zu einer reinen Phänomenologie und phänomenologischen Philosophie. Erstes Buch: Allgemeine Einführung in die reine Phänomenologie. Zweiter Halbband: Ergänzende Texte (1912–1929)". In: *Husserliana*. Vol. III/2. The Hague: Nijhoff.
Husserl, Edmund (1980): "Phantasie, Bildbewusstsein, Erinnerung: Zur Phänomenologie der anschaulichen Vergegenwärtigungen. Texte aus dem Nachlass (1898–1925)". In: *Husserliana*. Vol. XXIII. The Hague: Nijhoff.
Husserl, Edmund (2001a): "Die Bernauer Manuskripte über das Zeitbewusstsein (1917/18)". In: *Husserliana*. Vol. XXXIII. Dordrecht: Springer.
Husserl, Edmund (2001b): *Logical Investigations*. Vol. 1. London/New York: Routledge.
Husserl, Edmund (2001c): *Logical Investigations*. Vol. 2. London/New York: Routledge.
Husserl, Edmund (2012): "Zur Lehre vom Wesen und zur Methode der eidetischen Variation". In: *Husserliana*. Vol. XLI. Dordrecht: Springer.
Majolino, Claudio (2008): "Husserl and the Vicissitudes of the Improper". In: *The New Yearbook of Phenomenology and Phenomenological Philosophy* VIII, 17–54.
Majolino, Claudio (2010): "La partition du réel. Remarques sur l'eidos, la phantasia, l'effondrement du monde et l'être absolu de la conscience". In: Ierna, Carlo/Jacobs, Hanne/Mattens, Filip (eds.), *Philosophy, Phenomenology, Sciences*. Dordrecht: Springer, pp. 573–660.
Mohanty, Jithendra Nath (1997): *Phenomenology: Between Essentialism and Transcendental Philosophy*. Evanston IL: Northwestern University Press.
Park, Woosuk (1988): "The Problem of Individuation for Scotus: A Principle of Indivisibility or a Principle of Distinction?" In: Franciscan Studies 48, pp. 105–123.
Park, Woosuk (1990): "Haecceitas and the Bare Particular". In: Review of Metaphysics, pp. 375–397.
Smith, David Woodruff (2010): *Husserl*. London: Routledge.
Sowa, Rochus (2007): "Essences and Eidetic Laws in Edmund Husserl's Descriptive Eidetics". In: *The New Yearbook for Phenomenology and Phenomenological Philosophy* VII, pp. 77–108.
Suarez, Francisco (1982): *On Individuation* (transl. by J. J. E. Gracia). Milwaukee: Marquette University Press.

Robert Hanna
Transcendental normativity and the avatars of psychologism

Section I, chapter 2, Naturalistic misconceptions

What forces this dispute upon us is the fact that "Ideas," "essences," and "knowledge of essences" are denied by empiricism. Here is not the place to develop the historical reasons [*Gründe*] why precisely the victorious advance of the natural sciences has promoted philosophical empiricism (despite the extent to which, as "mathematical" sciences, they also owe their high scientific rank to an eidetic founding) and why their advance has made empiricism the prevailing conviction—indeed, almost the only reigning conviction—within the circles of those conducting empirical research. In any case, an animosity to ideas is alive in these circles and thus, too, among psychologists. In the end this animosity must endanger the progress of empirical sciences themselves, precisely because it hampers the eidetic founding of these sciences (a founding by no means completed already), the constitution, that may prove to be necessary, of new sciences-of-essences that are indispensable for the progress of empirical sciences. As will become clear later, what is said here concerns precisely the phenomenology that makes up the essential eidetic foundation of psychology and the humanistic sciences. Hence, some elaboration is needed in defense of our conclusions. (*Ideen* 34/40)

The scientific world conception is characterised not so much by theses of its own, but rather by its basic attitude, its points of view and direction of research. The goal ahead is unified science. The endeavour is to link and harmonise the achievements of individual investigators in their various fields of science. From this aim follows the emphasis on collective efforts, and also the emphasis on what can be grasped intersubjectively; from this springs the search for a neutral system of formulae, for a symbolism freed from the slag of historical languages; and also the search for a total system of concepts. Neatness and clarity are striven for, and dark distances and unfathomable depths rejected. In science there are no 'depths'; there is surface everywhere: all experience forms a complex network, which cannot always be surveyed and, can often be grasped only in parts. Everything is accessible to man; and man is the measure of all things. Here is an affinity with the Sophists, not with the Platonists; with the Epicureans, not with the Pythagoreans; with all those who stand for earthly being an d the here and now. The scientific world–conception knows no unsolvable riddle. Clarification of the traditional philosophical problems leads us partly to unmask them as pseudo-problems, and partly to transform them into empirical problems and thereby subject them to the judgment of experimental science. The task of philosophical work lies in this clarification of problems and assertions, not in the propounding of special 'philosophical' pronouncements. The method of this clarification is that of logical analysis; of it, Russell says (*Our Knowledge of the External World*, p. 4) that it "has gradually crept into philosophy through the critical scrutiny of mathematics... It represents, I believe, the same kind of advance as was introduced into physics by Galileo: the substitution of piecemeal, detailed and verifiable results for large untested generalities recommended only by a certain appeal to imagination." (Ernst Mach Society 1929, Sect. 2)

1. Introduction

Logical truth, logical validity, logical soundness, logical laws, mathematical truth, the power-set operation over denumerably infinite collections, non-denumerable infinity or transfinite magnitude, strict moral obligation, absolute goodness, the moral law, aesthetic perfection or the absolutely beautiful, maximality in general, necessity in general, a priori knowledge of necessary truth, acting with a good will, and a priori knowledge of moral principles–what do all of these deeply important notions have in common?

First, they all specify the *highest* ends, goals, ideals, standards, and values of various different kinds of rational human activity. And second, they all specify items or notions which, if they exist, are *unconditional and strictly universal*. Following Husserl's terminology in *Ideas 1* and elsewhere, I will call such items or notions capital-I *Ideas* or *essences*. And following Kant's groundbreaking discussions of these matters in his theoretical and practical Critical philosophy, I will call the complete collection of these Ideas or essences, i.e., the unconditional and strictly universal highest ends, goals, ideals, standards, and values of various different kinds of rational human activity, *categorical normativity*.

What does it mean to say that categorical normativity exists? By saying that something "exists," I mean (i) that it has *ontic status*, (ii) that it can be picked out by *meaningful directly referential terms* in true atomic singular judgments or propositions (and that therefore it can also be quantified over in true particular or universal general propositions), and (iii) that it can be known by means of perceptual or rational *intuition*. Existence or ontic status per se should be sharply distinguished from *factual* existence, which implies *occurrence in actual spacetime and in actual causal connections*, and also entails *modal contingency*. That which factually exists, *might not have* factually existed: it really could have been or happened otherwise. By sharp contrast, categorical normativity, if it exists, does so unconditionally and strictly universally: it really necessarily is. Amongst the factually existing things are all those that are also knowable exclusively by means of sense perception and other empirical methods, especially including those of the natural sciences: let us call those facts *the empirical facts*. But if categorical normativity exists, i.e., if Ideas or essences exist, then they are *not* empirical facts, and they can be known only by rational intuition.

Now, with direct reference to Husserl's much later, but also fully Kant-inflected, and in its own way groundbreaking, discussion of these matters in his 1913 *Ideas 1*, part I, chapter 2, "Naturalistic Misconceptions," let us call the three-part compound thesis (i) that everything that exists in the world is an empirical fact (the ontological sub-thesis), (ii) that categorical normativity does not exist (the skeptical sub-thesis), and (iii) that all empirical facts are exclusively knowable and completely explicable by means of sensory experiences and/or the natural sciences (the epistemic sub-thesis), *scientific naturalism*. And correspondingly, let us call the corresponding three-part compound contrary thesis (i*) that *not* everything existing in the world is an empirical fact, because at least some existing things are Ideas or essences (the ontological counter-sub-thesis), (ii*) that categorical normativity *does* exist (the anti-skeptical sub-thesis), and (iii*) that *not* everything in the world is exclusively knowable and completely explicable by means of sensory experience and/or the natural sciences (the epistemic counter-sub-thesis), *strong anti-naturalism*. Strong anti-naturalism is also a *rationalist* thesis, because it dierctly entails that a priori knowledge of Ideas or essences by means of rational intuition is really possible (cf., e.g., Chapman et al. 2013; Hanna 2015).

Finally, let us call the three-part compound thesis (i) that categorical normativity exists, (ii) that categorical normativity requires *the actual or really possible existence of innately-specified rational human minds*, and (iii) that categorical normativity is knowable a priori by means of rational intuition in *phenomenology*, the thesis of *transcendental-phenomenological* (TP) *normativity*, a.k.a. the thesis of TP normativity. Obviously, the thesis of TP normativity is a strongly anti-naturalist thesis, an idealist thesis, and also a rationalist thesis.

With all that as background, in this chapter I want to argue that in part I, chapter 2 of *Ideas 1*, "Naturalistic Misconceptions," Husserl presents the strongly anti-naturalist and rationalist thesis of TP normativity and uses it as a primitive premise and philosophical starting-point in order to argue against *all* varieties of scientific naturalism, which in turn he sees as avatars–i.e., incarnations or re-incarnations–of *psychologism*, which he had criticized in much detail and at great length in the first volume of the *Logical Investigations*, the *Prolegomena to Pure Logic* (cf. Hanna 1993; Hanna 2006, ch. 1; Hanna 2008, pp. 27–42; Kusch 1995). In so doing, in 1913 in *Ideas 1*, Husserl also prepares the basic groundwork for his 1936 *Crisis of European Sciences*, which Dermot Moran very aptly calls Husserl's "counter-proposal to the Manifesto of the Vienna Circle that promoted the adoption of a scientific worldview" (Moran 2012, p. 14)–namely, the Circle's co-authored 1929 pamphlet, *The Scientific Conception of the World*. According to Moran, the *Crisis* "builds on Husserl's earlier critiques of naturalism" (Moran 2012, p. 14); and not only that, but in my opinion the *Crisis* builds *fundamentally* on both Husserl's critique of Psychologism in the *Prologomena to Pure Logic* and also the "Naturalistic Misconceptions" chapter in *Ideas 1*.

In turn, my focus on TP normativity as the core of Husserl's anti-scientific naturalistic arguments in the "Naturalistic Misconceptions" chapter, not only broadly conforms to, but, I think, also deepens and extends the central claims of Steven Crowell's important recent book, *Normativity and Phenomenology in Husserl and Heidegger*. According to Crowell, "the normative is found wherever we can speak of rules, measures, standards, exemplars, ideals, concepts, and so on," and these things,

> like phenomenological 'essences,' ... possess a kind of normative claim that precludes our thinking of them simply as entities that turn up in the world, whether as part of the latter's causal nexus, as social facts, or as elements of the subject's psychological outfitting. It is this that makes the normative a basic concern in phenomenology, since it belongs squarely within the scope of the latter's distinctive sort of anti-naturalism. (Crowell 2013, p. 2)

It is precisely phenomenology's "distinctive sort of anti-naturalism," as grounded in *transcendental* normativity, that I want to zero in on. Crowell correctly points out that by 1913 Husserl had come to see [psychologistic] naturalism ... as an instance of a much more pervasive naiveté that would undermine the effort to establish a radically self-responsible, presuppositionless philosophy. (Crowell 2013, p. 45)

What I want to argue is that this "much more pervasive naiveté" is nothing more and nothing less than what The Vienna Circle called *the scientific conception of the world*. So if Husserl is correct about strong anti-naturalism, and I am correct about what Husserl is saying in *Ideas 1*, chapter 2, then no matter what we might think about *the rest* of Husserl's controversial metaphysics of transcendental-phenomenological idealism, nevertheless his thesis of TP normativity *on its own* is sufficient to undermine scientific naturalism and the scientific conception of the world. Or in other words, I am saying that Husserl's thesis of transcendental-phenomenological *normativity* can to an important extent be logically detached from his own metaphysics of transcendental-phenomenological *idealism*, and exploited philosophically on its own. Even if Husserl's transcendental-phenomological idealism is *false*, nevertheless his thesis of transcendental-phenomenological normativity could still be *true*, if there are other more philosophically defensible and weaker versions of transcendental idealism that can be substituted for Husserl's own version (cf., e. g., Hanna 2013).

2. "The natural attitude": A disambiguation

Before I get properly underway, however, and in order to avoid misunderstandings, I think that it is crucial to note that Husserl's notion of *the natural attitude* is importantly ambiguous. On the one hand, it can mean

(i) *our common sense or ordinary orientation to* the world, to other human persons, and to ourselves,

and on the other hand, it can mean
- (ii) *the natural-scientific conception of the world*, other persons, and ourselves.

In other words, these two Husserlian notions of "the natural attitude" are as fundamentally distinct as Wilfrid Sellars's *Manifest Image* and *Scientific Image* of the world, other persons, and ourselves (cf. Sellars 1963, p. 1–40). To keep these two very different aspects of "the natural attitude" distinct in our minds, I propose that we call them, respectively, (i) the *everyday* attitude, and (ii) the *naturalistic* attitude. I think that Husserl is absolutely correct that these two attitudes are fully *consistent with* one another, insofar as, in our not only modern but also *post*-modern, post-Galilean, post-Newtonian, post-Einsteinian, post-quantum-mechanical, post-industrial, technology-driven 20th and 21st Euro-American Western socio-cultural context, the everyday attitude *can also be* importantly and to a large extent non-self-consciously *determined by* the naturalistic attitude. We might call this *the hegemony of the scientific conception of the world*. But this hegemony of the scientific conception certainly *does not have to be* the case, as Sellars's seminal discussion of the two Images makes self-evident. And I also think that Husserl's later notion of the "lifeworld" or *Lebenswelt* in the *Crisis* was a serious attempt *to detach* the notion of the everyday attitude from the naturalistic attitude, and isolate the everyday attitude for philosophical investigation into its nature and epistemic force. In any case, in this chapter I will be concentrating exclusively on Husserl's critique of the *naturalistic* attitude, not on his theory of the everyday attitude.

3. § 18–The thesis of TP normativity asserted

In § 18, Husserl asserts the thesis of TP normativity as I have spelled it out in section I. That is clear enough from this text:

> The general elaborations that we have put forward in advance about essences and a science of essences (in contrast to facts and sciences of facts) treated the essential foundations for our construction of the idea of a pure phenomenology (that according to the Introduction is supposed to become, indeed, a science of essences) and for the understanding of its place in relation to all empirical sciences, including psychology. All intrinsic determinations must be understood, however, in the right sense; much depends upon this. It must be stressed quite emphatically that in [making] them [those determinations], we have not lectured from some foregone philosophical standpoint; we have not made use of philosophical doctrines that have been passed down to us, however universally they are acknowledged. Instead we have carried out a few *principled expositions* in the strictest sense;

that is to say, we have merely given faithful expression to distinctions that are directly given to us in *intuition*. (*Ideen* 33/39)

Is Husserl rationally entitled to assert this thesis? In one sense, obviously *yes:* he can assert any logically consistent thesis he likes, thereby taking it *seriously*, and then spell out its implications. But although Husserl is certainly doing that, he is also clearly doing *more* than that. He starts with the prima facie existence of an open-ended collection of prima facie fundamentally important things, taken as rational human phenomenological data or givens: logical truth, logical validity, logical soundness, logical laws, mathematical truth, the power-set operation over denumerably infinite collections, non-denumerable infinity or transfinite magnitude, strict moral obligation, absolute goodness, the moral law, aesthetic perfection or the absolutely beautiful, maximality in general, necessity in general, a priori knowledge of necessary truth, acting with a good will, and a priori knowledge of moral principles. Then he argues that the thesis of TP normativity is a philosophically *better explanation* of the prima facie existence of these things than scientific naturalism, which must ultimately not only *deny the real existence* of Ideas and essences (skepticism), but also somehow *explain away their prima facie existence and provide an "error theory" of our belief in them* (eliminativism). If Husserl is able to show that scientific naturalism fails in this reductive project, then he does not even have to appeal to an inference to *the best* explanation, but instead only to an inference to *a better* explanation, in order to prove his case for TP normativity. I particularly emphasize this methodological point because I think that it is all too easy for the scientific naturalist to load up Husserl with a rationally unfair burden of proof, and then claim a cheap philosophical victory by default: not only does Husserl have to show that the thesis of TP normativity beats scientific naturalism in a one-to-one philosophical competition, he also has to provide a positive metaphysics and epistemology for *grounding* TP normativity. But that is clearly an uncharitable demand, and far more than Husserl actually needs to do in this context.

At the end of the day, with scientific naturalism safely out of the way, we might then critically analyze and evaluate Husserl's positive metaphysics and epistemology for grounding the thesis of TP normativity. And indeed, in §§ 21–24, Husserl does formulate initial responses to the three standard criticisms of the thesis of TP normativity: that it entails a psychologistic version of idealism; that its version of Platonism is a metaphysical and epistemic mystery; and that it unacceptably entails "fictionalism" or the irreality of Ideas or essences. But it is crucial to re-emphasize that in order to show that TP normativity is a better philosophical theory than scientific naturalism, Husserl does not *have to* carry out the grounding task *here*.

4. §§ 19 and 20–Against scientific naturalism, a.k.a. empiricist Naturalism, a.k.a. positivism

Scientific naturalism, as we have seen, contains three basic elements: (i) an ontological sub-thesis (necessarily, all existing things are empirical facts), (ii) a skeptical sub-thesis (necessarily, there are no Ideas or essences), and (iii) an epistemic thesis (whatever is knowable and explicable, is knowable exclusively and explicable completely by means of sensory experience and/or natural science). In *Ideas 1*, part I, chapter 2, Husserl's basic labels for scientific naturalism are "empiricist naturalism" (*Ideen* 34/41) and "positivism" (*Ideen* 38; 44–45/45; 51–53). The "positivist" label is particularly apt and prescient, since it anticipates The Vienna Circle and its 1929 Manifesto by more than 15 years.

The critical upshot of § 19 is a direct refutation of the ontological sub-thesis and the epistemic sub-thesis of scientific naturalism = empiricist naturalism = positivism. Via these sub-theses, scientific naturalism = empiricist naturalism = positivism asserts that necessarily, all things are empirical facts, and also that whatever is knowable and explicable is knowable exclusively and explicable completely by means of sensory experience and/or natural science. But since, by the thesis of TP normativity, Ideas and essences exist and are a priori knowable by means of rational intuition, and since Ideas or essences are not facts, it follows that scientific naturalism = empiricist naturalism = positivism is false:

> The fundamental mistake of empiricist argumentation lies in identifying or, better, confusing the basic demand of a return to the 'things themselves' [*die 'Sachen selbst'*] with the demand that knowledge be justified in every instance by *experience*. Accepting the conceptual, naturalistic restriction of the framework of knowable 'things,' he takes for granted without further ado, that experience is the only act in which things themselves are given. But *things* are *not* without further ado *things of nature*; actuality in the usual sense is not without further ado actuality in general; and of the acts that give [things] in an originary sense, the one that we call *experience* refers *only to the actuality of nature*. Making these identifications [for example, of things with things of nature]–and treating them as allegedly self-evident–means casting aside, without looking, distinctions that can be given with the clearest insight. Hence, the question: on *which* side do the prejudices lie? Genuine presuppositionlessness does not demand straightaway the rejection of 'judgments foreign to experience'; [it does so] only when the *proper sense* of the judgments *demands* justification by experience. To *claim* directly that *all* judgments allow for, indeed, even demand, justification by experience, without previously having subjected the essence of the judgments to a *study* (in accordance with the fundamentally different sorts of them) and without, thereby, having weighed whether this claim is not in the end *absurd*–that is a 'speculative, a priori construction,' one that does not become any better by issuing this time from the empiricist side. Genuine science and the genuine presuppositionlessness proper to it demand, as the underpinning of all proofs, immediately valid judgments as such, judgments

that draw their validity directly from *intuitions that give things in an originary way.* [...] *Immediately 'seeing'–not merely sensory, empirical seeing* but *seeing in general, i.e., any kind of consciousness that gives* [something] *in an originary fashion*–is the ultimate source of legitimacy of all rational claims. (*Ideen* 35–36/41–43)

In § 20, Husserl goes after the *skeptical* sub-thesis of scientific naturalism = empiricist naturalism = positivism, which says that necessarily, there are no Ideas or essences. Since scientific naturalism = empiricist naturalism = positivism simply helps itself, without further argument, to the epistemic methods of both the natural sciences *and* the formal sciences of mathematics and logic, it presupposes that both inductive inference and deductive inference are legitimate and valid. But the basic principles of induction and deduction are themselves a priori necessary truths, hence Ideas or essences, and knowable only by means of rational intuition. Hence scientific naturalism = empiricist naturalism = positivism presupposes the truth of the thesis of TP normativity, and is self-refuting. As Husserl puts it:

> Moreover, one easily recognizes that to make the case for this identification [of science in general with empirical science] and dispute the validity of purely eidetic thinking, leads to a skepticism that, as genuine skepticism, cancels itself because of its absurdity. One need only ask the empiricist for the source of the validity of his universal theses (for example, 'all valid thinking is grounded on experience as the intuition that alone affords [things]') and he becomes entangled in a demonstrable absurdity. Direct experience affords only singular individualities and no universalities; hence, it does not suffice. He cannot appeal to insight into essences [*Wesenseinsicht*] since he disavows that. He can, it is true, still appeal to induction and thus in general to the complex of intermediate manners of inference, by means of which empirical science acquires its universal propositions. Yet how do matters stand, we may ask, with the truth of the intermediate inferences, whether they be deductive or inductive? Is this *truth* itself–indeed, we could even ask, already for the truth of any singular judgment, is it itself–something that can be experienced and, thus, in the end something perceivable? And how do things stand with the *principles* underlying the manners of inference, to which one appeals in the case of dispute or doubt? How do things stand, for example, with the syllogistic principles, the principle of 'transitivity' and so forth, to which the validity of every manner of inference leads back in the end? Are they themselves in turn empirical generalizations or does not such a construal entail the most radical absurdity? (*Ideen* 37/43–44)

5. § 21–Against psychologistic idealism

In an important sense, by the end of § 20, the philosophical heavy lifting of chapter 2 is already finished: it has already been shown that if the thesis of TP normativity is true, then scientific naturalism = empiricist naturalism = positivism is false, and also that the thesis of TP normativity provides a better philosophical explanation of the prima facie existence of Ideas and essences. So at this point Husserl could simply pick up his philosophical toys and go home. But as I mentioned above, in this chapter Husserl *also* wants to address, in at least a preliminary way, the three standard worries about the thesis of TP normativity: that it entails a psychologistic version of idealism; that its version of Platonism is a metaphysical and epistemic mystery; and that it unacceptably entails "fictionalism" or the irreality of Ideas or essences. In § 21, he addresses the first worry, i.e., the one about psychologistic idealism.

Psychologism is the thesis that the laws of logic (or more generally, the categorically normative laws, or canons, of authentic knowledge and science as such) are reducible to the laws of empirical natural science. And idealism is the thesis that everything, especially including the objects of human knowledge, is in some way mind-dependent. Now there are several different ways of formulating the worry about psychologistic idealism–e.g., as a worry about solipsism, as a worry about relativism, or as a worry about reducing objective reality and truth to the subjective experiential evidence for objective reality and truth. And in the *Prolegomena to Pure Logic*, the first volume of the *Logical Investigations*, Husserl very carefully and indeed pretty much exhaustively critically covers the entire psychologistic-idealistic terrain. Interestingly, here in *Ideas 1*, he focuses on the *third* worry about psychologistic idealism, namely the worry about reducing objective reality and truth to the subjective experiential evidence for truth:

> One speaks, to be sure, of evidence but instead of bringing it as discerning into *essential connections* with seeing [*Sehen*] in the usual sense, one speaks of a '*feeling of evidence*,' a kind of mystical *index veri* [indicator of the true] that supposedly lends the judgment an affective coloring. Such construals are possible only insofar as one has not learned to analyze kinds of consciousness by way of looking at them in an unadulterated way and in keeping to what is essential [*rein schauend und wesensmäßig*] instead of making theories about them from on high. These alleged feelings of evidence, of the necessity of thinking, and whatever else they might be named, are nothing more than *theoretically concocted feelings*. Everyone who has brought any case of evidence to the point where she actually sees [its] givenness, and has compared it with a case where the evidence for a judgment with the same content is lacking, will recognize this. One immediately notices, then, that the tacit presupposition of the theory that evidence is a feeling is fundamentally erroneous (namely, the presupposition that a case of judging is colored by one's feelings at one point in time and at another is not, yet otherwise is the same, as far as the rest of its psychological essence is concerned.) One notices that it is far more the case that one and the same top layer, that of the same asserting (as merely expressing *the meaning*) conforms in the one case, step for step, to an intuition 'clearly discerning' the state of affairs, while in the other case a completely different phenomenon, a non-intuitive, at times completely confused and unstructured consciousness of the state of affairs is functioning as the lower layer.

Thus, [if one were to make that erroneous presupposition] in the empirical sphere, one could with *the same* right grasp the difference between a clear and faithful perceptual judgment and an arbitrary, vague judgment of the same state of affairs, in such a way that the former is merely endowed with a '*feeling of clarity*,' the other is not. (*Ideen* 39 – 40/46 – 47)

The simple but fundamental point that Husserl is making here is that authentic evidence (*Evidenz*), a.k.a. self-evidence, is necessarily veridical, whereas the mere subjective experience of evidence, a.k.a., the feeling of evidence, or the feeling of clarity, is not necessarily veridical. The feeling of evidence or the feeling or clarity is perfectly consistent with illusion and falsity. Hence to confuse authentic evidence, which entails objective reality and truth, with the mere subjective experience of evidence, which is perfectly consistent with illusion and falsity, as the psychologistic idealist does, is to make a basic mistake. But the thesis of TP normativity does not confuse these two essentially different kinds of evidence. So even if the thesis of TP normativity is idealistic–as indeed it is, as transcendental-phenomenological idealism–it is not psychologistically idealistic. Again, it is crucial to remember that it would be rationally unfair, in this context, to require Husserl to provide and prove a positive metaphysics of idealism in order to make this fundamental point.

6. § 22–Is this mystical Platonism? No.

In § 22, Husserl addresses the second standard worry about the thesis of TP normativity, i.e., that its version of Platonism is a metaphysical and epistemic mystery. He responds to this worry in two steps.

First, he repeats the crucial point that the class of things that have *ontic status* is larger than the class of things that have *factual existence*, especially including the even narrower class of *empirical facts*, and that his version of Platonism is committed only to the highly plausible cognitive-semantic thesis that necessary truths in logic, mathematics, and other a priori sciences contain directly referential singular terms and quantify over the objects picked out by those terms:

> If *object* and *real*, *actuality* and *real actuality* are one and the same, then the construal of Ideas as objects and actualities is, to be sure, an absurd 'Platonic hypostasizing.' If, however, both are sharply separated as was done in the *Logical Investigations*, if object is defined as anything at all, thus, for example, as the subject of a true (categorical, affirmative) assertion, what offense can then remain–unless it be of the sort that stems from obscure prejudices? Also, I did not, indeed, invent the general concept of object, but instead only reinstated the concept demanded by all purely logical propositions. At the same time, I pointed out that it is an intrinsically indispensable concept and, hence, one that has also shaped general scientific discourse. (*Ideen* 40/47)

Second, Husserl explicitly avoids commiting himself to metaphysical and epistemic mysticism about Ideas or essences, i.e., he explicitly *avoids committing himself* to the mystical thesis that Ideas or essences occur essentially *outside of* and essentially *such as to exclude* spacetime and the causal order, and also *explicitly restricts himself* to claiming that any attempt to *psychologize* Ideas or essences by making them into "concepts" in the special and indeed specious sense of *mental constructs* must fail:

> What lies factually before us can only be real, mental occurrences of '*abstraction*' that latch onto real experiences or presentations. As a result, 'theories of abstraction' are then zealously constructed, and psychology, proud of [its grounding in] experience, expands here, *as in all intentional spheres* (that still make up the main themes of psychology), with *concocted phenomena*, with *psychological analyses that are not analyses at all*. Ideas or essences, it is said, are thus '*concepts*' and concepts are '*mental constructs*,' 'products of abstraction,' and as such they play, to be sure, a large role in our thinking. [...]
>
> We reply: certainly essences are 'concepts'–provided one understands by 'concepts' what this polyvalent word permits, namely, essences, and provided one makes clear to oneself that *then* talk of mental products is nonsense as is talk of concept-*formation* [*Begriffsbildung*], understood in the strict and literal sense. Occasionally one reads in a treatise that the series of numbers is a series of concepts, and then, a bit further, that concepts are constructs [*Gebilde*] of thinking. Thus, the numbers themselves, the essences, are initially designated as concepts. But, we ask, are the numbers not what they are, whether we 'construct' [*bilden*] them or not? Certainly, I do my enumerating; I construct my numerical representations in adding 'one and one' [to make two]. The representations of the number are then these, and, if I repeat the same construction another time, they are then others. In this sense, there are sometimes no numerical representations, sometimes many, arbitrarily many numerical representations of one and the same number. But precisely by this means we have, indeed, made a distinction (and how could we avoid it). A representation of a number is not a number itself; it is not the *Two*, this sole member of the series of numbers, the member that, like all such members, is a non-temporal being. To designate it as a mental construct is, accordingly, absurd, an offense against the completely clear sense of arithmetical discourse, discourse that is always discernible as valid, thus, *prior to* all theories. If concepts are mental constructs, then such things as pure numbers are not concepts. But if they are concepts, then concepts are not mental constructs. Hence, new terms *are needed*, precisely in order to resolve equivocations as perilous as these. (*Ideen* 41–42/48–49)

In other words, Husserl is saying that the version of Platonism required by the thesis of TP normativity *requires* that Ideas or essences are non-reducible to empirical facts, but does *not* require that Ideas or essences occur essentially outside of or exclusive of the spatiotemporal or causal order, and also *rules out* the possibility that Ideas or essences are mental constructs. So according to Husserl's version of Platonism, Ideas or essences are non-factual, non-empirical, non-transcendent, non-mental objects that are the truth-makers of necessary truths in the a priori sciences.

Of course, a fully adequate and defensible metaphysics of non-mystical Platonism would ultimately have to say more than this, and would ultimately have to answer the $64,000.00 question: "So what precisely *are* these non-factual, non-empirical, non-transcendent, non-mental objects that are the truth-makers of necessary truths in the a priori sciences?" Contemporary Kantians, naturally, will look to some or another version of transcendental idealism to provide the answer (cf., e.g., Chapman et al. 2013, part 2; Hanna (2015, chs. 6–8). But the crucial methodological point to reiterate is that Husserl does not have to answer *that* question here, in order to provide an effective preliminary response to the standard anti-Platonist criticisms.

7. § 23–Is this fictionalism? No.

In § 23, Husserl addresses the third and final standard worry about the thesis of TP normativity, namely that it unacceptably entails "fictionalism" or the irreality of Ideas or essences. In view of what Husserl has argued in § 22, his response to the third worry can be short and sweet: Only if one held that Ideas or essences are "concepts" in the special and specious sense of mental constructs, would it follow that Ideas or essences are fictional or irreal; but the thesis of TP normativity does not hold this view about Ideas or essences; therefore the thesis of TP normativity does not entail fictionalism or the irreality of Ideas or essences (*Ideen* 42–43/49–50). The critical dialectic is made somewhat complicated here by the fact that Husserl, as a *cognitive semanticist*, a.k.a. a theorist of intentionality, is *also* committed to a theory of concepts in the non-special and non-specious sense, and *also* committed to a sharp distinction between the mental acts of conceptualization and imagination. "Mental constructs" are indeed possible, but only as *objects of acts of imagination*, not as *objects of veridical conceptualization* that pick out Ideas or essences, which in turn are more analogous to acts of veridical sense perception than to acts of imagination:

> One can perceive, remember, and thereby be conscious of things as 'actual'; or in modified acts one can be conscious of them as doubtful, nothing (illusory); finally, in a completely different modification, one can also be conscious of them as 'merely hovering about' and hovering about *as if they were* something actual, were nothing, and so forth. The situation is completely similar for essences, and this is tied to the fact that, like other objects, they also can be meant at times correctly, at other times falsely as, for example, in the case of thinking falsely in geometry. Comprehension and intuition of essences, however, is a polymor-

phic act; in particular, the *discernment of an essence is an act that affords [it] in an originary way*, and, as such, it is the *analogue of sensory perceiving* and *not of imagining*. (*Ideen* 43/50)

Whatever one thinks of Husserl's cognitive semantics or his theory of intentionality, it is crucial to recognize that the thesis of TP normativity is *not* affected by the critical vicissitudes of this theory. Ideas or essences are the *objects* of acts of conceptualization, even if acts of conceptualization do indeed have *intentional contents* that are themselves Ideas or essences of a certain kind; but Husserl's thesis of TP normativity does *not* itself depend on his theory of intentional content.

8. § 24–Rational intuition and the principle of all principles–TP normativity again

In § 24, Husserl steps back from his responses to the standard critical worries about the thesis of TP normativity, and simply re-states the thesis in a nutshell that he calls "the principle of all principles," which says that categorical normativity (i.e., the domain of "principles") exists insofar as Ideas or essences exist, and Ideas or essences are knowable by veridical acts of rational intuition in the a priori sciences:

> But enough of erroneous theories. No conceivable theory can make us stray from the principle of all principles: that each intuition affording [something] in an originary way is a legitimate source of knowledge, that whatever presents itself to us in 'Intuition' in an originary way (so to speak, in its actuality in person) is to be taken simply as what it affords itself as, but only within the limitations in which it gives itself there. Let us continue to recognize that each theory in turn could itself draw its truth only from originary givennesses. Thus, every assertion that does nothing further than give expression to such givennesses through mere explication and meanings conforming precisely to them is actually, as we put it in the introductory words of this chapter, 'an absolute beginning,' called upon to lay the ground in the genuine sense, a principium. This holds in particular measure, however, for the general knowledge of essences, knowledge of the kind for which the word 'principle' is usually restricted. (*Ideen* 43/51)

It is crucial to remember yet again that the thesis of TP normativity is basically being put forward by Husserl as a theory about knowledge in the sciences that is a *better* explanatory theory of the relevant data than scientific naturalism = empiricist naturalism = positivism; and since it has already been shown that natural scientists themselves presuppose a priori principles of logic, mathematics, and induction, then scientific naturalism = empiricist naturalism = positivism is self-undermining, and the thesis of TP normativity is *clearly* the better theory, no matter what one might think about Husserl's idealism, Platonism, and theory of intentionality.

9. § 25–Scientism can't explain science

In § 25, Husserl goes on the critical offensive again, and points out a striking irony which follows directly from the recognition that scientific naturalism = empiricist naturalism = positivism is self-undermining: *scientism has to be a false theory of the formal and natural sciences, precisely because it clearly cannot explain what it clearly presupposes, namely that the formal and natural sciences include principles that are themselves objectively valid, necessary, and a priori*. Or as Husserl puts it,

> The positivist rejects knowledge of essences *de facto*, only where he reflects 'philosophically' and lets himself be deluded by the sophisms of empiricist philosophers. But he does not reject them when, as a natural scientist, he thinks and justifies [things] in the normal attitude of natural science. The reason for this is the fact that he allows himself to be guided there to a very broad extent by insights into essences. Everyone is, indeed, familiar with the fact that the purely mathematical disciplines, the material disciplines like geometry or phoronomy, the formal (purely logical) disciplines like arithmetic, analysis, and so forth, are the basic means of theorizing in the natural sciences. That these disciplines do not proceed empirically, that they are not justified through observations and experiments on experienced figures, movements, and so forth, is obvious. Empiricism, of course, does not want to see this. (*Ideen* 44/51–52).

In other words, in order to take science seriously, it does *not* follow that one must defend scientific naturalism = empiricist naturalism = positivism. On the contrary, in order to take science seriously, one must *reject* scientific naturalism = empiricist naturalism = positivism and *defend* some or another version of the TP normativity thesis. But the critical bottom line is: *scientism can't explain science*. If any Husserlian claim deserves to be posted on the wall in every philosophy department in the world, this is it.

10. § 26–Dogmatic vs. philosophical standpoints on science

In § 26, the final section of the "Naturalistic Misconceptions" chapter, Husserl explores a seemingly simple but all-too-easily overlooked implication of the strikingly ironic critical point he made in § 25. The implication is that *doing science per se* and *philosophically recognizing the nature of science* are sharply distinct and should not be confused. This is what Husserl calls the crucial difference between (i) the "dogmatic" standpoint on science insofar as one is a working scientist, and (ii) the "philosophical" standpoint on science. It is simply a fallacy to think that the theories *framed* by the sciences are the best theories *of* the sciences. In other words, it is simply a fallacy to think that the best natural scientific theory of *the physical world* is a fortiori the best theory of *physics*, far less the best theory of logic, mathematics, or philosophy. And the reason why it is so important to recognize this fallacy is that if it is committed, *it leads to skepticism about science itself*:

> It is necessary to draw an unavoidable and important distinction in the realm of scientific research. On the one side stand the *sciences in the dogmatic attitude*, turned toward their subject matters [*Sachen*], unfazed by any epistemological or skeptical sort of problem. They start from the originary givenness of their subject-matters (and repeatedly return to the latter, in testing what they know), and they ask what the subject matters immediately afford themselves as and, on the basis of this, ask what can be inferred in a mediated way about these subject matters and those of the domain in general. On the other side stands scientific research in the epistemological attitude, the *specifically philosophical attitude* that pursues the skeptical problems regarding the possibility of knowledge, and initially resolves them in an intrinsically universal way in order then to apply the attained solutions and draw the consequences for the assessment of the ultimately valid sense and epistemic value of the results of the dogmatic sciences. At least *at the present time* and as long generally as a highly developed critique of knowledge is lacking, one that has grown to the point of utter rigorousness and clarity, it is *right to seal the borders of dogmatic research off from 'critical' inquiries*. In other words, it is for philosophical science to decide on the legitimacy and illegitimacy of epistemological (and, as a rule, skeptical) prejudices, but they need not trouble the dogmatic scientist. Yet, it is precisely typical of skepticisms to dispose [researchers] to unfavorable hindrances of this kind. Hence, it seems appropriate to us now to see to it that these prejudices do not hinder the course of the scientist's research. (*Ideen* 46/54–55)

In other words, scientific naturalism = empiricist naturalism = positivism sells *formal and natural science themselves* down the river, just as surely as it sells *philosophy* down the river.

Husserl's point here seems clearly, distinctly, and undeniably true. But why has it been so difficult for other philosophers, and especially for his scientistic, empiricist, naturalist, and positivist critics, even to recognize *what* his point is, quite apart from accepting it? My own view is that other philosophers and critics have mistakenly assumed that the distinction between (i) the dogmatic standpoint on science and (ii) the philosophical standpoint on science is the same as the distinction between (i*) doing science unreflectively, and (ii*) being reflective about science. But that is not what Husserl is saying. *Of course* working scientists are reflective investigators. Hence the philosophical standpoint is *not* the same as being reflective. What Husserl is saying is that the philosophical standpoint is the same as taking an inherently transcendental-phenomenological and categorically normative standpoint on science. The philosophical standpoint is investigating "the conditions of the possibility" of science, i.e., it is investigating what is *necessarily and a priori true* about science, i.e., it is investigating *the Idea or essence of science*. In order to move from the dogmatic standpoint on science to the philosophical standpoint on science, it is not sufficient merely to *reflect* on science: one must also *reject* scientism, empiricism, naturalism, and positivism and *accept* some or another version of transcendental idealism together with its commitment to categorical normativity and rationalism. No wonder, then, that other philosophers and especially his scientistic, empiricist, naturalist, and positivist critics, have not even *recognized* Husserl's point, much less accepted it. How could they even recognize it, without already having moved from a dogmatic to a philosophical standpoint on science?

In one sense, given the scientistic, empiricist, naturalist, and positivist default assumptions of mainstream contemporary professional philosophy in the teens of the 21st century, this is a depressing insight. For until the sociological profile of mainstream professional philosophy radically changes, to be a Kantian or a Husserlian is to be a barely-tolerated and even outright despised philosophical outsider. But in another sense, and bracketing the slings and arrows of the profession and its conventional wisdom, it is still nice to be on the side of the philosophical angels.

11. Conclusion

So we are back to where we started, namely with the thesis of TP normativity and its self-evident philosophical superiority over scientific naturalism. Or, to put the upshot of this chapter as a philosophical advertising slogan: Kant's critical philosophy, Husserl's *Logical Investigations*, *Ideas 1*, and *Crisis*, transcendental-phenomenological normativity, and the demise of scientific naturalism and the scientific conception of the world–it *doesn't get much better than this*.

References

Benacerraf, Paul (1973): "Mathematical Truth". In: *Journal of Philosophy* 70, pp. 661–679.
Chapman, Andrew/Ellis, Addison/Hanna, Robert/Hildebrand, Tyler/Pickford, Henry W. (2013): *In Defense of Intuitions: A New Rationalist Manifesto*. London: Palgrave Macmillan.
Crowell, Steven (2013): *Normativity and Phenomenology in Husserl and Heidegger*. Cambridge: Cambridge Univ. Press.
Ernst Mach Society (1929): *The Scientific Conception of the World*. Available online at URL <http://evidencebasedcryonics.org/pdfs/viennacircle.pdf>.
Hanna, Robert (1993): "Logical Cognition: Husserl's *Prolegomena* and the Truth in Psychologism". In: *Philosophy and Phenomenological Research* 53, pp. 251–275.
Hanna, Robert (2006): *Rationality and Logic*. Cambridge, MA: MIT Press.
Hanna, Robert (2008): "Husserl's Arguments against Logical Psychologism". In: Mayer, Verena (Ed.): *Edmund Husserl: Logische Untersuchungen*. Berlin: Akademie Verlag, pp. 27–42.
Hanna, Robert (2013): "Transcendental Idealism, Phenomenology, and the Metaphysics of Intentionality". In: Ameriks, Karl/Boyle, Nicholas (Eds.): *The Impact of Idealism*. Cambridge: Cambridge Univ. Press, pp. 191–224.
Hanna, Robert (2015): *Cognition, Content, and the A Priori*. Oxford: Oxford Univ. Press.
Kusch, Martin (1995): *Psychologism*. London: Routledge.
Moran, Dermot (2012): *Husserl's Crisis of the European Sciences and Transcendental Phenomenology: An Introduction*. Cambridge: Cambridge Univ. Press.
Quine, Williard Van Orman (1969): "Epistemology Naturalized". In: Quine, Williard Van Orman: *Ontological Relativity*. New York: Columbia Univ. Press, pp. 69–90.
Sellars, Wilfrid (1963): "Philosophy and the Scientific Image of Man". In: Sellars, Wilfried (Ed.): *Science, Perception, and Reality*. New York: Humanities Press, pp. 1–40. Also available online at URL = <http://www.ditext.com/sellars/psim.html>.

Andrea Staiti
The melody unheard: Husserl on the natural attitude and its discontinuation

Section II, chapter 1, The thesis of the natural attitude and its suspension

> Quis est, qui complet aures meas tantus et
> tam dulcis sonus?
> Cicero, *De Republica*, VI, 18.

In book six of Cicero's *De Republica* the protagonist of the dialogue, Scipio Aemilianus, encounters the spirit of his adoptive grandfather, Scipio Africanus, in a dream. The old Roman general shows his grandson the firmament from an unspecified vantage point above it and exhorts Scipio to live a life of honor and justice, so as to receive his reward after death and dwell forever among the blessed in the Milky Way. As Scipio gazes upon the starlit night sky and contemplates the revolution of planets and stars fixed in nine diaphanous concentric spheres, he exclaims in amazement, "What is this sound, so loud and yet so sweet, that fills my ears?" (Cicero 1998, p. 90) Africanus explains: "That [...] is the sound produced by the impetus and momentum of the spheres themselves. [...] Filled with this sound, people's ears have become deaf to it." (Cicero 1998, p. 90)

There are fascinating similarities between the myth of the celestial melody and Husserl's conception of the natural attitude, which is the theme of this chapter. The natural attitude is our default way of being in the world. In the natural attitude we take for granted the existence of the world and ourselves in it. Thereby we fail to catch hold of the marvelous dynamics of transcendental constitution in which the being of the world (including our being as humans in the world) is essentially grounded. Filled with the plenitude of readily available beings that saturate the horizon of their experience, humans are fundamentally deaf to the 'melody' of transcendental constitution, i.e., the infinite array of harmonious syntheses of experience underpinning the world's being.

Additionally, there is no way to 'perceive' the unheard melody of transcendental constitution within the boundaries of natural life. In a similar way, Scipio Aemilianus only awakens to the melody of the spheres in the context of a strange dream. For Husserl a special kind of initiation is required to visualize the transcendental field: the phenomenological *epoché*. Strictly speaking, however, there is nothing within the natural attitude that prepares the terrain for the performance of the phenomenological *epoché*. There is no natural remedy for the congenital naïveté caused by uninterrupted exposure to the fact of being, just like there is no natural remedy for the congenital deafness caused by uninterrupted exposure to the celestial melody. The phenomenological *epoché* thus comes onto the scene of Western philosophy completely un-announced and un-prepared, putting Husserl in the uncomfortable situation of playing both Scipios at once. On the one hand Husserl is like Aemilianus, amazed at the new horizon of experience that lays open before him and immersed in the contemplation of it. On the other hand Husserl needs to be Africanus, too. He must attempt to explain to himself and his contemporaries the meaning and the conditions of possibility of such novel experience, and he must look for ways to connect the phenomenological attitude, at least 'retrospectively,' to life in the natural attitude. This difficult task occupies Husserl for most of his mature philosophical life, especially in the 1920s and 1930s. The first book of *Ideas*, however, is the venue where the phenomenological *epoché* is presented to the public for the first time, thus initiating a philosophical debate that continues to this day.

Husserl's introduction of the natural attitude occurs in the first chapter of section two of *Ideas*. This chapter is deceptively short. There is hardly another piece in twentieth century philosophy to which Kant's witty remark about the length of books really depending on how long it takes to understand them rather than the number of pages more aptly applies: it would be much shorter if only it were a little longer! Even a master of hermeneutics like Paul Ricœur considers it "enigmatic" and recommends inexperienced readers to "leave it behind" (Ricœur 1996, p. 39) and move directly to chapter two. Being aware of the hermeneutic challenge posed by the chapter's brevity, my attempt in what follows will not be to summarize or recapitulate it, but rather to expand on what I take to be its three main themes: (1) the natural attitude (§§ 27–30); (2) Cartesianism (§ 31) and (3) the phenomenological *epoché* (§ 32). Given the complexity of the first theme I will break it down into two parts: (1a) the world of natural experience, and (1b) the general thesis of the natural attitude.

1. The world of natural experience

At the beginning of § 27 Husserl introduces the natural attitude as the way in which "human beings naturally live" and argues that an elucidation of it is "best conducted in the first person." (*Ideen* 48/56) In the natural attitude humans are constantly aware of the world as an existing totality, but neither do they thematically know about this awareness, nor do they have reasons to question it.

Scholars have been puzzled by the somewhat abrupt opening of this section. Paul Ricœur, for instance, argues that the logical and ontological considerations of the previous section can be considered as a detachable prelude, and that the book actually starts here (cf. Ricœur 1996, p. 37).[1] However, while this section undeniably reads as a second beginning, if we had not been previously instructed about essences and how to discern them we would likely miss a crucial point. These opening statements have to be read as expressions of eidetic laws. In other words, it does not just so happen that human beings naturally live in the natural attitude. They do so essentially. Husserl is more explicit about the state of affairs in later texts, where he insists that in the natural attitude "subjectivity is human," and "something different is unthinkable," (Husserl 1962, p. 489) thus making explicit the conceivability criterion that legitimates eidetic insights. He even goes on to propose an explicit equation: "Being in the natural attitude means finding oneself as a human being in the world" (Husserl 2002, p. 156). Realizing the essential link between human subjectivity and natural attitude is key to understanding Husserl's contention that genuine epistemological questions can only be raised in a completely different attitude, that is, one in which subjectivity does not feature as human. Given that human subjectivity in the natural attitude interprets itself as an entity in and of the world (thus taking the fact of the world for granted), either the world is bound to remain an ultimately unquestionable presupposition in every philosophical inquiry, or there is a way to look at the world from a different perspective, one that interrogates the world *as world*. The phenomenological attitude comes forward as the only viable resource to realize the latter possibility.

As for the first person perspective adopted to describe the world of the natural attitude, both the style and the substance of § 27 recast the opening sections of Richard Avenarius' *Der menschliche Weltbegriff* (1891). As Manfred Sommer (1985), and, more recently, Emanuele Soldinger (2010) convincingly showed, Avenarius and the philosophical school of empirio-criticism had a tremendous impact on the development of Husserl's thought. Husserl mentions Avenarius explicitly in the lecture course *Basic Problems of Phenomenology* (1910/11) (cf. Husserl 2006a) as a major source of inspiration for his own understanding of the world as a philosophical problem. Let us hear the opening section of Avenarius' book, in order to then draw a short comparison between the two thinkers:

> I with all my thoughts and feelings find myself in the middle of an environment. This environment consists in a variety of elements, which stand reciprocally in a variety of rela-

---

[1] Ricœur suggests that the reader "can provisionally omit" (Ricœur 1996, p. 37) section one and return to it at a later point.

tions of dependence. To this environment belong also fellow humans, expressing a variety of assertions. What they say, in turn, stands mostly in a relation of dependence with the environment. Moreover, fellow humans speak and act like me. They answer my questions like I answer theirs. They pursue the various elements of the environment or avoid them. They alter such elements or endeavor to maintain them unaltered. They designate with words what they do or stop doing, and they explain as deed or interruption of a deed their reasons and plans. All this they do like me, as well. Therefore I couldn't think otherwise: fellow humans are entities like me–and I myself am an entity like them. (Avenarius 1891, p. 4)

The similarity with the opening paragraph of § 27 is striking:

I am conscious of a world, endlessly spread out in space, endlessly becoming and having become in time. I am conscious of it, and that means above all that I immediately find it intuitively, I experience [erfahre] it. Through seeing, touching, hearing and so forth, in the various manners of sensory perception, corporeal things in some sort of spatial distribution are *simply there for me*; in the literal or figurative sense of the word they are 'on hand,' whether or not I am particularly attentive to them and engaged with them, observing, thinking, feeling, willing. Animals, including humans, are also immediately there for me; I look at them, I see them, I hear them approaching, I grasp them by the hand; speaking with them, I immediately understand what they are imagining and thinking, what sorts of feelings are stirring in them, what they wish or want. They, too, are on hand in my field of intuition as actualities, even if I do not pay attention to them. (*Ideen* 48/56)

In very brief compass Avenarius' project can be characterized as a positivistic critique of metaphysical constructions distorting the original nature of our actual experiences. His philosophical strategy consists in contrasting theorization and experience, and then proceeding to determine what structures and regularities characterize experiencing prior to all theorizing. Avenarius pursues a descriptive rehabilitation of what he terms the natural or *pure* experience of the world as the basis of all scientific inquiry, be it good or poor, successful or unsuccessful. Using language that should strike phenomenologists as remarkably familiar, in his earlier *Critique of Pure Experience* (1888) Avenarius recommends that empiriocriticist philosophers take their departure "directly in the things, rather than in books" and "only grant validity to the thing at issue (*die Sache*)." In so doing, they should make an effort to "take up the thing as much as possible in the way in which it gives itself." (Avenarius 1888, p. xvi) The influence of Avenarius' vocabulary and project on Husserl is thus unmistakable.

Avenarius defends a kind of neutral monism of sensation, according to which the traditional distinction of outer and inner experience is derivative. The unadulterated 'thing' of pure experience, for Avenarius, is a complexion of sensations prior to the metaphysically driven ascription of these sensations to an 'inner' or 'outer' realm, and even prior to their construal as discrete mental or physical items. In a way that anticipates later positivistic thought, such as Carnap's *Aufbau*, for Avenarius what counts as 'world' for us is constructed by way of a progressive complexification of simple, 'pure' experiences. However, like Husserl, Avenarius is not a sensualist. He admits that part of our immediate, original experience is also determined by past experience and the concepts springing from it.[2]

However, here is where Avenarius and Husserl part ways. First, as Soldinger emphasizes (cf. Soldinger 2010, p. 204), Husserl considers pure experience as already organized in perfectly intuitable classes, such as Perception, Expectation, Feeling, Judgment, etc. The ability to discriminate between, say, my act of seeing my room and my act of remembering my decision to buy a new desk does not stem from tacit psychological theorizing or conceptual construction. It is a phenomenological given. Second, Husserl's world of the natural attitude is a much thicker and more diversified environment than Avenarius would readily concede. Starting with the perceptual level, Husserl maintains that our actual experience always includes a lot more than the momentary appearance of data in our perceptual field simple, or standing in conceptual (subsumptive) function. As he eventually explains in § 35, our concrete experience is always organized around a focal point, to which an act of explicit, attentive grasp (or *cogito*) is directed. While we are implementing a *cogito*, however, a variety of objects are perceived (but not attended to) in the background, ready to be perceived the moment we elect to redirect our attention toward them. To use an important distinction from a later chapter, these unattended objects are intentionally present and even "*given in an originary way*" or "in person," although certainly not given '*as* themselves' or self-given (*selbstgegeben*) (*Ideen* 122/142).

Beyond the strict sphere of presence with its background and foreground objects, Husserl highlights "a *horizon of indeterminate actuality, a horizon of which I am dimly conscious.*" (*Ideen* 48/57) This horizon is both spatial and temporal and

---

[2] In any case, for Avenarius concepts are cut of the same cloth as sensations. As Manfred Sommer puts it: "Experience, and even 'naïve' or 'original' experience, for Avenarius is more than a sequence of impressions. It is more than the succession of data. Experience always means also apperception, apprehension of the given on the basis of the pre-given, subsumption of singular sensory presentations under general concepts. Concepts, however, are nothing other than such singular presentations, and they carry their title only because of their additional function. A singular presentation (*Einzelvorstellung*) becomes a concept when it does not only exhibit (*präsentiert*) that which it presents (*vorstellt*), but also apperceives what it does not present. A singular presentation is not general. It becomes generalized to the extent that new items are subsumed under it. The concept comes about as concept only in the subsumption." Sommer 1985, p. 37)

it correlates with a horizon of experienced potentialities in the subject (which Husserl sometimes calls a *Könnenshorizont.*) I know that at any time I can access past objects in memory, that I can enact the appropriate movements to reach distant objects, and that I can direct anticipatory expectations toward future objects. I do not *need*, however, to actually produce memories, or move in space in order for past or distant objects to become part of my experience. They already *are* part of my experience. They are dimly and indeterminately present all the time. For instance, I have never been to Beijing but there is a sense in which Beijing is present in my experience *now*. It is an actually existing place, which I know includes existing buildings, streets, people, etc. If I actually resolved to go there, the progress in my experience would *not* be a leap from absolute absence to absolute presence, but rather a transition from obscure, dim presence to clear, intuitive presence. Similarly, I have no actual memory of what I did on November 8th, 1989. However, even in this case there is a sense in which that day is part of my present experience. I know at least that I did *something*. I can eventually make an effort to fill out this nearly completely empty intention with at least some intuitive content. For instance, I know that I presumably went to school, and if I did I must have worn the uniform that we used to wear, etc. I could use external aids and the testimony of other people to help me fill out that memory, if it were necessary, for instance, if I were a key witness in a trial, and so forth.

The important thing here is to point out that the structure of this ever-present horizon for Husserl is *non-inferential*. It would be phenomenologically incorrect to describe our experience of objects beyond the scope of our current perceptual field as the conclusion of an inference having the existence of presently perceived objects as its premise. To say that I am somehow 'inferring' that my apartment must still exist while I am packing to go home after class would just be a bad description of what I am actually doing. Neither did the certainty of my apartment's existence ever subside over the course of the day, nor did the apartment itself actually ever leave the sphere of my experience, so that I would somehow need to regain cognitive possession of it with the aid of inferential reasoning. The apartment and the certainty associated with it were part of the horizon of my experience all along.

Husserl's analyses of horizon-consciousness progress with increased sophistication throughout his career. As Saulius Geniusas argues, it is only in the years after *Ideas* that Husserl develops them into proper thematizations of the *world*. Thus in *Ideas I* "the world-horizon remains unexplored, even though the world is the original figure of the horizon in this work." (Geniusas 2012, p. 63) In 1925, in his lectures on *Phenomenological Psychology*, Husserl arrives at the sharpest formulation of his conception of the world and its horizons as integral to our experience. Husserl states, in open contrast to Kant:

> Kant insists that the world is not an object of possible experience, whereas we continually speak in all seriousness of the world precisely as the all-inclusive object of an experience expanded and to be expanded all-inclusively. I cannot acknowledge the Kantian proposition, no matter how the concept of experience is formed, if it is to remain serviceable. For us, real single things are experienced, but the world is also experienced; and the two are even inseparable. (Husserl 1976, p. 71)

Not only does Husserl's natural world of experience include temporally and spatially remote objects. It also includes non-sensuous objects such as values and numbers. As he continues his description in § 27: "This world is not thereby here for me as mere *world of things* [*Sachenwelt*]; instead, with the same immediacy, it is here as *a world of values, a world of goods, a practical world*." (*Ideen* pp. 49 – 50/58) And furthermore, in § 28: "The world of numbers is likewise here for me, precisely as the field of objects of the arithmetic pre-occupation." (*Ideen* 51/59) But what does it mean that both values and numbers are "here for me" in the natural experience of the world as much as physical things or other human beings? Husserl is adamant that items like values and numbers, if the appropriate conditions obtain, are actually perceived. The phrase *Wertnehmung*, literally taking-in-of-value, which Husserl frequently uses, is deliberately construed as a parallel of *Wahrnehmung*, the ordinary German word for perception. This can be somewhat irritating, especially if one holds fast to the equation of 'perception' and 'sensory perception' characterizing much philosophy and the ordinary usage of the term. David Carr, for instance, finds Husserl's insistence on the direct perceptual experience of the world of culture and its characteristic, value-laden objects troubling. Therefore, in his view, "[s]uch terms as 'pre-predicative,' 'immediate,' 'intuitively given' are clearly out of place" (Carr 2004, p. 367) if applied to the items like values, numbers, and cultural formations. However, if we stick to the definition of perception provided at the very beginning of *Ideas*, in § 1, as simply "the experience that affords [the objects] in an originary way," (*Ideen* 9/11) then there is nothing strange about calling the experience of values or numbers 'perception,' provided that it affords such objects in an originary way. Suppose, for instance, that I am holding in my hands a copy of Dante's *Divine Comedy* and I form in my mind the judgment 'This is a masterpiece!' In Husserl's description, if I am forming the judgment in full awareness of the poem's aesthetic value, then this value itself is present perceptually for me, it is given in an originary way. We can legitimately draw distinctions of emptiness and fulfillment in the value-directed intention, in a way entirely analogous to sensory perception. Compare, for instance, a college student holding his copy of the *Divine*

Comedy and thinking 'This is a masterpiece!' and a Dante scholar holding the same book and forming the same judgment. Both the scholar and the student are intending the same value,[3] but the degree of fulfillment is (at least presumably) greater for the scholar's intention. Similarly, if one actually forms the complex intention '2 + 2 = 4,' and thereby *sees* with evidence that this equation is correct, then the numbers and operations composing it are not merely thought, but actually given originarily or, in a sense, perceived.

Lastly, note that the necessity to receive some kind of training in order to be able to catch hold of numbers or the aesthetic value of the *Divine Comedy* does not pose any particular problem to Husserl's contention that we can perceive such items. Sensory perception, too, requires that the perceiver enact certain procedures in order to grasp perceptual objects. If I want to perceive the painting hanging on the left side of my room I have to turn my head appropriately. In an analogous way, if I want to perceive the aesthetic value of the painting I have to learn certain things about art and develop an artistic sensibility. Needless to say, turning one's head to the left is infinitely easier (at least for most human subjects) than learning art history or cultivating an artistic sensibility. In both cases, however, certain kinds of objects appear as correlates of the appropriate 'moves,' a simple kinaesthetic move in the case of a sensuous object and a set of much more complex theoretical and practical 'moves' in the case of aesthetic values.

After enunciating the kinds of objects encountered in our natural experience of the world (essentially four kinds: physical things, human and non-human animals, values, and mathematical/ideal objects) Husserl remarks that for the purposes of the book he is not interested in an exhaustive analysis:

> …we do not set for ourselves the task of continuing the pure description and escalating it to the level of a systematically comprehensive characterization of what is found in the natural attitude (together with all the attitudes that can be coherently interwoven with it), exhaustively characterizing it thereby in all its breadth and depth. Such a task can and must–as a scientific task–be undertaken. It is an extraordinarily important task, even though it has been scarcely noticed before now. It is not our task here. (*Ideen* 52/60–61)

---

[3] I am deliberately simplifying the phenomenological description here. In a more accurate description one would want to take into account the difference between the experience of an object *as valuable* and the experience of the *value itself*, as a distinct object in its own right. Accordingly, one could experience the *Divine Comedy* as valuable without necessarily intending explicitly the distinctive aesthetic value attaching to it, and perhaps equally attaching to works written in the same style, language, etc. At any time, however, we can redirect our intention from the valuable object to the value itself. Husserl addresses this distinction in § 37, cf. *Ideen* 64–66/75–77.

Famously, a few years later Heidegger would claim that his own work *Being and Time* (1927), produced such a systematic description of the natural experience of the world, which Husserl envisioned but never really carried out. *Pace* Heidegger, however, we know that Husserl himself became increasingly engrossed in this task, which culminated with his late formulation of lifeworld ontology as the royal road into transcendental phenomenology. In a recent paper Dermot Moran proved that these early analyses in *Ideas I* are systematically linked to Husserl's later work on the lifeworld. Moran stresses a "direct continuity, despite the gap of a quarter century, between *Ideen I* and *Krisis*." (Moran 2012, p. 121) Needless to say, the concept of the lifeworld in *The Crisis of the European Sciences and Transcendental Phenomenology* (1936) and in the manuscripts surrounding this work is much more refined and complex than the world of natural experience roughly characterized in *Ideas I*. Moran, however, is right to see Husserl working on these issues as early as *Ideas I*, and possibly even earlier.

Before I move to analyze the actual core of this section, i.e., Husserl's concept of a *general thesis* undergirding our experience of the world in the natural attitude, I would like to advance a suggestion. I believe that part of the reason why Husserl's later concept of the lifeworld is so much more complex (and even problematic) than its earlier formulation in *Ideas I* is that in the last decade of his life Husserl used the lifeworld problematic to engage a variety of thinkers and themes at the same time. While, as argued above, the natural concept of the world in *Ideas I* is developed primarily out of a critical appropriation of Avenarius' empirio-criticism and it revolves around the notion of a pure experience prior to all theory, Husserl's later concept of the lifeworld engages simultaneously the work of philosophers as rich and diverse as Dilthey, Rickert, Simmel, and Heidegger. The lifeworld either responds or claims to respond to problems in the theory and history of natural and human science, the theory of knowledge, the philosophy of psychology, the philosophy of history, and even metaphysics. It is little surprise, then, that as the analyses developed in embryo in these sections of *Ideas I* increase in scope and ambition, difficulties and tensions correspondingly multiply.

2. The general thesis

Moving into § 30 Husserl gets at the perhaps most difficult, but also most critical claim advanced in this chapter. The claim is that the natural attitude is characterized by what he calls a *general thesis*:

> I find constantly on hand opposite me the one spatio-temporal actuality to which I myself belong, as do all other human beings who find themselves in it and related to it in a similar way. I find the 'actuality' (the word already says as much) *to be there* in advance and *also take [it] as it affords itself to me, as being here*. No doubt or rejection of anything given in the natural world changes anything in *the natural attitude's general thesis*. As an actuality, 'the' world is always there; at most it is here or there 'other' than I supposed; this or that is to be stricken *from it*, so to speak, under the title of 'illusion,' 'hallucination,' and the like, stricken from it as the world that–in the sense of the general thesis–is always there [*immer daseiende Welt*]. (*Ideen* 52/61)

From this dense passage we learn three interconnected things about the world as experienced in the natural attitude: (i) it is always "there in advance," or *vorgegeben*; (ii) its being there in advance is connected to something called "the general thesis;" (iii) this general thesis is immune to doubt or resection. Commenting on this paragraph, Paul Ricœur registers a certain disappointment. He writes:

> This paragraph is somewhat disappointing if one expects of it a radical definition of the natural attitude. It doesn't answer the most elementary questions: (a) Why use the word *thesis* or *position* (*Thesis = Setzung = Position*) for this attitude which consists in *finding there an existing world and accepting it as it is given,* as existing? In brief, how is *finding there* equivalent to *positing*? (Ricœur 1996, pp. 87–88)

Ricœur is asking the right questions, and he is correct that Husserl is not answering them here. This is partly because a full phenomenological elucidation of the relationship between givenness-in-advance (*Vorgegebenheit*), thetic or positional consciousness, and non-emendability of our overall consciousness of the world belongs in *genetic phenomenology,* whose theme is "to make understandable how, in the development proper to the structure of every stream of consciousness [...]–how those intricate intentional systems develop, through which finally an external world can appear to consciousness and to the ego." (Husserl 2001a, p. 62) Husserl does not develop his genetic phenomenology until the 1920s. However, we can find some helpful indications to clarify these issues already in his earlier work.

To say that the world is 'there in advance,' means that, unlike individual things, the world does not enter or leave the scene of our experience. It is always there before we turn our attention to this or that particular object and before we engage in any practical or theoretical activity. This is, of course, not a temporal 'before.' It expresses a 'logical' relation of priority and not a temporal one. There are many new things we can discover about the world, or in the world but the world itself is not the sort of thing that can be discovered. It is the ground of every possible discovery, which is not itself a discovery. Whatever we decide to busy ourselves with, the world is always 'there,' readily available to us for further operations. Unlike things and people in the world, the world does not admit of 'degrees' of availability and does not become 'available' (or fails to do so) depending on our contingent plans and purposes. It is always 'available' prior to all plans and purposes. What does it mean, then, that the world is 'posited,' as the phrase 'general thesis' suggests? Or, to reiterate Ricœur's question, "how is *finding there* equivalent to *positing?*" (Ricœur 1996, pp. 87–88).

In order to understand the meaning of Husserl's *positing* we have to consider the philosophical lineage of this crucial notion. It leads back to Hume's *Treatise on Human Nature*, Kant's introduction of "*setzen*" as an appropriation of Hume in his pre-critical and critical writings, Herbart's continuing usage of Kant's vocabulary, and finally Brentano's resort to the notion of positing in his original theory of judgment. A thorough exploration of this lineage would exceed the scope of this chapter so let me just focus briefly on Hume and Kant, to whose original theories Husserl's notion of "*setzen*" stands in closest relationship.

Hume is the first philosopher to devote a thorough analysis to the phenomenon of *belief*. In the *Treatise* he observes that there are three fundamentally different ways in which we can entertain an idea. (1) We can merely form the idea in our imagination; (2) we can form the idea and conceive the corresponding thing as existent; (3) we can form the idea, conceive the corresponding thing as existent and also *believe* in the existence of the thing. Hume famously states that moving from (1) to (2) and (3) does not add anything to our initial idea at the level of content:

> 'Tis [...] evident that the idea of existence is nothing different from the idea of any object and that when after the simple conception of any thing we wou'd conceive it as existent, we in reality make no addition to or alteration on our first idea. [...] But I go farther; and not content with asserting, that the conception of the existence of any object is no addition to the simple conception of it, I likewise maintain, that the belief of the existence joins no new ideas to those, which compose the idea of the object. (Hume 2000, pp. 65–66)

Believing a certain thing, thus, does not alter or restructure the content of the corresponding idea merely representing that thing. It is a new "manner of our conceiving" (Hume 2000, p. 67) the idea, or a new "operation of the mind" (Hume 2000, p. 68) carried out on the original idea. In this new manner of conceiving the idea we make a commitment, we 'posit' the corresponding thing as existent. Let us leave aside the difficulties and obscurities in Hume's attempt to account for such new operation of the mind within the framework of his psychology. For the purpose of this chapter it is important to notice that for Hume calling belief an "operation of the mind" does not mean that belief is something we actively bestow on or withdraw from our ideas as we wish. Rather, belief is "something *felt* by the mind." (Hume 2000, p. 68) Especially when we directly experience something in perception, belief is an immediately felt characteristic attached to our sensory experience. Everything else that we believe, in Hume's account, draws its force from the sphere of present sensory experience, which is the venue where 'belief' manifests itself in strongest and most irresistible fashion.

It is this Humean sense of belief as a mental operation adding no new content to a given idea that Kant's notion of '*Setzung*,' and in particular simple or absolute *Setzung* translates. In his celebrated refutation of the ontological argument for the existence of God he points out:

> Being is obviously not a real predicate, i.e., a concept of something that could add to the concept of a thing. It is merely the positing of a thing or of certain determinations in themselves. [...] Now if I take the subject (God) together with all his predicates [...] and say God is, or there is a God, then I add no new predicate to the concept of God, but only posit the subject in itself with all its predicates, and indeed posit the object in relation to my concept. (Kant 1998, p. 567; A599/B627)

If I believe that God exists, then I posit an existing entity corresponding to my concept (Hume would say 'idea') of God. In a recent contribution Wayne Martin advances the following suggestion to elucidate Kant's usage of 'positing':

> "Posit" translates Kant's *setzen*–to put or to place. These are themselves the Latin and German equivalents of the Greek 'thesis' [...], whose primary meaning is also to place or set. "Thesis" is, of course, itself an etymon of syn-thesis: to put or place together. In thinking about its application here, it is useful to have in mind the mathematical sense of positing–as when I posit a number in the course of a proof ("Posit an integer greater than n ..."). Kant's claim, then, is that in judging Pierre to be wise I combine my concepts, but in judging that he exists I posit him. (Martin 2006, p. 52)

This analogy with mathematical reasoning, however, can be slightly misleading. The act of positing in mathematical reasoning is a deliberate intellectual act. However, when I 'posit' the existence of Pierre, for example, when I meet Pierre on the street I do not engage in a deliberate intellectual act. My positing of Pierre simply 'happens.' In Humean idiom, it is a felt operation of the mind whose occurrence I witness. For Kant, of course, already at the perceptual level 'positing' involves the work of conceptual capacities and a spatiotemporal system of reference, which is entirely absent in Hume. This however, does mean that the act of positing for Kant involves any kind of deliberate reasoning, as is the case with mathematical (or metaphysical) claims.

Moreover, positing in mathematical reasoning does not necessarily involve believing in the existence of what is posited. For example I can 'posit' an uneven number that is divisible by two, just in order to prove that there is no such number. I can 'posit' all sorts of mathematical entities and relations just for the sake of argument. However, there is a much more fundamental and original sense of positing that both Hume and Kant have in mind. It has nothing to do with intellectual reasoning in that it is woven into the very fabric of our perceptual experience of things.

This fundamental sense of positing prior to all judgment and conceptualization is precisely what Husserl has in mind. Here is a helpful passage from a research manuscript that makes clear why, to address Ricœur's question, 'finding there' is equivalent to 'positing':

> In experience, and ultimately in perception, we are conscious of what is experienced as being. That which is experienced is valid for us, the subjects of experience, as being. This means that the very process of experiencing harbors within itself a 'positing of being' (*Seinssetzung*), the 'belief-in-being' (*Seins-'Glauben'*) issuing from the I. Only through experiencing and on the basis of such belief a world is 'there' for us, as something existing. (Husserl 2008, p. 266)

As we stated above, Husserl 'positing' is not primarily something accomplished in judgment. In other words, judgment reflects at the logical, predicative level a dynamic of consciousness that happens originally in perception. We do not 'posit' exclusively the existence of unobserved things or mathematical entities via inferential reasoning. First and foremost we 'posit' the existence of things encountered in simple perception, and we do not do so on the basis of actual judgment. This Humean/Kantian sense of positing is already clear in earlier texts such as *Logical Investigations*, where Husserl describes 'positing' as a mode of *belief* attaching to certain acts of presentation. In particular, 'positing' or 'nonpositing' is a mode pertaining to what Husserl labels 'act-quality,' and it enters into the overall definition of an act of consciousness. This distinction is meant to capture the contrast between merely imagining something or entertaining a thought and actually seeing something. When I merely imagine a crocodile, my act of consciousness intending a crocodile does not *posit* the crocodile. The imagined crocodile is not experienced with the compelling force of *belief*. Things are different when I actually perceive, or actually expect to perceive a crocodile, say, at the zoo. If I was to describe the act of consciousness intending the perceived or expected crocodile, I should take into account my actual *believing* that there is a crocodile, my *positing* a crocodile as opposed to merely entertaining an imaginative act having a crocodile as its intentional correlate.[4]

---

4 In order to dispel every possible misunderstanding of the phenomenological notion of positing, it would be helpful to contrast Husserl with yet another philosopher who abundantly em-

The phenomenological description of *thesis* or positing at the level of single acts of consciousness yields one further, important eidetic insight: "*To each positing act there corresponds a possible non-positing act having the same matter, and vice versa.*" (Husserl 2001b, p. 151) In other words, we can transform in thought every possible act of consciousness into a mere 'presentation,' i.e., the mere entertaining of a thought or understanding of a proposition. In this regard, the same presentational matter 'my dog in the garden' can underlie a positional act, in which I take my dog to really be in the garden, or the corresponding non-positional act, in which I merely think about my dog in the garden.

One of the difficulties connected to extending the analysis of *thesis* in individual acts of consciousness to the *general thesis* pertaining to the world is that the general thesis does not attach to one specific act of consciousness. For this reason, we cannot possibly think of the *general thesis* converted into a *general non-thesis*, whereby the same presentational matter 'world' would underlie a non-positional total act, one in which the world is merely thought about. Husserl is very well aware of this difficulty as he states at the beginning of § 31:

> The general thesis, by virtue of which we are constantly conscious of the real environment (not merely in keeping with apprehension in general but as an 'actuality' *that is there*), naturally does *not* consist *in one distinctive act*, in one articulated judgment *about* existence. It is, indeed, something obtaining persistently during the entire duration of the attitude, i.e., during the natural, waking life directed towards it. What is respectively perceived, what is clearly or dimly envisaged, in short, everything from the natural world of which we are conscious experientially and prior to thinking, bears in its entire unity and in terms of every articulated saliency the character of [being] 'there,' 'on hand.' An explicit (predicative) existential judgment, in unison with this character, may be essentially grounded on it. When we say this, we nonetheless know that in doing so we have only made into a theme and predicatively grasped what somehow already lay unthematically, unthought, unpredicated

---

ploys the term *setzen*, but, unlike Husserl, gives it a strong metaphysical connotation, i.e., Fichte. We should not think of Husserl's *Setzung* as somehow analogous to Fichte's *Tathandlung*, as an original metaphysical 'deed' flowing from the spontaneity of an absolute ego. Unlike Fichte, Husserl does not want us to subvert the way in which we ordinarily think about objects and suggest that in reality we somehow unconsciously create the objects of our experience. While Husserl *does* maintain that the objects of experience are *essentially* and not only contingently related to our experiences of them, and while this does commit him to the view that objects are *constituted*, this has nothing to do with his notion of positing, *thesis*, or *Setzung*. Again, let us not think of *Setzung* as a kind of *fiat* issued by the subject and bestowing existence on what would otherwise be a mere jumble of disconnected sensations. For Husserl, *thesis*, positing or *Setzung* is a descriptive character of some acts of consciousness, in particular, nominal acts (acts containing meanings of the genus 'noun') intending perceptually existing physical things, or at least perceptual things that we take to exist.

in the original experiencing [*Erfahren*] or better lay in what is experienced [*Erfahrenen*] with the character of what is 'on hand.' (*Ideen* 53/62)

If we take the general thesis to be the distinctive feature of the natural attitude,[5] and the fundamental mode of our experience of the world in it, then it is appropriate to stress with Sebastian Luft the foundational function of the natural vis-à-vis every other possible worldly attitudes:

> All attitudes implicitly and tacitly bear the belief that the world they are in, or dealing with in some way or the other, exists. They might believe in it in different ways, as this or that, but they believe always that it exists. If this thesis is inherent in all attitudes it is, of course, never explicit, we are naive towards it. To paraphrase this, we can vary Kant's famous statement by saying: *the belief that the world exists must accompany all my attitudes*. (Luft 1998, p. 163)

---

5 In a wide-ranging study of *Ideen* Jean-François Lavigne criticizes Husserl's characterization of the natural attitude in terms of a 'general thesis.' He argues that this characterization is a veritable "deformation" (*gauchissement*) (Lavigne 2009, p. 63) of the natural attitude, which knows nothing of a subjective accomplishment as the origin of our consciousness of being (Lavigne 2009, p. 91). According to Lavigne, in the natural attitude we always encounter being as "absolutely autonomous" or "for itself" (*perséité*) (Lavigne 2009, p. 45), as "positing itself through itself," and not as "the correlate of a doxic position" (Lavigne 2009, p. 92). According to Lavigne, perceptual experience in the natural attitude has no doxic quality whatsoever. Something like a doxic quality, or belief character, only "appears in perceptual judgment" (Lavigne 2009, p. 93), such that Husserl is illegitimately reading back into simple perception a feature that only pertains to judgment. In Lavigne's narrative, this "phenomenological falsification" (Lavigne 2009, p. 91) of the natural attitude amounts to a "psychological pre-reduction of being in the natural attitude to the world of phenomena," and to an "an elimination of the surplus of being" vis-à-vis all appearance (Lavigne 2009, p. 65). This illegitimate operation, for Lavigne, sets the stage for and sustains logically Husserl's transcendental idealism. What to make of Lavigne's argument ultimately depends on how much ontological robustness one is willing to attribute to the natural attitude. If it is a good description of experience in the natural attitude to say that in it being comes forward as absolutely autonomous and independent from consciousness, then Lavigne is right. However, it seems to me that Lavigne is attributing an excessive ontological commitment to the natural attitude, thus reading back into it a kind of strong realism that is actually a philosophical theory, and not an innocent description of how we naturally experience things. Husserl's description is more convincing than Lavigne's because the natural attitude is primarily driven by practical concerns, and practical concerns do not take their ontic correlates ('beings') as absolute or completely alien to consciousness. In the natural attitude beings are precisely that: correlates for our activities, and as such they always appear in some modality of belief. The world is the overarching ground for such beliefs, and our attitude toward it is a 'thesis' in that *we take it* to be there for us.

Note that, in the same sense in which the world for Husserl does not reduce to the world of physical things, the all-encompassing general thesis of the natural attitude does not pertain exclusively to the world of physical things. In a somewhat odd way, the general thesis stretches to affect indirectly also items that are not strictly speaking *in* the world, such as numbers or imagined entities. Prior to a serious phenomenological investigation, we take mathematical judgments and their subject matter to be somehow 'about the world,' and even our most unbridled fantasies are obscurely taken to occur 'in the world,' to be somehow part of the world.[6] This is because the general thesis is the diffuse and unchanging foil against which we implicitly read everything we encounter or embark upon.

One last aspect of Husserl's presentation of the general thesis remains to be discussed: its immunity to doubt, illusion and rejection. This is a direct consequence of the fact that the general thesis does not attach to one distinctive act having one distinctive intentional object. In order to fully clarify this point we should address Husserl's analyses of *modalization* and doxic modalities in §§ 103–105 of *Ideas*.[7] Husserl develops these analyses in full in later works, such as *Experience and Judgment* and the aforementioned *Analyses Concerning Passive and Active Synthesis*, where he takes into account the temporality and associative dimensions of perception. This is not the place to expand on Husserl's genetic phenomenology, a dimension entirely absent in *Ideas I*, but it is perhaps a good place to hint at how a genetic analysis of perception is unavoidable in order to clarify the sense of the world's indubitableness.

A genetic analysis of perception is one in which perception is not investigated exclusively in terms of its structural components (act-matter, act-quality, *belief*-character, attentional mode, intentional object, etc.), but it is rather seen as a concrete *process unfolding in time*. As such, perception is characterized by anticipatory components, which in turn can be either confirmed or contradicted by further experience. To paraphrase freely one of Husserl's favorite examples, let us imagine being at the shopping mall and deciding to approach one of the attendants to ask for information. We identify what we take to be the attendant and walk towards her. At this point the modality of our perceptual experience is, in accordance with the general thesis, 'certainty of existence.' If we were to express this with words in an explicit judgment we would say: 'there is a store attendant.' To be certain of the existence of a store attendant includes having certain expectations regarding the further unfolding of our experience. We expect to start no-

---

[6] Saulius Geniusas aptly talks about an "imprint of worldliness" that characterizes even abstract entities such as numbers or values in the natural attitude, cf. Geniusas 2012, p. 57.
[7] See Nicolas De Warren's chapter in this book.

ticing certain movements, imperceptible from afar, as we approach; we expect the attendant to hear our voice when we call her, to turn around, etc. If this happens, our certainty of being is confirmed and strengthened.

However, it could also happen otherwise. We may start realizing that the 'shop attendant' displays a strange fixity, that she does not respond to our calling, etc. Instead of being confirmed our certainty of being starts to waver. The new data coming from our experience conflict with the previous ones, and a new possible way of apprehending what we are seeing pushes to supplant the one we held heretofore. We start *doubting* that what we are seeing is a human being and contemplating the possibility that it may be a mannequin. Our certainty undergoes, in Husserl's language, a modalization. Finally, when we get close enough, we realize that, indeed, it was a mannequin. The foregoing way of apprehending what we saw is correspondingly changed. We realize that we underwent a perceptual *illusion*, and, correspondingly, we *strike* or *cross out* the previous stretches of perceptual experience. This small perceptual trauma is retained in time-consciousness as an illusory episode in our perceptual life as our experience moves on.

Note that, while experiences like the one just described may occur frequently in our life, none of them leads us to ever question or doubt the existence *of the world*. It is impossible to think about our total consciousness of the world undergoing a modalization like the one just described, i.e., one that begins with the certainty of the world's existence, eventually faces conflicting data, goes through a phase of doubt, 'crosses out' the existing world as illusory, and finally *replaces* the world previously believed to exist with *another world*, which we now take to be the truly existing one. Even if we imagine fantastic scenarios, like the one described in the famous movie *The Matrix*, a total modalization of the general thesis is out of question. Even if the revision of Neo's beliefs in the movie was overwhelmingly broad, 'the world' simply turned out to be different than he had expected it to be. It was not replaced by a second world. The one, non-emendable world simply turned out to have a new, emendable face.

We could then conclude that, in consideration of the logic of illusion, the sentence: "the world is an illusion" is countersensical, and based on *metabasis*. A category pertaining to the genetic analysis of single perceptual acts is applied outside of its legitimate sphere of validity. Contrariwise, the sentence "the world exists" is analytically true every time I pronounce it and regardless of the perceptual circumstances in which I pronounce it.

This final statement should likely puzzle some readers. How can Husserl hold this view about the world and still be a Cartesian? This leads us to the next section.

3. Cartesianism

Husserl opens § 31 quite abruptly stating: *"Instead now of remaining in this attitude, we want to alter it radically."* (*Ideen* 52/61) He continues, stating that, given the aforementioned convertibility of the general thesis into an existential judgment, "[w]e can proceed with the potential and not explicit thesis, precisely as we do with the explicit thesis of a judgment." (*Ideen* 53/62) If we want to discontinue the general thesis in order to inaugurate a new attitude, Husserl recommends, we have to follow Descartes and attempt to doubt universally. This, he says, "belongs to the realm of our *perfect freedom*." (*Ideen* 53/62) In keeping with Descartes's characterization of *assent* as an act of freedom, Husserl is arguing that we can withdraw it at will. But doesn't this stand in sheer opposition with the above argument? How can Husserl hold both that 'the world exists' is analytically true and that we can withdraw our 'assent' to the general thesis underlying this existence, as Descartes would have it?

Sympathetic interpreters and critics alike often complained about Husserl's allegiance to Descartes in these passages. In spite of his subsequent efforts in this section to distinguish the genuine sense of the *epoché* from Descartes's doubt, Husserl has often been characterized as a Cartesian by virtue of his alleged commitment to the philosophical viability of hyperbolic doubt. As one recent commentator puts it, "It remains nevertheless the case that the phenomenological reduction is carried out not so much against doubt as through it, less as an alternative to an alternative to (*sic!*) Descartes's path as a way of taking it further." (Romano 2012, p. 436; for a critique of Romano see Staiti 2015)

As a way of responding to this criticism, a somewhat standard narrative about the development of Husserl's thought sees him as beginning as a Cartesian and then later departing from Cartesianism, as argued in a famous essay by Husserl's assistant Ludwig Landgrebe (cf. Landgrebe 2005). This narrative finds some support in Husserl's texts, in particular, in the much-cited passage from the *Crisis*, where he looks back critically to his earlier work:

> I note in passing that the much shorter way to the transcendental epoché in my Ideas toward a Pure Phenomenology and Phenomenological Philosophy, which I call the 'Cartesian way' [...], has a great shortcoming: while it leads to the transcendental ego in one leap, as it were, it brings this ego into view as apparently empty of content, since there can be no preparatory explication; so one is at loss, at first, to know what has been gained by it, much less how, starting with this, a completely new sort of fundamental science, decisive for philosophy, has been attained. Hence also, the reception of my Ideas showed, it is all too easy right at the very beginning to fall back into the naïve-natural attitude–something that is very tempting in any case. (Husserl 1970, p. 155)

As I argue at length elsewhere, however, I have reservations about this narrative (cf. Staiti 2012). First, *pace* Husserl's retrospective self-interpretation, strictly speaking there is no full-fledged Cartesian way at work in *Ideas*. In the same way in which one swallow does not make a spring, one reference to Descartes does not make a Cartesian way. If by the *Cartesian way* we mean a specific pedagogical strategy devised to introduce the apprentice phenomenologist to the transcendental field of inquiry, then, again, there is no such thing in *Ideas I*. The Cartesian way into phenomenology, as exemplified, for instance in the lectures on *First Philosophy*, begins with Husserl setting up the ideal of absolutely self-responsible and presuppositionless knowledge. Husserl then proceeds to examine candidates potentially fitting such an ideal. He highlights the essential presumptiveness of external perception and its corresponding inadequacy. He then concludes noticing how in the examination of the structures of external perception that revealed its inadequacy the reflective gaze underwent a significant shift. The structures and configurations of experiences were examined as a subject matter in its own right, without presupposing the validity of worldly being. This is enough to introduce the apprentice phenomenologist to the new field of inquiry and in so doing remove (at least tentatively) the blinders of the natural attitude (cf. Husserl 1959, pp. 17–80).

In *Ideas I* we do not find such an introduction to phenomenology through the Cartesian way. As Toine Kortooms shows in a compelling paper (cf. Kortooms 1993), what we found in *Ideas I* is rather a tenuous version of the psychological way, or, as I would be more inclined to put it, a description of how a reflection that begins as psychological can ascend to the level of transcendental philosophy after performing the phenomenological *epoché* and the reductions. Regrettably, there is nearly no pedagogical concern at work in *Ideas I*, as the abrupt intimation at the beginning of § 31 to just alter the natural attitude more than eloquently indicates.

This lack of pedagogical concern is lamentable, but it can be at least understood considering the intended audience of the book. We have to remember that *Ideas* was written as the opening essay for Husserl's newly founded phenomenological yearbook. It was meant to be a kind of methodological manual written for scholars who *already practiced* phenomenology. It was certainly not meant to be, say, an introduction to phenomenology for college students. It is then perfectly understandable that Husserl would move rather quickly on the basics, in order to then spend more time communicating his recent discoveries and clarifying their sense. It is also perfectly understandable that the place to look for Husserl's more pedagogical approaches to phenomenology are his lectures, where he could not presuppose familiarity with or, for that matter, benevolence toward his work in the audience.

Second, is it true that in *Ideas* Husserl is committed to the viability of Cartesian doubt, as Romano argues? An attentive reader will notice that Husserl always talks about the *"attempt to doubt universally"* (*Ideen* 53/62) and even italicizes the word 'attempt.' He maintains that "[i]t is possible for us to *try to doubt* anything and everything," (*Ideen* 53/62) and not that we can actually do it. In later texts informed by genetic phenomenology, Husserl goes as far as to say that Descartes's method is "quite dubious" (Husserl 2008, p. 254) and even "laughable." (Husserl 2008, p. 236) This is because, as we argued above:

> Every verification or contradiction of a thing presupposes the being of another thing, and ultimately, therefore, the being of the world. [...] *Hence, the fact that every individual thing is susceptible to doubt is not equivalent to the fact that the totality of the world is susceptible to doubt.* (Husserl 2008, pp. 255–256)

These statements are perfectly consistent with Husserl's characterization of the general thesis in *Ideas* and they explain why he uses the word *alteration* or *modification*, and not the word *modalization* to describe the effect of the *epoché* on the natural attitude. This in turn explains his insistence that, unlike Descartes:

> *We do not give up the thesis that we have posited, we alter nothing in our conviction.* That conviction remains in itself as it is, as long as we do not introduce new motives for judgment, which is precisely what we do not do. And nevertheless it undergoes a modification—while it continues to be in itself what it is, *we place it as it were 'out of action,'* we 'suspend it,' we 'bracket it.' It is still here as before, like the bracketed in the brackets, like the suspended outside the context of the suspension. We can also say: the thesis is an experience, *but we make 'no use' of it*, and that is to be understood naturally not as privation [...]. (*Ideen* 54/63)

To conclude this section let us ask, then, what is it about Descartes that Husserl valorizes? Can we locate exactly the place in the *Meditationes* that Husserl would recommend imitating, and maybe also the place where the two thinkers part ways? Based on Husserl's statements in *Ideas* and other writings, I believe that what Husserl has in mind is not Descartes's famous examination of external experience, in which he decrees that it might as well be happening in a dream, but rather the very initial lines of the first meditation, in which Descartes resolves to call into question all his foregoing convictions in order to evaluate them. It is the act of shifting one's attention from the objects of the world to our experience of the world *for the sake of examining it*, and thus provisionally suspending its validity, that characterizes the *attempt* to doubt. This, and nothing else, is what Husserl finds masterfully exemplified at the beginning of the *Meditationes* and this, and only this, is the minimal measure of Cartesianism he is committed to and recommends to his readers.[8] True, in subsequent chapters other key elements of Descartes's philosophy are presented and justified, such as the notion of inner experience's indubitability. However, for the sake of clarity we have to distinguish the methodological dimension from the specific doctrines advanced by Descartes. Moreover, even when the letter of Husserl's work seems to match almost verbatim the letter of Descartes's work we have to bear in mind that the meaning of Husserl's statements undergoes a transformation in accordance with the reduction.[9]

4. The phenomenological epoché

We are now left with one last item to clarify, the phenomenological *epoché*, although the contrast with Descartes's method of doubt in the foregoing section already shed some light on this matter. Husserl describes the *epoché* in just a few brushstrokes in § 32:

> *We put out of action the general thesis belonging to the essence of the natural attitude*; we put in brackets anything and everything that it encompasses in an ontic respect: *thus this entire natural world* that is constantly 'there for us,' 'on hand,' and that will ever after remain here as an 'actuality' in keeping with consciousness, even if it pleases us to bracket it.
>
> If I do this, as I am completely free to, then I *do not negate* this 'world,' as though I were a sophist; *I do not doubt its existence*, as though I were a skeptic. But I exercise the 'phenomenological' ἐποχή that *utterly closes off for me every judgment about spatiotemporal existence*. (*Ideen* 55–56/65)

Considering Husserl's background in mathematics, it is appropriate to spend some time thinking about the mathematical metaphors he employs in order to clarify the structure of this thoroughly peculiar operation. In spite of Husserl's preferred language of bracketing, it is not clear that the corresponding mathematical operation really shares any relevant feature with the *epoché*. The use of brackets or parentheses in mathematics does not really change anything about the numbers or letters bracketed. It merely marks the order in which to carry out certain operations in case this order is not already obvious or is irrelevant. Similarly, the metaphor of changing sign, or transforming the value of

---

[8] On this matter I am in complete agreement with Julien Farges, who recently wrote: "[T]he *epoché* is not a certain kind of doubt, but rather the suspensive moment to which doubt owes what we could call its dubitative efficacy, i.e., its ability to throw doubt on anything." (Farges 2012, p. 100)
[9] See Burt Hopkins' chapter in this book.

what undergoes the *epoché* (cf. *Ideen* 136/159) is potentially confusing. If we think about it applied to the above distinction between positionality and non-positionality, then it seems that the *epoché* would transform positional acts into non-positional acts... and vice versa! For the reasons explained above, this cannot possibly be what Husserl has in mind. Paul MacDonald has suggested, correctly in my view, that the brackets Husserl is thinking about here may be the brackets of a different mathematical operation, namely, absolute value (cf. MacDonald 2000, p. 160). The analogy is all the more plausible because in both absolute value and the phenomenological *epoché* the 'value' associated with a certain item is left out of consideration. Moreover, absolute value does share some features with the *epoché*, such as idempotence. In other words, performing the *epoché* on an already reduced act does not change anything in the reduced act at issue.

These mathematical analogies, however, only hint at the eidetic specificity of the *epoché*. As was already the case with the notion of positing, the most expedient way to study the *epoché* is to begin with single acts of consciousness. *Epoché*, in fact, can be considered a distinctive modification intervening on an act of reflection. It is, in Husserl's words, "an act [*Aktus*] that affects an[other] act [*Aktus*]." (Husserl 2002, p. 149) In the natural attitude we sometimes carry out acts of reflection. As we contemplate a beautiful landscape we may shift the focal point of our mental regard to contemplate and rejoice at the delightful perceptual experience we are having. In memory, we can remember a conversation we had with a colleague and start reflecting upon it, maybe in order to evaluate how bad an involuntary *faux pas* actually was. Or we can focus on our perception to reevaluate what turned out to be an optical illusion.

In natural reflection, the act of reflection generally co-effectuates or co-implements the belief-character contained in the underlying straightforward act reflected upon. As Husserl puts it in *First Philosophy*:

> In the normal case of a reflection upon my naively implemented perception of a house, in my reflective perception I do not simply look at the act 'I perceive this house.' Rather, *I also partake in the perceptual belief* of the underlying ego. I as a reflective ego co-implement the belief of the house-perceiving ego. (Husserl 1959, p. 91)

In some cases, such as in perceptual illusions, I may occasionally reject the belief of the underlying ego, and realize in reflection that what I believed to be a house a minute ago was actually a hologram or the like. Both in the more frequent cases of co-implementing the pre-reflective belief and in the occasional cases of rejecting this belief, the ego of reflection in the natural attitude is characterized by an "*interest in the being of the object* [...]. Even if the ego's comportment is that of not co-implementing the belief [...], it is nonetheless a stance-taking toward being" (Husserl 1959, p. 95). The specific characteristic of *epoché* is that of dropping the interest in being or non-being altogether and merely considering the objects under scrutiny as phenomena manifested to an ego endowed with a certain index of belief, but one in which the phenomenological oriented ego refuses to participate (cf. Ströker 2004, p. 255). Husserl puts this shift of perspective in the following, helpful terms in a later manuscript:

> In the *epoché* I have the consciousness of the world and the conscious world modified, that is, modified precisely in the mode of abstaining from the natural life in the world in all its interests. A new interest should be activated, the interest in the universe of subjectivity, in which the world has its ontological meaning [*Seinssinn*] for me, in which therefore also my human being itself receives its ontological meaning [*Seinssinn*]. (Husserl 2006b, p. 125)

The language of activating a new interest is very helpful and it corrects the distorting tendency to see the *epoché* as somehow a loss or an arbitrary and potentially detrimental narrowing of phenomenology's field of inquiry.

As with *thesis*, the fact that it is possible to carry out *epoché* on single acts of consciousness does not immediately guarantee that it is possible to carry out a universal *epoché* spanning the whole breadth of our consciousness of the world and suspending in one blow the general thesis underlying it. This is a life-long problem Husserl struggled with. He believes that ultimately we do have an actual consciousness of our life as a whole, and it is precisely thanks to this consciousness of life as a whole (as documented for instance in the possibility of making life-spanning ethical decisions) that we can uphold the *epoché* as an enduring habit of thought encompassing the entirety of our life (cf. Husserl 1959, pp. 153–154; Staiti 2013; Jacobs 2013).

The difficulties connected with the phenomenological *epoché* in its double form, particular and universal, are not addressed in *Ideas I*. This, however, has a lot to do with the originally 'performative' character of this operation, which is more than just methodological. The *epoché* is not simply a methodological device designed to investigate an already available field of inquiry, e.g. human consciousness. Husserl conceives of the *epoché* primarily as opening up a new field of being for theoretical inquiry, one that could ideally be described and studied according to different methods. Rather than thinking about *epoché* as a method to practice, Husserl wants us to think of *epoché* as a fundamental stance to take toward our own life and the world around us. In so doing, a previously unseen field for research opens up and becomes available for our philosophical questions.

5. Conclusion

The first chapter of the second section of Husserl's *Ideas* is certainly one of the most challenging in the entire book. However, not only it entails the essential theoretical moves that set the stage for the detailed phenomenological analyses of later chapters. It also entails *in nuce* all themes, difficulties and concerns that drive Husserl's phenomenological inquiry for the rest of his life.

Bibliography

Avenarius, Richard (1888): *Kritik der reinen Erfahrung. Erster Band.* Leipzig: Reisland.
Avenarius, Richard (1891): *Der menschliche Weltbegriff.* Leipzig: Reisland.
Carr, David (2004): "Husserl's Problematic Concept of Lifeworld". In: Embree, Lester/Moran, Dermot (Eds.): *Phenomenology. Critical Concepts in Philosophy. Vol. I.* London/New York: Routledge, pp. 359–374.
Cicero, Marcus Tullius (1998): *The Republic. The Laws.* Trans. Rudd, Niall. Oxford: Oxford University Press.
Farges, Julien (2012): "Réduction et cartésianisme." In: Grandjean, Antoine/Perreau, Laurent (Eds.): *Husserl: La science des phénomènes.* Paris: CNRS editions, pp. 93–113.
Geniusas, Saulius (2012): *The Origins of the Horizon in Husserl's Phenomenology.* Dordrecht: Springer.
Hume, David (2000): *A Treatise of Human Nature.* Oxford: Oxford University Press.
Husserl, Edmund (1959): "Erste Philosophie (1923/24). Zweiter Teil: Theorie der phänomenologischen Reduktion". In: *Husserliana.* Vol. VIII. The Hague: Nijhoff.
Husserl, Edmund (1962): "Phänomenologische Psychologie. Vorlesungen Sommersemester 1925". In: *Husserliana.* Vol. IX. The Hague: Nijhoff.
Husserl, Edmund (1970): *The Crisis of European Sciences and Transcendental Phenomenology. An Introduction to Phenomenological Philosophy.* Evanston IL: Northwestern University Press.
Husserl, Edmund (1976): *Phenomenological Psychology.* Nijhoff: The Hague.
Husserl, Edmund (2001a): "Analyses Concerning Active and Passive Synthesis–Lectures on Transcendental Logic". In: *Collected Works.* Vol. IX. Kluwer: Dordrecht.
Husserl, Edmund (2001b): *Logical Investigations.* Vol. II. London/New York: Routledge.
Husserl, Edmund (2002): "Zur phänomenologischen Reduktion. Texte aus dem Nachlass (1926–35)". In: *Husserliana.* Vol. XXXIV. Dordrecht: Springer.
Husserl, Edmund (2006a): "Basic Problems of Phenomenology". In: *Collected Works.* Vol. XII. Dordrecht: Springer.
Husserl, Edmund (2006b): "Späte Texte über Zeitkonstitution (1929–1934). Die C-Manuskripte". In: *Husserliana. Materialien.* Vol. VIII. Dordrecht: Springer.
Husserl, Edmund (2008): "Die Lebenswelt. Auslegungen der vorgegebenen Welt und ihrer Konstitution. Texte aus dem Nachlass (1916–1937)". In: *Husserliana.* Vol. XXXIX. Dordrecht: Springer.

Jacobs, Hanne (2013): "Phenomenology as a Way of Life? Husserl on Phenomenological Reflection and Self-Transformation". In: *Continental Philosophy Review* 46. No. 3, pp. 349–369.
Kant, Immanuel (1998): *Critique of Pure Reason*. Trans. and ed. by Guyer, Paul/Wood, Allen W. Cambridge: Cambridge University Press.
Kortooms, Toine (1993): "Following Edmund Husserl on One of the Paths Leading to the Transcendental Reduction". In: *Husserl Studies* 10, pp. 163–180.
Landgrebe, Ludwig (2005): "Husserl's Departure from Cartesianism". In: Bernet, Rudolf/Welton, Donn/Zavota, Gina (Eds.): *Edmund Husserl: Critical Assessments of Leading Philosophers*. Vol. I. New York: Routledge.
Lavigne, Jean-François (2009): *Accéder au transcendental? Réduction et Idéalisme transcendantal dans les Idées I de Husserl*. Paris: Vrin.
Luft, Sebastian (1998): "Husserl's Phenomenological Discovery of the Natural Attitude". In: *Continental Philosophy Review* 31, pp. 153–170.
MacDonald, Paul (2000): *Descartes and Husserl: The Philosophical Project of Radical Beginnings*. Albany: SUNY Press.
Martin, Wayne (2006): *Theories of Judgment: Psychology, Logic, Phenomenology*. Cambridge: Cambridge University Press.
Moran, Dermot (2012): "From the Natural Attitude to the Life-World". In: Embree, Lester/Nenon, Thomas (Eds.): *Husserl's Ideen*. Dordrecht: Springer, pp. 105–124.
Ricœur, Paul (1996): *A Key to Husserl's Ideas I*. Milwaukee: Marquette University Press.
Romano, Claude (2012): "Must Phenomenology Remain Cartesian?". In: *Continental Philosophy Review* 45, pp. 425–445.
Soldinger, Emanuele (2010): "Husserls Auseinandersetzung mit Avenarius und Mach und ihr Verhältnis zur Lebensweltproblematik". In: Merz, Philippe/Staiti, Andrea/Steffen, Frank (Eds.): *Geist–Person–Gemeinschaft. Freiburger Beiträge zur Aktualität Husserls*. Würzburg: Ergon Verlag, pp. 189–217.
Sommer, Manfred (1985): *Husserl und der frühe Positivismus*. Frankfurt a. M.: Klostermann.
Staiti, Andrea (2012): "The Pedagogic Impulse of Husserl's Ways into Transcendental Phenomenology. An Alternative Reading of the Erste Philosophie Lecture". In: *Graduate Faculty Philosophy Journal* 33. No. 1, pp. 39–56.
Staiti, Andrea (2013): "A Grasp From Afar: *Überschau* and the Givenness of Life in Husserlian Phenomenology". In: *Continental Philosophy Review* 46. No. 1, pp. 21–36.
Staiti, Andrea (2015): "On Husserl's Alleged Cartesianism and Conjunctivism: A Critical Reply to Claude Romano". In: *Husserl Studies* 31. No. 2, pp. 123–141.
Ströker, Elisabeth (2004): "The Problem of the *Epoché* in Husserl's Philosophy". In: Embree, Lester/Moran, Dermot (Eds.): *Phenomenology. Critical Concepts in Philosophy*. Vol. I. London/New York: Routledge, pp. 252–264.

Hanne Jacobs
From psychology to pure phenomenology
Section II, chapter 2, Consciousness and natural actuality

In the first book of *Ideas for a Pure Phenomenology and Phenomenological Philosophy* Husserl aims to establish nothing less than a new science that he terms pure phenomenology. In order to define the domain of this new science, Husserl distinguishes phenomenology from other existing sciences in a twofold way (*Ideen* 5–6/6). In contrast to empirical sciences such as physics and empirical psychology, which deal with facts, Husserl claims that pure phenomenology is a science that is concerned with essences–phenomenology is what Husserl calls an eidetic science. But in contrast to other eidetic sciences such as the material ontology of nature and descriptive psychology, which are sciences of the essences of transcendent reality, Husserl asserts that pure phenomenology is an eidetic science of *irreal* or transcendentally purified phenomena.[1]

The first two sections of the first book of *Ideas* ("Essence and Knowledge of Essence" and "The Fundamental Phenomenological Consideration") provide an initial glimpse of the distinctive eidetic and transcendental character of phenomenology. The first section provides an account of pure essences and eidetic knowledge in general. And the second section provides an initial characterization of the method that yields the transcendentally purified phenomena of which phenomenology is an eidetic science–the so-called phenomenological *epoché* (§§ 31–33).[2]

In the paragraphs immediately following the introduction of the method of phenomenological *epoché* (§§ 34–46), however, rather than applying this new method, Husserl provides a series of psychological descriptions on the basis of psychological reflection. This is surprising for at least two reasons. First, since Husserl has already distinguished phenomenology from psychology (both empirical and eidetic), it is not clear why he would engage in psychological reflection and description at this point in the book. Second, the psychological descriptions that Husserl provides in these paragraphs are of consciousness–specifically, our consciousness *of* something. But, as Husserl indicates at several points in the first book of *Ideas*, and as he more fully develops in the

---
[1] Correspondingly, Ströker 1983, pp. 12–16, points out that Husserl's transcendental phenomenology is "pure" in a double sense insofar as it is eidetic and transcendental.
[2] For accounts of the transcendental character of Husserl's phenomenology, see Luft 2011 and Zahavi 2003a, pp. 43–77, and for an account of Husserl's eidetics see Sowa 2011.

1912 pencil manuscript of the second book of *Ideas*, the object of psychology is, strictly speaking, not consciousness but the soul (*Seele*) considered as empirical reality (*Realität*).[3] Thus, since Husserl explicitly states that he is engaged in psychological descriptions in these pages, it is not immediately clear why he discusses consciousness and remains silent about the soul, which he considers to be the object of psychology.

In what follows, I first develop how these two interpretative difficulties can be overcome if we consider the overall aim of the second chapter–namely, to establish that consciousness has its own kind of being and hence essence. Then, I elucidate how exactly Husserl establishes this in this chapter and show how it entails a radical rethinking of the distinction between and relation of consciousness and world.

1. The aim of the second chapter of the second section of *Ideas*

Let us first consider why Husserl provides a series of psychological descriptions at this point in the progression of the second section of the first book of *Ideas*. It is curious that Husserl does this because, by not employing the method of *epoché* in these paragraphs, Husserl seems to surrender the ground that he has gained by the beginning of the second chapter of the second section. Specifically, in § 33 Husserl already states that the bracketing of the entire world including ourselves as natural entities leaves us with "'pure experiences,' 'pure consciousness,' with its pure 'correlates of consciousness' on one side and its 'pure ego' on the other" (*Ideen* 57/67). But instead of further describing these pure experiences or instead of elaborating in what sense the phenomena of a phenomenological science are different from psychological phenomena, Husserl proceeds without further ado to describe the phenomena of psychology. As he explicitly states at the outset of § 34:

---

[3] In what follows, I refer to the pencil manuscript of 1912 (Mss. F III 1/5–85), which is the earliest manuscript on which large parts of the current edition of the second book of *Ideas* are based. My reasons for using this manuscript are twofold. First, the manuscript was composed from October to December of 1912 and thus coincides with the composition of the first book of *Ideas*. Second, a new edition of the second book of *Ideas* consisting of the original texts on which the currently available 1952 edition is based is currently in preparation. Since the passages that are being referred to from the pencil manuscript are included in this 1952 edition, I refer to the 1952 edition here.

> Let us begin with a series of observations in which we do not trouble ourselves with any phenomenological ἐποχή. We are directed at the 'external world' in a natural manner, and, without leaving the natural attitude, we carry out a psychological reflection on our ego and its experiencing. (*Ideen* 59/69)

Given Husserl's insistence in the introduction that phenomenology can by no means be identified with psychology (*Ideen* 4/4), this way of proceeding is not immediately understandable, and this difficulty has not escaped the attention of commentators.[4]

One way of overcoming this first interpretative difficulty is to understand Husserl as not just engaged in securing the delineation of the domain of a new phenomenological science of transcendental phenomena but at the same time as concerned with establishing what kind of transcendent realities there are. More specifically, one might interpret the descriptions in these sections as providing an account of the phenomena with which other sciences deal–in particular, psychology, which deals with consciousness psychologically understood, and physical science, which deals with the material world. This is an understandable way of progressing, for, as Husserl states in the introduction, phenomenology "relates to all these 'phenomena,'" albeit "in a completely different attitude" (*Ideen* 3/3). If phenomenology somehow concerns itself with all the different phenomena with which the different sciences deal, it is important for Husserl to make clear what he understands the phenomena of these already established sciences to be in order to delineate the pure phenomena of his phenomenology. Given the fact that in Husserl's view what delineates a science is

---

4 See, for example, Ströker 1983, p. 17, and Brainard 2002, pp. 76–78. Some have questioned whether Husserl leaves the psychological level in the second section of *Ideas I*. So, for example, Ricœur 1996, p. 39, states that "the most important analyses of the second section are below the level of reduction, and it is not certain whether, following Fink, the analyses of the third and fourth sections go beyond a vague level between preparatory psychology and truly transcendental phenomenology." Ricœur 1996, p. 39, further wonders: "Toward what does this analysis tend–an analysis that can be called phenomenological in the broad sense of a description of phenomena, as they present themselves to intuition, but not in the strict sense of transcendental phenomenology introduced by reduction and constitution?" Husserl himself laments that many readers did indeed consider *Ideas I* to be a psychological work, Husserl 1959, p. 481. In contrast, De Boer 1978, p. 383, argues that "we must not regard the work of the second and third chapters [of the second section of *Ideas I*, H.J.] as a piece of intentional psychology that must afterwards be brought to the transcendental level through a 'change in attitude' (*Einstellungsänderung*)." Others have attempted to understand these analyses in light of Husserl's understanding of psychology in the 1920s. For example, Lavigne 2009, pp. 123–124, argues for a distinction between pure phenomenology and transcendental phenomenology and identifies the former with a psychological phenomenology.

an eidetic matter, his description of the essential differences between our psychological experiences and the world we experience in these pages can be understood as securing the delineation of the domains of psychology and physical science respectively.

Moreover, the fact that Husserl begins with a series of psychological descriptions appears even less surprising if we consider that Husserl claims that it is from experiences taken as "real occurrences in the world" or "as experiences from animal beings" that "the new domain arises through the new attitude" (*Ideen* 57/67) through the reductions that "'purify' the psychological phenomena of what lends them reality" (*Ideen* 6/6). That is, if the transcendental or irreal phenomena with which phenomenology deals are obtained by purifying the real phenomena that are the object of psychology, then it is as important to correctly understand the domain of psychology as it is to understand how we purify this domain in and through the method of bracketing, thus obtaining the domain of pure phenomenology. More strongly put, it is important for Husserl to show *that* psychology has its own object. And he does so by showing what essentially distinguishes the being of consciousness from the being of material things or by establishing that consciousness has its own kind of being and hence essence.[5] Doing so, moreover, establishes that while consciousness has its own kind of being it is nevertheless related to worldly things insofar as it is intentional consciousness or consciousness *of* something. As Husserl states at the outset of his psychological reflections in the second chapter of the second section: "What we need is a certain general discernment of the essence of *consciousness as such*, and especially of consciousness insofar as, in itself and in keeping with its essence, one is conscious of 'natural' actuality" (*Ideen* 58/68). And as the paragraphs in the chapter under consideration show, an eidetic psychological description of consciousness suffices to meet this need.

---

[5] As Ricœur 1996, pp. 93–94, points out: "Intentional psychology lays the foundation for fundamental phenomenology by showing that such a thing as consciousness exists." This is by no means an evident position at Husserl's time. See, for example, James's 1904 piece entitled "Does 'Consciousness' Exist?" which argues that "consciousness [...] is the name of a nonentity, and has no right to a place among first principles", James 1904, p. 477. James 1904, p. 478, immediately adds: "I mean only to deny that the word stands for an entity, but to insist most emphatically that it does stand for a function." This is not to say, however, that there are not important parallels to be drawn between Husserl's transcendental phenomenology and James's philosophy, even in this particular article, which speaks of consciousness as pure experience and conceives of consciousness as a relation. See, for example, most recently Cobb-Stevens 2014. The point is merely that, on Husserl's account, when considered from a psychological point of view conscious experiences are taken as real states of a real entity called soul (see below).

However, this way of addressing the first interpretative difficulty leads to the second – namely, the apparent inconsistency between these psychological descriptions and Husserl's account of the object of psychology later in the book. Although it is rarely noted, Husserl's first book of *Ideas* does not only propose a new conception of phenomenology as transcendental and eidetic but also a new conception of the object of psychology.[6] As Husserl mentions in passing in § 85, while we might be tempted to identify the object of psychology with intentional acts or the stream of consciousness in general, we should instead acknowledge that the soul is the object of psychology. Husserl writes:

> It is impossible, however, to avoid designating as 'psychic' or as objects of psychology the real bearers of this psychic dimension, the animal entities or their 'souls' and the real properties of their souls, respectively. 'Psychology without a soul' confuses, so it would seem to us, the suspension in general of the entity designated a soul (in the sense of some kind of nebulous metaphysics of the soul) with the suspension of the soul altogether, i.e., with the psychic reality factually given empirically, the *states* [or *conditions: Zustände*] of which are the experiences. This reality is in no way the mere stream of consciousness bound to the body and empirically regulated in certain manners. (*Ideen* 168/195–196; see also *Ideen* 68/80 and § 53)

Now, if the soul correctly understood is the object of psychology, and if this reality cannot be identified with the mere stream of consciousness, why does Husserl in his *psychological* descriptions in the chapter under consideration stick to a description of the stream of consciousness, a consciousness that he does not only describe in its eidetic structure but that he also claims to be absolute (§ 43)?

In order to address this difficulty, let us consider: the historical context of Husserl's redefinition of the object of psychology and how this redefinition of the object of psychology is obscured in §§ 34–38; why this neglect is justified given the aim of the chapter under consideration (i.e., the aim to establish that consciousness has its own being and hence essence); and how Husserl establishes that consciousness has its own being and essence.

2. Psychology and consciousness

Husserl's definition of the soul as the object of psychology in § 85 is introduced by way of a critique of Brentano's distinction between psychological phenomena

---

[6] For a discussion of the relation between psychology and phenomenology in *Die Idee der Phänomenologie*, see Drummond 2008. For a discussion of the relation between psychology and phenomenology at the time of *Krisis*, see Majolino 2008.

(e.g., the hearing of a tone or the seeing of a color) and physical phenomena (e.g., the tone or the color).[7] Specifically, while acknowledging Brentano's formative influence on the development of phenomenology, Husserl claims that Brentano did not succeed in his attempt to delimit the domains of psychology and physical science in drawing this distinction between different phenomena. According to Husserl, psychology is not, as Brentano proposed, a science of psychological phenomena or acts. Instead, Husserl claims, psychology deals with the soul, which is a psychological reality (*Realität*), and intentional acts are the soul's states (*Zustände* or *Zuständlichkeiten*). Further, according to Husserl, this psychological reality is accessible in experience–specifically, in psychological reflection. As a reality that is accessible to experience, the soul is both the object of a rational and empirical psychology. While rational psychology is the eidetic science that articulates the eidetic laws that no empirical psychological investigation can violate or establish,[8] empirical psychology is a science of fact that investigates the soul as empirical reality.[9]

This definition of psychology as a science of the soul is as much a critique of Brentano, who equates the object of psychology with psychological phenomena, as it is a critique of Husserl's own earlier definition of psychology in *Logical Investigations*. In this work Husserl identifies the object of descriptive psychology or phenomenology with consciousness as the bundle or unity of psychological experiences (i.e., the phenomenological I or consciousness in the broadest sense), which, in Husserl's view, comprises both intentional acts such as seeing or thinking and sensations such as the sensation of color or sound.[10] In *Logical Investigations* Husserl leaves open the possibility that, in addition to this phe-

---

[7] The expression "psychology without a soul" in the previously cited passage is a reference to Brentano, who uses this phrase, which was coined by F. A. Lange, when in the process of delineating the domain of psychology from natural science. Brentano's main concern is not so much to deny the existence of the soul as it is to assure the reader that his definition of the object of psychology does not stand or fall with the position one takes on the soul. Brentano writes: "Denn mag es eine Seele geben oder nicht, die psychischen Erscheinungen sind ja jedenfalls vorhanden [...] Es steht also nichts im Wege, wenn wir, statt der Begriffsbestimmung der Psychologie als Wissenschaft von der Seele, die jüngere uns eigen machen. Vielleicht sind beide richtig," Brentano 1874, p. 23.

[8] So, for example, Husserl states in the 1912 pencil manuscript of the second book of *Ideas:* "Rationale Psychologie ist eine große Wissenschaft, und sie umgrenzt die apod<iktisch> gesetzlichen Möglichkeiten, an deren absolut festen Rahmen die psychologischen Wirklichkeiten gebunden sind," Husserl 1991, p. 55; see also Husserl 1971, pp. 22–23, 42, 70.

[9] See section 4 below for a further discussion of the soul.

[10] On Husserl's conception of phenomenology at the time of *Logical Investigations*, see, for example, Moran 2005.

nomenological unity of mental acts or experiences, the psychological I could be a thing-like unity (*Einheit*) in the metaphysical sense, which would amount to there being a causal connection (*Band*) between the experiences (Husserl 1901, p. 332). Regardless of whether there is such a thing-like entity, the stream of consciousness has its own unity, and it is this stream of experiences that is the object of phenomenology or descriptive psychology. In contrast to a phenomenology that describes this stream of consciousness, genetic or empirical psychology deals with the causal nexuses that obtain between these conscious experiences (Husserl 1901, p. 336). If a thing-like unity in the metaphysical sense could be posited, it would have to be dealt with by genetic psychology. And because Husserl remains undecided in *Logical Investigations* as to whether we are justified in positing such a unity, he settles on delineating the domain of psychology and physical science by means of the phenomenological distinction between the descriptive content of intentional acts (i.e., the experiences or consciousness in the broad sense) and the intended object (i.e., the objects that are intended in transcendent acts) (Husserl 1901, p. 339).[11]

Thus, Husserl's conception of the object of psychology changes by the time of *Ideas* in that he comes to posit the soul as the object of psychology. However, this change is somewhat obscured in the text of the chapter under consideration. That is, Husserl states that his descriptive analyses of consciousness on the basis of a psychological reflection are to be understood as eidetic descriptions of our "*consciousness of something*" (*Ideen* 59/69), and these descriptions do not seem to be different from the ones provided in *Logical Investigations*. In comparison to this earlier work, Husserl does venture new analyses of actual or attentive intentional acts in contrast to our conscious awareness of what remains in the background (§§ 34–37).[12] And he also discusses how, in contrast to theoretical acts, our acts of valuation (*Wertung*) are, strictly speaking, not objectifying, even though, in contrast to his position at the time of *Logical Investigations*, Husserl contends that the value of an object that I appraise can be objectified as value and that axiological and practical acts are positing acts in the broad sense (§ 37).[13] Nevertheless, when describing psychological life in these sections, Hus-

---

[11] On the delineation between psychology and the physical sciences in *Logical Investigations* in relation to Brentano, see Fisette 2010.

[12] Husserl's concrete analyses of the phenomenon of attention from 1893–1912 are published as volume 34 of the *Husserliana*.

[13] Between *Logical Investigations* and *Ideas* Husserl elaborates his account of the structure of theoretical, axiological, and practical intentionality in a series of manuscripts (entitled *Studien zur Struktur des Bewusstseins*) that will soon be published in the *Husserliana* series. For an ac-

serl sticks to a description of what "we find immanently in" (*Ideen* 57/68) consciousness or what belongs to the stream of experiences. And while Husserl remarks that the experiences are real events (*reale menschliche Fakta*) insofar as they belong to a human being that is as real as any other object in the natural world (*Ideen* 59/69), he does not mention that, on his account of the object of psychology at the time of *Ideas*, psychological events do not just belong to a human being in the world. Rather, as I have mentioned, at the time of *Ideas* Husserl conceives of psychological events as states of a reality that he calls soul.

Nevertheless, there are some indications in the chapter under consideration that psychology does not just deal with real experiences but with a psychic reality. Specifically, at the outset of his psychological descriptions of conscious life, Husserl acknowledges that it is always me who perceives, remembers, imagines, judges, feels, desires, and wants. However, he immediately adds that the I or ego is not considered in what follows: "We leave out of consideration (and, indeed, in every sense) the I itself, to which those formations are all related, or that 'lives' 'in' them in very diverse ways" (*Ideen* 59/70). Insofar as Husserl is engaging in psychological descriptions here, the I is a psychological I or subject that is given in psychological reflection and is what he subsequently calls the "*real ego-subject*" (*Ideen* 100/117). It is this I that Husserl also calls soul or, more precisely, the soul-I.[14] And it is this I or soul that Husserl excludes at this point from the description.

However, insofar as Husserl claims that our psychological experiences are what is being purified when performing the *epoché*, and insofar as the *epoché* consists in a bracketing of reality, it is not clear why Husserl would not here, as he does later in *Ideas*, contrast the reality of the soul that is the object of empirical and rational psychology with the purified intentional experiences and their intentional correlates that are of concern for a transcendental phenomen-

---

count of the relation between theoretical acts and axiological and practical acts, see Drummond 2004 and 2009, Melle 1990 and 2012, and Rinofner-Kreidl 2013.

14 Husserl differentiates between the soul and the soul-I (*das seelische Ich*). So, for example, in the 1912 pencil manuscript of the second book of *Ideas*: "Beide Ausdrucksweisen Seele und seelisches Subjekt können bald identischen Sinn haben, und das gibt den einen Ichbegriff (wir sagen Seele), bald verschiedenen, wonach das seelische Subjekt zur Seele gehört, aber sich nicht mit der vollen Seele deckt. Dann unterscheidet sich ein neuer Ichbegriff, den wir als seelisches Ich bezeichnen werden," Husserl 1991, p. 120; see also Husserl 1971, p. 116. The I is the wakeful I that is described in §§ 34–37 and that is attentively engaged with the world of which it is aware. In contrast, a sleeping subject would not have such an I or ego. This notion of the soul as the subject of conscious life can also be found in Pfänder 1904. According to Schuhmann, Husserl read Pfänder's *Einführung in die Psychologie* between July 1904 and July 1905, Schuhmann 1973, p. 39. On Pfänder and Husserl in this respect, see also Marbach 1974, pp. 234–241.

ology. This would both elucidate why Husserl begins with a series of psychological descriptions and why phenomenology is nevertheless different from psychology. That is, while both psychology and phenomenology deal with experiences, the former takes them as psychological states of a soul and the latter deals with these experiences and their intentional correlates insofar as they are purified. So why does Husserl focus on the stream of experiences in his psychological descriptions and remain silent about the soul? This silence is striking given the fact that Husserl himself advises that we should speak of the soul in a passage that was written around the same time as the first book of *Ideas*:

> One can remain silent about the soul, one can scornfully call it a *façon de parler:* the soul is nevertheless what leads the apprehension and is what determines the [psychological] investigation with the correlative ideas that belong to it. But it is better to speak correctly and not interpret away what must, insofar as one is thinking correctly, always remain alive. (Husserl 1971, p. 19)

Husserl's silence on the object of psychology in his psychological descriptions can be understood in light of the aforementioned aim of these psychological analyses in the first book of *Ideas*. Rather than being occupied with accounting for the kind of reality that consciousness psychologically understood is, Husserl aims to establish that consciousness has its own kind of being that is different from the being of the world of which it is intentionally aware. And what characterizes its essence remains identical whether or not consciousness is considered as a reality (*Ideen* 100/117) or when this reality is bracketed (*Ideen* 58/68). Correspondingly, Husserl indicates that the psychological descriptions he is about to give are limited. That is, he states: "In these studies we go as far as is necessary to achieve the targeted insight, namely, the insight *that consciousness in itself has a being of its own that is not affected in its own absolute essence by the phenomenological suspension*" (*Ideen* 58/68; see also *Ideen* 100/117; *Ideen* 154/179). Given the aim of these psychological descriptions, which Husserl later characterizes as "immanent psychological" (*Ideen* 152/177), it is then not surprising that Husserl does not discuss how, from the psychological point of view, our experiences are to be considered as states of a psychological subject, I, or soul, as he does in the 1912 pencil manuscript of the second book of *Ideas*.

In order to further elaborate how Husserl establishes that consciousness has its own kind of being and essence, let us consider the sections in which he explicitly discusses the being of the world in contrast to the being of consciousness and their essential differences. Specifically, let us begin with Husserl's account of the being of the world that is the object of physical science, which is as unconventional as his account of the object of psychology and which allows him to rethink the distinction and relation between consciousness and world in a radical way.

3. The world and physical science

In the paragraphs that follow his outline of some essential features of our consciousness of something as we can access it in psychological reflection, Husserl proceeds to differentiate between two conceptions of the world: one that belongs to our naive worldview (§ 39) and another that belongs to our natural-scientific worldview (§ 40). The naive conception of the world is the one that Husserl renders in his description of how we experience the world and ourselves within the natural attitude in §§ 27–29. According to this everyday conception, the world consists of colored extended things that have different axiological and practical predicates, and we encounter others and ourselves as human beings in this world. The scientific conception of the world, in contrast, considers what appears in perception to be mere appearance. What truly is (*wahres Sein*), according to this natural-scientific conception of the world, is rather "an empty X that becomes the bearer of mathematical determinations and relevant mathematical formulas" (*Ideen* 70/83). What is important here is that while Husserl differentiates between the appearing thing of the sensory *imaginatio* and the physical thing that is the object of natural science, he also provides a warning against a certain way of understanding the relation between them in § 52 that hinges on a subtle distinction between two senses of the term "subjective." And this distinction plays a pivotal role for understanding how Husserl establishes both the essential difference and relation between consciousness and the world in this chapter.

The appearing world in its so-called primary and secondary qualities is, from the perspective of a physical science that seeks to determine reality in itself, subjective in the sense that how the world appears to me depends on the specific body I am and on the spatial location my body has at a certain point in time. However, Husserl insists, the perceptual thing and its appearing primary and secondary qualities are therefore not subjective in the sense of being part of consciousness, "as if the perceived things were in the qualities of the perception of it or as if these qualities were themselves experiences" (*Ideen* 94/110). Differently stated, it is not because the way in which things appear to me in both their secondary and primary qualities is relative to the position of my body and the functioning of my organs that the perceived thing is part of or immanent to consciousness. That is, as Husserl insists, the thing that I perceive is transcendent to consciousness, and it is this very thing that is the object of natural scientific investigation: "in the method of physical science the *perceived thing itself*, always and in principle, *is exactly the thing that the physicist investigates and scientifically determines*" (*Ideen* 95/111–112). And even though the qualities with which things appear are subjective in the epistemological sense, they are nevertheless transcendent to consciousness–that is, the appearing qualities are not subjective as my conscious experiences are, nor are they a real (*reell*) part of them.

Because the perceived thing is the object of science, according to Husserl, and given the fact that he is interested in establishing that consciousness has its own being and essence, Husserl can proceed by just considering the difference between transcendent things as they appear to us in perception and the intentional acts in which they appear. As he writes:

> Let us then exclude physics in its entirety and the entire domain of theoretical thinking. Let us stick to the framework of a straightforward intuition and the syntheses pertaining to it, to which perception belongs. It is then evident that intuition and intuited, perception and the thing in perception are, to be sure, essentially related to one another but they *are not one and combined* as a matter of an intrinsic necessity in a really obtaining and essential manner. (*Ideen* 71/84)

In contrast, a position that conflates what is subjective in the sense of being part of or immanent to consciousness, on the one hand, and what is subjective from the epistemological point of view of natural science (appearing primary and secondary qualities), on the other, fails, in Husserl's view, to appreciate that perception and the perceived thing are not one and thus overlooks the "fundamentally essential difference [...] between *being as experience* and *being as thing*" (*Ideen* 74/87).

Thus, Husserl argues that the object of physical science is the world that we see, and he further supports this argument by distinguishing between what is subjective in the sense of being immanent to consciousness and what is subjective in the epistemological sense. While a position that does not make this distinction would be able to draw an essential distinction between the being of consciousness and the being of the world, it would do so in a different way than Husserl intends to. That is, it would draw a distinction between a world in itself and the subjective representation of the world (including both the appearing things and our consciousness of things). In contrast, Husserl insists that the things we perceive are nothing but the object of physical science, and he thus insists on drawing the distinction between the being of consciousness and the being of the world differently–specifically, as a distinction between experience and what is intended in and transcendent to experience, be it a colored and extended thing or this thing as understood by physical science.[15]

By emphasizing the difference between these two notions of subjective and by insisting on the essential difference between perceiving consciousness and the transcendent things that are perceived, Husserl discredits a certain form of realism that identifies what is subjective from the epistemological point of view of natural science with what is subjective in the sense of being immanent to consciousness (*Ideen* 94/110). According to this form of realism, the appearing thing is a mere appearance that is caused by the world in itself, and this appearance is a mental image or sign of the 'true' physical thing that causes it (*Ideen* 97/114).

Against this account of causation and perception, Husserl formulates three arguments. First, Husserl argues against an image or sign theory of intentionality in general on the basis of the essential difference between our consciousness of images or signs and perception (*Ideen* 76/89–90; *Ideen* 96/112–113; *Ideen* 179/207–208). Second, as Husserl elaborates later in the book (§ 90), to conceive of perception in terms of a consciousness of an image (or sign) leads to an infinite regress since the representation of the image or sign presupposes perception, for which we in turn would have to call on a consciousness of an image (or sign) and so on (*Ideen* 179/208).[16] And third, Husserl argues that if the physical world were the cause of the appearing thing that we naively take for the true thing, this cause would have to be perceivable in principle through appearances, which

---

[15] In this sense, against Heidegger's suggestion, Heidegger 1979, pp. 139 ff., Husserl's distinction between immanence and transcendence is not like Descartes's distinction between *res cogitans* and *res extensa*.

[16] Husserl already rejects the sign theory of consciousness in the *Beilage zu den Paragraphen 11 und 20* in the Fifth Logical Investigation. There he points out the question-begging character of such an image or sign theory. For something to function as an image or sign it needs to be represented in a certain way (in a *Bild-* or *Zeichenbewusstsein*). As Husserl writes: "Erst durch die Fähigkeit eines vorstellenden Wesens, sich des Ähnlichen als Bildrepräsentanten für ein Ähnliches zu bedienen, bloß das Eine anschaulich gegenwärtig zu haben und statt seiner doch das Andere zu meinen, wird das Bild überhaupt zum Bilde," Husserl 1901, p. 397. Consequently, and in line with Husserl's infinite regress argument in *Ideas*, we cannot in turn call on images or signs to account for representation or intentionality itself. Husserl then goes on to argue that it is equally misguided to think of the intentional object as an image or sign of the transcendent object. In order to substantiate his argument Husserl states that the intentional object *is* the transcendent object and is not something like an image or a sign of this transcendent object. This identification is repeated in *Ideen* 178/206–207, and Husserl's account of the relation between the perceived thing and the object of physical science further curtails the attempt to differentiate between the intentional object and the transcendent object.

would also lead to an infinite regress (because these appearances would in turn be caused) (*Ideen* 95/111).[17]

As others have argued, Husserl's rejection of this specific form of realism is directed at Helmholtz and the natural-scientific realist tradition he engendered.[18] Now, Husserl's critique of this way of conceiving the distinction and relation of consciousness and world and his alternative characterization of the essential distinction and relation between consciousness and world is certainly relevant for his account of the distinction of the domain of psychology (experiences taken as states of the soul) and the domain of physical science (the perceived things considered in their mathematizable features). But in what way is Husserl's insistence on the distinction between the being and essential characteristics of consciousness (psychologically understood), on the one hand, and the world, on the other, relevant in light of his attempts to delineate the domain of his new phenomenological science?

First, by differentiating between them in the way he does, Husserl shows how consciousness and world are related through intentionality. And by bringing intentionality into view as an essential characteristic of certain kinds of conscious experiences, such as perceiving, remembering, or scientifically knowing, Husserl already indicates what will not be affected by the methodological performance of the *epoché*–pure consciousness and its pure intentional correlates.

---

17 On Husserl, causation, and perception, see Soffer 1996. Hardy 2013, pp. 139–141, questions the cogency of the latter argument.
18 The historical background of § 52 of *Ideas* is extensively and carefully developed by Rang 1990, pp. 341–373. Rang includes Wilhelm Wundt, Oswald Külpe, Carl Stumpf, as well as Ludwig Boltzman and Max Planck in this tradition. Husserl's critique of the view that equates appearing things with defective images or signs of a reality that causes them also implies a critique of Brentano. That is, even though Brentano did distinguish between the two aforementioned senses of subjective by differentiating between psychological phenomena (e.g., external perception) and physical phenomena (e.g., color, tone, and landscape), he nevertheless inherited the view according to which a physical phenomenon is a sign for a reality that causes it. Indeed, Brentano claims that physical phenomena that are the object of natural science arise on the basis of a causation that runs between the real material world and the real living organism, e.g., Brentano 1874, p. 128. And Brentano in turn characterizes physical phenomena as signs of the world that causes them, e.g., Brentano 1874, p. 24. Thus, while Brentano cannot be accused of conflating what is subjective in the psychological sense (i.e., the psychological phenomena) and subjective in the epistemological sense (i.e., physical phenomena), his psychology or, better, the claims he makes concerning physical phenomena, entail the realism that Husserl targets in *Ideas*. This is also pointed out by Rang 1990, p. 345. In addition, Husserl also faults Brentano for not disambiguating between sensations (e.g., sensation of color) and appearing objective moments (e.g., appearing color), *Ideen* 167/195. On Husserl's view, the latter are transcendent to consciousness and the former are immanent to consciousness, but Brentano conflates them.

That is, as Husserl states: "[t]he essence of experience itself entails not only that it is consciousness, but also of what it is the consciousness" (*Ideen* 63/74). This characterization is pivotal for the delineation of the domain of pure phenomenology, which does not just describe intentional experiences but also what is intended as intended–that is, the "noema" or *cogitatum qua cogitatum*.

More specifically, Husserl's turn to psychological reflection in the chapter under consideration is necessary because the eidetic characterization of intentionality in terms of *cogito* and *cogitatum* is not something that is available within the naive or scientific world-conception as Husserl understands them. That is, in the attitude of everyday life, insofar as in this attitude we are primarily concerned with the world that is perceived, consciousness appears not to have its own essence. As Husserl states, consciousness appears as "a case of an object being emptily looked upon by an empty 'ego' that is remarkably in touch with that object" (*Ideen* 69/81). The essence of consciousness as intentional is equally given short shrift in a certain philosophical interpretation of the natural-scientific conception of the world–specifically, when the appearing things and consciousness are conflated and both are considered as caused by the thing in itself. And, more problematically, on this philosophical view, it remains unclear how this account could allow us to understand the possibility of our consciousness being consciousness of a transcendent world. Specifically, if all we have are signs or images, how do we know that there is a world that causes them, and how do we know whether these signs and images represent this world?

Thus, it is Husserl's psychological reflections that reveal the essence of consciousness as intentionality and thereby secure the possibility of an eidetic science of consciousness. In addition, by identifying the object of physical science with the perceived thing, Husserl also already takes a decisive step toward securing the difference between a transcendental-phenomenological science of intentionality and a psychological description of the essence of consciousness. That is, if the object of physical science is the perceived object, and if the perceived object is what is intended in consciousness, phenomenology as a science of pure consciousness and its pure intentional correlates is, unlike psychology, also concerned with the world in itself of physical science. Even though a transcendental phenomenological description considers this world as intended (and not straightforwardly), Husserl thus guarantees what he already states in the introduction–namely, that phenomenology will be a science of *all* phenomena, albeit in an entirely different attitude. Concretely, transcendental phenomenology describes the essential structures of the experiences in which the world is accessed and describes how we arrive at a natural scientific understanding of the world (including ourselves) on the basis of our perceptual awareness of the world. However, the way that Husserl presents immanence and transcendence in §§ 42–46 leaves both the overall aim of these paragraphs and the sense in which phenomenology concerns itself with all phenomena vulnerable to misunderstandings.

4. Immanence and transcendence

Given the fact that Husserl has already introduced the method of *epoché* that would disclose the domain of phenomenology, one would expect that after his discussion of the essential difference and relatedness of consciousness and world Husserl would proceed to bracket what he has laid out to be real–not just the material world but also our consciousness of the world insofar as it is taken as a real event or psychological state of a real subject or soul. And since, as Husserl already stated, the domain of phenomenology is nothing less than purified experiences and their intentional correlates, it seems that the stage is finally set to exchange the natural attitude for the phenomenological one.

This is not, however, how Husserl proceeds in §§ 42–46, or at least not explicitly. Instead of proceeding to explicitly perform the methodological bracketing of the world, Husserl in fact proceeds, as the title of § 42 indicates, to contrast "*consciousness* and *reality*" (*Ideen* 74/88). Thus, even though he begins this chapter by describing the essence of what he claims are our conscious experiences that "belonged to the natural world as real occurrences" (*Ideen* 68/79), in these pages Husserl proceeds to contrast consciousness to reality as such, which might seem to suggest that at some point Husserl has surreptitiously exchanged the natural for the phenomenological attitude. If this were the case, however, Husserl would be allowing his psychological analyses to bleed into phenomenological descriptions made under the reduction, thereby obfuscating the distinction between psychology and pure phenomenology. What is more, in § 44 Husserl contrasts the being of consciousness, which he claims is absolute, to the being of the transcendent world, which is said to be merely phenomenal. In this way, Husserl risks that his position be mistaken for the position he criticizes in § 52–namely, one that identifies the world that appears in transcendent perception with mere appearance. And, finally, by not clearly differentiating between psychology and phenomenology *and* by speaking of reality in terms of appearance, Husserl risks that his position be mistaken for a subjective idealism that would dissolve the world into a succession of mental appearances. Given the fact that Husserl further on vehemently denies that this is what his position amounts to (*Ideen* 102–103/120–121), we should be clear about what Husserl has in mind when he speaks of the "[m]erely phenomenal being of the transcendent" (*Ideen* 77/91) and specify in what sense consciousness is absolute.

A first thing to keep in mind is that Husserl's characterization of the being of the transcendent world as merely phenomenal cannot be understood as a contrast between the "merely" phenomenal being of transcendent things to something else that is real. On the one hand, consciousness as brought into view by the method of *epoché* is not something real. On the other hand, Husserl is also not saying that anything worldly is real while the perceived world is not. That is, as I have elaborated, in Husserl's view, the perceived thing is the object of physics. In what sense then is the being of the world phenomenal? The being of the perceived thing is phenomenal not because it can be contrasted to a thing in itself but because, according to Husserl, what is transcendent can in principle be perceived in external perception. That is, as Husserl states:

> To assume a transcendence that dispensed with the described link (i.e., the link by way of coherent motivational connections with the respective sphere of my current perception) would be completely groundless; to assume a transcendence that *intrinsically* dispensed with the like would be *nonsense*. (*Ideen* 82/96)

The phenomenality of the transcendent thing does not exclude the reality of the thing; rather, for Husserl, the transcendent reality of things implies their phenomenality. That is, the actual reality of the thing entails that the thing can in principle appear in external perception, even though it currently or practically need not or cannot do so (*Ideen* 71/84).[19] And when something appears in perception we do not indirectly infer what we perceive but perceive it directly through the manifold of appearances in which the thing appears to us.[20] And to appear in this way is essential to worldly things, which implies, according to Husserl, two further essential characteristics of transcendent things.

First, a thing can never be exhaustively or adequately given in a single perception or in a finite continuum of perceptions (*Ideen* 77–78/91–92). That is, because it is of the essence of things to be accessed through appearances, they are always presented to consciousness from a certain point of view or perspective,

---

[19] That is, as Levinas 1963, p. 49, nicely points out: "Le grand intérêt de la conception de Husserl serait donc localisée dans son point de départ (le point de départ phénoménologique par excellence): avoir cherché l'existence de la chose extérieure non pas dans son opposition à ce qu'elle est pour la conscience, mais dans l'aspect sous lequel elle se présente dans la vie consciente concrète." See also Zahavi 2003b and 2010. Recently, Yoshimi 2014 has taken issue with Husserl's claim that transcendent being entails phenomenality.

[20] See Drummond 2012 for a phenomenological critique of representationalism and a defense of what he terms phenomenology's presentationalism.

which excludes and occludes other perspectives. The amount of perspectives that can be taken on things is, in Husserl's view however, infinite, and, as a consequence, the fully determined thing is the correlate of an infinite continuum of perceptions of it (*Ideen* 87/101–102).

Second, even if a given perception or phase of perception is veridical in some respect, the perceived thing that appears to this consciousness in this respect remains transcendent to it. This means that in the case of transcendent perception consciousness and its object never form a unity, and the transcendent object (or any of its features) is never immanent to consciousness (*Ideen* 66–67/78; see also § 41). Instead, according to Husserl, our perception of transcendent things consists in an apprehension (*Auffassungen*) of contents that are immanent to consciousness, such as sensations of color or shape that by being apprehended bring the objective color and shape of a thing to appearance and in this way adumbrate the thing.[21]

Because the object of transcendent perception is never immanent to consciousness, and instead presents itself in profiles (*Ideen* 77–78/91–92), our consciousness of transcendent things is fallible or open to doubt since we always presume more about the thing than what is currently visible to us. Consequently, even if nothing currently speaks against the way in which I take something, Husserl insists: "it is clear in every way that everything that is there for me in the world of things is in principle *only a presumptive actuality*" (*Ideen* 83/98). Differently stated, what I took to be a certain way might turn out to be different than I took it to be or it might turn out not to exist at all.[22] Importantly, however, Husserl immediately adds:

> by contrast, *I myself*, for whom that world is there (with the exception of what 'of me' is included in the world of things) or, better, the current actualization of my experience is an *absolute* actuality, given through an unconditioned positing that cannot be canceled or superseded in any way. (*Ideen* 83/98)

---

21 Husserl's theory of transcendent perception as consisting in the apprehension of contents of sensation, Husserl 1901, pp. 550–551, 562–566, has been criticized. See, for example Drummond 1978 as well as Hopp 2008.
22 One could wonder whether the mere fact that we could be wrong about how something is warrants the conclusion that the actuality of the thing is presumptive or that "every experience [*Erfahrung*], no matter how far-reaching, leaves open the possibility that the given *does not exist*" and that therefore "*thingly existence* [...] is in a certain way always *contingent*" (*Ideen* 83/97). Developing in what sense it is or is not and what this entails for Husserl's transcendental project falls, however, outside of the scope of this chapter. See McKenna 1982.

But what then of me is exactly included in the world of things? And what of me is absolute in the sense that the positing of myself cannot be canceled?[23]

Husserl's descriptions in §§ 42–46 contrast the world that is perceived in transcendent perception to consciousness. However, as Husserl himself indicates at the outset of this chapter, consciousness itself is considered as real in the natural attitude. In order to understand what exactly is bracketed in the *epoché* when it comes to consciousness itself, it is thus important to finally clarify in what sense consciousness is real. I have already stated that Husserl considers our psychological experiences as states of a soul and that he thinks that this soul cannot be identified with the stream of consciousness. In what sense then is the soul real or worldly? And how does the soul relate to the stream of consciousness that is accessed in immanent perception and that would not be affected in its being by the methodological bracketing of everything that is real or the suspending of the thesis that posits the world including ourselves as psychological realities?

Husserl can consider our conscious experiences to be real states of a psychological reality because he conceives of reality in a way that is broader than extended reality. Indeed, in the 1912 pencil manuscript of the second book of *Ideas* Husserl provides the following definition of reality: "unity of lasting properties in relation to pertinent circumstances" (Husserl 1991, p. 137). What this means is that, contrary to what Husserl's discussion of the spatiality of the thing in contrast to the perception of the thing in this chapter might suggest (*Ideen* 75/88–89), what essentially characterizes reality is not just extension (*res extensa*) but also causality (*Ideen* 299/347–348). More precisely, what is real (including its real properties) remains the same in changing circumstances that bring about a change in the state of what remains the same. Thus, even if a material thing with specific material properties (*Eigenschaften*) changes its state (*Zustand*) in different causal circumstances, it has one and the same property throughout these changes (e.g., elasticity). The thing is nothing but the unity of all these material properties and is what Husserl calls a "substance" (Husserl 1971, p. 4). The question is, consequently, whether we can also speak of a soul as a reality with real properties that depending on the circumstances will be in a certain psychological state. Husserl answers this question by drawing an analo-

---

[23] In what follows, I restrict myself to a consideration of Husserl's discussion of the way in which consciousness is absolute in §§ 42–46. However, as Majolino 2010 shows, when Husserl concludes in § 49, after the thought experiment of the nullification of the world, that consciousness is absolute, the term absolute has taken on a new meaning. That is, in that context, Husserl shows by means of eidetic variation that a nullification of the world entails a modification of consciousness, but does not affect its existence.

gy between the material thing and the soul. As he states in the following passages from 1912: "By emphasizing the substantial reality of the soul, we mean that the soul is, in a sense, similar to the material thing, a substantial-real unity" (Husserl 1991, 120). And again: "The subject is now a substrate of properties (personal properties in a determinate, very broad sense) analogous to the way a material thing is a substrate of thing-like real properties" (Husserl 1991, 121).

While the soul is not extended, in Husserl's view, it can nevertheless be considered as having real properties–*provided* that we relax the condition for reality and consider as real not only what remains identical amidst changes in causal circumstances but also what remains the same in what Husserl calls conditional circumstances, which are of a psycho-physical (pertaining to changes in the body or organs) and psychological (pertaining to the soul itself) nature.[24] Just as a change in the causal environment will bring about a certain change in the material state of an object with certain real properties in a certain way, a change in the sense organs, the brain, or in my psychological state will condition a certain change in my psychological state depending on the real properties that are characteristic of my soul. These properties or dispositions manifest themselves (*bekunden*) in my psychological states. Concretely, considered from a psychological point of view, depending on my intellectual, practical, or sensorial dispositions, I will experience something rather such than so, and this psychological state directly reveals my dispositions. Thus, even though they are not spatial or extended, our psychological states are nevertheless apperceived or taken as manifestations of something that does not fall together with the mental state in question. More precisely, in psychological reflection and empathy, experiences are taken as psychological states (*Zustände*) when they are taken as manifesting certain psychological features (Husserl 1991, 122). This means that these experiences are experienced as regulated in the sense that given certain psychological features I will be in certain psychological states in certain (psycho-physical and psychological) circumstances (Husserl 1991, 124).[25]

If consciousness is absolute in the sense that my positing of it in reflection cannot be cancelled (*Ideen* 83/98), what I posit when I reflect on my psychological life in the above described way is not absolute in this sense because I apper-

---

[24] On the distinction between causality and conditionality, see, for example, Bernet 2013.
[25] This is not to say that there are also not important differences between the soul and material things. See Husserl 1991, pp. 126. What is more, Husserl complements the naturalistic conception of the personal subject as a soul with real properties with an account of the person that participates with others in different forms of communities. For an account of the distinction between the personalistic and the naturalistic attitude in relation to the transcendental attitude, see Jacobs 2014.

ceive my experiences as states of a psychological subject with specific psychological properties. Accordingly, the knowledge we acquire of what kind of psychological properties we have is fallible. Nevertheless, we can easily bracket this transcendence by restricting ourselves to the experiences without apperceiving them as psychological states. As Husserl writes: "We can limit our eidetic analysis to the *experiences in themselves*, disregarding what characterizes them as states, as manifestations [*Beurkundungen*] of a real soul-unity with soul properties" (Husserl 1971, p. 39; see also Husserl 1991, p. 131). This bracketing yields something absolute, and it is consciousness thus considered that is pure or irreal and that Husserl contrasts to reality "whatever genus it may be" (*Ideen* 78/92)– either material things or myself as a psychological subject with certain psychological properties. At the same time, however, insofar as transcendentally purified consciousness is also a consciousness of something, this something of which it is conscious is entailed in the essence of the intentional act as and insofar as it is intended. It is this consciousness that is further described in its particular noetico-noematic structure in the third second of *Ideas*, while the fourth section, which provides the outlines of a phenomenology of reason, in turn inquires into the way in which we acquire evidence for our intending something in a certain way.

5. Pure phenomenology

In §§ 34–46 Husserl shows that consciousness has its own kind of being that is different from the world while being intentionally directed at this world. And while the chapter under consideration might initially seem to introduce more confusion than clarity, it plays a pivotal role in establishing the possibility of a new phenomenological science that concerns itself with the essence of consciousness. Specifically, the bracketing of everything that is real in and through the phenomenological *epoché* results in "*gaining a new region of being, one that has not previously been circumscribed in its distinctiveness*" (*Ideen* 58/67). This region can be described in the language of *Cartesian Meditations* as *ego cogito cogitatum*. That is, by bracketing the world, ourselves included, we retain pure consciousness with its intentional correlate and egoic centering, which are not two things but one correlation.[26]

In addition, if we understand this chapter in the context of Husserl's overall effort not just to establish a pure phenomenology that would provide insight into

---

26 See Drummond 2003, pp. 71–75, for a more detailed account of the correlation.

how we acquire knowledge of different kinds of ontological entities but also to further develop the correlated ontologies of the different kinds of objects there are, we can perhaps understand Husserl's way of proceeding in these sections. That is, by describing what is experienced in psychological reflection as different from what is experienced in transcendent perception, and by clarifying the relation between the perceived thing and object of physics, Husserl significantly broadens the scope of reality. In this way, he also significantly broadens the scope of his transcendental phenomenology, which, as a phenomenology of reason, spells out how knowledge is possible of individual realities that fall under different ontological regions or highest genera of reality (i.e., material thing and soul).

As it appears, transcendent being is for Husserl even more multiform than he lets on in these passages. As both his initial description of the natural attitude and his concluding remarks on the task of a phenomenology of reason indicate, in addition to experiencing things and ourselves as psychological subjects, we experience objects that are practical and of value, and we experience ourselves as persons that are part of different kinds of communities (linguistic, social, political, historical, etc.). And each type of transcendent being or "phenomenon" has a corresponding phenomenological analysis that describes how this particular kind of objectivity (e.g., nature in itself, soul, value, community, person) shows up for us and describes how we can acquire insight and knowledge of it in the corresponding empirical and eidetic sciences (*Ideen* 305/354–355).

In his 1930 afterword to *Ideas*, Husserl points out: "That the world exists [...] is entirely beyond doubt. But it is quite another matter to understand this indubitability which sustains life and positive science and to clarify the ground of its legitimacy" (Husserl 1989, p. 420; Husserl 1971, pp. 152–153). It is to such an understanding that Husserl's transcendental phenomenology aspires. The chapter under consideration aids in this understanding insofar as it opens the transcendental dimension, the eidetic description of which allows us to acquire insight into the way that different kinds of objectivities are accessed in different kinds of conscious experiences and how knowledge can be had of them.

References

Bernet, Rudolf (2013): "The Body as a 'Legitimate Naturalization of Consciousness'". In: *Royal Institute of Philosophy Supplement* 72, pp. 43–65.
Brainard, Marcus (2002): *Belief and Its Neutralization. Husserl's System of Phenomenology in Ideas I*. Albany: State University Of New York Press.

Brentano, Franz (1874): *Psychologie vom empirischen Standpunkt*. Leipzig: Duncker & Humblot.
Cobb-Stevens, Richard (2014): "William James on Consciousness and the Brain: From Psycho-Physical Dualism to Transcendental Philosophy". In: Heinämaa, Sara/Hartimo, Mirja/Miettinen, Timo (Eds.): *Phenomenology and the Transcendental*. London: Routledge, pp. 235–254.
De Boer, Theo (1978): *The Development of Husserl's Thought*. The Hague: Martinus Nijhoff.
Drummond, John J. (1978): "On the Nature of Perceptual Appearances, or Is Husserl an Aristotelian?". In: *The New Scholasticism* 52. No. 1, pp. 1–22.
Drummond, John J. (2003): "The Structure of Intentionality". In: Welton, Donn (Ed.): *The New Husserl: A Critical Reader*. Bloomington: Indiana University Press, pp. 65–92.
Drummond, John J. (2004): "'Cognitive Impenetrability' and the Complex Intentionality of the Emotions". In: *Journal of Consciousness Studies* 11. No. 10/11, pp. 109–126.
Drummond, John J. (2008): "The Transcendental and the Psychological". In: *Husserl Studies* 24, pp. 193–204.
Drummond, John J. (2009): "Feelings, Emotions, and Truly Perceiving the Valuable". In: *The Modern Schoolman* 86. No. 3, pp. 363–379.
Drummond, John J. (2012): "Intentionality without Representationalism". In: Zahavi, Dan (Ed.): *Oxford Handbook of Contemporary Phenomenology*. Oxford: Oxford University Press, pp. 115–133.
Fisette, Denis (2010): "Descriptive Psychology and Natural Sciences: Husserl's Early Criticism of Brentano". In: Ierna, Carlo/Jacobs, Hanne/Mattens, Filip (Eds.): *Phenomenology, Sciences, Philosophy. Essays in Commemoration of Edmund Husserl*. Dordrecht: Springer, pp. 221–253.
Hardy, Lee (2013): *Nature's Suit: Husserl's Phenomenological Philosophy of the Physical Sciences*. Athens, Ohio: Ohio University Press.
Heidegger, Martin (1979): *Prolegomena zur Geschichte des Zeitbegriffs*. Frankfurt am Main: Klostermann.
Hopp, Walter (2008): "Husserl on Sensation, Perception, and Interpretation". In: *Canadian Journal of Philosophy* 38 No. 2, pp. 219–245.
Husserl, Edmund (1901): *Logische Untersuchungen. Zweiter Teil: Untersuchungen zur Phänomenologie und Theorie der Erkenntnis*. Halle: Niemeyer.
Husserl, Edmund (1959): "Erste Philosophie (1923/24). Zweiter Teil: Theorie der phänomenologischen Reduktion". In: *Husserliana*. Vol. VIII. The Hague: Nijhoff.
Husserl, Edmund (1971): "Ideen zu einer reinen Phänomenologie und phänomenologischen Philosophie, 3: Die Phänomenologie und die Fundamente der Wissenschaften". In: *Husserliana*. Vol. V. Dordrecht: Nijhoff.
Husserl, Edmund (1989): "Ideas pertaining to a Pure Phenomenology and to a Phenomenological Philosophy. Second Book. Studies in the Phenomenology of Constitution". In: Rojcewicz, Richard/Schuwer, André (Trans.): *Collected Works*. Vol. 3. Dordrecht/Boston/London: Kluwer Academic Publishers.
Husserl, Edmund (1991): "Ideen zu einer reinen Phänomenologie und phänomenologischen Philosophie, 2: Phänomenologische Untersuchungen zur Konstitution". In: *Husserliana*. Vol. IV. Dordrecht: Kluwer.

Jacobs, Hanne (2014): "Transcendental Subjectivity and the Human Being". In: Heinämaa, Sara/Hartimo, Mirja/Miettinen, Timo (Eds.): *Phenomenology and The Transcendental*. London: Routledge, pp. 87–105.
James, William (1904): "Does 'Consciousness' Exist?". In: *The Journal of Philosophy, Psychology and Scientific Methods* 1 No. 18, pp. 477–491.
Lavigne, Jean-François (2009): *Accéder au transcendantal? Réduction et idéalisme transcendantal dans les Ideen I de Husserl*. Paris: Vrin.
Levinas, Emmanuel (1963): *Théorie de l'intuition dans la phénoménologie de Husserl*. Paris: Vrin.
Luft, Sebastian (2011): "Husserl's Method of Reduction". In: Luft, Sebastian/Overgaard, Søren (Eds.): *The Routledge Companion to Phenomenology*. London/New York: Routledge, pp. 243–253.
Majolino, Claudio (2008): "Des signes et des phénomènes: Husserl, l'intrigue des deux psychologies et le sujet transcendantal". In: Gandt, François de/Majolino, Claudio (Eds.): *Lecture de la Krisis de Husserl*. Paris: Vrin, pp. 161–195.
Majolino, Claudio (2010): "La partition du réel: Remarques sur l'eidos, la phantasia, l'effondrement du monde et l'être absolu de la conscience". In: Ierna, Carlo/Jacobs, Hanne/Mattens, Filip (Eds.): *Phenomenology, Sciences, Philosophy. Essays in Commemoration of Edmund Husserl*. Dordrecht: Springer, pp. 573–660.
Marbach, Eduard (1974): *Das Problem des Ich in der Phänomenologie Husserls*. The Hague: Nijhoff.
McKenna, William R. (1982): *Husserl's "Introductions to Phenomenology": Interpretation and Critique*. The Hague: Nijhoff.
Melle, Ullrich (1990): "Objektivierende und nicht-objektivierende Akte". In: Samuel Ijsseling (Ed.): *Husserl-Forschung und Husserl-Ausgabe*. Dordrecht: Springer, pp. 35–49.
Melle, Ullrich (2012): "Husserls deskriptive Erforschung der Gefühlserlebnisse". In: Breeur, Roland/Melle, Ullrich (Eds.): *Life, Subjectivity, and Art. Essays in Honor of Rudolf Bernet*. Dordrecht: Springer, pp. 51–99.
Moran, Dermot (2005): "The Meaning of Phenomenology in Husserl's *Logical Investigations*". In: Banham, Gary (Ed.): *Husserl and The Logic of Experience*. New York: Palgrave Macmillan, pp. 8–37.
Pfänder, Alexander (1904): *Einführung in die Psychologie*. Leipzig: J.A. Barth.
Rang, Bernhard (1990): *Husserls Phänomenologie der materiellen Natur*. Frankfurt am Main: Klostermann.
Ricœur, Paul (1996): *A Key to Husserl's Ideas I*. Trans. Vandevelde, Pol. Milwaukee: Marquette University Press.
Rinofner-Kreidl, Sonja (2013): "Husserls Fundierungsmodell als Grundlage einer intentionalen Wertungsanalyse". In: *Metodo. International Studies in Phenomenology and Philosophy* 1 No. 2, pp. 59–82.
Schuhmann, Karl (1973): *Husserl über Pfänder*. Den Haag: M. Nijhoff.
Soffer, Gail (1996): "Perception and Its Causes". In: Nenon, Thomas/Embree, Lester (Eds.): *Issues in Husserl's Ideas II*. Dordrecht: Kluwer Academic Publishers, pp. 37–56.
Sowa, Rochus (2011): "Eidetics and its Methodology". In: Luft, Sebastian/Overgaard, Søren (Eds.): *The Routledge Companion to Phenomenology*. London/New York: Routledge, pp. 254–265.

Ströker, Elisabeth (1983): "Phänomenologie und Psychologie. Die Frage ihrer Beziehung bei Husserl". In: *Zeitschrift für philosophische Forschung*, 37 No. 1, pp. 3–19.
Yoshimi, Jeff (2014): "The Metaphysical Neutrality of Husserlian Phenomenology". Forthcoming in: *Husserl Studies*.
Zahavi, Dan (2003a): *Husserl's Phenomenology*. Stanford: Stanford University Press.
Zahavi, Dan (2003b): "Phenomenology and Metaphysics". In: Zahavi, Dan/Heinämaa, Sara/Ruin, Hans (Eds.): *Metaphysics, Facticity, Interpretation*. Dordrecht-Boston: Kluwer Academic Publishers, pp. 3–22.
Zahavi, Dan (2010): "Husserl and the Absolute". In: Ierna, Carlo/Jacobs, Hanne/Mattens, Filip (Eds.): *Phenomenology, Sciences, Philosophy. Essays in Commemoration of Edmund Husserl*. Dordrecht: Springer, pp. 71–9.

Burt C. Hopkins
Phenomenologically pure, transcendental, and absolute consciousness

Section II, chapter 3, The region of pure consciousness

The third chapter of Part two of *Ideas for a Pure Phenomenology and Phenomenological Philosophy. First Book: General Introduction to Pure Phenomenology*, "The Region of Pure Consciousness," represents the first significant foray into the topic announced by the second part of the first half of its general title, or so I want to argue. Pure phenomenology, relative to all other sciences, has on Husserl's view a "unique position" (*Ideen* 3/3), and it is his intention "to demonstrate it to be the fundamental science of philosophy." (*Ideen* 3/3) As such, "phenomenology must lay claim, in keeping with its essence, to being 'first' philosophy and providing the means for every rational critique [*Vernunftkritik*]" (*Ideen* 117/136). That said, Husserl's view in 1913 was apparently that the third and concluding book of his *Ideas for a Pure Phenomenology and Phenomenological Philosophy* would "awaken the insight that genuine philosophy, the idea of which is to realize the idea of absolute knowledge, is rooted in pure phenomenology" (*Ideen* 7/8) Taken literally, Husserl's words here suggest that–prior to the projected third book of the *Ideas*–pure phenomenology's relation to philosophy will not have been awakened, which is at the very least paradoxical, given Husserl's view of its philosophical priority announced in the second sentence of *Ideas I*. The paradox being how it's possible to present a general introduction to the fundamental science of philosophy, pure phenomenology, a science that properly understood proves to be coincident with first philosophy, without awakening the insight into pure phenomenology's philosophical status.

For my argument to gain any traction then, that is, for my claim that prior to the projected third book of the *Ideas* pure phenomenology's significance for phenomenological philosophy is addressed in Chapter Three of Part Two of *Ideas I*, this paradox needs to be recognized. Specifically, what needs to be recognized is that as a general introduction to the eidetic science of pure consciousness, the immediate concern of *Ideas I* is *not* to awaken, or better, to thematize its philosophical significance for a phenomenological philosophy. Once this is recognized, the oddity of Husserl's step-by-step presentation of pure phenomenology and pure phenomenological knowledge in *Ideas I* without necessarily addressing its philosophical significance becomes less so, and perhaps assumes greater coherence and consistency than it would otherwise, especially when read anachronistically.

My claim, then, is that this chapter goes beyond a general introduction to the science of pure phenomenology by thematizing the significance of that science for phenomenological philosophy. It does so to the end of exposing the "mythology" (*Ideen* 97/114) behind "a worldview founded on natural science" (*Ideen* 92/108) and the "*absurdity* [*Widersinn*, B.H., not italicized in the original]" (*Ideen* 103/120) of "construing the world *philosophically* as absolute" (*Ideen* 103/120) rather than consciousness (secured by pure phenomenology, of course). Despite Husserl's attribution of 'transcendental'[1] to the latter's philosophical status, he does not understand the phenomenological philosophy that would have to establish its truth to have done so using indeterminate "philosophical notions from the top down." (*Ideen* 103/121) Rather phenomenological "knowledge," which has been "condensed into universally stated descriptions," (*Ideen* 103/121) is aimed in this chapter at making transparent "some general thoughts that can be of help in acquiring the idea of the transcendentally pure consciousness" (*Ideen* 104/121). This idea, or more precisely, "absolute consciousness as a field affording sense" (*Ideen* 103/120 – 121), is presented by Husserl as something that, when recognized following the "radical considerations" (*Ideen* 92/108) that drive phenomenological reflection, provides, "in the face of the philosophical misery [*des philosophischen Elends*][2] in which we labor away in vain under the

---

[1] The first mention of "transcendental" (§ 33, *Ideen* 58/68) in *Ideas I* occurs in connection with pure consciousness, and refers to "[i]mportant motives grounded in a set of epistemological problems [that, B.H.] justify our designation of this consciousness '*transcendental consciousness*' as well" (*Ideen* 58/68). Husserl's marginal note in *Copy D* characterizes these motives as "modern." Husserl's next mention of "transcendental" in this connection occurs subsequent to his argument that pure consciousness is essentially independent of and therefore existentially prior to worldly, natural being. That is, it occurs within the context of the modern epistemological–and thus "philosophical"–problems that Husserl mentions with the introduction of the term "transcendental" to his text.

[2] Daniel Dahlstrom's translation of *Ideas I* (Hacket) corrects the previous two English translations, which render "Elends" incorrectly as "poverty." The difference is significant, as "poverty" in this context suggests a lack of philosophical resources whereas "misery" suggests philosophical pathos.

The phrase "Misery of Philosophy" can be found in the title of Marx's 1847 pamphlet written in response to Proudhon's 1846 work, *Système des contradictions économiques, ou, Philosophie de la misère* (*System of Economical Contradictions, or, Philosophy of Misery*): Marx's title, *Misery of philosophy. Response to the philosophy of misery of Mr. Proudhon* (*Misère de la philosophie. Réponse a la philosophie de la misère de M. Proudhon*), is thus born in his clever reversal of the relationship between 'philosophy' and 'misery' in Proudhon's title. Claudio Majolino, Daniele De Santis, and Emiliano Trizio, fellow faculty of the Phenomenology and Phenomenological Philosophy Summer School [Italy], provided me with the substance of this note.

fine name of a worldview founded on natural science" (*Ideen* 92/108), the antidote to this philosophical misery.

Some 100 years after *Ideas I*'s path-breaking presentation of pure phenomenology as the foundation of a phenomenological philosophy grounded in pure, transcendental, and absolute consciousness, the "philosophical misery" from which it was supposed to liberate us is arguably a thing of the past. But rather than being a cause for celebrating the success of Husserl's transcendental turn, its absence from today's philosophical scene is, on the contrary, a cause of profound concern for those who still find philosophical value in laboring away under the fine name of phenomenologically transcendental philosophy. After more than three quarters of a century of sustained and fundamental critique, there appears to be little philosophical life left in Husserl's idea of the transcendentally pure consciousness. Not only is the world back on top in contemporary phenomenology, but, also, and in line with this, causally determined "facts" derived from its transcendent sphere of reality are increasingly accorded phenomenological–*phenomenological!*–legitimacy as cognitive contents capable of trumping philosophically transcendentally constituted units of sense and meaning.

In considering this state of affairs, the question naturally arises, whence Husserl's philosophical misery in the face of "a world-view founded on natural science," (*Ideen* 92/108) that is, in the face of 'naturalism'? Put differently, what is it about grounding putative *philosophical* claims in those of natural science that in 1913 elicited not just Husserl's philosophical misery but also his confidence that he was not alone in being affected thus while laboring in its "face"? Moreover, the related question likewise arises naturally, whether the "developments" of natural science in the intervening century are such that beyond updating phenomenology's relationship to natural science the nature of the relationship of its cognitive claims to those of natural science are in need of fundamental revision? Indeed, if the answer to this last question were positive, it might not only explain but also justify the lack of philosophical misery felt by today's phenomenologists who labor not in vain but undisturbed and indeed quite profitably in the face of a world-view anchored in natural science.

As mentioned, this chapter is the first one that thematizes the philosophical significance of pure phenomenological knowledge. The knowledge involves the radical considerations that transform reflection on consciousness into a *phenomenological* reflection on pure consciousness together with the resultant foundational discoveries of pure phenomenology. The philosophical significance involves Husserl's claims, on the one hand, that nature is inseparable from pure consciousness, while, on the other hand, that pure consciousness is separable from nature. This separability, indeed, grounds pure consciousness' epistemological and existential priority over natural knowledge and indeed over nature "itself." As also mentioned, Husserl understands these claims to be presented without using philosophical notions from the "top down" but rather universal statements whose cognitive content issues from the bottom up, insofar as they have their basis in knowledge already established by pure phenomenology. Thus, to the extent that Husserl presents 'arguments' for a phenomenological philosophy—and that extent is considerable—he understands their basis to reside in concrete cognitive implications rather than conceptual inferences. To take a pertinent and telling example: he argues conscious lived-experiences are not conceivable in relation to nature in the way that color is conceivable in relation to extension: namely, that while color is inconceivable without extension, conscious lived-experiences are conceivable without nature. For Husserl nothing in the concepts of 'color' or 'extension' entail the inconceivability of the former in relation to the latter, while, likewise, in the case of the concepts of 'conscious lived-experience' or 'nature' nothing entails the former's independence from the latter. In both cases, it is only knowledge of the *phenomena* relevant to these concepts that permits their relationship to be articulated cognitively. And in this chapter, Husserl argues that the phenomena of pure consciousness and nature establish that while nature is inconceivable apart from pure, transcendental consciousness, transcendental consciousness is conceivable apart from nature and thus exhibits epistemic and existential priority over it.

The sine qua non of the knowledge proper to the relevant phenomena requires a phenomenological reflection, in the sense of "acts of the second level" (*Ideen* 91/107) that are directed at the acts "carried out" in straightforward perceiving and experiencing, together with the determinate transcendencies of "unities of things [that, B.H.] appear and not only appear but instead are given with the character of being 'on hand [*vorhanden*, B.H., not italicized in the original],' 'actual [*wirklich*, B.H., not italicized in the original].'" (*Ideen* 91/107) Moreover, acts of excogitation likewise straightforwardly directed but founded in an "empirical-logical way" in perception and experience, yield "inferences […] to new transcendencies" (*Ideen* 91/107) that also compose that to which the second level acts of phenomenological reflection are directed. As already mentioned, acts of phenomenological reflection are distinguished from the reflections that anyone can effect by pure phenomenology's "radical considerations" (*Ideen* 92/107). These considerations, the self-imposed abstinence from "*carrying out*" (*vollziehen*) (*Ideen* 91/106) these determinate perceptions and experiences and the excogitations founded upon them, are therefore considerations that "'bracket' the acts carried out" such that "for the new investigations, 'we do not go along with these theses.'" (*Ideen* 91/107) The reflected content of the *phenomenological* reflection that is driven by such radical considerations is emphatically not 'conceptual' on Husserl's view. No amount of "reflection" on the concepts of 'perception,' 'experience,' 'empirical-logical excogitation,' 'determinate' and 'inferential' transcendencies,' is capable of yielding knowledge of the acts that fall under these concepts. Only phenomenological description can do so, can exhibit these acts' contents, which otherwise remain unnoticed when straightforwardly carried out.

The phenomenological method, as Husserl will later put it, therefore "moves entirely in acts of reflection" (*Ideen* 139/162). This doesn't mean, however, that the phenomena uncovered by phenomenology are *intrinsically* 'reflective.' All sorts of phenomena, for instance, the world-horizon or retentionally modified acts of consciousness and their objects, are exhibited by the reflective modification of pure lived-experience requisite for phenomenological reflection as always already there, ready to be perceived, prior to the advertence of the phenomenological reflection that exhibits them. This priority, however, is not temporal but what can only be called "phenomenological:" the "how" of the givenness to phenomenological reflection of such phenomena can only be described in terms of their manifesting themselves–at the very the moment of their reflective modification–in terms of their non-thematic "*unreflectively lived*" (cf. *Ideen* 144/168) modality independent of this moment. But this does not mean–notwithstanding almost a century of Neo-Kantian, Hermeneutic, and French critique–that the phenomena of pure phenomenology are somehow pejoratively "objectified" in a way that mitigates against Husserl's claims of their descriptive purity. From the inseparability of their mode of givenness as the *reflected* content of a phenomenological reflection, it does not follow that that content has been transformed by phenomenological reflection into an objective mode of being, which is to say: transformed into a mode of being putatively estranged from the phenomenon's mode of manifestation independent of such reflection.

Despite their diversity, a common presupposition runs through all these critiques, and that's that each has some kind of *methodical* or otherwise cognitive access to the very phenomenon in question that is not reflective, and that what it discloses is that Husserlian reflection is guilty of distorting it. But when asked, the proponents of these critiques are unable to tell us how, for instance, they *know* that reflection stills the stream, or is guided by the prehension of *Vorhandensein*, or is made possible by the flesh of the world, or excludes alterity, or différance, etc. What is behind all these critiques, I submit, is their mistaking the same for the other, that is, reflection unmodified by pure phenomenology's radical considerations, for a reflection so modified. Thus the dialectic of 'reflective' and 'pre-reflective' (or, worse, 'unreflective) that is behind the common presupposition I've identified here, when it (this dialectic) is itself exhibited as a phenomenon, presupposes rather than addresses what is at issue in Husserl's account of a phenomenological reflection responsible for the modification of an unreflectively lived-experience into the reflected phenomenon of the same. That is, this dialectic presupposes a thematic mode of awareness of that dimension of some phenomenon that is putatively unreachable or otherwise distorted by phenomenological reflection, which is to say, it presupposes a thematic mode of awareness of what is both reflected and supposedly unreflected. And the point is that this mode of awareness cannot but be 'reflective' in the pure phenomenological sense.

Returning now to Husserl's introductory presentation of pure phenomenology in *Ideas I*, as mentioned, what I am claiming is that the significance of its knowledge for philosophy, which is to say with Husserl, for genuine and indeed first philosophy, is not its immediate concern. Thus what I am arguing for here is that it's not until Husserl draws in this chapter (the for some infamous) conclusions about the *being* of the world and the *being* of consciousness on the basis of this knowledge, that he makes thematic the significance of pure phenomenology's ideas about the world and consciousness for a phenomenological philosophy. The pure phenomenological knowledge in question concerns, on the one hand, the descriptive content of the phenomenon of the world, and, on the other hand, the descriptive content of the phenomenon of pure conscious lived-experience. The former content is manifest in terms of transcendencies given through profiles and "intentional unities in manifolds of appearances" (*Ideen* 85/100). The latter content is manifest in terms of "experiential manifolds" (*Erfahrungsmannigfaltigkeiten*) (*Ideen* 88/103) in which the world's intentional unities are given in correlation, such that "[a]n object, being in itself, is never such that would not involve [anginge] consciousness and ego-consciousness" (*Ideen* 86/101). Phenomenological reflection uncovers the correlation in question as an essential one, meaning that the reflected phenomena of manifolds of appearances are inseparable from the reflected manifolds of the experience in which they appear. From this descriptive state of affairs Husserl draws the pure phenomenological conclusion that the manifolds of objective transcendencies are inconceivable apart from the manifolds of conscious experiences. Their recognition as such, I want to stress, is not based in the concepts of experiential or objective manifolds but rather in what is *seen* by the reflection on the acts in which such manifolds are found and thus on the basis of their *reflected* manifestation to pure phenomenological reflection.

Husserl reports that a significant aspect of what is seen in the case of objective manifolds is "the possibility of not-being (inherent essentially in every instance of a transcending thing)" (Husserl 2014, pp. 88–89/104), a possibility manifest in the profiled manner in which the transcending thing's objective intentional unity is given, that is, through appearances. In the case of experiential manifolds, however, Husserl reports "[e]very current [*aktuelle*, B.H.] experience points beyond itself to possible experiences that point themselves in turn to new possible experiences, and so on ad infinitum" (*Ideen* 87/102). This is the case for Husserl, because "*The possibility of being experienced never designates an empty logical possibility*, but instead one motivated in an experiential connection" (*Ideen* 86/101) that is itself the connection of the "'*motivation*.'" (*Ideen* 86/101) By "motivation" Husserl understands "the specification of the purely phenomenological sphere" (*Ideen* 86, note/101, note), which, "as a contrast to the concept of causality related to the transcendent sphere of reality," is a "*universalization* of the very concept of motivation, in keeping with which we are able, for example, to say that 'wanting some purpose' motivates 'wanting the means.'" (*Ideen* 86, note/101, note) Experiential manifolds of lived experiences are therefore manifest not only as continuous, but also in a manner that can always be continued. Owing to their "motivation," they bring about the unity of the transcendent thing's "one-sided" appearance through profiles, being motivated as it were by this "purpose"–i.e., the 'unity' appearing through the manifold profiles–to provide the means for its realization–i.e., the 'one' transcendent thing appearing "ever more perfectly" (*Ideen* 75/89).

Husserl's description of the pure phenomenological difference between these two modes of givenness in the chapter immediately preceding the one under consideration zeros in on the indeterminateness that is inseparable from the appearance, through objective manifolds, of the profiles proper to something transcendent, in contrast to the determinateness of the manifold lived-experiences in whose givenness is presented the unitary transcendency of that which is transcendent. Inseparable from the presentation of something transcendent is what the preceding chapter characterizes as "a horizon of determinable indeterminacy" (*Ideen* 78/92). In sharp contrast, the continuous "stream" of lived experience that forms the transcendency of the transcendent, owing to its un-presented mode of givenness, "*is given as something absolute*," in the precise sense that its reflected content manifests to pure phenomenological reflection "something absolute, it has no sides that could display themselves one time one way, another time another way." (*Ideen* 79/92) As such, the manifold of lived-experiences is given as "immanent" (*Ideen* 79/93). Husserl draws two conclusions from the pure phenomenological knowledge that he presents as providing for the next chapter, that is, Chapter Three of Part Two, "the most important premises for the conclusions that we wish to draw for the intrinsic detachability of the entire natural world from the domain of consciousness" (*Ideen* 84/99). The first is that the thesis of the world is 'contingent,' in the sense that the existence of the transcendent thing is "*never an existence necessarily demanded by the givenness*" (*Ideen* 83/97) posited in the manifold of objective appearance. What appears is inseparable from the possibility of experiential correction in the further course of experience. The second conclusion is that "[c]onflict, semblance, being otherwise–these have no place in the absolute sphere." (*Ideen* 83/98) Hence "[t]*he 'contingent' thesis of the world thus stands over against the 'necessary' thesis of my pure ego and life as an ego*, a thesis that is utterly indubitable." (*Ideen* 83/98)

Because these conclusions have their basis in knowledge obtained in the pure reflection that reflects the phenomenal content of the objective and experiential manifolds that posit respectively the world thesis and the thesis of lived experience, Husserl rules out "rational motivations" (*Ideen* 84/98) from the dubitability of the former and "pure essential necessity" (*Ideen* 83/98) from necessity of the latter. The world is dubitable "because the possibility of not-being, as a possibility in principle, is never excluded" from what is "*thinkable*" (*Ideen* 84/99) in relation to the manifold in which it is given. The necessity of the being of any current lived-experience is not the eidetic particularization of an eidetic law but the necessity of an essential law that "plays a part in the factum, and, of course, here in its existence as such," (*Ideen* 84/98) of a lived-experience. The essential law in this case arising as "[t]he ideal possibility of a reflection that has the essential character of an evidently incontrovertible thesis of *existence* is grounded in the essence of a pure ego *in general* and an experience *in general*." (*Ideen* 84/98)

So much, then, for Husserl's initial articulation of the philosophical significance of pure phenomenological knowledge for a phenomenological philosophy. This knowledge may be summarized in terms of the descriptive, reflectively exhibited possibility of appearing otherwise that is inseparable from the appearance of the one transcendent thing posited in the unity of the objective manifold, and the correlative impossibility of being otherwise proper to the experiential manifolds whose motivation is responsible for positing the unity through which the one thing appears. On the basis of this knowledge, Husserl draws two interdependent and interrelated thematically *philosophical* conclusions. One, that the meaning of the being of the natural world is "a *merely intentional being* [...], a being that is in principle only capable of being intuited and determined as something identical on the basis of motivated manifolds of appearance [*Erscheinungsmannigfaltigkeiten*, B.H.]–but *beyond this is* a nothing" (*Ideen* 90/106). Two, "that consciousness, considered in '*purity*,' has to hold as a *connection of being that is, for itself, closed off*, i. e., as a context of *absolute being* into which nothing can penetrate and from which nothing can slip away, a context that has no spatiotemporal outside and can exercise causality on nothing." (*Ideen* 90/105)

Husserl's confidence that a phenomenological philosophy is able to take care of the naturalism responsible for our philosophical misery rests, as already mentioned, on the "bottoms up" status of the universality of the pure phenomenological principles that he argues warrants these two phenomenologically philosophical conclusions. And as I've already hinted, the received wisdom today is that these principles do not warrant Husserl's conclusions. On the one hand, from the non-perspectival mode of givenness of conscious lived experiences the critical claim is made that it does not follow that that consciousness' *being* is absolute–in the sense of "nulla 're' indiget ad existendum" (*Ideen* 89/ 104)–any more than it follows from the posited mode of givenness of the meaning proper to transcendent nature that its *being* is relative to that of the consciousness that posits it. Husserl, so the criticism explains itself, conflates 'being' in the sense established by his phenomenology, that is, 'being given,' with 'substance' in the sense of Scholastic metaphysics, that is, "a thing which exists in such a way as to depend on no other thing for its existence [*quam rem quae ita existit nulla alia re indigent ad existendum*]." (Descartes 1985, p. 210)[3]

Really? If indeed it's the case that the transcendence of 'nature,' conceived in terms of both the Cartesian *imaginatio* proper to sensible perception and the *intellectus* proper to mathematical physics, is inseparable from its appearance in

---

3 I.e. Descartes, *Principles of Philosophy*, Pt. I, § 51. Heidegger, for instance, argues that "absolute being [in the sense of its independent existence, B.H.] [...] does not determine the entity itself [consciousness, B.H.] in its being but rather sets the region of consciousness within the order of constitution and assigns to it in this order a formal role of being earlier than anything objective" (Heidegger 1985, pp. 105–106). Heidegger's point being that the Cartesian definition of substance doesn't permit the ontological distinction between the region of objectivity (nature) and that of consciousness to be "grounded" because this ground is presupposed by Husserl's appeal to the order of constitution. Marion, to cite a more recent criticism, argues that the implicit appeal to Descartes in Husserl's "*nulla 're' indigent ad existendum*" actually contradicts Descartes on two crucial points. The first involves Husserl's elision of "*alia*" from Descartes' original phrase and the placing of "*re*" in quotation marks, which, according to Marion, "prove that Husserl utilizes in Descartes an insufficient and unsuitable definition" (Marion 1998, pp. 82–83), as "*alia (res)* would imply that consciousness was itself and first a *res*" (Marion 1998, p. 82), which of course is precisely what Husserl is intent on denying with his opposition of consciousness and *realitas*. The second contradiction involves Descartes' understanding of both *res cogitans* and *res extensa* to be substances, and, indeed, substances relative to the substantiality of God. I will suggest below that these criticisms are beside the point, if one identifies that point as I argue it should be identified with the phenomena in question and not Husserl's misguided self-interpretation of them in terms 'substance.' Crucial to these phenomena is their motivated manifestation as essentially correlated unities of objective and subjective manifolds, the correlation of which is one-sidedly founded on the manifolds and unities proper to the subjective pole of this correlation. Tellingly, neither Heidegger nor Marion mention Husserl's account of the phenomena of 'motivation' or 'unities of manifolds' in their criticisms.

the manifold of pure consciousness, then the "mythology" of a world-view founded on natural science seems to me to be exposed and not just for the state of natural science in 1913 but for all time. That is, insofar as the presuppositions behind this world-view exposed by Husserl are inseparable from natural science's intrinsic meaning, then no amount of scientific development or progress would be capable of surpassing their cognitive limitations. On the basis of pure phenomenological knowledge, Husserl first shows that the two *philosophical* theses that compose these presuppositions, that of "an unknown world of things as realities in themselves" (*Ideen* 97/114) and that of cognitive legitimacy of "the *causal* explanation of appearances," (*Ideen* 97/114) amount to a story without a proper philosophical foundation. The first presupposition is refuted for all time on the basis of the phenomenon of the motivated structure of all appearances, or, better, on the basis of the eidetic law that governs the pure phenomenon of motivation. More precisely, it is so refuted if it is *philosophically* "true" that both the meaning (*Sinn*) of sensible and physical nature, namely, the transcendence of nature as it appears through sensible things as well as its manner of appearance through the mediation of mathematical physics, presupposes the motivational 'unity' of the manifold of experience and the motivated 'unit' of the transcendent appearance (the latter's being 'one'). Likewise so refuted is the second presupposition, if it is *philosophically* true that inseparable from the meaning of 'causality' is "that [it, B.H.] intrinsically belongs to the connection of the constituted, intentional world" (*Ideen* 98/114), that is, to the relations between the transcendent units of appearances that compose this world. For if this is true, then the putative 'causal' bond between "'objective' physical being" (*Ideen* 98/114) and "the absolute experiences of appearing that constitute them" (*Ideen* 97/114) is indeed "mythical."

The rub, of course, is how to establish the truth of these philosophical claims, claims that for Husserl amount to establishing "the absurdity in rendering physical nature absolute, this intentional correlate of thinking that determines things logically, and likewise the absurdity in taking this nature that determines the directly intuitive world of things in an experiential-logical [*erfahrungslogisch*, B.H.] fashion and that is completely *familiar* in this function […] and making it into an unfamiliar reality, indicating itself only mysteriously, a reality that *itself* can never be grasped […] a reality to which one imputes the role of a *causal* reality in relation to the elapsing instances of subjective appearances and experiences experiencing them [*erfahrende Erlebnisse*]" (*Ideen* 98/114 – 115). In short, the absurdity at issue here "stems from construing the world *philosophically* as absolute" (*Ideen* 103/120).

Husserl's way of establishing the truths of these claims in 1913, to argue that the phenomenologically motivated status of all appearances renders it conceivable that the objective manifold of the appearances of sensible and physical nature is capable of annulment, while it is inconceivable that the manifold unity of pure consciousness responsible for the *appearing* of these appearances as intentional units of 'being' would not exist following nature's annulment, is, as already mentioned, supposed to involve an equivocation and therefore to commit an informal fallacy. To wit, the equivocation of identifying 'being' with both the phenomenological unit of meaning relative to consciousness and the ontological or metaphysical substance capable of independent existence.

One hundred years hence, it is apparent that the framing of this putative equivocation is itself rife with unwarranted philosophical and phenomenological presuppositions. Philosophically, the "traditional" meaning of being as 'substance' presupposes the Latin negation of Aristotelian οὐσία as the way of being belonging to anything that has attributes but is itself not an attribute of anything, and thus is χωριστόν (separate) and τόδε τι (a this). That is, as the capacity to have predicates, *substantia* as the translation of οὐσία negates the meaning of the Greek word it is supposed to be translating.[4] Phenomenologically, the mode of the givenness of both nature's transcendence and transcendental consciousness' immanence as unities of manifolds situates the most proximate traditional precedent of their phenomenal manifestation in neither Scholastic nor Aristotelian metaphysics but in Plato's late non-Socratic philosophy. In contrast to Plato's Socratic presentation of philosophy, whose interrogation of εἴδη is mediated by images, Plato's late thought is concerned with the unity of the multitudes that appear beyond being and so appear otherwise than exclusively through the medium of images (cf. Hopkins 2011a, part I, chs. 1–2).

For my purposes, it will be enough to point out that the late Platonic precedent to Husserl's antidote to the philosophical misery induced by naturalism has nothing to do with the Socratic opposition between 'being' and 'becoming'..' But, rather, it has everything to do with the κοινωνία (community) between the unity of the unlimited multitude responsible for the soul's κίνησις (motion) and the unity of the limited multitude responsible for the κοινωνία τῶν εἰδῶν (community of *eidê*) in ἐπιστήμη (apodictic knowledge).[5] My point here, howev-

---

4 The fact that Husserl's "*nulla 're' indigent ad existendum*" was no doubt invoking the Scholastic notion of substance takes nothing away from my argument to follow that the absoluteness of pure, transcendental consciousness is beyond being and thus not adequately captured by 'substance' or any other concept of being. In this as in all matters of transcendental phenomenology, the decisive "truth maker" is not the appeal to what Husserl himself really thought about a given phenomenon but the appeal to the phenomenon in question.
5 Cf. Plato, *Sophist*, 249a-c; 253b-257a; cf. Klein (1934) and Klein (1936), ch. 7. For the English translation cf. Klein (1968) and Hopkins (2011b), ch. 19.

er, is neither that Husserl's antidote to naturalism self-consciously drew its inspiration from Plato nor that it is somehow analogous to Plato's late philosophy of the unities and multiplicities that compose and are therefore somehow "beyond" being. What is significant for my purposes is that once the Platonic precedent for a philosophy that, like Husserl's, wasn't conceived by its originator as an ontology is established, it is easier to see today, some 100 years after the fact, that Husserl's antidote to naturalism was not administered 'ontologically' but in the philosophically more–and, indeed, most–fundamental sense of the recognition of the horizon of multitudes from out of which both all posited and all apodictically demonstrated unity of knowledge emerges. Moreover, once this is seen, then the visibility of the epistemic and ontological priority assigned by both Plato and Husserl to the unities manifest in the multitudes that compose the soul's knowledge over the unities posited and established in the multitudes that are other than those of the soul also becomes manifest.

Whether Husserl's 'beyond being' antidote to naturalism presented some 100 years ago will appear as any more philosophically compelling today than it did then in the light of its reassessment in terms of its proper Platonic precedent, depends upon whether one shares Husserl's–and, for that matter, Plato's–philosophical *pathos* in the face of a world-view founded on natural science. The common source of their *pathe*, I submit, is the congenital blindness–for all time–of natural science (whether mediated by mathematics or not it makes no difference) to the intelligible sources of its cognitive pretensions. Because it is necessarily generated in the absence of the original vision of the unities that compose these sources, natural knowledge, whether in the hands of the naturalist or the philosopher, can only be "related" to them through a forever-misguided *a posteriori* appeal to causalities. To labor in the face of the putative *singularity* of a world-view founded in efficient causality's epistemically unavoidable fragmentation of the singularity it is supposed to explain–without realizing that to do so is to labor in vain–is something neither Plato nor Husserl were capable of. And they were both so for the simple but profound reason that each experienced philosophical pathos in the face of the fragmented knowledge capable of yielding neither universal knowledge nor the one philosophy inseparable from the exalted idea of knowledge's universality. Thus whatever their philosophical differences, Plato and Husserl seem to have been pathologically united by their shared response to naturalism.

Bibliography

Descartes, René (1985): *The Philosophical Writings of Descartes*. Trans. Cottingham, John/Stoothoff, Robert/Murdoch, Dugald. Cambridge: Cambridge University Press.
Heidegger, Martin (1985): *History of the Concept of Time. Prolegomena*. Trans. Kisiel, Theodore. Bloomington: Indiana University Press.
Hopkins, Burt C. (2011a): *The Philosophy of Husserl*. Durham: Acumen.
Hopkins, Burt C. (2011b): *The Origin of the Logic of Symbolic Mathematics. Edmund Husserl and Jacob Klein*. Bloomington: Indiana University Press.
Klein, Jacob (1934): "Die griechische Logistik und die Entstehung der Algebra". In: *Quellen und Studien zur Geschichte der Mathematik, Astronomie und Physik*, Abteilung B: Studien 3, 1, pp. 18–105. [Part I]
Klein, Jacob (1936): "Die griechische Logistik und die Entstehung der Algebra". In: *Quellen und Studien zur Geschichte der Mathematik, Astronomie und Physik*, Abteilung B: Studien 3, 2, pp. 122–235. [Part II]
Klein, Jacob (1968): *Greek Mathematical Thought and the Origin of Algebra*. Trans. Brann, Eva. Cambridge, Mass.: MIT Press. [Reprint: New York: Dover, 1992]
Marion, Jean-Luc (1998): *Reduction and Givenness: Investigations of Husserl, Heidegger, and Phenomenology*. Trans. Carlson, Thomas A. Evanston: Northwestern University Press.

Sebastian Luft
Laying bare the phenomenal field: The reductions as ways to pure consciousness

Section II, chapter 4, The phenomenological reductions

1. Introduction

Chapter Four, "The Phenomenological Reductions," is the last chapter of Section II, *The Fundamental Phenomenological Consideration*, of *Ideas* I. Its systematic locus at this point in the work is both a summary of the previous discussions and a further fleshing out of the methodological reflections pertaining to the entryway into the very enterprise of pure phenomenology. After these fundamental considerations, Husserl moves on to more specific issues pertaining to pure phenomenology, such as the distinctions between sensual *hylé* and intentional *morphé* or between noesis and noema, in Section III (*On the Method and Problems of Pure Phenomenology*). But in order to move on "safely," Husserl wants to make sure that the field of this new science has been clearly laid bare and, more importantly, sharply demarcated. These efforts of demarcation are remarkable, since phenomenology as a philosophical endeavor is not new at this point, neither to Husserl nor to his contemporaries, and Husserl was seemingly unconcerned in the past about this methodological *caveat*. What is new, as of *Ideas* I, is the emphasis on the *purity* of consciousness, which Husserl finds hard to make comprehensible, both (presumably) to himself and (given the reception of this work, obviously) to his readers. Conversely, to secure this purity, what is to be avoided are contaminations from the "outside." Since we ourselves, as creatures living first and foremost in pre-theoretical life, are always "out there" and since attaining this purity requires such a difficult change of view from the normal way of seeing, this sophisticated new task has to be conceived with utmost care. Husserl admits that his past attempts have been vulnerable to this threat of contamination, and in *Ideas* I, as a manifesto of the Phenomenological Movement and the first volume of the new series he has just inaugurated with other first-row phenomenologists (cf. Schuhmann 1990), Husserl wants to make certain, beyond any doubt, that phenomenology is clearly understood as the descriptive-eidetic science of pure or transcendental consciousness, and that it *cannot* be anything else if it wants to come forth as a rigorous science.

The way Husserl presents this method of demarcation is by laying bare the field of pure consciousness. This process, however, is at the same time the product of exclusions, which, *ex negativo*, leave standing the phenomenal field, the field of labor for phenomenology, in its purity. In this task of excluding what is *not* to be taken as the field of phenomenology, Husserl uses the term "reductions," though his understanding of the term here is synonymous with that of "exclusion," "bracketing," or *epoché*. This becomes clear when he speaks of "the phenomenological reduction as the suspension of the natural attitude or, better, its general thesis" (*Ideen* 104/121), something which he earlier explicitly calls phenomenological *epoché* (cf. *Ideen* 55/65). In light of the use of the term "reduction" in Husserl's late period (cf. Husserl 2002 and Luft 2011, pp. 52–81) , where it is used in the singular as a label for the transcendental-phenomenological method *in general,* it may strike a reader of the later Husserl as curious that in the present chapter four, he speaks of "reductions" in the plural.[1] It is fair to say that Husserl's vocabulary at this point, and with respect to this problem, was not as stable as later, which is somewhat regrettable given the history of its reception. Indeed, to this day, hasty readers of *Ideas* I lump together as one and the same thing the *epoché*, the transcendental reduction and even the eidetic variation.[2] This is a gross misreading, as readers of Husserl know, but also an indication of the transitional nature at least of Husserl's terminology in *Ideas*. Whether the reduction as a method itself significantly changes in later years is a different question; one which, however, cannot be answered in this context. Suffice it to say that, while Husserl's thinking was in flux until the end, the reduction as *general title of and principal method into* phenomenology does not experience any fundamental changes, while Husserl, nonetheless, conceives different ways and strategies to lead into phenomenology as a science of transcendental consciousness.[3]

In the present text, Husserl presents the so-called Cartesian way by way of a reduction to the ego as the last "bastion" that remains after all exclusions (in paragraphs 27–32). Yet already in the discussions regarding the domain of phenomenological research in this chapter IV, it becomes clear that the path follow-

---

[1] The present author has written extensively on Husserl's (mature) method of the phenomenological reduction. For my most extensive treatments, I refer esp. to Luft (2002) and Luft (2011), here esp. Part I. For a very general overview over the problem of reduction in the late Husserl, cf. also Luft (2012).

[2] An especially egregious example of a fundamental misunderstanding of Husserl's method is to be found in the–unfortunately classical–study by Adorno (1984), but many readers of Husserl have relied on this erroneous reading.

[3] On the ways into the reduction, cf. the classical article Kern 1977.

ing Descartes' path of "hyperbolic doubt" may be, as Husserl later deems it, the "most direct" path to transcendental phenomenology and therefore retains its right (cf. Husserl 1993, pp. 425–426, esp. p. 426). But Husserl's alleged "Cartesianism" ends here, as the sphere of phenomenological research is not to be construed as an ultimate ego which provides an ultimate grounding of any knowledge claims. Nevertheless, Husserl's use of Cartesian terminology and his wavering between this "Cartesianism" and the actual descriptive work of the phenomenological domain make this text a somewhat confusing read, especially when it comes to his discussion of the "pure ego."

Regarding the actual method of getting at this region, lots of ink has been spilled on the alleged distinctions between the *epoché* and the reduction as different parts or methodological steps of the way into phenomenology. However, in a charitable reading one should say that the two methodological components of excluding the general thesis of the natural attitude and of leading back (*reducere*) to the field germane to phenomenology can indeed not be as sharply separated as one might desire. If, however, one sees the exclusion of the general thesis of the natural attitude and the reduction to pure consciousness as two organic steps in the process of uncovering the field of pure consciousness, the distinction between both need not, and indeed cannot, be kept apart so strictly. Excluding something is at the same time the opening up of something new, for which appreciation is sought. This opening up occurs, formally, with the *epoché*, "in one blow," but what exactly is contained therein requires clarification. In this sense, one can say that the present chapter four, dealing with reductions, is an enumeration of the further bracketings of *moments of* the natural attitude, some of which are *already* and *obviously* entailed in the original bracketing (or "exclusion") of the natural attitude, which Husserl spells out once again just to make sure all bases are covered. Others, however, are *not obviously* entailed therein, and perhaps *not at all* included in the first *epoché* and where the question may be raised whether an exclusion is possible at all. These paragraphs 56–62, thus, have the purpose of clarification and of addressing misconceptions from the outset, before the real work of phenomenology gets underway, though they may leave the reader with some questions, some of which will be discussed at the end of this chapter.

I will first give an overview over the seven paragraphs, summarizing what Husserl accomplishes here. In a concluding part, I will point to what I take to be the most interesting and at the same time most controversial points that require, if not a detailed elucidation, at least an orientation to discern the crucial points, (1) the question of the pure ego; (2) the exclusion of pure logic; and (3) the status of phenomenology as an eidetic science.

There are five areas that Husserl wishes to exclude: (1) all sciences (natural sciences and human sciences or humanities [*Geisteswissenschaften*]), (2) the pure ego, (3) God, (4) transcendent eidetics and pure logic (formal eidetics), and (5) transcendent material eidetics. Discussing these sharpens both the method of phenomenology as well as the nature of its subject matter. After this discussion, Husserl adds two paragraphs where he reflects on the methodological meaning of these reductions and discusses epistemological consequences for what is to come.

To assess these further reductions, let us briefly recall why the *epoché* as bracketing of the natural attitude is necessary and what it accomplishes.

The insight into the purity of consciousness of which phenomenology is to be the science, necessitates making explicit the stance we ordinarily take unto the world. In this stance, we do not and cannot get pure consciousness into view, because we are directed at things in the world, and take ourselves as part of this world, one object among others. We take consciousness, in other words, as an empirical and worldly fact. As an empirical fact, experienced in our normal way of viewing it, it is contaminated by worldly "matter," for instance, my personal first-person access (and my personal history, my character etc.). As such a fact, it is also viewed as one "thing" next to others in the world, and not as that agent that is privileged among all other things as that which *experiences* the world. To view it as that which *has* the world as its object and is not itself another object in the world and in its purity (consciousness as such), we need to suspend this view in its entirety. This pre-phenomenological view is called the natural attitude.[4] How is the suspension of this view accomplished? It is not negated or doubted, since we cannot avoid returning back to it. The natural attitude is, thus, not comparable to, for instance, a Platonic or Hegelian view of common sense of the everyday life, which is shown to be wrong and fundamentally misguided ("inverted") from the philosophical standpoint. It has its relative right but needs to be suspended to get into view what it never can get into view; thus it is bracketed, held in suspension for the time in which phenomenology is being done. We withhold judgment as to its existence, veracity, and knowledge claims.

Thus, the bracketing of the natural attitude entails the bracketing of the general thesis underpinning the former. The general thesis is never explicitly stated but is, metaphorically speaking, an unheard base line that goes along every particular act, and if made explicit, it would state, simply, that the world and the

---

[4] For an extensive discussion of the constitutive moments of the natural attitude, cf. Luft (2011), pp. 37–50.

objects in it (including myself) *exist* (cf. Husserl 1959, pp. 36–43). This thesis is not issued on the part of anyone's individual consciousness, but is the attitude of consciousness *as such* to the world. It comes with birth, as it were, that we take the world to exist, and that means, moreover, to exist independently from ourselves. In all acts of the natural attitude, the world is *taken to be* existing. The statement "the world is," thus, is not strictly speaking a statement with respect to the world, but a statement concerning consciousness' taking of the world, namely to consider it to exist mind-independently. It is not an ontological but a transcendental proposition, and hence the "bracketing" is a suspension of the ontological claim that the world *exists*. The general thesis of the natural attitude, then, may be interpreted as a transcendental statement comparable to the Kantian "I think" that must be able to accompany all my representations, only on a more basic level (cf. *Ideen* 104/123).

As a result, we are now reduced, as investigators, to the experience of the world, the first-person perspective. Consequently, once this general thesis is bracketed, what remains is not the world as the totality of things and thus as an idea, but the region of the individual experiences that experience the world, *also excluding* the *objects* of the world itself which are taken to be equally mind-independently. Hence, with the bracketing, we gain access to the region of consciousness in which the world is experienced or–to put it differently–the space in which the world can manifest itself to an experiencing agent. This does not have to be a human agent, but I must necessarily use my personal first person access to gain the first person access as such, in its purity, just as the mathematician uses numbers viewed on a page as access to numbers-as-such. Phenomenology is the a priori science of the region of the first person experience in its purity and generality, eidetic science of pure consciousness. Since this is what remains after the exclusion of the general thesis, Husserl also calls it a "residuum" (*Ideen* 56/66) of bracketing, a term he later regrets using, because what remains is not some "tag-end of the world" (Husserl 1991, p. 63)[5]; rather, something completely other-worldly is opened up, a region *sui generis*. It is not another region *within* the world but the space *in which* the world can be experienced and in which it constitutes itself for us *in* our experience (taken as the widest possible manner of having evidence of something–in phenomenological terms, intentionality).

---

5 In this passage, Husserl overtly criticizes Descartes for this mistake, but from the context it becomes clear that he also wishes to distance himself from Descartes in this respect and avoid a misconstrual of his method as following this Cartesian mistake.

2. § 56–Natural and human sciences

What is bracketed, in chapter one of the *Fundamental Phenomenological Consideration*, is the natural attitude as that what all special attitudes, all acts have in common, and that is the general thesis that the world exists. This is now where § 56 takes up the question as to what is included in this initial bracketing. Given the name, the "*natural* attitude," it suggests that *nature* is that which is bracketed. But what about consciousness or "spirit"? Since nature has its own scientific disciplines dealing with it, the question becomes what sciences are included in this bracketing. Obviously all natural sciences, as dealing with objects of nature, are excluded. But phenomenology is not, then, a human science, a *Geisteswissenschaft*, as Dilthey or a Neo-Kantian like Windelband might define all other sciences that are not about nature (cf. Makkreel 2009). Contrary to such a distinction between sciences with respect to nature and what-is-not-nature, Husserl declares, *all* objects of the world that are taken to be existing, including cultural objects, are to be excluded as well, and hence *all sciences* pertaining to them. This is not to deny that cultural objects such as buildings or art works have their own meaning; rather, as existing of natural matter, such as stone or wood, they, too, are taken as existing as independently of human experience in the natural attitude, regardless of whether they were made by us as opposed to self-subsisting nature. Thus, regardless of their cultural meanings, cultural objects, too, are part of the world of the natural attitude insofar as they exist in the world *of* the natural attitude.

Although this sounds like a rather obvious point, given his definition of the natural attitude, this amounts to a rejection of a Neo-Kantian philosophy of culture, which had great currency in Husserl's day, when Husserl dismisses all "cultural *facta*" as starting points for an investigation of the field of pure consciousness, since these *facta* all are taken as existing, thus belonging to the natural attitude. They might be taken into consideration as "unities of validity" (cf. *Ideen* 104/122), that is, as something that has a "spiritual" dimension, i.e., something not already existing in the world but something constituted by minded creatures that is somehow "appended" to the physical object. As such, a cultural object might be, for instance, an "index" of the ingenious mind who created it. But the access point, from this cultural object, into the "mind of the artist," does not give us access to consciousness in its purity, at best into the individual consciousness of this artist. As opposed to sciences of lawful relations (in nature or culture), the Southwest Neo-Kantians (esp. Windelband) posited sciences of individual events as a different, but equally valid scientific ideal (cf. Windelband 2015). A discipline such as historiography is interested precisely in these individual events (the specific event in Sarajevo, which triggered World War I), not in lawful relations or generalities. The implicit point that Husserl makes here is that phenomenology is beyond the distinction between the domain of consciousness as bound through idiographic facts and the domain of nature as bound by nomothetic laws. Phenomenology is the eidetic (i.e., lawful) science *of* consciousness. The *natural* attitude, then, pertains to the way we *naturally* experience the world writ large, not just *nature*. Nature, too, is, as an object of experience, a product of constitution, and natural science (besides other theoretical or other human activities) is a product of our doing, hence *itself* an object of culture. Phenomenology, too, is a product of minded creatures by that standard, but it studies not the world and its objects, but the *constitution* of the world in consciousness.

The natural attitude is the default, taken-for-granted stance vis-à-vis the world, which includes nature as well as culture, and thereby, accordingly, natural as well as cultural or human sciences. To bracket it has similarity with the Socratic ignorance with respect to dogmatic assumptions about the world, Descartes' hyperbolic doubt, leaving over as indubitable only the *ego sum*, or Kant's Copernican Turn away from the world as a thing in itself to the world as phenomenon. In aligning himself with these predecessors makes Husserl's attempt a truly philosophical endeavor. But its purpose, to clear the way for phenomenology, distinguishes it radically from these philosophical endeavors (though Descartes and Kant, in Husserl's estimation, darkly anticipated the field of pure consciousness). To bracket the natural attitude, finally, can by no means mean to do away with all presuppositions and prejudices. It neither wants to do this nor claims this is possible. Its purpose is to analyze consciousness in the way it experiences the world, not the world itself or (natural or cultural) things in it.

3. § 57–The pure ego

Next, does the exclusion of all factuality include the thinking ego who performs this very action? Or does the exclusion of the personal (empirical) ego leave as a result a pure (transcendental) ego? If so, what kind of entity, then, is this pure ego? Here, one has to distinguish the ego that currently experiences, of which a reflection upon experience would be another experience (and create a new ego), and the ego as a self-same identity as that to which *all* experience is *in principle and necessarily* related. Thus, regarding the question, whether we find "an ego" after the exclusion of the human being as a natural-cultural being or psycho-physical unity, the question is falsely put. What we find are experiences in a stream of consciousness, in which we experience conscious things, or episodes with things, that come and go. Certainly there is a "who" of these experiences that stays identical in this constant flux; yet it is not something that can itself be experienced but is the condition of the possibility of experience. It is in this sense that Husserl endorses the Kantian formula, "the 'I think' must be able to accompany my representations" (cf. *Ideen* 105/123). The moment I reflect upon it, it vanishes as a pure ego and becomes an experience (*Erlebnis*) with its own stream of consciousness upon which I reflect by means of an "I think." In his 1923/24 lecture *First Philosophy*, Husserl gives a phenomenological description of such an activity under the title of "splitting of the ego" (*Ichspaltung*), which creates new streams of consciousness in the course of each such splitting, when I, for instance, reflect on my earlier stream of consciousness and disapprove my earlier actions (cf. Husserl 1959, pp. 86–92). As he says here, in a striking metaphor, the ego is not some block of wood that can be chopped up into pieces. Rather, I always live, consciously, in a stream and can reflect on another, but in the act of reflection, the ego remains latent, while making another stream patent. In each case, the pure ego as the conscious ego-center is elusive, but must be assumed to exist as the "radiating center" of acts.

However, as a unit of such identity and, in case of the concrete ego I am, as the bearer of certain personal traits, as a style by which experiences are had and enacted, one can speak of a pure ego as *pure* correlate of a *personal* ego, and as such Husserl calls it a peculiar "*transcendence in immanence*" (*Ideen* 105/124), which, however, plays no role for "many investigations" within phenomenology, as he claims. One can imagine that this is indeed the case of, e. g., time-consciousness, which is a rather "austere" description of the formal structure of temporal experience in primal impression, pro- and retention. It becomes hard to imagine, however, that questions of a transcendent ego play no role in a phenomenology of the lived-body or memory and imagination. All of these dimensions of subjectivity entail rich dimensions of experience, which cannot be simply "pealed away" to reveal a pure ego without losing what is essential to them. Nonetheless, such a pure ego must be presupposed as that to which all experiences are relative, as the experiencing agent.

At this point Husserl, as well as in the second edition of the *Logical Investigations* of 1913, takes back his critique of Natorp, whom he criticized for an "ego-metaphysics" (cf. *Ideen* 106, note/124, note). This fear of such a metaphysics made Husserl shy away from an account of the pure ego earlier, whereas he now admits it as necessary, albeit in the Kantian sense as a regulative idea of the unitary origin of all acts. It should be noted that this critique hardly applies to Natorp's ego-conception. The latter's project of a "reconstructive psychology" in Natorp's *Allgemeine Psychologie* of 1912 (cf. Natorp 2013)[6], which Husserl admits not having studied at the time he publishes *Ideas*, is actually much closer to a phenomenological ego-conception that rejects the notion that the ego is a *substantial* unit that can be grasped and understood like an external object (like the piece of wood). I shall return to this point in the critical discussion. For now we can record that with the admission of a pure ego, Husserl is implicitly aligning himself with a Kantian conception of a transcendental subject, which nonetheless must be distinguished from this ego's field of experience which is the real domain of phenomenological analysis.

4. § 58–God

Regarding the question of God[7], Husserl's position (philosophically, not in terms of personal religious belief) can be called Kantian. God is, by definition, that which is absolutely transcendent, hence it cannot be an object of experience. It can perhaps, "wondrously," be experienced mediately by the teleology we discover in nature (this, too, is Kant's idea). As being part of what the natural sciences discover, such a teleological structure putatively leading to a divine being, too, has been excluded. This point can be made rather quickly. Absolute reality that is the definition of the divine is transcendent in an absolutely different sense of the transcendence of the world. But Husserl uses the question regarding the absolute for a reminder as to the nature of the region of phenomenology. For the question as to the final goal of the world can also raise the question as to an absolute ground for the "facticity ... of the constituting consciousness" (*Ideen* 107/125). I suspect another reference to Natorp, for whom the primal origin of the subject lies in unbounded, ineffable life, when Husserl rejects such an "absolute" notion of absolute consciousness that would indeed be analogous to a divine consciousness on the "opposite" side of the spectrum. Pure consciousness after the reduction *is* absolute, but in an entirely different, but also less metaphysically problematic sense. It is absolute insofar as everything that is and can be experienced is relative to an experiencing consciousness. That everything that is exists must be construed as experienceable, at least in principle, to an ex-

---

[6] On the influence of Natorp on Husserl, cf. the editor's introduction to the new edition of this work Natorp (2013), pp. xi-xxxviii.
[7] The Husserliana volume in which Husserl reflects on God and the possibility of a phenomenological theology (though mostly from later periods) has just been released, cf. Husserl (2014b). Cf. also Held (2010) for a discussion of God in Husserl's phenomenology.

periencing consciousness, that everything is relative to the latter, which is thereby the absolute, is a statement expressing Husserl's transcendental idealism.[8] This rather modest concept of the notion "absolute" must be emphasized when some philosophers want to go beyond Husserl in wanting to posit absolute life or manifestation as an absolute beneath or prior to consciousness, as something Husserl took for granted. To Husserl, they become guilty of a dogmatic metaphysics by disrespecting the exclusions enacted by the reduction. For, to go beyond consciousness is to transcend, in the opposite direction, absolute consciousness as the space for the manifestation of the world, its manifestation in experience. That there would be a manifestation beforehand that would enable such a manifestation in experience may be an intriguing thought, but not one that can be entertained within the boundaries set by the reduction.

5. § 59–Formal eidetics and pure logic

The next two paragraphs form a unity, insofar as they discuss the necessity, or even possibility, of excluding certain scientific disciplines that are neither natural nor human (thus empirical or factual), but eidetic. There are formal and material eidetics. Formal eidetic sciences would be, for instance, mathematics or geometry, but also formal logic; material-eidetic disciplines are disciplines which correspond to regional ontologies, for instance the region of bodies or colors. In the present paragraph, Husserl discusses formal-eidetic disciplines, in the next material-eidetic ones.

Insofar as the reduction excludes all kinds of objectivities, it must also exclude those objectivities that are of the nature of *essences*. Yet, as Husserl cautions at the outset, a complete exclusion of *all* essences cannot be possible, for then a science of pure consciousness, which is by definition eidetic (or pure) as well, would be impossible. The question thus becomes, what kind of eidetic sciences need to be excluded. To all spheres of being belong material ontologies, which have to be excluded as belonging to that region of being that has been bracketed. To these material ontologies belong necessarily the formal ones "object as such" and the formal logic with respect to "object as such." The question becomes whether one can exclude something like formal logic, since the phenomenologist, too, has to perform acts of thinking with respect to what

---

[8] On Husserl's conception of the "absolute," cf. Boehm (1959) (a classical essay, still well worth reading) and Zahavi (2010), who summarizes earlier research but essentially agrees with Boehm's interpretation.

she experiences. It seems that formal logic as that which rules thinking in its most formal manner cannot be suspended. "Every pure experience is also subsumed under the logically widest sense of object" (*Ideen* 108/126), would be the conclusion of this argument. This, however, is an erroneous line of thought. For, phenomenology does not proceed *constructively*, as in formal logic or formal mathesis, but *intuitively*. For this reason, formal logic needs to be excluded as well as all formal mathesis (algebra, theory of numbers, theory of manifolds). The bracketing of formal logic, thus, makes it clear that "phenomenology is then in fact a *purely descriptive* discipline, thoroughly investigating the field of transcendentally pure consciousness in *pure Intuition*" (*Ideen* 108/127). Instead, phenomenology is beholden to the principle of all principles, "*to lay claim to nothing other than what we are essentially able to make transparently evident to ourselves in consciousness itself,* in pure immanence" (*Ideen* 109/127).

6. § 60–Material eidetics

Things stand differently with respect to material eidetics. Insofar as consciousness is not only comprised of formal structures but first and foremost a material sphere of experience, the eidetic science of this region cannot be excluded. Phenomenology is an eidetic, not an empirical science, of pure consciousness; but as being pure, it is for that reason not formal.[9] In general, every empirical science stands under an a priori science with respect to the region of which it is science. What we want to describe is the a priori of consciousness, and this description can, thus, only be by way of a science of essences. But the essences are not transcendent but immanent. "Thing," "shape," "movement" are *transcendent* essences, and hence eidetic sciences of these transcendent essences, such as rational psychology and sociology, are excluded. Here Husserl adds that these sciences have, up to now, lacked a proper grounding, judging from their rather recent histories; whether Husserl's judgment would stand a century later remains an open (and quite interesting) question. Phenomenology is, thus, "*absolutely independent of all material-eidetic* sciences dealing with *transcendent* essences" (cf. *Ideen* 110/129) That means, by way of exclusion, phenomenology is a material-eidetic science of *immanent* essences, those, thus, that belong to the immanence of the stream of consciousness, insofar as this stream of conscious-

---

[9] That purity is identical with formality may be considered Kant's understanding when he critiques *pure* reason: purity refers to forms of intuition and forms of the understanding.

ness experiences individual, material experiences that have to be investigated as to their material-immanent *general universality*.

7. § 61–Meaning of the systematics of the reductions

The purpose of these reductions, Husserl says by way of summary, was to demarcate the radically different spheres of being and cognition, that of worldly being and transcendental being, or world and consciousness, and that any reaching over of one into the other is an impermissible, faulty *metabasis*. These careful reductions are needed precisely to clarify the radically new nature of the field of phenomenology, which requires its own and radically new attitude vis-à-vis the natural attitude. Husserl lists some pitfalls for a proper appreciation for the field of phenomenology. The first is a psychological understanding of these immanent essences. They are as little psychological facts as are numbers. Such a mistake is simply the inability to distinguish between the eidetic and the factual, as was psychologism's mistake. Next, therefore, one must distinguish between immanent and transcendent essences, thus, "on the one side [are] essences of configurations of consciousness itself; on the other side essences of individual occurrences that transcend consciousness, i.e., essences of the sort that 'announce' themselves only in configurations of consciousness, for example, those that are 'constituted' in consciousness through sensory appearances" (*Ideen* 112/131). Here, Husserl self-critically mentions that he himself, in the *Logical Investigations*, was initially not entirely consistent in the latter distinction and that he, as all other "born dogmatists" (*Ideen* 113/132), initially had difficulties learning the distinctive seeing necessary for doing phenomenology, and consequently to maintain at all times the attitude necessary for giving eidetic descriptions of the pure immanence of consciousness.

8. § 62–The "dogmatic" and the phenomenological attitude

To distinguish, in conclusion, phenomenology from all other sciences, Husserl reverts to a distinction between the natural and phenomenological attitudes, which he now calls, in variation and slightly different emphasis, the dogmatic and the critical attitudes. All non-phenomenological disciplines are dogmatic in the sense of taking the being of their region for granted, i.e., as standing on the ground of the natural attitude. Once the natural attitude is suspended, one is in principle in an attitude that is radically different from it, and reverting to Kant, he calls it "critical" in that this new attitude engenders a critique of which the sciences of the natural attitude are by their very nature incapable, for which they are blind. But as critique, it not only is able to open the pathway to pure phenomenology, with respect to its own subject domain, but also to applied phenomenology, as a critique of the sciences of the natural attitude. Phenomenological critique is in this sense "first philosophy" as, for every individual science, it provides the "ultimately evaluating [*letztauswertende*] critique and, along with the latter, in particular the ultimate determination of the sense of 'being' of its objects and the intrinsic clarification of its methodology" (*Ideen* 113–114/133) and as such, as he says with some pathos, phenomenology is the "secret longing of all modern philosophy" (*Ideen* 114/133), something that all the great modern philosophers wanted but were unable to accomplish. Husserl considers his philosophy the grand synthesis of rationalism, empiricism and criticism, as being a rational science of experience, which he occasionally also calls, in a grand synthesis, "transcendental empiricism." Previous forms of scientific philosophy are sublated [*aufgehoben*] in his transcendental-eidetic phenomenology. Though Husserl was not an avid reader of Hegel, at least in this ambition of satisfying modern philosophy's "secret yearning," he is quite comparable to the philosopher of the absolute.

9. Discussion of specific problems

I now move on to the discussion of a few points that strike me as particularly interesting and also problematic in Husserl's exposition.

9.1. The question of the pure ego

In the question as to the exclusion of the pure ego, Husserl first has to define it, and he characterizes it as a pole of rays emanating from it, characterizing it further as a "peculiar–non-constituted–transcendence, a transcendence *in immanence*" (*Ideen* 105/124). Regarding this pure ego, he adds in the famous footnote (repeated in similar tone and content in the 2nd edition of *Logical Investigations*, published the same year, 1913) that he no longer maintains a skepticism with respect to the pure ego and that he no longer worries about the "degenerations [*Ausartungen*] of an ego-metaphysics" (Husserl 1984a, p. 374, note). What is somewhat puzzling about this statement is Husserl's phrasing of this position–the affirmation of a pure ego–as metaphysical. What kind of metaphysics is this that phenomenology, initially, needs to steer clear of, but later can be unconcerned about, assuming it is no longer "degenerate"? It is known here that Husserl initially takes issue with Natorp. In order to untangle this knot, let us see what Natorp's position is and Husserl's rendering of it. It turns out that this story is somewhat complicated.

In § 8 of the Fifth *Logical Investigation* Husserl discusses Natorp's conception of consciousness. The passages he quotes from the latter's 1888 booklet *Einleitung in die Psychologie nach kritischer Methode* are a fair presentation of his view, so before we can see what exactly Husserl takes issue with, let us briefly present Natorp. Natorp's project in this book, as well as his more mature *Allgemeine Psychologie nach kritischer Methode* of 1912 (cf. Natorp 2013), is to construe a psychology "according to critical method," i. e., within the boundaries of transcendental philosophy. Transcendental philosophy, according to the Marburg School, should be about the logical reconstruction of cultural *facta*, according to the logical structure that construct each sphere of reality. Culture as the sum total of these facts is this school's title for reality. Since what is sought for are these logical structures, the starting point for a transcendental philosophy of culture must be from a science of each region, where these structures have crystallized. Hence, in terms of synthetic a priori cognition, transcendental philosophy must start out from the factum of mathematical-exact natural science; in the case of ethics, the starting point is legal science, jurisprudence (cf. Luft 2014). Natorp's idea of a transcendental psychology is now, if these *facta* are constructed, they must be constructed starting from some-"thing," which can only be consciousness as that which accounts for these constructions in minded creatures (or what he calls simply "life"). So if construction moves the path towards something made, finished, this process can also be reversed and undone, by way of re-construction. I can go in the *positive or negative*, plus or minus direction on a vector, as he says metaphorically. Going the negative way I can recover the subjective life from which the objects became constituted.

But what I arrive at, following the subjective direction, is not a new *factum*, but that to which all *facta* are opposed, what Natorp also calls a *facere* (the *factum* is a *fieri*, something being made). Thus, the reconstructive path of psychology discovers no new *factum* but that to which all *facta* are given. It is in this sense nothing but a restatement of the Kantian I-think, when Natorp says,

> We have ceased calling it I insofar as we think it as an object. To be Ego does not mean being an object but to be that which is opposed to all objectivity as that what to which something is an object (quoted in Husserl 1984a, p. 373).

Natorp's aim in his psychology is, said differently, to resist reifing the ego or viewing it as some sort of substance. All we can say about it reconstructively is that, since all objects are objects for an ego, it must be the "subjective center of reference" (*Beziehungszentrum*, Husserl 1984a, p. 372) for all objects insofar as they are given or givable to a subject. As such it is the eye which must be assumed as seeing something but which cannot see itself. Since this is not itself experienced but that to which experience is related, it is a transcendental ego in the Kantian sense, with Natorp's addition that it is an ideal center of all that is conscious, as an ideally assumed center. Consciousness thus is defined as "the fact of being conscious" (Natorp coins the term *Bewusstheit*, Natorp 2013, p. 29) and not something that itself can *become* conscious to itself. It is always conscious *of something*. Its "nature" is, in other words, intentional.

How this can be called "metaphysics" is quite questionable, since Natorp's point is exactly Kantian, that it is *not* an object of experience, only something that *has* experience. That Natorp calls it a "basic *fact* of consciousness" (*Grundtatsache*) should not unfairly be interpreted as slipping into some form of substantiality again. When Husserl thus takes this to mean, asking rhetorically, that "this, what is noticed, does it not become content? Does it not become object-like (*gegenständlich*)?" (Husserl 1984a, p. 373), then one must answer with Natorp: no, it does not. It is an ideally (re-)constructed point of origin that stands on the opposite end of the vector and what "is" there, in both directions, is an infinitely distant point: just as we never arrive at the thing in itself, we never arrive at the "ego in itself." They are two extreme directions of reality. To not grant this point is to overlook that Natorp here makes use of the Kantian notion of the regulative idea.

Thus, regarding Natorp's position and Husserl's critique, three things need to be pointed out:

First, the allegation of a "metaphysics" at play here is quite implausible. For, if anything, Natorp's idea of the ego being something radically different from all objectivity (not a supreme form of it, nor something beyond objects), and that objectifying the ego is an improper *metabasis*, is something that Husserl should enthusiastically agree with.

Secondly, though Husserl would have to agree with Natorp in that the ego is something different from objects in the world, where they differ is that, to Husserl, subjectivity *can* be experienced; but what is experienced is not an ego as a substantive unit, as another "middle-sized dry good." What Husserl wants to describe phenomenologically is the structure of acts in the flow of consciousness. Hence, the subject is construed as subjectivity, a temporally structured field of consciousness. That objects are experienced in this flow of consciousness by an experiencing I is, at best, trivially true. And since, as Natorp himself claims, the subject cannot itself be experienced, to claim it exists in a substantial way, as just another object, is a meaningless proposition. Thus, the *horror metaphysicus* that befell Husserl can be mitigated in this way, that neither Natorp nor Husserl intend to posit some kind of hidden substance behind a veil. Indeed, taken in this modest sense of claiming that all acts stem from an unknown and unknowable center is something that Husserl would not object to in *Ideas*. He more or less repeats Natorp's position, then, when he says that the pure ego can "*in no sense* ... count *as a really obtaining piece* of the experiences themselves *or an inherent aspect* of them" (*Ideen* 105/123).

Thirdly, one possible explanation for why Husserl might have seen in Natorp a degenerate metaphysics nonetheless and which presumably was the reason he might have been put off by Natorp's conception from the beginning, is precisely the larger philosophical agenda that drove the Marburg School, namely its philosophy of culture, to which Natorp's psychology was to be (to Natorp at least) the finishing capstone. If all cultural *facta* are constructed as stemming from a common center from which they emanate centrifugally, then Husserl rightfully had the impression that this was some grand metaphysical scenario that was being laid out. It is plausible to assume that Husserl knew enough of the larger philosophical agenda of the Marburg School in general and Natorp in particular, who went off into a mystical direction shortly after publishing the *Allgemeine Psychologie* and developed a speculative "panmethodism" uniting both methods (constructive, reconstructive) to construe a "logic of origin."[10] Thus, the more modest claim of Natorp, that the ego is not an object and may not be treated as one, is certainly one that Husserl would underwrite, and hence the apologetic words to Natorp are certainly more than niceties to a philosophical "antipode" he nevertheless greatly admired philosophically and towards whom he was personally disposed to in a friendly manner. It is quite likely, however, despite the "great premonition" (*große Vorahnung*, Husserl 2002, p. 4) of phenomenology which Husserl later attributes to Natorp, Natorp's philosophizing after 1912 presumably would have put off Husserl even more than the alleged ego-metaphysics of his *Psychology According to Critical Method*. Thus, in spite of Husserl's unfair allegation in *this* respect, the *larger-scale* instinct that, in all likelihood, drove Husserl to his negative assessment of Natorp is in the end correct.

---

10 Cf. once again the editor's introduction to Natorp (2013), esp. pp. xxxiii-xxxv.

9.2. The exclusion of pure logic

In all of these exclusions, perhaps the most puzzling one is Husserl's exclusion of pure logic. This claim is responsible for the often-voiced critique of phenomenology as being a sort of mystical experience or seeing, which defies any logical justification or rational oversight.[11] It also flies into the face of Husserl's claim that phenomenology should be a pure logic and *mathesis universalis.* So how can he, after all, claim this? According to Husserl, the phenomenologist must bracket even such logical axioms as the principle of non-contradiction (cf. *Ideen* 108/127). This claim is so hard to accept because—to mention just one concern—the phenomenologist, once she starts to put her findings in pure intuition into words, has to use words of an ordinary language that stands under formal laws, make inferences, avoid contradiction, and so on. The presumed demand to purify ordinary language to create an ideal phenomenological vernacular does not make things easier, since such a language would have to be construed as, precisely, ideal, and it is not clear that such a language would be anything other than pure logic (setting aside the somewhat absurd possibility of a "pure phenomenologeze," which would function according to completely different rules).[12] Husserl's insistence that the "general and absolute validity" of the principle of non-contradiction, which he does *not* deny, "could render discernible via examples in its own [stock of] givennesses" (*Ideen* 108–109/127) from a phenomenological standpoint, does not seem to solve the problem. For the claim that the evident principle of non-contradiction could be made evident through the givennesses proper to pure intuition creates a problem familiar since Plato's theory of the forms. How would one be able to identify in intuition the principle of non-contradiction if one did not already have prior knowledge of such a principle? Surely an explanation of a pre-existence of the soul would be beyond the pale to Husserl. So it seems that this exclusion is, for one, not possible, and secondly, stands in contradiction with his earlier claim that phenomenology yields "the 'sources' from which the basic concepts and the ideal laws of *pure logic* stem" (Husserl 1984, p. 7).

Arguably, there are two ways one can respond to this critique, if one does not want to simply say that Husserl was merely overstating his case here for some rhetorical flourish. For one, it has to be clear what Husserl means with phenomenology as a *descriptive* discipline. As descriptive, it relies purely on intuition,

---

[11] Again, cf. Adorno's pamphlet regarding this allegation (Adorno 1984).
[12] It was Husserl's assistant Fink who theorized about the possibility of such a phenomenological language in which all ordinary meanings (stemming from the natural attitude) would be "radically transformed." Husserl was radically opposed to this idea, cf. Luft (2002).

i.e., on a description of that which manifests or displays itself in experience. It is a description of what manifests itself in experience *in the first person perspective*. Another way of saying this is that the phenomenologist *witnesses* what manifests itself in consciousness, and then gives an eidetic account of it *insofar as it is experienced*, not as what it is as something transcendent. In this sense, something like the principle of non-contradiction would also be something transcendent. And, the latter manifests itself in consciousness in principle in no other way than does an object of visual perception. An object of perception is of interest to the phenomenologist only immanently, as how it is experienced as seen in adumbrations. The same goes for the experience of the principle of non-contradiction. It gives itself as apodictic; it is thus experienced as absolutely valid, in an analogous way that the object's given front side is given, "in the flesh." The task of the phenomenologist is, in the case of the perceptual object, to formulate laws of givenness, such as the law of adumbration (that physical objects give themselves in profiles, *Abschattungen*). Immanent objects, now (Husserl claims), do not adumbrate themselves, but they do manifest themselves nonetheless. The task of the phenomenologist then, in the case of the principle of non-contradiction, is a description of the way it is given. In this sense the phenomenologist *also* has to formulate the law of givenness, i.e., that it can be *experienced* as not-being-possible-otherwise. It is not about the nature of the principle from the third-person perspective, but about the way it is experienced, such that one could even say, "absolute *validity*" of a law, any law, is a statement about the *experience* of its apodicticity (since it would be validity-*for*-someone). Apodicticity, then, could be spoken of in a *logical* and *phenomenological* sense, respectively. In the latter sense, it would be a matter of descriptive phenomenology and has nothing to do with the absolute character of it as a logical axiom. It is not about logic but about the experience of logic. "Apodictic" just as "probable" or "dubious" are descriptors that can be experienced from the first-person perspective and correlate to logical entities from the third-person perspective that are constructed in any formal *mathesis*.

Secondly, the relation between the experience of apodicticity and apodictic laws themselves can also be construed as a path *from* one *to* the other. What is hinted at here is Husserl's genetic phenomenology, which is certainly not worked out at this stage, but which can be anticipated as telling a story as to how one gets from the former to the latter (cf. Husserl 1966).[13] Namely, it is not the case that one needs to accept the Platonic scenario, that the identification of a logical law requires a prior knowledge of this law. Rather, one can interpret, as Husserl

---

[13] For a thorough account of Husserl's late genetic phenomenology, cf. Welton (2002).

does, pre-logical or in general pre-predicative experience as implicitly, mutely containing, but *giving rise to* logical structures, not as causing but *motivating* them. So, the simple perceptive experience that something *cannot at the same time* have this or that color can be a first rudimentary experience of non-contradiction. The story a genetic account gives, then, is how we get *from* pre-predicative experience *to* explicit predicative structure in language and from there to the formalized version in a logical notation. This is what Husserl purports to do in his "transcendental logic," which is the *genetic* working out of the task of pure logic, *statically* conceived. This claim also entails that something like logical (or conceptual) structure is not *imposed on* the world through our capacity of judging with the help of pure categories (Kant), and it also rejects the notion that there is *no such thing* as pure, pre-predicative and hence pre-logical experience in favor of a thoroughgoing conceptualism (Hegel). Rather, its claim is that the world itself contains its material-eidetic structures that can manifest themselves in our consciousness (and can only do so there); structures, however, that *need to be made explicit by us for ourselves* through descriptive analysis of their experience in consciousness.

The latter claim speaks to Husserl's form of transcendental idealism, which is, at the same time (as he insists), a most robust realism: we do not create logical structures, but the world contains an a priori structure that, however, manifests itself and can *only* manifest itself in an experiencing subject. Both are not independent of one another, but form an a priori correlation.[14] We as experiencing subjects cannot experience the world other than as manifesting itself in consciousness, which means that phenomenology as a descriptive discipline of the experience of the world has to reconstruct how this structure manifests itself in our experience. As manifesting *itself* it can only be apprehended and comprehended *by us*. "Constitution" is a process of working out *for us* how the structure of the world is *when* it gives itself. Givenness is a term spoken from within the correlational a priori. Given the recent debate about non-conceptual content in contemporary philosophy (especially initiated by John McDowell), Husserl's strikingly original, but virtually unknown, position deserves attention.

9.3. Phenomenology as eidetic science of pure consciousness

Finally, Husserl is very adamant about construing phenomenology as an eidetic science. It has to come forth as an eidetic science in order to be truly philosoph-

---

14 Cf. Luft (2011), esp. the Introduction, concerning this correlation.

ical, i.e., to yield a priori truth about consciousness as such. It must be a science of essences, not of facts; a phenomenological empirical science is a "nonsense." But why is this so? Can it not *also* be a science of facts, a *Tatsachenwissenschaft*? Must one, and why must one by necessity, go the route to the eidetic? While remaining impressed by Husserl's grand ambition, can one not remain at the level of the factical and content oneself with a mere science of facts with a moderate level of generality, a general description of phenomena in the first-person perspective without the need to move on from here to the eidetic stage? Can I not remain at the level of an empirical science and simply leave essences aside? Would this moderation and humility not also be much more friendly to today's concerns on the part of phenomenologists and other philosophers studying the mind, who would likely ridicule what can at best be a pretense? And has not the eidetic ambition been the greatest obstacle in appreciating Husserl's phenomenology from the outset? It has been questioned, even rejected–fairly or not–as early as the 1920 s, when Heidegger started developing his own brand of phenomenology, as a "hermeneutics of *facticity*" and precisely not of eidetic structures *of* factical experience. These critiques are certainly in part unfair and rest on a great deal of misunderstanding; still they indicate problems that inadvertently arise.

Husserl scolded the notion of an empirical phenomenology as "picture book phenomenology" (*Bilderbuchphänomenologie*). But what is wrong with painting a coherent and faithful picture book of my way of seeing the world and ensuring that I can find co-seers who will be asked whether or not they agree with my picture, and accordingly help me improve it? In this way, we would arrive at a mutually agreeable account of what it is like to experience in different manners, an account that would be fallibilistic like all other empirical sciences, hence always in the process of modification and improvement, refinement, and so on.[15] And in some respects one can view the history of the phenomenological movement itself as such a process of ever-further modifications, with its changing fashions and recurring fads and themes like in any other science and–perhaps an asymptotic approach towards truth. Its own history suggests, thus, that it is an empirical science, a science with a clearly defined method, to be sure, but with respect to an empirical thing, consciousness.

Husserl's answer here is unambiguous, yet (I think) all but clear. His claim is not that this picture book phenomenology, while possible, does not satisfy the

---

[15] For a good summary of Husserl's notion of eidetics, cf. Sowa (2007). Sowa concludes, however, with the rather implausible claim that the task of eidetics can be squared with a Popper-style fallibilism.

demand for an eidetic science. So, it is *not* the case that such a picture book phenomenology may exist but does not hold up to the standards of eidetic science. Rather, his claim is that such a phenomenological *Tatsachenwissenschaft* is altogether impossible. He maintains, concerning the question as to a phenomenological empirical science, that it can "only be decided on the basis of eidetic phenomenology." As he explains, arguing for this claim,

> 'every attempt to start out naively from a phenomenological science of facts [*Tatsachenwissenschaft*] would be a nonsense *prior to* the execution of a phenomenological eidetic science. For it becomes plain that there cannot be a phenomenological science of fact *besides* the extra-phenomenological sciences of facts that is parallel and alongside these, and this is because the ultimate evaluation [*Auswertung*] of all sciences of facts leads to a unified concatenation [*Verknüpfung*] of all factical phenomenological nexuses and those motivated as factical possibilities corresponding to these sciences of facts, and this unified concatenation is nothing but the region of the sought-for phenomenological science of facts. To a main portion this science is, thus, the 'phenomenological revolution [*Umwendung*]' of the ordinary sciences of facts enabled by eidetic phenomenology, and the only question remains to what extent from there something further could be accomplished' (*Ideen* 114– 115/134, although I supply my own translation here).

Attempting to reconstruct Husserl's argument here is not easy. If I understand him correctly, his point is that there cannot be a phenomenological science of facts besides other sciences of facts, because phenomenology is situated in altogether different realm than mere facts, corresponding to its radically different subject matter. Put differently, it is a science of the first person perspective. All other sciences are of the third person perspective. For that reason they cannot exist alongside one another and they are not parallel as, for instance, phenomenological psychology is parallel to transcendental phenomenology, as Husserl later claims (cf. Husserl 1976a, p. 207)–a claim that is equally problematic. So far so good.

But Husserl goes further; he claims that there simply *is* no phenomenological science of facts that would be *distinct* from the phenomenological eidetics. Now there is a simple way of explaining this, which, however, does not get to the heart of the matter, I think, and a more complicated one (which is to be preferred anyway, hermeneutically). One way of reading this is that with the *epoché*, the exclusion of the natural attitude, one already arrives *automatically* at the eidetic, thus, the purification of consciousness is already its purification from all worldly (e. g., human) contaminations, and thus one is already dealing with eidetic states of affairs. But things are not that easy. For is it not the case that with the *epoché* I arrive at pure consciousness, but that this is initially still made up of individual experiences, whose essences, precisely, I am trying to find? Why else call phenomenology the *eidetic* science of pure consciousness? Finding essences of consciousness is the result of the eidetics, not something that is already there ready-made once the purification is complete.

To make things more complicated, the reason Husserl gives in the above quotation for why phenomenology must be eidetic actually dodges the issue in favor of another point, namely "that is because the ultimate evaluation [*Auswertung*] of all sciences of facts leads to a unified concatenation [*Verknüpfung*] of all factual phenomenological nexuses and those motivated as factical possibilities corresponding to these sciences of facts, and this unified concatenation is nothing but the region of the sought-for phenomenological science of facts." *This* seems to indicate the scenario according to which phenomenology is first philosophy in the sense that all worldly facts (*Tatsachen*) and their sciences have their ultimate authentication (*Ausweisung*) in their manifestations in the first person perspective. This idea is well known, but it seems to be a different point than before and still does not explain why there cannot be a phenomenological science of facts that is of the status, for instance, of a phenomenological anthropology, that it claims to be a phenomenological description of the general traits of the first person-experience of the species *homo sapiens*. One could even allow for some of these findings to be more than anthropological, when purified by eidetic variation. There are certainly some laws of experience that are easily seen as apodictic, for instance, that perceptual objects adumbrate themselves to any possible creature with the capacity for visual perception. These are some of the most impressive findings of Husserl, but they are also few and rare. So why not allow for a sort of hybrid phenomenology with results, some of which are empirical and prone to modification, some of which are apodictic, unthinkable otherwise? Would not the novelty of the region of pure consciousness allow for such an unorthodox concept of science that would be inconceivable in the sciences of the third-person perspective? Why strive for *absolute* purity, hence, and why not see the results of phenomenological description as more or less general generalities?

These questions ultimately ask for the feasibility of phenomenology in the way Husserl's ambitious plan foresaw it. The resistance against his phenomenology as a science of essences certainly stems from this specific difficulty of the subject matter itself. Granted that there are many misunderstandings due to this difficulty, and a thorough appreciation of Husserl's eidetic project is at this point still lacking. The claim here is not that the project is unfeasible; I merely wanted to point to some possible issues one could raise with respect to it and that would call for a more modest conception of phenomenology, that would not violate its claim to be a science, but that would consider the idea of an eidetic science negligible.

10. Conclusion

Husserl, although he wants to put up some methodological *caveats* of how not to misconstrue his phenomenology in this chapter, nonetheless makes some rather controversial and problematic claims, as the history of his reception has shown. Their problematic nature should in no way be dismissed in this presentation but rather brought to a full appreciation. Indeed, only when possible objections, such as the ones mentioned in the previous section, can be critically assessed and responded to, can Husserl's project get off the ground. A look at the history of the reception of *Ideas* shows, these and other objections were put to Husserl frequently, and he responded to them mostly in indirect ways. Generally, one can say, at any rate: To understand the history of the Phenomenological Movement is to know the history of the reception of *Ideas* I.

Despite all question marks, the reader gets a sense of the radicality involved in construing phenomenology as a descriptive-eidetic science of pure consciousness. The full title of the book is, to recall, *Ideas for a Pure Phenomenology and Phenomenological Philosophy*. Short of, as of yet, being fully unfolded as a phenomenological *philosophy*, it is clear that Husserl is intent on safeguarding phenomenology, first and foremost, as a *pure* discipline. As committed to such purity, the reductions that lead to this region of pure consciousness have to be most carefully executed and possible contaminations to this purity must be rigorously ruled out. Only a construal of the region of phenomenology as pure and of phenomenology itself as a discipline committed to such purity, can give rise to Husserl's sincere hopes that phenomenology can become a true philosophy that "must come forth as a science," to recall Kant's hopes for the future of critical philosophy. With the ideal to construe phenomenology as a rigorous science with the most pristine ideal of scientific inquiry–a priori or eidetic–Husserl is Kant's most ambitious but also most extreme heir.

Bibliography

Adorno, Theodor W. (1984): *Against Epistemology: A Metacritique. Studies in Husserl and the Phenomenological Antinomies* (Studies in Contemporary German Social Thought). Boston: MIT Press.

Boehm, Rudolf (1959), "Zum Begriff des Absoluten bei Husserl". In: *Zeitschrift für philosophische Forschung* 13, pp. 214–242.

Held, Klaus (2010): "Gott in Edmund Husserls Phänomenologie". In: Ierna, Carlo/Mattens, Filip/Jacobs, Hanne (Eds.): *Philosophy, Phenomenology, Sciences*. Dordrecht: Springer, pp. 723–738.

Husserl, Edmund (1959): "Erste Philosophie (1923/24). Zweiter Teil: Theorie der phänomenologischen Reduktion". In: *Husserliana*. Vol. VIII. The Hague: Nijhoff.
Husserl, Edmund (1966): "Analysen zur passiven Synthesis: aus Vorlesungs- und Forschungsmanuskripten 1918–1926". In: *Husserliana*. Vol. XI. The Hague: Nijhoff.
Husserl, Edmund (1976a): "Die Krisis der europäischen Wissenschaften und die transzendentale Phänomenologie: eine Einleitung in die phänomenologische Philosophie". In: *Husserliana*. Vol. VI. The Hague: Nijhoff.
Husserl, Edmund (1976b): "Ideen zu einer reinen Phänomenologie und phänomenologischen Philosophie, 1. Allgemeine Einführung in die reine Phänomenologie. 2. Halbbd.: Ergänzende Texte". In: *Husserliana*. Vol. III/2. The Hague: Nijhoff.
Husserl, Edmund (1984): "Logische Untersuchungen. 2. Bd., 1. Teil: Untersuchungen zur Phänomenologie und Theorie der Erkenntnis". In: *Husserliana*. Vol. XIX, 1. The Hague: Nijhoff.
Husserl, Edmund (1991): "Cartesianische Meditationen und Pariser Vorträge". In: *Husserliana*. Vol. I. Dordrecht: Kluwer.
Husserl, Edmund (1993): "Die Krisis der europäischen Wissenschaften und die transzendentale Phänomenologie. Ergänzungsband Texte aus dem Nachlass 1934–1937". In: *Husserliana*. Vol. XXIX. Dordrecht: Kluwer.
Husserl, Edmund (2002): "Zur phänomenologischen Reduktion. Texte aus dem Nachlass (1926–1935)". In: *Husserliana*. Vol. XXXIV. Dordrecht: Kluwer.
Husserl, Edmund (2014b): "Grenzprobleme der Phänomenologie. Analysen des Unbewusstseins und der Instinkte; Metaphysik; späte Ethik; Texte aus dem Nachlass; (1908–1937)". In: *Husserliana*. Vol. XLII. Dordrecht; Heidelberg: Springer.
Kern, Iso (1977): "The Three Ways Into the Transcendental-Phenomenological Reduction". In: Elliston, Frederick A./McCormick, Peter (Eds.): *Husserl. Expositions and Appraisals*. Notre Dame: Notre Dame University Press, pp. 126–149.
Luft, Sebastian (2002): *"Phänomenologie der Phänomenologie." Systematik und Methodologie der Phänomenologie in der Auseinandersetzung zwischen Husserl und Fink*. Dordrecht: Springer.
Luft, Sebastian (2011): *Subjectivity and Lifeworld in Transcendental Phenomenology*. Evanston: Northwestern U Press.
Luft, Sebastian (2012): "Von der mannigfaltigen Bedeutung der Reduktion nach Husserl. Neuere Reflexionen zur Grundbedeutung des zentralen Begriffs der transzendentalen Phänomenologie". In: *Phänomenologische Forschungen*, pp. 5–29.
Luft, Sebastian (2014): "Reassessing Neo-Kantianism. Another Look at Hermann Cohen's Kant Interpretation". In: *Philosophical Readings* VI. No. 1, pp. 90–114.
Makkreel, Rudolf A. (2009): "Wilhelm Dilthey and the neo-Kantians: On the Conceptual Distinctions Between *Geisteswissenschaften* and *Kulturwissenschaften*". In: Makkreel, Rudolf A./Luft, Sebastian (Eds.): *Neo-Kantianism in Contemporary Philosophy*. Indianapolis: Indiana University Press, pp. 253–277.
Natorp, Paul (2013): *Allgemeine Psychologie nach kritischer Methode*. Luft, Sebastian (Ed.). Darmstadt: Wissenschaftliche Buchgesellschaft.
Schuhmann, Karl (1990): "Husserl's Yearbook". In: *Philosophy and Phenomenological Research* 50, pp. 1–25.
Sowa, Rochus (2007): "Wesen und Wesensgesetze in der deskriptiven Eidetik Edmund Husserls". In: *Phänomenologische Forschungen*, pp. 5–37.

Welton, Donn (2002): *The Other Husserl. The Horizons of Transendental Phenomenology*. Indianapolis: Indiana U Press.
Windelband, Wilhelm (2015): "History and Natural Science". In: Sebastian Luft (Ed.): *The Neo-Kantian Reader*. London: Routledge, pp. 287–298.
Zahavi, Dan (2010): "Husserl and the 'Absolute'". In: Carlo Ierna, Filip Mattens, Hanne Jacobs (Eds.): *Philosophy, Phenomenology, Sciences*. Dordrecht: Springer (Phaenomenologica 200), pp. 71–92.

James Dodd
Clarity, fiction, and description
Section III, chapter 1, Methodological pre-considerations

1. The problem of method

The first chapter of *Ideas I*, Section III, bears the title "Methodological Pre-considerations" (*Methodische Vorerwägungen*); the title of Section III itself is "On the Method and Problems of Pure Phenomenology" (*Zur Methodik und Problematik der reinen Phänomenologie*). As a pair, these titles raise some questions for the reader: why does Husserl seem to embark, at just this point, on a series of *preliminary* methodological reflections? We are already rather deep into the text (so on p. 116 of the masterful new translation by Daniel Dahlstrom), at the start of the third of four sections, and immediately after the close of what one might think should be the methodological heart of *Ideas I*, namely the famous *Fundamentalbetrachtung* of Section Two (§§ 27–62). All the action, at least with regards to method, seems to have already taken place: the *epoché* of the natural attitude has been established (§§ 27–32), the region of pure consciousness and its being elaborated (§§ 33–55), the scope and tasks of the phenomenological reduction set (§§ 56–62). Is it not reasonable to expect that we should be standing squarely within the horizon of a methodologically secured phenomenological investigation proper? So why does Husserl instead seem to put the brakes on everything and choose to begin all over again?

There are two points to keep in mind when trying to make sense of the role that this chapter plays in the *Ideas I* as a whole. The first is that the situation at this point in Husserl's presentation is comparable to an important juncture in Descartes' *Meditations*, a similarity that is arguably not an accident. Husserl engages Descartes throughout the *Ideas*, and on many levels, from the explicit appropriation of Cartesian doubt in § 31 to the more subtle reflection on the problem of method that runs throughout *Ideas I*, and in many ways culminates in the beginning chapter of Section III.[1] The relevant moment in Descartes'' *Meditations* is the point early in the Second Meditation where, after the exercise of radical

---
[1] Descartes, and more generally what one might call "Cartesianism" as a broader set of philosophical motives and commitments, is of course a virtually constant presence in Husserl's writings. See Patocka (1989), and Landgrebe (1970) for illuminating elucidations of the problem.

doubt has led to the discovery of the certainty of the existence of the *ego cogito* as its absolute limit, Descartes still faces the question of just what the *ego cogito* is:

> *I am, I exist*, is necessarily true whenever it is put forward by me or conceived in my mind. But I do not yet have a sufficient understanding of what this 'I' is, that now necessarily exists. So I must be on my guard against carelessly taking something else to be this 'I', and so making a mistake in the very item of knowledge that I maintain is the most certain and evident of all. (Descartes 1990a, p. 17)

Establishing the certain existence of the ego as the subject of thinking (in this case the thought of a doubt) does not entail an immediate clarification, or even insight, into the *being* of the ego. Certainty of existence does not entail a comprehension of essence. Thus after having secured its existence, Descartes must in a way begin again, in order to address the essence of what will then serve as his *fundamentum inconcossum*. Of course, Descartes has a ready answer to this question in his concept of a thinking substance, giving the dramatic moment of the question of essence in the Second Meditation a bit of the air of being staged. But it is nevertheless important to recognize that Descartes is sensitive to the fact that the question needs to arise at all, even if in order to be immediately answered with the essential determination of the *cogitans*, for the establishment of existence can never in itself stand as a substitute for the labor of comprehending essence.

The opening of Section III represents a comparable moment in the progression of *Ideas I*. Like Descartes, for Husserl the basic orientation of method is not reducible to the simple affirmation of the existence of consciousness, even if the being of consciousness is characterized in the course of its coming into focus as "absolute being" (§ 54). Method nevertheless finds its more decisive determination, or direction in a decision about the essence of consciousness. Yet unlike Descartes, a decision regarding essence is not readily available, at least not in the same way, for Husserl does not simply adopt a traditional conception of the essence of subjective existence, even if modified, but instead subjects the decision to the method itself. That is, the determination of essence will be reached by way of an investigation of the field opened by the *epoché* and the reduction of transcendence. Again unlike Descartes, this introduces a peculiar circularity: the answer to the question of the essential characteristics of consciousness, which is necessary to guide phenomenological method, is itself the subject of phenomenological investigation. Here we begin to see the meaning of "preliminary" in the title to this chapter: the method must be deployed in a preliminary fashion, thus in a manner not fully established; phenomenology thus begins in a state of awaiting its own results in order to establish itself firmly as a method, or a science. It operates, in other words, with a chronically insufficient understanding of what consciousness "is."

Another way to frame the issue is to ask: what is there to *see*, once we have suspended the natural attitude and established the absolute independence of consciousness as a sphere of existence? How do we enter into this domain in a manner commensurate with the essential patterns of manifestation that fix its modes of access? Or, in Husserl's words:

> How do we find the right way to begin? The beginning here is, indeed, what is most difficult, and the situation an unusual one. The new field does not lie spread out before our view, with an abundance of distinct givennesses [*abgehobenen Gegebenheiten*], such that we could simply grab hold of them, and be certain of the possibility of making them the objects of a science (*Ideen* 116/135)

The second point to consider, which is a consequence of the first, is that the "preliminary" method to be employed in this context of finding our way into consciousness is for Husserl as equally vague and indeterminate as the object under investigation. As Husserl puts it, continuing the passage just quoted, not only does the "new field ... not lie spread out before our view," but there is also no question of "being certain of the method, by which we are supposed to proceed here." (*Ideen* 116/135) Husserl again goes beyond Descartes in that, whatever the question of method may be in the *Meditations*, it is never really about what the method *is* or *should be* for the exploration of subjective being; instead, the proof of the existence of the *ego cogito* is a part of a broader metaphysical argument that will provide justification for "the method" which, on its part, is assumed by Descartes to have been already articulated in its basic principles. Of course, the relation between method and the metaphysical argument in the Descartes writings is not as a result necessarily a simple one; for method and metaphysics in some sense each presuppose the other, and can thus only unfold together, as Jean-Luc Marion argues in a pair of elegant essays on this subject (cf. Marion 1999). What is striking about these sections in Husserl''s *Ideas I*, by contrast, is the idea that "method" can be something indeterminate, yet still operative; method can be in play before it has fully taken shape, as a kind of anticipation of its own forms and determinations of essence that in no way can be said to be fixed in advance.

One aspect of this indeterminacy of method is the apparent inapplicability of other examples of successful methods to the new domain opened by the *Fundamentalbetrachtung*. Husserl expresses this in terms of a lack of a context of familiarity, one that would allow examples of successful methods from other domains (say the empirical sciences, psychology pre-eminent among them) to provide guidance. But the lack of familiarity also operates on a more mundane level, which takes the form of a general lack of experience with dealing with what amounts to a new field of objectivities. We lack, in other words, those habits of seeing that form a seamless whole with traditional scientific methods, providing a ballast of familiarity that sustain them from within; for even when they encounter something unfamiliar, they nevertheless can rely on the familiar as a point of departure for investigation, for "here everything unfamiliar is in the horizon of something familiar." (*Ideen* 116/136).

> How different the situation is in phenomenology. It is not only the case that, already *in advance of* any method determining the subject matter, it needs a method precisely in order to bring the field of the subject matter [*Sachfeld*]–that of the transcendentally pure consciousness–into focus for it to be apprehended. Nor is it the case here that it is merely necessary to shift focus painstakingly from the kinds of natural givenness of which it is continuously conscious and which are, as it were, interwoven with the newly intended kinds of givenness (so that it is constantly in danger of confusing one with the other). In addition, it lacks everything that works to our advantage in the natural sphere of objects, namely, the familiarity through practiced intuition, the benefit of inherited ways of theorizing and discipline-specific methods. (*Ideen* 117/136)

On the other hand, one should note at this point that this entire drama in § 63 of naively stumbling into a new territory in which we only slowly learn to find our way about, struggling to bring into focus the terrain and its features, is something of a philosophical fiction. The same is of course true of Descartes' *Meditations* which, like Hobbes in his description of the state of nature in the *Leviathan*, is structured dramatically around a fictional account of an origin, or a beginning. In all three cases a fiction is employed in order to orient thinking to the problems unique to beginnings, out of a sense that such problems must be engaged in this way in order to illuminate something essential concerning our thinking, even if we never in fact have or will ever face such perfect beginnings pristine in their *naiveté*. Husserl is of course already quite familiar with this new land; he has set up residence here long ago, and has accordingly become thoroughly familiar with its flora and fauna. Nevertheless, in order to introduce the reader to the methodological challenges specific to the new science of phenomenology, he provides the reader with a rhetorical fiction that serves as a guide for finding one's way into phenomenology.

We will have much more to say about fiction later on, but for now, regardless of the status of the philosophical fiction of entering a new domain, the point remains that, once phenomenological investigation is underway, the investigation itself is always faced with a unique demand for clarification. All science requires clarity, but in the case of phenomenology, this requirement takes the form of a characteristic inner demand for a constant reflection on the *problem of method:*

"It [phenomenology, J.D.] does not merely have to develop the method to obtain new kinds of knowledge for the new kinds of subject matters; it also has to procure the uttermost clarity about the sense and validity of the method." (*Ideen* 117/136) This requirement for self-transparency regarding method is an unmistakable legacy of Descartes, for it represents the grounding gesture of "first philosophy" itself:

> In addition–and this is far more important because it is related to a matter of principle– phenomenology must lay claim, in keeping with its essence, to being 'first' philosophy and providing the means for every rational critique [*Vernunftkritik*] that needs to be carried out. Thus, it requires the uttermost presuppositionlessness and an absolute, reflective insight into itself. Its own essence requires it to realize the most perfect clarity concerning its own essence and thereby, too, concerning the principles of its method. (*Ideen* 117/136)

Phenomenology accordingly functions in a far more rarefied space than do the other sciences, in the sense that its preliminary lack of footing is not a mere effect of its relative youth, but an important problematic all its own, one basic to the manner in which it is to be established as first philosophy. This is not only because phenomenology operates under the demand to progress without presuppositions, but also because this demand itself, or how it might be even possible for a thinking to operate in such a uniquely self-transparent mode, is *by no means clear in advance*. And Husserl is being very deliberate in this respect in these sections: the meaning of the demand for clarity, or for the self-transparency of the method, requires an immanent, consciously problematic progression towards its full articulation.

This in turn helps to further elaborate the sense in which these are "preliminary" or even "preparatory" considerations. They are preliminary in the sense of being necessarily, inescapably *naive*. This *naiveté* can be understood to be an essential structure of beginnings: one only begins to understand by first engaging a relation to what one does not understand, a relation thanks to which a possibility of understanding opens. The specific form *naiveté* takes in the case of phenomenological reflection is complex, and can be highlighted in two steps. The first is Husserl's emphasis on the *obvious* part of what any phenomenological investigation involves, which he sums up in this way:

> If the aim now is for it to be a science *within the framework of immediate Intuition alone*, a purely '*descriptive*' science of essences, then the universal character of its way of proceeding is given in advance as something entirely self-evident. It has to place before its eyes pure occurrences of consciousness as exemplars; it has to bring them to ever more perfect clarity; within this clarity it has to analyze them and apprehend their essences, it has to pursue the patently discernible connections among the essences and take up what is re-

spectively seen into faithful conceptual expressions that allow them to dictate their sense purely through what is seen or generally discerned, and so forth. (*Ideen* 119/138)

Thus to the extent that any objectivity is available for clarification, so too are the objectivities of the transcendental field; this is obvious. The second step is to recognize how the pursuit of such an investigation, however obvious its general form may be, nevertheless remains ambiguous with respect to its *scientific* character, thus requiring a specific mode of reflection that seeks, at each step, to justify the method. This is the peculiar complexity inherent to phenomenological beginnings: it is obvious what we need to do, but not clear how to do it. Thus even as the method unfolds along the lines of what is predelineated in the obvious, it must do so under the aegis of a reflection on what it is thereby accomplishing in its very movement. Again Husserl:

> At first this procedure, naively at work, serves only to acclimate the researcher to the new domain, to practice seeing, apprehending, analyzing within it generally and to become a little acquainted with the kinds of givenness in it. But then scientific reflection–reflection on the essence of the procedure itself, as the essence of the kinds of givenness at play in it, on the essence, the accomplishment, and the conditions of perfect clarity and discernment as well as of a perfectly faithful and fixed conceptual expression, and so on–takes over the function of a general and logically rigorous justification of the method. (*Ideen* 119/138–139)

It is on this level of scientific reflection, with its focus not simply on clarity but self-transparency, that the questions arise–what is meant by "procedure" here? What "kinds" of givenness are germane to transcendentally reduced consciousness? What are the "conditions" for clarity in this sphere? What counts here as a "faithful" and "fixed" conceptual expression? That we move forward, and must move forward, without being able to initially answer such questions, since they can only be answered fully from what emerges from the investigation itself, is what constitutes the complex self-conscious *naiveté* of phenomenological method.

Another way to express this is to note that things like *clarity, insight* [*Einsicht*], and *expression* themselves become fundamental phenomenological problems, thus things to be clarified, understood, and expressed, even as they remain normative regarding how phenomenological problems in general are to be developed. (*Ideen* 119/138–139) In other words, the norms that emerge from the investigation of such phenomena are in turn norms under which the investigation itself stands, and stands *in principle*. This means that their "clarification" is never a question of local problems. A phenomenology of evidence, likewise a phenomenology of expression, inevitably set into motion the self-clarification of phenomenological method as such.

From this it becomes important to recognize a double, even a triple movement implicit in Husserl's reflections on method in these sections. One level involves bringing reduced consciousness into view: here reflection, understood as a kind of seeing, is oriented towards consciousness as such, without being trapped in the forward intentional movement towards the apprehension of its object. This is the essential contribution of the double accomplishments of *epoché* and reduction: the suspension of the influence for reflection of the sense of the world as pre-given coupled with the redirection of reflection in terms of the constitutive accomplishments of transcendental consciousness with respect to the being-sense of the world. The second level involves the attempt to put into words, and thereby to fix (*fixieren*), what there is to see, thanks to this new orientation, in stable, univocal expressions. This is in part comparable to the ordinary work of any science, and in cases of new sciences the task is of course the development of a vocabulary adequate to expressing the relations and features germane to the given theoretical domain under investigation. In the case of phenomenology there arises the basic question of what should guide the development of such a vocabulary, given again the characteristic lack of familiarity regarding the objects of phenomenological reflection: what is to guide our choice of expressions will only become gradually clear in the wake of having succeeded, at least in a preliminary form, in formulating the expressions themselves. But then this is precisely what leads, on a third level, and on the basis of the successful coincidence between given and expression, to the need to clarify, or bring to clarity, what has thereby been accomplished. This third movement represents for Husserl a properly *logical* activity that raises successful expression to the level of a science. But it also reveals that all this preparation for phenomenology (and so the *Ideas I* as a whole) is not merely a reflection that situates itself prior to phenomenology, but phenomenology itself: "[...] and so it is apparent that, in terms of content, this entire work–a work that purports to prepare the way to phenomenology–is itself phenomenology through and through." (*Ideen* 120/139)

2. Clarification and givenness

But how does logical clarification take place, thanks to which phenomenology comes into its own, as it were? Part of the task involves imposing a discipline on expressions, by way of the pursuit of rigorous, perhaps even univocal terms that give expression to explicit, clearly defined thinking or judgment (this is the theme of § 66). But it is important to stress that for Husserl clarification is not limited to language, or even to the act of judgment; more important is clarity on the side of the apprehension of essence: "Of greater interest to us are considerations concerning method that, instead of referring to the expression, refer to the essences and essential connections that it is supposed to express and that have to be apprehended first." (Beginning of § 67, *Ideen* 121141) Clarification is thus not simply a necessity when it comes to the technical deployments of language, nor does it accordingly achieve its most comprehensive form in scientific statements, but is always at work in the very seeing germane to any concrete scientific investigation.

Husserl will later, in § 16 of his 1929 *Formal and Transcendental Logic*, distinguish between two types of evidence that correlate to two types of "clarification." The first type of evidence belongs to the clarification, or in Husserl's terminology, *Verdeutlichung*, of judgment forms at the basis of formal apophantics; the second belongs to the clarification, or *Klärung*, of that which is judged in judgments, or what in judging one is seeking to aim at "through" the judgment. (Husserl 1969, p. 60; Husserl 1974, p. 65) The two need to be distinguished, for one involves the evidence of making explicit what is said (so the judgment), while the other the evidence of what is given in the judgment (so the judged):

> To judge explicitly is not *per se* to judge with '*clarity*': Judging with 'clarity' has at once *clarity of the affairs*, in the performance of the judgment-steps, and *clarity of the predicatively formed affair-complex* in the whole judging [*im ganzen Urteil*]. An unclear and a clear judging can judge one and the same judgment; thus evidence of the self-identity of the judgment can extend throughout essentially different modes of givenness. But only a *judging with full clarity* can be *actual present cognition*; and, as such, it is a *new evidence*, pertaining to a givenness originaliter of the affairs themselves, of the predicatively formed affair-complex itself, at which one aims in the judging that strives toward cognition [...]. (Husserl, 1969, p. 61; Husserl 1974, pp. 65–66)

It is a variant of the latter, more robustly epistemic sense of "clarity" that is of principal interest in these sections of *Ideas I*. This means that the issue is not so much the general relation between seeing and expression, thanks to which one succeeds or fails to find the words for what is seen, but the specific challenges presented by the task of phenomenological seeing itself. This is an issue, Husserl claims, since experience is characterized by a distinct tendency to be *unclear*: it resists not so much expression, as the original intuitive manifestation thanks to which it would lend itself to expression. "Experiences [*Erlebnisse*, J.D.] on which research focuses generally tend to present themselves with an *emptiness* and *vague remoteness* that renders them applicable neither to a singular nor to an eidetic determination." (*Ideen* 121/141) The point here is not that consciousness is essentially determined according to what Husserl, in his initial treatment of eidetic intuition in § 3, defines as the "inadequate" essence of categories such as "material thing." To be sure, this is also to some extent the case with lived experience, the manner of givenness of which is clearly saturated with unclarity, to such an extent that it is likely that its essential features will include characteristic ways of being precisely "unclear," "vague", or "remote." At this point, however, the question turns on the methodological problem posed by unclarity as a conditioning factor with respect to how lived experience is to be approached at all phenomenologically, and the threat that imperfect clarity, vagueness of presence, can only yield imperfect intuitions of essence. Thus a key methodological task is to situate the intuitivity of experience within a regime of clarification, one aimed at exploring the potentialities for clarifying the unclear, sharpening the vague, and bringing the remote near: "Hence, it is necessary *to bring* to normal proximity and make *perfectly clear* what in each case hovers before us in fleeting unclearness [*Unklarheit*], in greater or lesser remoteness from intuition [*Anschauungsferne*]." (*Ideen* 121/141) This is even the case if it turns out that what is to be brought near, or clarified, are the manifold ways of being unclear or "inadequately given" germane to the being of consciousness.

Yet the task of clarification thus understood does not occur independently of at least the beginnings of the essential determination of consciousness. The approach to consciousness by way of a clarification aimed at bringing it out of its obscurity is intertwined with the eidetic articulation of obscurity as an essential determination of consciousness. Clarification thus emerges as a necessity, and not simply one of those otherwise contingent difficulties of a young science first getting a foothold in its object domain. For consciousness, though originally present and reflectively available as a constant stream of experience, is also in an important sense present in such a way that it "itself," what it itself is, remains obscure, and with that present in a way that chronically lacks intuitivity. In § 67 Husserl describes this self-obscurity of consciousness as a *distance* that stands in contrast to a *proximity*. In the terminology he begins to fix here, "intuitive" consciousness coincides with clarity, or given as self-given, givenness of itself (*Selbstgegebenheit*); while non-intuitive givenness coincides with the remote, and in this sense the obscure. It is worth quoting the passage in full:

> Consciousness that affords [*gebendes Bewusstsein*, J.D.] in the precise sense of the term, intuitive in contrast to non-intuitive consciousness, clear in contrast to obscure consciousness–these all coincide. Something similar is the case for levels of givenness, intuitiveness, clarity. The zero-limit is obscurity [*Dunkelheit*, J.D.], the one-limit [*Einsgrenze*, J.D.] is full clarity, intuitiveness, givenness.
>
> Givenness, however, is not to be understood in this case as originary givenness; hence, it is not to be understood as in perception. We do not identify '*given as itself*' with '*given in an originary way*,' 'in person.' In the specifically designated sense, 'given' and 'given as itself' are one and the same, and the use of the latter, profuse expression should only serve to

exclude *givenness in the wider sense*, in terms of which it is said of whatever is represented that it is given in the representation (but somehow 'in an empty way'). (*Ideen* 122/142)

Originary givenness thus excludes only the emptily intended, or the empty presence of the non-given; it retains within its purview all possible modes of non-self presence or remoteness from clear determination that do not rely on empty presentations (*Leervorstellungen*). The fact that a distinction between self and originary givenness is at all in play anchors an important methodological ground of clarification: the bringing to proximity what is otherwise removed (of the self) in the remoteness that represents an essential characteristic of the originary givenness of lived experience (*Ideen* 122/142–143).

The result of this (provisional, we should say) terminological distinction is a conception of clarity that is in turn grounded in a conception of givenness that extends into the obscure, thanks to which "clarity" can be thought of as embedded in givenness *without reducing givenness to clarity*. Clarification thus emerges as an exploration of a manner of givenness that attempts to grasp, with insight, the essential laws according to which givenness lends itself to clarity–or by contrast remains firmly within the bounds of the unclear or obscure.

To elucidate what it might mean for givenness to be something that lends itself to clarity, take as an example Colin Turnbull's account of his Mbuti guide, a tracker raised following the signs and trails of the rainforest in the Congo, meeting his counterpart, a guide and tracker raised on the savannah (cf. Turnbull 2012). The tracker from the forest is familiar with how to read significant signs and marks from relatively short distances, and is puzzled when his counterpart, who is accustomed to operating in a much more expansive visual landscape, manages to pick out marks and signs crucial to the art of tracking as they are crossing the open savannah. Out in the open, the forest tracker can suddenly no longer track, not because the signs are not there, but because they have been obscured by being there in an unfamiliar manner. The signs can be made available only on the basis of set of visual patterns and cues that need to be learned–and can only be learned on the basis of their *originarily being there*, though in a mode of remoteness and intuitive distance (*Gegebenheitsferne*, to use Husserl's expression) that in a sense hides them in plain view.

A phenomenological reflection on consciousness is, *mutatis mutandis*, comparable to relearning how to see according to patterns that belong to a broader expanse, or a wider horizon of what is originarily present with respect to conscious life. For when it comes to consciousness, Husserl might argue, we are naturally more like the forest people, for whom clarity extends only just beyond the nearest tree, for it is only within those limits that we are accustomed to engaging what is possible within the horizon of originary givenenss. Extending these limits is not an extension of originary givenness itself, but it is an extension of the range of objectivities that we are able to encounter, have access to, and investigate within its domain.

Husserl extends his account of clarity in § 68, in which he distinguishes two fundamental processes of clarification. One is the process of bringing something to intuitivity, thus extending the domain of what has been clarified; the second is the enhancement of a clarity already gained, already accomplished (cf. *Ideen* 124/143–144). Taking §§ 67–68 together, it is important not to confuse the domain of clarity with the "originary giving intuition" (*originär gebende Anschauung*) from the principle of all principles in § 24: the domain of legitimate phenomenological investigation is not limited to what has been *clarified*, but *given* in its living presence. We investigate by clarifying, which entails already having secured what is to be clarified in a more original sense. This also implies, contrary to some readings of § 24, that the principle of all principles is not meant primarily to be a limiting constraint on phenomenological investigation, but on the contrary a principle that grants an *expansion* of objectivity. Consider again the formulation of the principle:

> No conceivable theory can make us stray from the *principle of all principles: that each intuition affording [something] in an originary way is a legitimate source of knowledge, that whatever presents itself to us in 'Intuition' in an originary way* (so to speak, in its actuality in person) *is to be taken simply as what it affords itself as, but only within the limitations in which it affords itself there.* (*Ideen* 43/51)

The distinction between originary and self-givenness articulated at the beginning of Section III determines the deeper meaning of this principle. For if we understand that the "limits" of *originary* givenness evoked by the principle of all principles are not equivalent to the limits of what is *clearly* intuited, or *in strictu sensu* the limits of *self*-givenness, then the "limitation" imposed on phenomenological investigation serves only to prevent us from overlooking the possible further expansion of clarity within the horizon of originary presence. The principle, in short, serves as a grounding leitmotif for the exploration of what remains unknown in the depth of presence, and not a restriction to what is immediately secure thanks to some mythical role of the intuitively given in cognition. It is meant to curtail our tendency to underestimate the depth of givenness, itself an expression of an age-old suspicion of appearances that becomes aggravated when coupled with an addiction to concepts and the stories we like to tell about how they function.

However, at the same time it is also important to emphasize, as Husserl does at the end of § 68, that the account of clarification he offers in these sections is already an idealization. There are no "purely" clarified intuitions, likewise there are no purely empty presentations passing over into intuitivity. The rule is rather that impure intuitions, established somewhere between clarity and obscurity, empty and full presentation, play the decisive role in phenomenological investigation. It is more of a matter of pushing against some tendencies and developing the rhythms of others, than transforming everything latent and possible in originary givenness into patent intuitive actuality.

3. Fiction and eidetics

The apprehension of *essences* adds another important dimension to Husserl's account of the practice of phenomenological clarification. As had already been argued in §§ 3–4, the intuition (and by extension clarification) of an essence is related, but not reducible to the intuition of its concrete instances. Husserl makes the important remark in § 69 that, even if the two progress together, nevertheless clarifications of essence can occur in cases where the "*underlying individual instances*" (*Ideen* 125/145) remain at a low level of clarity. This is in particular the case with very general differentiations of essence; Husserl here cites as examples the difference between color and sound, or will and perception. The idea is that certain essential determinations exemplified in an individual case can reach a degree of proximity, and with that clarification, even while other determinations remain in obscurity, even the vast majority of those that constitute the full determinacy of the *individuum*.

It is also important to stress that any process of the clarification of givenness is in turn embedded in the particular *kind* of lived experience germane to the givenness to be clarified, and the essential features of the kind of experience involved condition the possibilities (or impossibilities) of clarification. Perceptual experience stands out as particularly significant in this respect: perception provides a relatively stable field of a multiplicity of givens readily available for the logical work of clarification. Perceptions constantly accompany consciousness, they do not dissipate in reflection (as do other types of experience, such as anger (cf. *Ideen* 11/12–13)). It is obvious that perception for this reason will play a fundamental role in phenomenological investigation, as a kind of baseline set of examples and analyses that will serve as a reliable point of comparison for the investigation of objectivities that are not given in any kind of comparable stability (such as categorial objects and other idealities dependent upon a more active involvement of the ego).

Yet the stability of perception also comes at a price, at least from the point of view of the clarification of essence. Originarily given perception, while certainly open to modification (so one can redraw a figure, or rearrange the chairs in the room), nevertheless remains relatively locked down, limited within a certain given range of possible modifications determined by what can be repeated, and how, within the scope of perception. This means that one can engage the modifiability of form, thus the range of possible variations governed by essence, only in a very conditioned manner. In perception, one is ultimately bound to the particularity of what things can show themselves to be on the level of fact, thus restricting the potential to explore essences that can only be brought to intuitivity through the apprehension of a relatively unbounded range of differing instances.

This is why, Husserl argues, *phantasy* is essential for phenomenological research. The importance of phantasy however is for Husserl fundamental to *any* kind of eidetic research, so for example in geometry, which is only possible if one is free from the relative constraints of *perceptual* exemplification. Even in the case of the sketches of the geometer, it is really phantasy that is doing the work, since the sketches themselves remain limited to the constraints of perceptual manifestation:

> In actually sketching and modeling, however, he [the geometer, J.D.] is constrained, while in phantasy he has incomparable freedom in reshaping the fictitious figures at whim, in running through continuously modified possible configurations, thus in producing an unlimited number of new forms. This freedom opens up to him for the first time access to the expanses of essential possibilities with their infinite horizons of varieties of knowledge of essences. Thus, the sketches normally follow *after* the constructions of phantasy and the eidetically pure thinking that is carried out on their basis. (*Ideen* 126/147)

Things are no different for the phenomenologist: "Like the geometer, the phenomenologist can only make limited use of an originary givenness as a means of assistance." (*Ideen* 127/147)

As the example of geometrical sketches shows, originary perception and phantasy can work together: drawing a figure provides a point of departure for imaginative variation of geometrical form; or observing the gentle curling of smoke tendrils flowing out of a cigar a point of departure for imagining a range of topological variants. Husserl speaks of the perceived as "pollinating" phantasy, providing the first series of instances from which phantasied variations can flow in order to clarify the relevant essence. (*Ideen* 127/148) But pollination can also come from phantasy itself, as an example of a kind of self-pollination of fictions; more, a whole range of works of phantasy can be mobilized for the interests of the investigation of essence:

> Extraordinary profit is to be drawn from the offerings of history and, in even richer measure, from what art and, in particular, literature have to offer. Although these are products of imaginings [*Einbildungen*], they tower high over our own phantasy's accomplishments in regard to the originality of the new configurations, the fullness of individual features,

and the continuity of motivation. In addition, through the suggestive power of the artistic means of exhibition, they convert themselves with particular ease into perfectly clear phantasies, when we attempt to construe things in an intelligible way. (*Ideen* 127/148)

The pollination of imagination by perceptions is not about justification, about providing some anchor in the empirical world that would legitimate eidetic investigation. The point is not to think of phantasy as somehow a supplement to the empirical, the latter being the real touchstone of truth; rather, when it comes to essential determinations, everything has to do with providing the methodological ground for the broadest possible exploration of form. It is also worth noting that this does not imply that phenomenology must necessarily shift from an investigation of the constitution of the regions of real being, such as nature or social existence, to an investigation of art and literature. And of course there are few if any examples in Husserl's own corpus of an explicit engagement with the imaginative arts; even the use of Dürer's copperplate engraving "Knight, Death, and the Devil" hardly engages the work of art as an explicit accomplishment of the imagination. Rather the point is that fictions, what they accomplish and what they show us, are indispensible to navigating the specifically eidetic dimensions of the natural and the social; more, these accomplishments constantly accompany phenomenological investigation, as a ready store of associations and formulations that illuminate eidetic horizons of determination, even if they are not explicitly acknowledged. To insist on dissecting what we see thanks to perception from what we see thanks to imagination, to purify "real" perception from any stain of forms that ultimately have the origin of their articulation in the narratives of history, the worlds of literature and art, would hopelessly compromise the forward progression of any eidetic science.

Accordingly, phenomenology proceeds, not contingently but out of necessity, through a series of phantasized fictions, pollinated from whatever source is available–the clarification of the essence of pure transcendental consciousness can occur *in no other manner*. This leads Husserl to end § 70 with the following provocative passage:

> Thus, if one loves paradoxical talk, one can actually say–and if one properly understands the ambiguous sense involved, one can say in strict truth–that '*fiction*' *makes up the vital element of phenomenology, as it does of all eidetic science*, that fiction is the source from which knowledge of the 'eternal truths' draws its nourishment. (*Ideen* 127/148)

"A sentence that," as Husserl remarks in a footnote to this passage, "would be particularly well-suited as a quotation to ridicule, from a naturalistic point of view, the eidetic manner of knowing." (*Ideen* 127, footnote/148 fn.)

4. Descriptive eidetics

If a reliance on fiction is not unique to phenomenology, but is characteristic of all eidetic science, then this is not what sets phenomenology apart from other eidetic sciences such as geometry. What sets phenomenology apart is rather something else that bears a close relation to fiction–namely *description*. One could say that the entire reflection on the nature of clarification in this chapter is ultimately aimed at the scientific justification, or at least delimitation, of the role of description in phenomenology. Careful reflection here is necessary, for Husserl intends here to defend the very peculiar, even contradictory idea of a "descriptive eidetics": "*Is it correct to stick phenomenology with the aims of mere description? A descriptive eidetic*–is that not *something altogether perverse?*" (*Ideen* 128/149)

For Husserl, the contrast between phenomenology and eidetic sciences such as geometry and arithmetic plays a central role in this respect, and is the topic of discussion in §§ 71–72. Here Husserl argues that the phenomenologist cannot proceed as a geometer, as if it were possible to pursue something akin to a "geometry of experience." The geometer proceeds axiomatically, aiming at a fundamental set of core propositions or structures that define what Husserl calls a definite or mathematical manifold in the precise sense: namely a manifold of objects constructed in an exhaustive manner by being logically deduced from a set of axioms. In formal mathematics, axiomatics thus provide a rigorously fixed framework, or frameworks, within which phantasy does its work. The role that fiction plays in a formal science like geometry, in other words, is an organic part of a constructive-deductive method, for which description proper has no role: phantasy explores possible variations all of which are, in principle, constructible within the axiomatic structure established in advance (cf. *Ideen* 130/151–152).

Husserl argues that phenomenology is a concrete eidetic discipline, and insofar as it is eidetic, one can ask the question, as Husserl does: "is the stream of consciousness a genuine mathematical manifold?" (Husserl, 2014, p. 132/153–154) On one level this is a question of clarification, or whether clarification might yield a potential delimitation of a few basic forms that would serve as the foundation for all determinations of consciousness, thus allowing phenomenology to proceed eidetically-constructively. But there is something else to this: basic forms are not enough for construction. The issue is rather *what kinds of concepts* will arise thanks to any clarification of the essence of the stream of consciousness. Definite concrete manifolds are characterized by their being accessible through precise, exact, and univocal *concepts* that articulate the highest genera of a region, and which lend themselves to axiomatization only thanks to this precision. The possibility of exactness is conditioned by the essence of the particular region in question—namely, whether such essences are themselves "exact" or "precise." Husserl puts it thus:

> [...] to what extent 'exact' essences are to be found within the domain of essences–and whether exact essences figure at all in the substructure of all essences that can be apprehended in actual Intuition, and thus figure, too, in the substructure of all essential components–that is fully dependent upon the distinctiveness [*Eigenart*, J.D.] of the domain. (*Ideen* 132/154)

The point here is important: the very character of phenomenology as an eidetic science is relative to the essential characteristics of its domain, the life of transcendental consciousness, which has not yet been clarified sufficiently to determine logically the manner in which its rigorous investigation is to be understood. This leads Husserl, in § 74, to a reflection on the distinction between "descriptive" and "exact" or univocal concepts. His aim here is to defend the possibility that description, which is neither univocal nor exact, could nevertheless be the source of properly eidetic concepts. The issue is not the status of an imprecise description of something that would also lend itself to precise concepts, but rather of a type of description which, *as description*, is commensurate to a kind of essence that is itself *only morphologically accessible*–or as Husserl puts it, the issue has to do with the possibility of "concepts that are *essentially and not contingently inexact*, and *hence* unmathematical as well." (*Ideen* 133/155) Eidetic research is thus not limited to essences that define an ideal of perfect precision or exact determination, or to essences in the sense of "ideas in the Kantian sense," but in principle include essences that are morphological in the sense of cleaving closer, as it were, to what we can actually "see":

> Geometric concepts are '*ideal*' *concepts*; they express something that one cannot 'see.' Their 'origin' (and thus also their content) is essentially different from that of the *descriptive concepts* as concepts that immediately express essences taken from straightforward intuition; they express no 'ideals.' Exact concepts have their correlates in essences that have the character of '*ideas*' *in the Kantian sense*. As correlates of descriptive concepts, *morphological essences* stand over against these ideas or ideal essences. (*Ideen* 133/155)

In § 75, Husserl then sketches the movement basic to phenomenological description: given the flowing, fluctuating character of lived experience, it is impossible to fix for eidetic description the given morphology of individuated experiences, even in their eidetic constitution (qua what Husserl calls eidetic singularities); instead description unfolds on a "*higher level of specificity*," (*Ideen* 135/157) or the morphology of those determinations of lived experiences on a higher level of generality (so memory in general, perception in general, and the like). Here rigor is possible in a way not possible on the level of the reflection on the passage of individual lived experiences, but again this rigor is not tantamount in any way to the achievement of a set of properly exact concepts: the movement is instead conditioned by a specifically intuitive, and with that descriptive, mode of seeing that straddles the tension between fact and essence.

Clearly Husserl is beginning to show more of his hand, and letting on that phenomenology is more developed, more mature, than it might seem to be at the beginning of this chapter: it is at least mature enough to provide an important example of a specifically descriptive eidetics, or an object domain that lends itself to eidetic investigation only morphologically. Nevertheless, it is interesting to note that Husserl explicitly leaves the door open to the possibility of a future "geometry of experience," thus to a phenomenology that would, given the accomplishment of the maturation of a set of precise concepts from more morphological beginnings, be in a position to proceed axiomatically and not merely descriptively:

> Not answered by any of this, to be sure, is the pressing question whether or not in the eidetic domain of reduced phenomena (whether as a whole or in any domain of a part) *alongside* the descriptive way of proceeding, there could also be an idealizing way of proceeding that substitutes pure and rigorous ideals for what is given intuitively, ideals that then could serve as basic means for a mathesis of experiences–as the counterpart to the *descriptive* phenomenology. (*Ideen* 135/158)

There is still an indeterminacy here, basic questions that can be answered only in the course of phenomenological investigation itself. Thus the argument Husserl makes in § 75 is really just that we should not *begin* with the assumption that all eidetic sciences are in principle mathematical sciences, nor should we assume in advance that descriptive explorations of form cannot be taken as a methodological basis for the clarification of essence. Whether or not there might emerge the grounds for a more constructive approach to the same phenomena is left open, and can be left open since in no way does phenomenology as a descriptive eidetics require that we answer, in advance, whether or not a geometry of experience is possible.

In sum, the methodological posture that Husserl leaves us with at the end of this chapter is distinctively indeterminate, and must be such for fundamental reasons. Husserl outlines for us a methodological project of clarification through eidetic description, but where the very status of such description wavers between an ideal of precision and exactness and the possibility that phenomenological concepts will remain within the imprecise but rigorous bounds of a descriptive morphology. Precisely what could be definitive of the rigor of phenomenology, thus its very status as a science, remains a problem for phenomenology itself, as does the promise of phenomenology as a "first" philosophy. The *Ideas I* as a whole, one might argue, never grows beyond this self-conscious progression of method as something preparatory–a posture, one might argue, that is ultimately the source of its strength.

Bibliography

Descartes, René (1990): *The Philosophical Writings of Descartes*, Volume II. Trans.Cottingham, John/Stoothoff, Robert/Murdoch, Dugald. Cambridge: Cambridge University Press.

Husserl, Edmund (1969): *Formal and Transcendental Logic*. Trans. Cairns, Dorion. The Hague: Nijhoff.

Husserl, Edmund (1974): "Formale und Transzendentale Logik. Versuch einer Kritik der logischen Vernunft". In: *Husserliana*. Vol. XVII. The Hague: Nijhoff.

Landgrebe, Ludwig (1970): "Husserl's Departure from Cartesianism." In: Elveton, Roy O. (Ed.) *The Phenomenology of Husserl: Selected Critical Readings*. Chicago: Quadrangle Books.

Marion, Jean-Luc (1999): "What is the Metaphysics within the Method? The Metaphysical Situation of the *Discourse on Method*"; and "What Is the Method in the Metaphysics? The Role of the Simple Natures in the *Meditations*". In: *Cartesian Questions. Method and Metaphysics*. Chicago: University of Chicago Press.

Patocka, Jan (1989): "Cartesianism and Phenomenology (1976)". In: Kohak, Erazim (Ed.): *Jan Patocka. Philosophy and Selected Writings*. Trans. Erazim Kohak. Chicago: University of Chicago Press.

Turnbull, Colin (2012): *The Forest People*. New York: Random House

Dan Zahavi
Phenomenology of reflection

Section III, chapter 2, Universal structures of pure consciousness

In his book *Hermeneutik und Reflexion,* von Herrmann distinguishes *hermeneutic* phenomenology and *reflective* phenomenology and identifies the latter with Husserl's approach to phenomenology. For von Herrmann this classification is not intended as praise, but rather seen as a criticism and deficiency. Von Herrmann takes reflection to be an objectifying, interrupting and distancing procedure. It is a violent theorizing that deprives the experiences reflected upon from what is their own, namely their lived *"Vollzugshaftigkeit."* Thus, although Husserl's reflective phenomenology claims to be true to the phenomena, this is, according to von Herrmann, not at all the case. Being so dependent upon a reflective methodology as it is, it is prevented from accessing and disclosing the a-theoretical being of the experiential dimension (cf. von Herrmann 2000, p. 20).

Whatever one might hold of von Herrmann's ultimate verdict, I think he is quite right in considering reflection crucial to the Husserlian enterprise. This is also something that a close reading of the chapter *Universal Structures of Pure Consciousness* will confirm. As Husserl writes in § 77 of *Ideas I,* the phenomenological method is reflective. In the following, I will explore the role and status of reflection. I will first discuss the preconditions for reflective self-consciousness and then assess the descriptive and philosophical accomplishments of reflection.

1. The foundations of reflective self-consciousness

In § 77 of *Ideas I,* Husserl argues that every ego experiences or lives through its experiences. This does not mean that it is always grasping, or thematizing or objectifying the experiences. But every experience that isn't thematized can in principle be made into an object by an act of reflection. Furthermore, every act of reflection is itself an experience and consequently something that is lived through and something that in principle can be made into an object by a higher-order reflection. In the same paragraph, Husserl also points to the temporal character of reflection. When we reflect, the experience that we reflect upon is not simply given as existing here and now, but also as having already been given prior to reflection. That is, it is in the nature of reflection to grasp something that was already given prior to and independently of the grasping. Husserl's description in § 77 repeats claims made earlier in the text, for instance in § 38 and § 45:

> [L]iving in the cogito, we do not consciously have the cogitatio itself as an intentional object. Yet at any time it can become that. The intrinsic possibility of a *'reflective' shift of focus* is an essential property of it, and naturally [this is] a shift of focus in the form of a new cogitatio that is directed at it in the manner of simply apprehending it. In other words, any cogitatio can become the object of a so-called 'inner perception,' and then, as a further consequence, the object of a *reflective* evaluation, an approval or disapproval, and so forth. (*Ideen* 66/77)

> We see that experience has the kind of being that in principle can be perceived in the manner of reflection. (Ideen 81/95)

Let me present and contrast two very different interpretations of these statements.

In various previous publications, I have argued that Husserl just like Sartre is committed to the existence of pre-reflective self-consciousness (cf. Zahavi 1999, 2003a, 2004). According to this reading, rather than taking self-consciousness to be something that occurs only during exceptional circumstances, namely, whenever we reflect upon our conscious life, Husserl considers it a feature characterizing the experiential dimension as such, no matter what worldly entities we might otherwise be conscious of and occupied with.

Not everybody agrees with this interpretation, however. In a couple of recent texts, Christian Beyer has argued that Husserl must instead be appreciated as a defender of a dispositional higher-order representation theory of consciousness. To some extent, Beyer's proposal aligns itself with an older and well-established–though, in my view, obsolete–interpretation, according to which Husserl defends a reflection theory of self-consciousness. In *Selbstbewußtsein und Selbstbestimmung*, for instance, Tugendhat argued that Husserl defines self-consciousness as a relation between two different experiences, where one takes the other as its inner object (cf. Tugendhat 1979, pp. 52–53). For Tugendhat, Husserl consequently understood self-consciousness as a subject-object relation between two different experiences (a perceiving and a perceived), and in his view, Husserl never succeeded in explaining why such a relation should result in *self*-consciousness (cf. Tugendhat 1979, pp. 15; 17; 53). Similar views can be found in Henrich, Frank and Gloy, who all faulted Husserl's analysis of self-consciousness and argued that he never managed to escape the reflection-theoretical paradigm (cf. Henrich 1966, p. 231; Gloy 2004, p. 203). To quote Manfred Frank: "In any case, Husserl does not know any other concept of self-consciousness than the reflective one" (Frank 1991, p. 300). Frank even claimed that Husserl not only failed to provide a convincing analysis of self-consciousness, but that he also failed to understand the very problem (cf. Frank 1991, p. 45).

Although Beyer takes Husserl to be a higher-order representationalist, he does not share the negative assessment of these earlier critics. Moreover, he gives a quite original new twist to the interpretation by emphasizing what he takes to be the similarities between Husserl's view and the theory of Peter Carruthers, and by arguing that Husserl's analysis can provide a phenomenological motivation for the latter (cf. Beyer 2010, p. 27). This is in many ways a startling claim and runs counter to my own interpretation according to which the positions of Husserl and Carruthers are antithetically opposed.

The view that Carruthers has defended over the years is roughly the following: To speak of what an experience is like, or of its phenomenal feel, is an attempt to characterize those aspects of experience that are subjective. But to speak of the subjective aspects of experience is to speak of aspects that are available to the subject. What this means, according to Carruthers, is that they must be states of which the subject is aware and this obviously involves a certain amount of self-consciousness or self-awareness; in fact, according to Carruthers, it requires the ability to reflect upon, think about and conceptualize one's own mental states (cf. Carruthers 1996, pp. 155, 157). Carruthers consequently defends the view that the subjective feel of experience presupposes a capacity for self-awareness and as he writes, "such self-awareness is a conceptually necessary condition for an organism to be a subject of phenomenal feelings, or for there to be anything that its experiences are like" (Carruthers 1996, p. 152. Cf. Carruthers 1996, p. 154). Given the conceptual requirement, Carruthers ultimately argues that only creatures that are in possession of a *theory of mind* are capable of enjoying conscious experiences or of having mental states with phenomenal feels (cf. Carruthers 1996, p. 158). One implication of this is that animals and children under the age of three, who allegedly lack a theory of mind, are also blind to the existence of their own mental states. As Carruthers puts it, there is in fact nothing it is like for them to feel pain or pleasure (cf. Carruthers 1998, p. 216; Carruthers 2000, p. 203).

What is then the view held by Husserl according to Beyer? On the ascribed view, a conscious mental state is distinguished from an unconscious mental state by the fact that it is the object of a higher-order representation. According to the dispositionalist reading, the metarepresentation in question must be understood as an "Urteilsdisposition", i.e., as a disposition to judge (Beyer 2010, p. 20). Thus, a mental state is conscious if the subject based on that state (and if in possession of the relevant concepts) is disposed to make the non-inferential judgment that it itself is currently in that state (cf. Beyer 2011, p. 44; 53).

More specifically, for Husserl all my conscious mental states–all my *Erlebnisse*–are characterized by the fact that they can be taken as objects by inner perception, and it is this inner perception that then automatically disposes me to judge that I currently have the mental state in question (cf. Beyer 2011, p. 48). Now, Beyer concedes that inner time-consciousness also plays an important role in Husserl's account, and he argues that it is the non-intentional inner consciousness inherent in the *"Zeitempfindungen"* (time sensations) that makes the first-order mental state accessible to inner perception and to subsequent introspective judgment (Beyer 2011, p. 49):

> If Husserl's analyses are correct, then there is something that founds and makes explainable these dispositions: The sensing of time that is immanent in consciousness. This 'inner consciousness' doesn't constantly evoke 'inner perceptions' and subsequently, introspective judgments. However, it is constantly ready to motivate and found such reflective acts. (Beyer 2011, p. 53)

I think such a reference to inner time-consciousness is indeed unavoidable. Had Beyer failed to include it, his account simply could not be presented as a viable Husserl interpretation. Incidentally, this also points to one of the well-known lacunas in *Ideas I*. In that work, Husserl confined himself to an analysis of the relation between constituted objects and constituting consciousness. But as Husserl admits in § 81, his preceding discussion of constituting consciousness has not really been a discussion of the truly absolute. Rather, his analysis of constituting act-intentionality is an analysis of something that itself is constituted temporally in a profoundly different manner than the objects of intentionality. There is as such nothing problematic about this admission, nor about Husserl's desire to remain silent about this profoundly difficult topic, since an extensive exploration would have led him too far afield. What is problematic is rather Husserl's claim that temporality is the title for a *completely* independent realm of problems, one that he can push aside without jeopardizing the rigor of his investigation (*Ideen* 156–157/182). Given the pervasive significance of temporality and the fact that temporality is a universal form of experience, this is hardly convincing.

But back to Beyer. Does his reference to the motivating non-intentional inner consciousness not put pressure on the entire setup? How can one at the same time argue that inner consciousness is what motivates and founds the higher-order disposition and still defend a capacity-based explanation of consciousness, i.e., an account that argues that our mental states are conscious if and only if we have the capacity to judge that we are having them? Instead of arguing that a mental state is conscious because it possesses a dispositional metarepresentation, I think a far more natural move to make is to reverse the explanatory arrow and argue that a mental state possesses a dispositional metarepresentation because it is conscious. This also seems to be what Husserl is getting at in the following passage from *Formale und transzendentale Logik*:

> *An absolute existent* is existent in the form, an intentional life–which, no matter what else it may be intrinsically conscious of, is, at the same time, consciousness of itself. Precisely for that reason (as we can see when we consider more profoundly) it has at all times an essential ability to *reflect* on itself, on all its structures that stand out for it–an essential ability to make itself thematic and produce judgments, and evidences, relating to itself. (Husserl 1969, p. 273; Husserl 1974, pp. 279–80)

Thus, rather than saying that Husserl's account of inner time-consciousness provides a phenomenological motivation for Carruthers' dispositionalist higher-order theory as Beyer claims, I think the right conclusion to draw is that Husserl's account completely undermines Carruthers' theory. This is obviously not a conclusion that Beyer is willing to draw, and this is also why he ends both his articles on the topic by writing as follows: "Without the subject's capacity for metarepresentation, however, this sensing of time would remain blind" (Beyer 2010, p. 30); "Without the corresponding higher-order dispositions to judge, 'inner consciousness' would remain blind, and it would hardly be appropriate to designate it as 'pre-reflective self-consciousness'" (Beyer 2011, p. 53). However, I do not know of any places where Husserl endorses such a view and I do not think it is compatible with what Husserl elsewhere says about the self-constitution of the absolute flow. It would lead too far afield on this occasion to rehearse Husserl's analysis of time-consciousness, but let me end this first section with a few quotes that I take to support the claim that Husserl did endorse the existence of a non-objectifying pre-reflective self-consciousness:

> The flow of the consciousness that constitutes immanent time not only *exists* but is so remarkably and yet intelligibly fashioned that a self-appearance of the flow necessarily exists in it, and therefore the flow itself must necessarily be apprehensible in the flowing. The self-appearance of the flow does not require a second flow; on the contrary, it constitutes itself as a phenomenon in itself (Husserl 1991, p. 88; Husserl 1966a, p. 83).

> This all-encompassing time-consciousness, however, is obviously *no continuous, immanent perceiving* in the *precise* sense of the term, i.e., in the sense of a perceiving that is *currently positing*, which is, indeed, itself an experience in our sense, one lying in immanent time, presently enduring, constituted in time-consciousness. In other words, it is obviously not a continuous, inner reflecting, in which the experiences would come to be objectively *posited* in the specific sense, *apprehended currently as being*. (*Ideen* 220/255–256)

> We can reflect on each act and in so doing turn it into an object of an act of immanent "perception." Prior to this perception (to which belongs the form of the cogito), we have the "inner consciousness" which lacks this form. (Husserl 1989a, p. 125; Husserl 1952, p. 118)

> When I say 'I,' I grasp myself in a simple reflection. But this self-experience [*Selbsterfahrung*] is like every experience [*Erfahrung*], and in particular every perception, a mere directing myself towards something that was already there for me, that was already conscious, but not thematically experienced, not noticed. (Husserl 1973, 492–493)

> The actual life and lived-experiencing is of course always conscious, but it is not therefore always thematically experienced and known. For that a new pulse of actual life is necessary, a so-called reflective or immanently directed experience. This is not merely added to the previous life, to the respective experience or experiential thinking, rather it transforms it in a specific manner. (Husserl 1987, p. 89)

The last quote touches on the issue that I next wish to discuss, the transformative power of reflection.

2. Reflective transformations

One of the urgent methodological questions that phenomenology has to face up to is the question of whether and to what extent experiential subjectivity can be made accessible to direct examination. If subjectivity, rather than being an object that we encounter in the world, is the very perspective that permits any such encounter, can it then at all be grasped and described, or is it only approachable *ex negativo*? Will any examination necessarily take the subject as an object of experience and thereby distort it beyond recognition? Not surprisingly, this particular question is one that very much has been at the forefront in the debate about whether or not reflection is at all trustworthy. Does reflection give us access to the original experiential dimension or is there, on the contrary, reason to suspect that the experiences are changed radically when reflected upon? Is reflection, in reality, a kind of falsifying mirror or telescope that transforms whatever it makes appear?

In §§ 76 and 79, Husserl makes two very significant phenomenological remarks about methodology. He first states that the proper method rather than being something that is applied on a certain domain from the outside, is a norm that springs from and is motivated by the structures of the domain itself (cf. *Ideen* 138/161). And as he then adds, in a rather Aristotelian vein, every kind of being has its own kind of givenness and correspondingly its own proper and matching method of investigation. To treat essential characteristics of any domain as a deficiency is for Husserl a fundamental mistake (cf. *Ideen* 151/176). Husserl is consequently careful to point out that it is unacceptable to transfer demands we put on evidence in one domain to other domains where these demands are in principle incapable of being realized.

In § 78 of *Ideas I*, Husserl observes that reflection is the name for an act that allows us to analyze other experiences, and also the name for the more general method that we have to employ if we wish to obtain knowledge of consciousness (cf. *Ideen* 142/165).[1] Husserl further remarks that we need to distinguish different types of reflection and importantly that every reflection essentially modifies or transforms the experience reflected upon. Finally, Husserl states that the phenomenological task is to investigate systematically all the reflective modifications (cf. *Ideen* 143/167) or to put it differently, phenomenology has to explore the contribution of reflection in a more systematic fashion. It has to engage in a kind of meta-reflection. Towards the end of the paragraph, Husserl then states that it is absurd to propose that experiences as a result of being reflectively scrutinized are transformed beyond recognition. He insists that one ought not to let oneself be confused by or concerned with refined arguments, but that it is enough to stay true to the principle of principles and the findings of pure intuition (cf. *Ideen* 145/169).

Perhaps Husserl came to have some doubts about the cogency of this advice, since he in the following paragraph, 79, actually does engage argumentatively with a number of skeptical objections raised by H.J. Watt.

In a first step, Husserl makes it clear that phenomenology is not susceptible to some of the standard objections directed at introspectionism for the very simple reason that the phenomenological focus and concern is quite different from the one found in introspective psychology. In fact, as Husserl and many other phenomenologists have consistently pointed out, to identify phenomenology (and the phenomenological method) with introspectionism is to commit a fundamental mistake (cf. Husserl 1971, p. 38; Merleau-Ponty 1945, p. 72). The goal of phenomenology has never been to offer descriptions of idiosyncratic experiences—"here and now, this is just what I experience". Rather, part of the phenomenological ambition is to disclose invariant experiential structures that are intersubjectively accessible, and its analyses are consequently open for corrections and control by any (phenomenologically attuned) subject. Thus, phenomenology is concerned with principled claims such as "The experience of pain has a temporal duration." It is not making factual claims such as "I am currently having a toothache." Moreover, and this will be highlighted further below, contrary to a widespread misunderstanding, phenomenology isn't merely interested in the structure of experience, it also investigates the object of experience, and the cor-

---

[1] One question that this claim gives rise to is whether Husserl is hereby ruling out that we might be able to obtain knowledge about consciousness through empathy. For a more detailed discussion of Husserl's account of empathy, cf. Zahavi (2012).

relational a priori that holds between the object and the different modes of givenness (cf. Husserl 1954, pp. 169–170). Thus, the phenomenologist explores the correlational structure. She investigates how the disclosing performance of intentional consciousness allows the world to appear in the way it does and with the validity and meaning it has. This is why phenomenology is a form of transcendental philosophy and not a form of introspective psychology.

Still this clarification does not as such address the more fundamental question of whether reflection is trustworthy or whether it rather distorts whatever it makes appear. As Husserl is well aware, the scientific credentials of phenomenology hangs on its ability also to target the realm of the unreflected. Had it been unable to do so, had it been restricted to only making claims about experiences reflected upon, it would have been incapable of making eidetic claims about the structure of experiences per se (be they unreflected or reflected).

Husserl's first reply to this is that skepticism in general is self-refuting since it always presupposes what it seeks to deny. This also holds true for skepticism regarding reflection. To say, "I doubt the epistemic validity of reflection" is to make a reflective statement. In order for the statement to be valid, the utterer must reflectively know something about his doubt. At the same time, knowledge about unreflected experiences is also presupposed (in order to substantiate the claim that reflection distorts them). But such knowledge about the unreflected domain is precisely what is being called into question. In short, if the skepticism were valid there would be 1) no reason to believe in the existence of unreflected experiences, 2) no reason to believe in the existence of an act of reflection, and 3) no reason to believe that reflection transforms or distorts the lived experience (cf. *Ideen* 149/174).

It is at this point important not to misunderstand Husserl. Husserl's rejection of the skeptical worry does not commit him to the view that reflection is always trustworthy, all he is saying is that reflection cannot always be untrustworthy.

For Husserl, reflection is certainly constrained by what is pre-reflectively lived through. Reflection is answerable to experiential facts and is not constitutively self-fulfilling. To deny that the reflective self-ascription of intentional states is based on any experiential evidence whatsoever is implausible. If I am to describe and assess my beliefs and intentions, it is not enough that I have them, I must also be aware of them, that is prior to reflection, I cannot have been "mindblind." As Sartre would later write in *Being and Nothingness* on reflection, "It implies as the original motivation of the recovery a pre-reflective comprehension of what it wishes to recover" (Sartre 1956, p. 156). At the same time, however, Husserl does recognize that reflection qua thematic self-experiences does not simply reproduce the lived experiences unaltered. That is, he certainly does recognize that reflection rather than merely copying or repeating the original experience transforms it, or as he explicitly states, *alters* it (cf. Husserl 1950, p. 72; Husserl 1987, p. 89). But this is precisely what makes reflection cognitively valuable. To put it differently, had reflection simply reproduced the original experience faithfully, *reflection would have been superfluous*. As I see it, Husserl consequently situates himself between two extremes. On the one hand, we have the view that reflection merely copies the lived experience and on the other, we have the view that reflection distorts lived experience. The middle course is to recognize that reflection involves a gain and a loss.

Sometimes, Husserl writes that the experience to which we turn attentively in reflection acquires a new mode of being; it becomes accentuated (cf. Husserl 1966a, p. 129). He also speaks of reflection as a process that discloses, disentangles, explicates, and articulates all those components and structures that are implicitly contained in the pre-reflective experience (cf. Husserl 1984, p. 244; Husserl 1966b, p. 205). As Husserl puts it, in the beginning we are confronted with the so to speak dumb experience that must then be made to articulate its own sense (cf. Husserl 1950, p. 77). What is important, however, is that this articulation is not necessarily imposed from without; is not necessarily foreign to the experience in question. Rather than adding new distorting components and structures to the experience reflected upon, a reflection might, at best, simply be accentuating structures already inherent in the lived experience. In this case, the persistent fear that reflection is somehow prevented from attaining true subjectivity seems unfounded.

One way to avoid the skeptical conclusion might consequently be to see reflection as a form of attention, and to compare the relation between pre-reflective and reflective consciousness to the relation between marginal and focal consciousness. In both cases, the transition from one to the other can be understood in terms of an *attentional modification*. Our attentive examination of a bottle does not change the bottle beyond recognition, so why should the attentive examination of an experience of a bottle change the experience beyond recognition?

There is, however, also a limit to how far one might insist on the similarity between reflection and attention. First, the concepts of attention and attentional modification are taken from the domain of object-consciousness and are related to the distinction between thematic and marginal objects. The attentional modification is what is at stake when we shift our focus between different objects, bringing those at the margin into the center of attention. To simply identify the process of reflection with such an attentional modification would be to remain committed to the view that our pre-reflectively lived through experiences linger in the background as marginal objects, and such a view might best be avoided (cf. Zahavi 2004). Second, in *Ideas I* Husserl is clearly stating that whereas attention is a particular feature or mode of our primary act and not a new act (cf. *Ideen* 64–65/75–76), reflection is a new (founded) act, for which reason reflection always involves a relation between two different experiences (cf. *Ideen* 66–67/78). This is why, Husserl in some places speaks of reflection as entailing a kind of doubling or fracture or *self-fission* (cf. Husserl 1959, pp. 89–90; 111; 306). To some extent, reflective self-consciousness is distinguished by a certain detachment and withdrawal, since reflection deprives the original experience of its naïveté and spontaneity. To put it another way, reflective self-consciousness does not merely differ from pre-reflective self-consciousness by its intensity, articulation, and differentiation, but also by its quality of *othering*. Becoming a theme to oneself is also a matter of becoming divided from oneself. Reflective self-consciousness consequently involves a form of alienation. It is characterized by a type of *self-fragmentation* that we do not encounter on the level of pre-reflective self-consciousness.[2]

Rather than being an odd side- or aftereffect, this specific feature might actually count as one of the crucial accomplishments of reflection. Consider that one of the distinguishing marks of rationality is the capacity to subject our beliefs and actions (and emotional reactions) to critical assessment. But if we are to do this, it is not sufficient simply to be pre-reflectively aware of them. Rather, what we need is to deprive our ongoing mental activities from their automatic normative force by stepping back from them. As Moran has pointed out, this stepping back is a metaphor of distancing and separation, but also one of observation and confrontation. It is the reflective distancing, which Korsgaard also describes as involving a self-division, that allows us to relate critically to our mental states and put them into question (cf. Korsgaard 2009, p. 213; Moran 2001, pp. 142–143). Such an idea is not foreign to Husserl. He as well would emphasize the importance of critical self-assessment and often spoke of the evidence-based self-responsible life that phenomenology makes possible (cf. Husserl 1959, p. 167).

---

[2] One implication of this self-fragmentation is that there will always remain an unthematized, and to that extent anonymous, spot in the life of the subject. Every reflection will contain a moment of naïveté since it is necessarily prevented from grasping itself, cf. Husserl (1962), p. 478. As Husserl also writes, I cannot fully grasp my own functioning subjectivity because I am it; that which I am cannot be my *Gegen-stand*, cannot stand opposed to me, cf. Husserl (1959), p. 412. Although experiential life can thematize and disclose itself, it can consequently never do so exhaustively and completely. Does this outcome constitute a major problem for phenomenology? Is it a fatal shortcoming, or rather an unavoidable but quite harmless impasse? As already indicated, I take the latter to be the case. Reflection cannot apprehend the anonymous life in its very functioning, but neither is it supposed to. Its aim is to lift the naïveté of pre-reflective experience, and not to relive or reproduce it.

3. Reflection and reduction

Let me in a final step move on to consider the more overarching philosophical accomplishments of reflection. In § 76, the first paragraph of the chapter *Universal Structures of Pure Consciousness*, Husserl makes a number of important statements regarding the impact and scope of the phenomenological enterprise. After having stated that the most fundamental ontological distinction is the one between the being of consciousness and the being of that which reveals itself for consciousness–or between transcendental and transcendent being[3]–Husserl goes on to point out that this radical difference doesn't prevent the two types of being from being essentially related. Indeed, an "objectively" oriented phenomenology has as its main theme intentionality, and any proper investigation of intentionality must include an investigation of the intentional correlate (§ 84). To employ some of Husserl's distinctions, there is not only a hyletic-phenomenology and a noetic-phenomenology, but also a phenomenology that deals with the constitution of the objects of consciousness (cf. *Ideen* 169/196). Or as he puts it later in the text, there is a *hyletic*, a *noetic* and a *noematic* form of reflection (cf. *Ideen* 300/349). Husserl's distinction obviously relates to his more general understanding of what a proper investigation of consciousness must include. It should target the hyletic content, e.g., the bodily and perceptual sensations, which lacks intentionality of its own; it should examine the proper bearers of intentionality, the noeses, i.e., the meaning-giving, sense-affording or animating apprehensions; and finally it should investigate the noematic correlate of consciousness (cf. *Ideen* 165; 166 – 167; 174 – 175/192; 194; 203). Although, phenomenology according to Husserl is able to offer far richer analyses of the noetic than of the hyletic dimension, he also stresses that the greatest and most important problems in phenomenology are related to the question of how objectivities of different kinds, from the prescientific to those of the highest scientific dignity, are constituted by consciousness (cf. *Ideen* 169/196). Indeed, "investigating, in the most all-encompassing way, how objective unities of every region and category are 'constituted in keeping with consciousness' is what counts" (*Ideen* 170/198). It is for this very reason, that Husserl can write that there is not only a phenomenology of natural scientific thinking, but also

---

[3] One might wonder to what extent this rather clear statement undermines Heidegger's well-known criticism in *History of the Concept of Time,* where Heidegger argues that Husserl due to his exclusive interest in intentionality identified the Being of consciousness with the Being of objects, and consequently failed to uncover the unique mode of Being characterizing intentional subjectivity itself (cf. Heidegger 1979, pp. 143, 152).

a phenomenology of nature (qua correlate of consciousness). To think otherwise, is to misunderstand the character and purpose of the phenomenological reflection and reduction. This is also why, Husserl already in § 76 writes:

> At the same time, the suspension has the character of an alteration via an operation sign that transforms the value of what follows it, and, with this alteration, what is revalued is reclassified in the phenomenological sphere. To put it more figuratively, what is bracketed is not wiped off the phenomenological board but merely bracketed and thereby provided with a marker indicating as much. With this, however, it is a major theme of research. (Ideen 136–137/159)

To understand what is going on here, it will be helpful to consider some later texts by Husserl, where he is even more explicit about the non-excluding character of the reduction and about the fact that we by adopting the phenomenological attitude and by engaging in phenomenological reflection by no means effectuate an exclusive turn toward inwardness but rather continue to remain concerned with and focused on worldly objects.

In a text from 1931, for instance, Husserl remarks that the only thing that is excluded as a result of the *epoché* is a certain naïveté, the naïveté of simply taken the world for granted, thereby ignoring the contribution of consciousness (cf. Husserl 1989b, p. 173). Thus, the turn from a naïve exploration of the world to a reflective exploration of the field of consciousness is not a turning away from the world, but is rather a turn that for the first time allows us to study the world in a new and radical way, namely qua intentional correlate (cf. Husserl 1989b, p. 178). Such a reflective investigation obviously differs from a straightforward exploration of the world, but it remains an investigation of reality; it is not an investigation of some otherworldly, mental, realm.

As Husserl also makes clear in other texts from the same period, when the natural world is spoken of as "ausgeschaltet", as bracketed, what this means is merely that the transcendental philosopher must cease to posit the world naively (cf. Husserl 2002, p. 21). It does not imply that she cannot continue to observe, thematize and make judgments concerning the world, but she must merely do so in a reflective manner that considers the world as intentional correlate (cf. Husserl 2002, p. 58). In fact, as Husserl points out in *Erste Philosophie II*, it is better to avoid using the term "Ausschaltung" altogether, since the use of this term might easily lead to the mistaken view that the being of the world is no longer a phenomenological theme, whereas the truth is that transcendental research includes "the world itself, with all its true being" (Husserl 1959, p. 432). This is also why the often repeated assertion that the Husserlian reduction involves a suspension of all existential positings ought to be considered with some suspicion. There are reasons to think that the suspension in question is merely propaedeutic and provisional. As Husserl puts it in a text dating from 1930:

> If transcendental phenomenology has carried out its work, if, at least, it has encompassed the universal structure of being and world, then the *significance of the method of epoché*– whose import had to remain incomprehensible at the beginning–is also fully grasped. The epoché leads to that which is the primary absolute for me, i.e., to me as transcendental ego. Moreover, insofar as the epoché leads to the interpretation of this ego's concreteness in the primordiality, then to the clarification of the constitution of others as other human beings, and finally to the clarification of the constitution of myself as a human being in the world– which thereby also receives its own transcendental significance–insofar as these clarifications occur, the abstention from the positing of the world is systematically overcome. The transcendental presuppositions for the positing of the world, the transcendental foundations for the world are systematically revealed. They are revealed as transcendentally valid in transcendental evidence. And finally, the existing world emerges in ontic validity [*Seinsgeltung*], in the same ontic validity it had in the naïveté, but now merely with its transcendental horizons of presupposition disclosed. (Husserl 2002, p. 245)

In short, to perform the *epoché* and the reduction is not to dissolve or suspend the "Seinsgeltung der Welt" (Husserl 2002, p. 233), but rather to relativize this ontic validity. This incidentally might be one of the core implications of Husserl's transcendental idealism (cf. Jacobs 2013). Now, I am not claiming that all of this was already fully worked out and thought through by Husserl when he wrote § 76 of *Ideas I*, but I would suggest that this is where he was heading. A brief comparison of *Ideas I* with *Formal and Transcendental Logic* and *Cartesian Meditations* can incidentally serve as a good illustration of the development of his thinking. Whereas Husserl in *Formal and Transcendental Logic* would say that phenomenology is transcendental because it seeks to clarify the constitution of transcendence (cf. Husserl 1969, pp. 252–253; Husserl 1974, p. 259), and whereas he in *Cartesian Meditations* writes that the concepts transcendence and transcendental are correlated and that the task of transcendental phenomenology is to *elucidate* mundane transcendence through a systematic disclosure of constituting intentionality (cf. Husserl 1950, p. 32; 65), his formulation in § 86 of *Ideas I* is more ambiguous:

> On its own terrain, i.e., that of pure consciousness, and in its purely eidetic attitude, i.e., 'suspending' every sort of transcendence, phenomenology comes necessarily to this entire complex of *problems that are transcendental in the specific sense. Hence,* it deserves the name, *transcendental phenomenology. (Ideen* 170–171/198)

One thing though that Husserl was already quite explicit about in *Ideas I* was the fact that the performance of the phenomenological reduction allows for a tremendous discovery, namely the discovery of the constitutive accomplishments of consciousness. Whereas our ordinary natural lives are lives lived in states of self-alienation since we remain unaware of our own transcendentality, the performance of the reduction dissolves this self-alienation, and lifts subjectivity, as Husserl puts it in a text from 1932, to a new level of transcendental self-consciousness (cf. Husserl 2002, p. 399). This returns us to the issue of self-consciousness and closes the circle.

4. Conclusion

Let me end by quickly returning to von Herrmann. In the preceding, I have argued that there might be less reason to be critical of reflective phenomenology than von Herrmann suggests. But of course, part of von Herrmann's project is also to promote Heidegger's hermeneutic phenomenology. As he writes: "Hermeneutic phenomenology does not interrupt the primal intention of life and experience in order to objectify it reflectively; rather it grasps this primal intention in order to make it phenomenologically transparent and articulate" (von Herrmann 2000, p. 92). Von Herrmann consequently takes hermeneutic understanding to provide us with a completely new type of access to the experiences; an access that for the first time allows them to reveal themselves as they truly are (cf. von Herrmann 2000, p. 50). In contrast to reflection, this truly phenomenological understanding can be described as a being immersed in life, or being in sympathy with life. Ultimately, von Herrmann proposes a methodology based on "hermeneutic intuition" (von Herrmann 2000, p. 92) as a clear alternative to Husserl's reflective methodology. I would doubt the cogency of von Herrmann's distinction. I think there are good reasons to consider Heidegger's hermeneutic intuition as simply another name for phenomenological reflection. Let us not forget that hermeneutic phenomenology also seeks to thematize and articulate experiential structures, seeks to make us pay heed to something that we normally live through but fail to notice due to our absorption in the surrounding world (cf. Zahavi 2003b). If one accepts this conclusion, the further question is, of course, whether reflective phenomenology and hermeneutic phenomenology are really that different. If their difference were supposed to rest solely upon whether or not they employ reflection, I would argue that it is utterly artificial. But, of course, frequently the distinction is also taken to touch upon quite different issues as well, including the status of subjectivity, the role of the *epoché*, and the more general stance towards transcendental philosophy. Frequently the distinction is taken to be a distinction between a pure and transcendental type of phenomenology on the one hand, and an existential and hermeneutic kind on the other. Whether that distinction is artificial as well is a topic for a different paper.

References

Beyer, Christian (2010): "Husserls Bewußtseinskonzeption im Lichte der neueren Diskussion." In: Frank, Manfred/Weidtmann, Niels (Eds.): *Husserl und die Philosophie des Geistes*. Frankfurt: Suhrkamp, pp. 18–30.
Beyer, Christian (2011): "Husserls Konzeption des Bewußtseins." In: Cramer, Konrad/Beyer, Christian (Eds.): *Edmund Husserl 1859–2009*. Berlin/New York: de Gruyter, pp. 43–54.
Carruthers, Peter (1996): *Language, Thoughts and Consciousness. An Essay in Philosophical Psychology*. Cambridge: Cambridge University Press.
Carruthers, Peter (1998): "Natural Theories of Consciousness". In: *European Journal of Philosophy*, 6. No. 2, pp. 203–222.
Carruthers, Peter (2000): *Phenomenal Consciousness. A Naturalistic Theory*. Cambridge: Cambridge University Press.
Frank, Manfred (1991): *Die Unhintergehbarkeit von Individualität*. Frankfurt am Main: Suhrkamp.
Gloy, Karen (2004): *Bewusstseinstheorien. Zur Problematik und Problemgeschichte des Bewusstseins und Selbstbewusstseins*. Freiburg: Alber.
Heidegger, Martin (1979): "Prolegomena zur Geschichte des Zeitbegriffs". In: *Gesamtausgabe*. Vol. 20. Frankfurt am Main: Vittorio Klostermann.
Henrich, Dieter (1966), "Fichtes ursprüngliche Einsicht". In: Henrich, Dieter/Wagner, Hans (Eds.): *Subjektivität und Metaphysik. Festschrift für Wolfgang Cramer*. Frankfurt am Main: Klostermann, pp. 188–232.
Husserl, Edmund (1950): "Cartesianische Meditationen und Pariser Vorträge". In: *Husserliana*. Vol. I. The Hague: Nijhoff.
Husserl, Edmund (1952): "Ideen zu einer reinen Phänomenologie und phänomenologischen Philosophie. Zweites Buch. Phänomenologische Untersuchungen zur Konstitution". In: *Husserliana*. Vol. IV. The Hague: Nijhoff.
Husserl, Edmund (1954): "Die Krisis der europäischen Wissenschaften und die transzendentale Phänomenologie. Eine Einleitung in die phänomenologische Philosophie". In: *Husserliana*. Vol. VI. The Hague: Nijhoff.
Husserl, Edmund (1959): "Erste Philosophie (1923/24). Zweiter Teil. Theorie der phänomenologischen Reduktion". In: *Husserliana*. Vol. VIII. The Hague: Nijhoff.
Husserl, Edmund (1962): "Phänomenologische Psychologie. Vorlesungen Sommersemester 1925". In: *Husserliana*. Vol. IX. The Hague: Nijhoff.
Husserl, Edmund (1966a): "Zur Phänomenologie des inneren Zeitbewusstseins (1893–1917)". In: *Husserliana* Vol. X. The Hague: Nijhoff.
Husserl, Edmund (1966b): "Analysen zur passiven Synthesis. Aus Vorlesungs- und Forschungsmanuskripten 1918–1926". In: *Husserliana*. Vol. XI. The Hague: Nijhoff.
Husserl, Edmund (1969): *Formal and Transcendental Logic*. Trans. Cairns, Dorion. The Hague: Nijhoff.

Husserl, Edmund (1971): "Ideen zu einer reinen Phänomenologie und phänomenologischen Philosophie. Drittes Buch: Die Phänomenologie und die Fundamente der Wissenschaften". In: *Husserliana*. Vol. V. The Hague: Nijhoff.
Husserl, Edmund (1973): "Zur Phänomenologie der Intersubjektivität III. Texte aus dem Nachlass. Dritter Teil. 1929–35". In: *Husserliana*. Vol. XV. The Hague: Nijhoff.
Husserl, Edmund (1974): "Formale and transzendentale Logik. Versuch einer Kritik der logischen Vernunft". In: *Husserliana*. Vol. XVII. The Hague: Nijhoff.
Husserl, Edmund (1984): "Einleitung in die Logik und Erkenntnistheorie. Vorlesungen 1906/07". In: *Husserliana*. Vol. XXIV. Dordrecht: Nijhoff.
Husserl, Edmund (1987): "Aufsätze und Vorträge (1911–1921)". In: *Husserliana*. Vol. XXV. Dordrecht: Nijhoff.
Husserl, Edmund (1989a): *Ideas Pertaining to a Pure Phenomenology and to a Phenomenological Philosophy. Second Book. Studies in the Phenomenology of Constitution*. Trans. Rojcewicz, Richard/Schuwer, André. Dordrecht: Kluwer Academic Publishers.
Husserl, Edmund (1989b): "Aufsätze und Vorträge (1922–1937)". In: *Husserliana*. Vol. XXVII. Dordrecht: Kluwer Academic Publishers.
Husserl, Edmund (1991): *On the Phenomenology of the Consciousness of Internal Time (1893–1917)*. Trans. Brough, John Barnett. Dordrecht: Kluwer Academic Publishers.
Husserl, Edmund (2002): "Zur phänomenologischen Reduktion. Texte aus dem Nachlass (1926–1935)". In: *Husserliana*. Vol. XXXIV. Dordrecht: Kluwer Academic Publishers.
Jacobs, Hanne (2013): "Phenomenology as a Way of Life? Husserl on Phenomenological Reflection and Self-Transformation". In: *Continental Philosophy Review* 46. No. 3, pp. 349–69.
Korsgaard, Christine M. (2009): *Self-Constitution: Agency, Identity, and Integrity*. Oxford: Oxford University Press.
Merleau-Ponty, Maurice (1945): *Phénoménologie de la perception*. Paris: Éditions Gallimard.
Moran, Richard (2001): *Authority and Estrangement: An Essay on Self-Knowledge*. Princeton: Princeton University Press.
Sartre, Jean-Paul (1956): *Being and Nothingness*. Trans. Barnes, Hazel Estella. New York: Philosophical Library.
Tugendhat, Ernst (1979): *Selbstbewußtsein und Selbstbestimmung*. Frankfurt am Main: Suhrkamp.
von Herrmann, Friedrich-Wilhelm (2000): *Hermeneutik und Reflexion. Der Begriff der Phänomenologie bei Heidegger und Husserl*. Frankfurt: Vittorio Klostermann.
Zahavi, Dan (1999): *Self-awareness and Alterity. A Phenomenological Investigation*. Evanston: Northwestern University Press.
Zahavi, Dan (2003a): "Internal time-consciousness and pre-reflective self-awareness". In: Welton, Donn (Ed.): *The New Husserl. A Critical Reader*. Indiana University Press, pp. 157–180.
Zahavi, Dan (2003b): "How to investigate subjectivity: Natorp and Heidegger on reflection". In: *Continental Philosophy Review* 36. No. 2, pp. 155–176.
Zahavi, Dan (2004): "Back to Brentano?". In: *Journal of Consciousness Studies* 11. No. 10–11, pp. 66–87.

Zahavi, Dan (2012): "Empathy and mirroring: Husserl and Gallese". In: Breeur, Roland/Melle, Ullrich (Eds.): *Life, Subjectivity & Art: Essays in Honor of Rudolf Bernet*. Dordrecht: Springer, pp. 217–254.

Dermot Moran
Noetic moments, noematic correlates, and the stratified whole that is the *Erlebnis*

Section III, chapter 3, Noesis and noema

> We shall continue to look around further in the sphere of consciousness and attempt to become familiar with the noetic-noematic structures in the chief modes of consciousness. In the actual demonstration we shall assure ourselves at the same time, step-by-step, of the *thoroughgoing* trenchancy of the fundamental correlation between noesis and noema [*der durchgängigen Geltung der fundamentalen Korrelation zwischen Noesis und Noema*].
> - Ideen 181/211

> In the sphere of essence there are no contingencies [*gibt es keine Zufälle*]; everything is linked by eidetic connections [*Wesensbeziehungen*], thus, in particular, noesis and noema.
> - Ideen 186/216

The chapter on "Noesis and Noema" (*Ideen* §§ 87–96), Chapter Three of Section Three of *Ideas*, a Section that has the overall title "On the Method and Problems of Pure Phenomenology," lies at the center of the entire book. This third chapter aims to illustrate the phenomenological method applied to the close analysis of intentional experience. Here Husserl identifies various eidetic (essential) laws and conceptual distinctions that can be discovered by phenomenological analysis, in particular giving a first account of noesis and noema, but also discussing the intentional nature of judgments and even makes some remarks concerning the phenomenology of attention. It is in this chapter also that Husserl speaks for the first time of a "correlation" (*Korrelation* § 90) between noesis and noema. The concept of this essential correlation is initially introduced only tentatively (§ 91), as something whose complete validity still needs to be ascertained. Furthermore, although he focuses primarily on the analysis of perception and imagination (fantasy), he moves on to the noesis-noema structure in judgment and willing, extending his analysis to the "widest spheres of intentionality" (§ 91).

Husserl is emphatic in this chapter that his phenomenological investigations are merely initial explorations (see § 96), "purely introductory meditations" (*emporleitende Meditationen, Ideen* 192/223). *Ideas* stands at the "portal to phenomenology" (*Eingangstor, Ideen* 161/187–88; "entry portal", *Eingangspforte, Ideen* 52/61). As he frequently proclaims:

> Here, in the context of our meditations that merely lead up to phenomenology, the task cannot be to expound its components systematically (*Ideen* 192/223)

There is, furthermore no ideal route–no "royal road" (*Königsweg, Ideen* 193/223)– into phenomenology. Each set of problems has to be tackled in its own way. The current exploration is provisional; Husserl likens himself to an explorer mapping out a new territory (§ 96). A systematic exposition is a long way off and Husserl is not even sure what will remain of his current claims which are tentative at best. It is important then to see this chapter as an initial, exploratory effort to tackle the noematic-noetic structure of intentionality.

Husserl is also empathic that it is decisive to give a faithful description of everything that is given and to exclude "all interpretations that transcend the given" (§ 92). In particular, he is worried that our very use of certain words to name things, e.g. the "psychical" (*das Psychische*) already misleads. Even the term "phenomenology" is now familiar as a term whereas the "matter" (*die Sache*) it intends to pick out is not understood. Husserl will seek to introduce a new language. All the old terms "sense", "meaning", "intention" are loaded with ambiguities such that one must be very distrustful of ordinary and even scientific language:

> Yet transferences among them have encumbered all these words with so many equivocations–and not least with the sort that stem from gliding over into these correlative layers, which science is supposed to keep rigorously and systemically separate–that the greatest precaution is in order in relation to them. (*Ideen* 191/222)

Words can mask or distort the phenomenological findings. Yet he seems not to want to abandon language altogether but rather to develop wider senses that are phenomenologically vindicated through evidential seeing:

> Our new terms and the accompanying analyses of examples certainly serve us better for the generalities we are considering. (*Ideen* 191/222)

Husserl then is not proposing an unambiguous ideal language such as developed in the Vienna Circle by Rudolf Carnap and others, rather he wants as far as possible to have terms that can be clarified intuitively although the manner of this intuitive evidence is also a matter of dispute. Husserl struggles both to invent new terms and to fix the meanings of others. He is not very successful and some of his attempts, e.g. "hyletic data", "matter", "*hyle*", "content", and the wonderful technical term "stuff" (*Stoff*), have led to only greater confusion and disagreement among his readers. In this chapter, the term "noema" is given an initial outline.

The central focus is on the key phenomenological concept that Husserl took over from Brentano, namely intentionality: the fundamental fact that all conscious experiences, e.g. perceptions, thoughts and feelings, are *about* something or *directed towards* something. Husserl begins by saying that everyone understands in general terms what is meant by the expression "consciousness of something" (*Bewusstsein von Etwas*) but elucidating its phenomenological character is a great challenge. He also complains that the phenomenological approach, with its peculiar internal or immanent mode of approaching conscious experiences, has not yet been properly understood. Therefore, in this chapter, Husserl proposes to elucidate intentionality in a radically new way, couched in the new language of noesis and noema (the term "noema" receives its first published airing in this chapter), thereby offering a major advance over his earlier treatment of the topic in the *Logical Investigations* (1900/1901), especially the Fifth Investigation. In the last paragraph of the chapter, *Ideas* § 96, Husserl says that he wants to work out "in general the difference between noesis (i.e., the concretely complete intentional experience, designated with the emphasis on its noetic components) and noema because apprehending and mastering this difference are of the greatest import for phenomenology" (*Ideen* 192/222).

In this chapter also, Husserl continues to document the a priori essential, structural features of conscious experiences (*Erlebnisse*), as understood from within the phenomenological perspective, i.e., from within the *epoché*, and excluding all knowledge drawn from psychology, logic or ontology. According to Husserl, the *epoché* or what he also, in the Introduction to *Ideas*, calls the "method of phenomenological reductions" allows access to experiences in their pure form, "in phenomenological purity" (*in phänomenologischer Reinheit, Ideen* 187/217).[1] The reduced experience is still a concrete entity that includes or embodies a noetic act (all acts are or embody noeses) that has its own noetic content to which there corresponds what Husserl calls "'noematic content" or, in short, the "noema" (*noematischen Gehalt ... Noema, Ideen* 174/203). Husserl as-

---

[1] I agree with Sebastian Luft in his contribution that Husserl does not firmly distinguish between the epoché and the phenomenological reduction in the text of *Ideas*. His main concern is to bracket or suspend the "general thesis" that pervades experience in the natural attitude.

sumes we can move further through an eidetic reduction to consider the experience in its generality. In this chapter Husserl employs the phenomenological *epoché* and the concept of "bracketing" or "parenthesis" (*Einklammerung, Ideen* § 88, § 94). Thus Husserl writes:

> Not to be overlooked thereby is the phenomenological reduction [*die phänomenologische Reduktion*] that requires us 'to bracket' ['*einzuklammern*'] [the actual process of] making the judgment, insofar we want to obtain just the pure noema of the experience of judgment. (*Ideen* 187/217)

It is clear, then, that the chapter is explicitly written from *within the phenomenological perspective*. Husserl here distinguishes the "phenomenological attitude" from both the "natural attitude" and the "psychological attitude" (an equally valid attitude that picks out the noema in its own way). In the phenomenological attitude there is, as he says repeatedly, an "exclusion" or "switching off" (*Ausschaltung*) in operation and the application of "brackets" (*Klammer, Ideen* § 88). This switching off should be understood in the manner in which an electrician will first power-off a device and unplug it before investigating it further. It must be disabled. Bracketing, on the other hand, is a metaphor drawn from mathematics. One can carry what is in brackets from one operation to another without altering its internal structure. This bracketing is explicitly an exclusion of "actuality" (*Wirklichkeit, Ideen* § 30), of what he calls "this thetic actuality" (*Ideen* 176/204), an exclusion of the "thing in nature" (§ 89), of the "entire physical and psychic world" (§ 88). We shall discuss further below the "general thesis" that is being excluded.

The investigation is this chapter, then, takes place in an explicitly *transcendental* register, with Husserl referring at the outset to the "uniqueness of the transcendental attitude" (§ 87). This means that Husserl wants to consider experiences in their mode of givenness (*Gegebenheitsweise*, i.e. the manner they are displayed to the experiencing subject) purified of everything "transcendent", as he puts. In fact, the *transcendental* nature of phenomenology had already been made explicit in *Ideas* at the end of the preceding § 86, where he says that the purely eidetic attitude proceeding in immanence with all transcendences excluded deserves the name "transcendental phenomenology" (*Ideen* 170–171/198). The opening section § 87 of Chapter Three offers an excursus on the difficulties of securing the "phenomenological attitude" (*die phänomenologische Einstellung*), which is here identified with "the transcendental attitude" (*die transzendentale Einstellung, Ideen* 172/200). The chapter begins with a discussion of "the most difficult of problems", whose sense (*Sinn*) is hidden, and how difficult it is to approach *experiences* from the right phenomenological attitude in order to yield an "eidetic finding". Many of Husserl's earlier students at Göttingen, who had considered phenomenology to be a form of realism, were deeply dismayed by Husserl's apparent embrace of transcendental idealism in *Ideas*. But Husserl in fact had been using the language of transcendental philosophy in his lectures from 1907, although it appears for the first time in print in *Ideas* (1913) and will be thenceforth a permanent stance of the mature Husserl.

Husserl begins by invoking "what is distinctive about intentional experience in terms of its generality" (*Die Eigentümlichkeit des intentionalen Erlebnisses*, *Ideen* 172/200). But he is impatient with simply invoking intentionality as if the mere reference to the idea of relatedness to an object gave any special insight into consciousness. He acknowledges that intentionality has been discussed in philosophy since the Middle Ages but genuine advances have not been made. The scholastic distinction between "immanent" or "intentional" object and the "actual" object, for instance, Husserl maintains, does pick out something essential, but this needs to be phenomenologically clarified (§ 90). Husserl, therefore, proposes a fresh start, promising exacting and painstaking new investigations.

As mentioned above, this chapter marks Husserl's first use of the term "noema" (German: *Noema*)-plural "noemata"-in print in his published work, although the term did appear briefly earlier in his 1906/7 lectures, *Introduction to Logic and Theory of Knowledge* (see Husserl 2008, p. 126 n. 2) and his more extensive 1908 lectures on *Theory of Meaning* (*Vorlesungen über Bedeutungslehre*) where he speaks of the "meant as such" (Husserl 1987, p. 217). The term 'noema' is taken from the Greek and means 'that which is thought'. Husserl uses it very broadly to mean whatever is the object of a conscious act (this could be a perceptual thing or quality or even a state-of-affairs, e. g. *that it is raining now*) in so far as it is apprehended as correlated with that act (see Bernet 1990). The Greek term 'noesis' means 'the act of thinking' and again Husserl uses it very broadly (he often speaks of "noetics" as the theoretical exploration of cognitive acts) to include not just acts of judgment and cognition but all conscious acts including perceivings, rememberings, and so on. In this chapter of *Ideas* he explains that noesis is to be understood as "the concretely complete intentional experience, designated with the emphasis on its noetic components" (*Ideen* 192/222). The noesis, then, is the lived experience (*Erlebnis*) taken as a whole but understood in terms of its "noetic" nature, e. g. it is taken as a perceiving, a remembering, a hoping, a doubting, and so on. In *Ideas* § 92, Husserl will speak, for instance, of a "noesis of perception" or a "noesis of remembering" and of what happens in the transition from one state to the other. Elsewhere in *Ideas* (§§ 33, 34) Husserl will use the Cartesian term *cogitatio* (Latin, "a thought") as equivalent.

Husserl will also draw attention to the crucial distinction between noesis and noema and their correlation in his Foreword to the Second Edition on the *Logical Investigations* (also published in 1913), where he states that the First Edition did not sufficiently distinguish between the noetic and noematic dimensions of what he there ambiguously calls "meaning":

> As a further defect of this Investigation [he is referring to the First Investigation], only understood and corrected at the end of the volume, we must note that it has no regard to the distinction and parallelism between the 'noetic' and the 'noematic': the fundamental role of this distinction in *all* fields of consciousness is first fully laid bare in the *Ideas*, but comes through in many individual arguments in the last Investigation of the old work. For this reason, the essential ambiguity of 'meaning' [*Bedeutung*] as an Idea is not emphasized. The noetic concept of meaning is one-sidedly stressed, though in many important passages the noematic concept is principally dealt with. (Husserl 2001a, p. 7).

Husserl is here claiming that the notions of noesis and noema actually were first treated (though not under those names) in *Logical Investigations*. Furthermore, he believes that most of the attention there went on the noetic side. Husserl wants to clarify how the notion of noema differs from the notion of meaning understood "as an idea" or simply as an ideal sense. *Ideas* § 94 echoes this passage in the Foreword of the *Logical Investigations* and refers to the Fifth Logical Investigation § 21, where the difference between the "intentional essence" and "epistemic essence" (*das erkenntnismässige Wesen*) of an intentional act is discussed.[2] This distinction is an attempt to show that there is more to the intentional structure of the act that epistemology or logic acknowledges. Husserl now thinks the earlier discussion was primarily noetic whereas a noematic interpretation is also required.

In this chapter of *Ideas* Husserl offers a surgeon-like dissecting of the phenomenologically reduced intentional "experience" (*Erlebnis*), that is, the experience as considered abstracted from all assumptions concerning its actuality in the world as a real psychic episode interacting with physical entities. He says that he wants to "conduct phenomenological discriminations [*Ausscheidungen*] and clarifications [*Klärungen*], by means of which, too, the sense of the problems

---

[2] In the Findlay translation of the *Logical Investigations*, "epistemic essence" is translated somewhat misleadingly as "semantic essence" (see Husserl 2001b, p. 123). Husserl thinks of the intentional essence as the combination of act quality and matter in the act, whereas the epistemic act includes reference to the intended object and is responsible for the "meaning" of the experience. Even the quality and matter do not exhaust the intentional essence. Husserl's discussion in the Logical Investigations is most complicated and he himself was dissatisfied with it and regards the noesis and noema terminology as a step forward in clarification. For further discussion of the epistemic essence, see John J. Drummond's contribution to this volume.

to be solved here can first be made intelligible" (*Ideen* 193/223). In this regard, Husserl begins with a fundamental distinction between the "components proper" of the mental process and the "intentional correlates", between *genuine components* of intentional experiences understood as temporal events and their *intentional correlates*, i.e. the objects the experiences aim at in some way. This reiterates a distinction already made in the Fifth Logical Investigation § 16 between what he calls there the "real (*reelle*) or phenomenological" and the "intentional" parts. His example there was illuminating. In an act of speaking, the spoken sound has its real components and abstract parts that can be descriptively analyzed–quite distinct from the physical sound vibrations, parts of the ear and so on (Husserl 2001b, p. 112). But distinct from these "real" parts are also the ideal parts–the identical meaning that is communicated by the sounds. In the Second Edition Husserl is clearer that besides these "real" components there are also "intentional components" including the intentional quality, matter, the intentional object, intentional essence, and so on, parts that can be identified in phenomenological rather than psychological analysis. He now calls these latter parts "phenomenological" (whereas in the First Edition he called the "real" parts "phenomenological") and he refers to the present chapter in *Ideas* for clarification (see the footnote in the Second Edition, Husserl 2001b, p. 354 n. 24).

Every experience has parts or components in several different senses. Following the analysis of the Third Logical Investigation § 2 there are "independent" or "dependent" (literally: "non-independent") parts. Independent real parts are also called "pieces" (*Stücke*). The head of a horse, for example, is a real part that can be detached from the horse (as in *The Godfather* movie) and will continue to exist as an independent object. The color of the horse, however, is not detachable from the colored surface, although it can be separated in thought and considered as distinct. This is therefore a "dependent" or "non-self-standing" part (*Ideas* § 88), something that can be distinguished as opposed to being separated from the whole and presented separately on its own.

Every conscious experience can be thought of as a "real" psychic event in the world, one that takes place primarily in worldly time, with its own specific temporal phases. On the other hand, an intentional experience aims at or is about something, and that thing (the intentional object, in Husserl's language) is not a real part of the intending act. I see the apple tree in an act of seeing, and not just the side that I currently apprehend. But the apple tree is "outside" of the experience and moreover has the "sense" of being an external or "transcendent" thing. An apple tree is an enduring spatio-temporal physical thing in the world. It is through focusing on precisely the intentional parts of the experience that I can gain knowledge both of the essential or necessary features of the act

(e. g. what belongs to perception as such) and the essential features of an intentional object (e. g. a perceived spatial object reveals itself in profiles). As Husserl writes:

> ... the intentional experience is consciousness of something [*Bewusstsein von etwas*], and it is so, according to its essence [*Wesen*] (e. g., as memory, as judgment, as will, and so forth). Hence, we can ask what essentially is to be said on the side of this 'of something.' (*Ideen* 174/202)

Among the most important contributions will be Husserl's recognition of key problems, including the 'manner of being of the noema, the way it "lies" in experience, the way one is supposed to be "conscious" of it' (*Ideen* 192/222).

In general, in this chapter, it should be noted that despite his mention of the intentional act or noesis, Husserl is primarily oriented towards the object side of the experience, namely, to the noema. He deliberately postpones discussion of the noesis to the chapters following. Furthermore, there is almost nothing in this chapter about the ego or "I" that somehow "lives in" and across the flow of *Erlebnisse*. (Husserl had already briefly discussed how the pure ego–which is itself without content–lives in the interwoven stream of experience at *Ideas* § 80) He does, however, make some remarks concerning "attention" (*Aufmerksamkeit*, § 92) in regard to intentional experience and the "radiating focus" (*Blickstrahl*) of the ego, about which we will have more to say later in our discussion.

Finally, it is in this chapter (§ 88) that Husserl makes use of his example–one of the few concrete examples in the whole of *Ideas*–of the perception of the blossoming apple tree in the garden that is often taken as paradigmatic for the understanding of the noema in general. Husserl's discussion of the apple tree has been interpreted in different ways. He seems to distinguish the "tree in actuality" (*Baum der Wirklichkeit*, see § 97), "the tree simply, the thing in nature" (*Der Baum schlechthin, das Ding in der Natur*, *Ideen* 176/205) and the noema "tree". He compounds this by saying (at § 89) that the actual tree can burn up whereas the sense (*Sinn*) "tree" cannot. This has led to an understanding of the noema as a kind of ideal entity (a Fregean sense which is an abstract ideal object which acts to determine the reference of a thought) whose only relation to the actuality is that the latter instantiates it.[3] Husserl does think that the ideal sense (*Sinn*) is

---

[3] The classic discussion of noema as a Fregean sense (*Sinn*) is to be found in Føllesdal 1990. There is now a huge literature on this topic, see *inter alia* Smith/McIntyre 1982; McIntyre 1987; Welton 1987; Sokolowski 1987; Drummond 1990; and especially the essays in Drummond/Embree 1992. See also John Drummond's contribution in this volume.

one component of the noema, the "noematic core", which guarantees sameness of reference across different thoughts of the same entity, but this identical sense is not identical with the noema as a whole. It is at best one layer (*Schicht*) of the noema. We shall examine Husserl's somewhat ambiguous statements about the noema further in this paper.

To set this chapter in context, Chapter Three follows on from two earlier chapters in the Third Section. Section Three Chapter One (§§ 63–75) reviews the phenomenological method, the self-suspension (§ 63) of the phenomenologist's natural attitude and the adoption of pure description of whatever is given in immanence (§ 65), the nature of intuition, clarification the degrees of givenness (*Gegebenheit* § 67), vagueness and clarity (§ 68), the nature of intuitions of essence (*Wesensschau*; *Wesensintuition* § 67), the notion of free fantasy variation (§ 70), the nature of the 'eidetic sciences' (§ 72), and the difference between exact and morphological essences, exact and inexact description. Chapter Two (§§ 76–86), entitled "Universal Structures of Pure Consciousness", develops further the concept of pure phenomenological reflection, the differences between such reflection and psychological introspection (§ 79), the nature of the pure ego (§ 80), time and time-consciousness (§ 81), the nature of horizons (§ 82) on mental processes, intentionality (§ 84), *hyle* and *morphé* (§ 85), and the nature of "function" (in relation to a brief discussion of one of Husserl's former teachers, the descriptive psychologist Carl Stumpf, 1848–1936). Both these chapters cover many of the main themes of the phenomenological method and there is a degree of repetition and moving in "zig-zag", as is Husserl's wont, going backwards and forwards over the same areas but uncovering new insights. The introduction of the noesis-noema structure in Chapter Three, however, opens up an entirely new way of doing phenomenology, one that will be retained by the mature Husserl in his later works. Husserl's new terminology is meant to clarity and belong exclusively within the phenomenological sphere. For this reason, the noesis-noema correlation cannot be simply taken as equivalent to the act-object or psychic-physical distinction in Brentano's analysis of intentionality. Indeed Husserl himself says that what he trying to get at is not what is available "in the natural attitude" (*in die natürlichen Einstellung*, *Ideen* 175/203).

Chapter Three on "Noesis and Noema" is, therefore, in many respects, a revolutionary chapter. Although it is interwoven with the other themes being investigated in the book, and in fact, in several places explicitly refers back to the *Logical Investigations*, which Husserl was revising at the same time, the chapter has a stand-alone quality and presents in condensed form many of the themes of *Ideas* overall. There is an explicit and important rethinking of intentionality as discussed in the *Logical Investigations*, with reference, in particular, to the Fifth Investigation (especially § 16). The chapter does refer back to the earlier discussion of intentionality in Section Three Chapter Two, where he discusses intentionality as "the main theme [*Hauptthema*] of phenomenology" (*Ideen* 161/187). His earlier "eidetic analysis" of *Ideas* Section Two concerning cogitation as act has now to be revisited.

Husserl emphasizes at this stage that it is not at all clear how phenomenological investigations align with ontological or other investigations of consciousness. It is not a case of "simply" performing the phenomenological reduction. Perhaps even more than in the case of perception, as he discusses later in the chapter, the case of judgment requires one to sharply distinguish between the *psychological* process of judging and judging considered in its essence, where normally one focuses on the judgment itself, i.e. what is judged which is a universal:

> Those of a psychologistic bent will take exception here throughout; they are already disinclined to distinguish between judging as an empirical experience [*Urteilen als empirischem Erlebnis*] and judgment as an 'idea,' as an essence [*Urteil als 'Idee', als Wesen*]. For us this distinction no longer requires any justification (*Ideen* 187/217)

Husserl is here expressing his agreement with the anti-psychologistic views of Bolzano and Frege. As Husserl had insisted already in the *Prolegomena* to the *Logical Investigations*, logic is not in any way interested in the psychological process but only in the judgment understood as a proposition, a statement. But now Husserl wants to move beyond both psychology and logic. He even allows himself a rare biographical remark right at the outset in *Ideas* § 87:

> In fact (if I may be allowed a judgment based on my own experience), it is a long and thorny path that leads from purely logical insights, from insights into the theory of meaning, from ontological and noetic insights, likewise from the usual normative and psychological epistemology to the apprehension of immanently-psychological [*immanent-psychologischen*] and then phenomenological givennesses [*phänomenologischen Gegebenheiten*] in the genuine sense, and leads finally to all the essential connections [*Wesenszusammenhängen*] that render transcendental relations [*transzendentalen Beziehungen*] intelligible to us a priori. (*Ideen* 172–73/201)

As the last sentence here makes clear Husserl wants to uncover a priori essential relations and connections, which as we have seen, he now also designates as "transcendental" relations. As he puts it, at the beginning of § 92, he has identified

> ... remarkable changes in consciousness [*Bewusstseinswandlungen*] that crisscross [*kreuzen*] with all other kinds of intentional occurrences, and thus make up a completely universal

structure of consciousness [*eine ganz allgemeine Bewußtseinsstruktur*], a structure with its own dimension. (*Ideen* 182/211)

Husserl now wants more precisely to investigate the essential structure of intentional experiences, including the key forms–perception, willing, emoting, valuing or judging–experiences delineated in essence, or as Husserl says 'as an 'Idea" (*als Idee, Ideen* 187/217) or '*as eidos*' (*Ideen* 187/217).

While the term "noema" is new in *Ideas*, Husserl had already been using the term 'noetic' from much earlier. The term "noetic" occurs already in the *Logical Investigations* (Husserl 2001a, § 32), for instance, and there is a longer discussion of "noetics" as a science of cognitive acts in the 1906/07 lectures on *Logic and the Theory of Knowledge* (Husserl 2008, §§ 25–33). In *Ideas* § 94 Husserl also speaks of "normative, logical noetics" which is consistent with what he says in 1907. However, what exactly is meant by noetics is not entirely clear, but Husserl is insistent that a phenomenological approach will look at the whole noetic/noematic complex rather than solely at the noetic operations and ideal senses with which logic is concerned.

Developing from the discussion of intentional content in the Fifth Logical Investigation, in *Ideas* § 88 Husserl introduces the noema and seeks to identify the "components of the lived experience" (*Erlebniskomponenten*). He begins with a fundamental distinction between the "components proper" and the "intentional correlates" of the experience. This time he speaks of the "real" (*reelle*) components as precisely those "parts and moments" that the *Erlebnis* may be said to have. Husserl uses the term "moment" for a non-independent part. In the First Edition of the *Logical Investigations* (1901) Husserl speaks of the *real* (*reell*) and the *ideal* content, but in the Second Edition of 1913, which he was working on at the same time as he was writing *Ideas*, the distinction is recast as the distinction between *phenomenological* and *intentional* content (Husserl 2001b, § 16). In the First Edition of the *Logical Investigations* Husserl writes:

> By the real phenomenological content of an act we mean the sum total of its concrete or abstract parts, in other words, the sum total of the *partial experiences* that really constitute it. (Husserl 2001b, p. 112).

In this Second Edition reformulation, Husserl has moved from considering the 'real' psychological state, understood as a psychic occurrence that takes place in time, to a consideration of the reduced state considered in isolation from all reality or actuality. This will enable him to focus on the essential attributes of this experience.

Husserl's overall aim is to provide an a priori essential analysis of the structure of the intentional *experience (Erlebnis)*. He is seeking to capture at least some of the essential (or eidetic), a priori laws that govern the temporal flow of conscious experiences and account for their ability to intertwine and interweave with one another in the seamless flow of a unified conscious life. Already in § 80 Husserl had noted the "two-sidedness" of an *Erlebnis*-it has a subjective and an objective side. These will now be renamed noesis and noema.

With the doctrine of intentionality of conscious experiences, Husserl is interested in the constitution of objectivity and in the manner in which objects, their properties and contexts (horizons), manifest themselves in the flow and maintain their stability across changing mental states and attitudes. Of course, here he is explicitly operating under the phenomenological reduction and is not interested in psychological information about the "psychic act" [in quotation marks] and also the object in a transcendent sense. He is interested as he says in "'objectivity meant as such", the objectivity in quotation marks' (*die "vermeinte Objektivität als solche", die Objektivität in Anführungszeichen, Ideen* 185/215). He is interested in "the essential question" (*die Wesensfrage*), namely, what is the "perceived as such"? (*das "Wahrgenommene als solches, Ideen* 176/205). The perceived as such is identified with the noema of the act of perception. Husserl is also interested in the nature of the intentional relation. He will try to separate the intentional relation to an object from the real causal relation.

Throughout this chapter Husserl progressively identifies and specifies a number of the eidetic laws governing the intentionality of conscious lived experiences:

> Every intentional experience is noetic, thanks precisely to its inherent noetic moments. (*Ideen* 174/202)

In other words every mental act or state is marked out as what it is–is defined essentially–by the noetic side of that state. Something is a perception, a remembering, a fantasizing, and so on, precisely because of this immanent noetic character. This is an ineliminable part of every experience. Secondly, it belongs to the essence of a lived experience "to have a sense" (§ 88). Husserl thus articulates a second eidetic law:

> Like perception, *every* intentional experience has its 'intentional object,' i.e., its objective sense–that is precisely what makes up the fundamental component [*Grundstück*] of intentionality. (*Ideen* 177/206)

He will elaborate other eidetic laws throughout the chapter:

> There is no inherent noetic aspect without an inherent noematic aspect specifically pertaining to it–so reads the essential law that is corroborated in every case. (Ideen 185/215)

Husserl does subscribe to another eidetic law that he does not articulate here but which was already stressed in the *Logical Investigations,* namely, that each *Erlebnis* has a single if multilayered noema. There is, so to speak, always a single state of affairs aimed at in the intention, perhaps a very complex one, intended by a single and perhaps very complex noesis. The "sense" of an experience is always a unified nexus or complex.

Husserl is clear that the various transformations that go on in consciousness are "never contingent, but instead essentially rule-governed" (§ 91). Furthermore, different kinds of acts have different correlated noemata. The noemata vary structurally with the acts. So a perceptual noema is necessarily different from a memory noema, although the memory noema will in some sense be dependent on the perceptual noema. Husserl writes:

> A noematic sense 'inhabits' each of these experiences, and however much this sense may be related in the diverse experiences, indeed, however essentially alike it may be in terms of its core composition [*Kernbestand*], in experiences of different kinds it is a noematic sense of a different kind in each case. (*Ideen* 181/210)

Another eidetic law, always assumed by Husserl and articulated explicitly earlier in *Ideas* (see § 42, for instance, where he says that every experience can seize itself in an inner perception) is that every conscious process can reflect on itself and apprehend its constituent moments. Husserl writes regarding experiences (or cogitations):

> The intrinsic possibility of a '*reflective*' *shift of focus* is an essential property of it, and naturally [this is] a shift of focus in the form of a new cogitatio that is directed at it in the manner of simply apprehending it. (*Ideen* 66/77)

Similarly in Section Three Chapter Four Husserl says:

> At first place, every experience is so fashioned that it is possible in principle to shift the focus to it and its really obtaining components [*seinen reellen Komponenten*], and likewise in the opposite direction to the noema, e.g. to the seen tree as such. (*Ideen* 198/229)

It is crucial that Husserl thinks it is possible not just for an experience to become, as it were, self-transparent or self-conscious, but also that our direction of attention can be altered at will to traverse the experience from the subjective towards the objective side, e.g. from scrutiny of the act of remembering to the event remembered. We can also take the attentional focus outside of the experience altogether–as is normal in the natural attitude (introduced at § 27)-and simply focus on the things transcendent to our intuiting of them. Nevertheless, it is the reflective apprehension of experience that allows for the possibility of disciplined phenomenological reflection in the full technical sense that Husserl is promoting.

In analyzing the structure of perception, Husserl does acknowledge that there is what he calls in *Ideas* § 88 a "real relation" (*ein reales Verhältnis*, *Ideen* 175/204)–presumably a causal relation–between the seeing and the object seen, between the act of perceiving (*die Wahrnehmung*) and the object perceived as such (*das Wahrgenommene als Solche*), but in the "phenomenological attitude" (*Ideen* 176/205) one takes no interest in this real relation. The relation as real is bracketed or excluded: "the real relation that actually obtains between perception and what is perceived is suspended" (*ausgeschaltet*, *Ideen* 175/204). Instead, Husserl attends specifically to "the phenomenologically reduced experiences of perception and enjoyment, just as they fit in the transcendental stream of experience" (*der transzendentale Erlebnisstrom*, *Ideen* 175–76/204). A new concept has been introduced here–the "transcendental stream of experience" which has to be grasped "in pure immanence" (*in "reiner Immanenz"*, *Ideen* 175/204). Husserl here means the stream of the experience as experienced in its first-personal way, with its own unique inner temporality, its sense of beginning and ending, its own internal structure and components, and so on, with every reference to the external world stripped away. The natural attitude, Husserl reminds us, has a certain view not only of objects in the natural world but of subjective experiences. *Erlebnisse* as natural events are essentially temporal events; they belong to the stream of experience and can be studied by psychology or possibly even by some kind of neurophysiology. The phenomenological focus, however, is on the individual lived experience (however that is to be defined, since in fact experiences are not sharply differentiated in the flow of consciousness) and the need to abide with it, staying loyal to what it gives precisely in the manner in which it gives itself. With meticulous carefulness one must pay attention to ensure nothing is inserted into the experience other than what is actually contained or lies in [*einlegen*] the essence of it, just exactly as it "lies" [*liegt*] therein (§ 96). Unfortunately, the language of "lying in" is somewhat misleading as it suggests that the objects of experience are embedded in the experiencing. Brentano too had spoken of the "indwelling" (*Einwohnen*) of the intentional content or object in the act, and this had led to an assumption that the intentional object is immanent in the act, whereas Husserl means precisely the opposite.

As we have seen, focusing on the phenomenologically reduced *Erlebnis* involves a disruption of the natural "direction" (*Richtung*) of attention that is usually toward the intentional object of experience. This leads Husserl in this chapter to offer some remarks on the nature of "attention" (*Aufmerksamkeit*)–a topic to which he devoted many reflections over the years (see Husserl 2005). In the natural attitude, one's focus is normally outwards towards the transcendent, one's everyday dealings in the world. Using Husserl's own example, one attends to the blossoming apple tree (*der blühende Apfelbaum*) and not primarily to one's perceiving with pleasure, although the observer is basking in the pleasurable viewing. Even in ordinary natural attitude reflection, one can shift attention to the felt qualitative character of the perceiving. I can say that I am looking *dreamily* or *wistfully* or *admiringly* or *questioningly* at the apple tree. So it is not just the object that, as it were, visible in the natural attitude, the mode or manner of perceiving is also manifest. Normally we do not separate these kinds of givenness and our natural attitude can focus back and forward across the experience, which, as we see from § 97, is conceived of as an extended temporal process, a process that takes time. One can enjoy the apple tree in its brilliant blossoming and also, in a shift of focus, savor the enjoyment (perhaps while aware of its fleeting nature). Indeed, even in his discussion of this famous example of seeing the apple tree in the garden, Husserl is also discussing seeing the apple tree in an appreciative way, basking in the vision of the apple tree, as it were. He speaks of "looking with enjoyment" (*wir blicken mit Wohlgefallen*) and of the "perception and the accompanying enjoyment" (*die Wahrnehmung und das begleitende Wohlgefallen*, *Ideen* 175/203).[4] So, it is not a case of simply looking in a neutral manner–although he does say he wants to remain "for simplicity" with straightforward perceiving. Husserl is deeply aware that all our conscious states are closely intertwined and interwoven and layered with other states. The phenomenological regard will pry the components apart and see how they are interrelated, what depends on what, and so on.

As he deepens the analysis, Husserl notes that the *Erlebnis* is suffused with a natural credence or belief-in-being, what he later will call *Seinsglaube*, that is a component of every intention in the natural attitude. This might be regarded as another eidetic law:

Every experience is characterized by a thesis or natural positing.

The mature Husserl will later speak of "belief in being" (*Seinsglaube*, see, e.g., *Cartesian Meditations* § 8) but this term does not occur in *Ideas*. He speaks here of a specific experience called a "thesis" (*Thesis*, § 31). In the natural attitude, we naïvely put credence in the actuality of our world and our experience in a "general positing" (*Ideen* § 30). The world is always already there in our expe-

---

4 The German term *Wohlgefallen* normally means "satisfaction, pleasure, enjoyment".

rience (§ 32), there for us, "on hand" (*vorhanden*), it is experienced as "actual" (*wirklich*).[5] Of course, not all experiences are thetic, but–and Husserl is not yet clear on this-in so far as experiences are formed in the natural attitude, they are suffused with this thetic character. In *Ideas*, furthermore, Husserl had not yet fully articulated the concept of the horizonality of our experience and of the world as a backdrop for all experience, but he does acknowledge that we take for granted an environment that exists for all (§ 29).[6] This general positing, moreover, does not disappear in the activity of switching to the phenomenological attitude. Nor is it distorted or changed into a different kind of noetic act such as doubting, presupposing or surmising (§ 31). Moreover, the "thesis" is not the judgmental act of positing existence, but a generalized assumption concerning actuality, something that suffuses the natural attitude at all times. This "thesis" remains what it is, but it now gets "modified" or "placed in brackets" and "put out of work". The thetic character or positing still belongs to the *Erlebnis* as an integral structural feature, but now our conscious noesis does not go down the line of endorsing it, of *living in acceptance*, as Husserl puts it. Husserl is explicit that "the thetic actuality is, indeed, not there for us in the way of a judgment" (*Die thetische Wirklichkeit ist ja urteilsmässig für uns nicht da*, Ideen 176/204), repeating what he had said in § 31. In other words, we now deliberately and as a matter of conscious decision, take a stance within the very *Erlebnis* itself–we do not externally sit in judgment on the *Erlebnis*, decide that the perception is in fact a hallucination or illusion, or whatever, we somehow shift focus within the *Erlebnis* itself and take it first as a phenomenon with its own structure and component parts, and also as a token of a type.

After the reduction, we find in the remembering the remembered as such, in expecting the expected as such, in the fictionalizing fantasy the fantasized as such. The key term here is "as such" (*als Solches*). We are moving to the sphere of the necessary and the a priori rather than the sphere of fact. We are uncovering essence.

Husserl's account of suspending the natural attitude through the "universal" *epoché* is actually more complex that many commentators realize. The "thesis" or "general positing" suffuses the whole natural attitude as we have seen, and it is also as it were a component feature of each experience. It seems that the *epoché* not just suspends the natural attitude but it, as it were, unplugs the be-

---

[5] As Sebastian Luft has pointed out in his contribution, Husserl does not define the "general thesis" in *Ideas* but it is really the assumption of the actuality of the world that pervades all experiencing in the natural attitude.
[6] Husserl does discuss the concept of "horizon" in relation to what is "co-given" in experience in Ideen § 44. For a useful discussion, see Geniusas 2012.

lieving-component in the reduced experience. A new form of reflection is brought to bear on the reduced experience. Husserl is not completely clear on the relation between the overall natural attitude (and its general thesis) and the phenomenologically reduced experience which has its internal thesis or credence suspended. It seems that the overall neutralization of the natural attitude has the effect of bracketing (without removing altogether) the belief-in-being of the experience itself.

Furthermore there are continuing "shifts" or "variations" in attention (§ 92), as Husserl calls them, going on which activate or de-activate certain qualities or aspects of the object and presumably also highlight or alter the noetic approaches to the object. One can be perceiving the apple tree, and pay attention to the component memory of the apple tree, the quality of the memory. One can have various further reflective engagements with the experience: is it clear or confused, singular or mixed with other memories, and so on? Obviously, the application of the *epoché* onto an original experience (*Erlebnis*) actually itself involves a new experience that superimposes itself, alters, or modifies, or in some way marks out or indexes, the prior *Erlebnis*, in this case the visual perception of the blossoming tree. The exercise of the phenomenological *epoché*, furthermore, according to Husserl earlier (*Ideen* § 31), involves an act of deliberate willing, a will to resist the pull of the natural attitude. This act of willing is of course a new experience which is now brought to bear on the existing experience, e.g. the perceiving of the apple tree, so that one now sees without any interest in worldly actuality. One is not just seeing-in-credence, as it were, but performing a new act of *attending* to the original seeing, not now in natural reflection but in transcendental reflection, which involves a kind of schooled, hyper-vigilance that brackets all existence assumptions. Husserl's critics were skeptical that one could really effect such a complete bracketing of actuality, but Husserl himself always insisted it was an absolutely essential part of phenomenological viewing.

Husserl thinks of an *Erlebnis* not as an instantaneous act but rather as one that takes place over a period of time, and in the process, one can become aware of different aspects of our own awareness and start to consciously check them. Thus, Husserl makes clear, the "fixing of attention" is inherent in the *Erlebnis* (§ 92). Husserl seems to think that suspending the thesis or credential component of the experience enables one to scrutinize it better from the point of view of sustained reflection. Consider the case of someone aiming a rifle at a target and looking through the telescopic sights and as they observe the target, they become conscious perhaps that their handgrip is too tight or that their breathing will disrupt the shot, and so they make conscious alterations of bodily stance [not just physical adjustments but possibly "psychic" or mental changes e.g. allowing the mind to empty, consciously relaxing, and so on]. In this case, the act of paying attention and concentration allows for a certain reviewing of component mental acts. Something like this is what the phenomenological *epoché* is supposed to provide. It is, to use another analogy, like the manner in which, in Zen sitting meditation, the meditator proposes to attend to the experience but not engage with it, simply notice it, note it, and pass on. One should avoid deliberately seeking to banish the intruding thought, end the reverie or whatever. One should simply abstain, not be drawn into it, or be drawn to resist it. Husserl, similarly, wants the meditating phenomenologist to disengage the general positing in order to bring the focus completely to the necessary structures in play in the what he calls the "transcendental stream". This new kind of modified attention that is alert to its own "shifts in attention" as well as to the "parts and components" of the experience, is what will be worked in the rest of Chapter Three.

This reflective modification of the experience in the phenomenological *epoché* is meant to bring both the nature of the noesis and its accompanying noema to light. Moreover, this new modified attending is supposed to bring to light the necessary a priori "correlation" between noesis and noema, Husserl's new terminology, introduced in this Chapter Three. Husserl has chosen the term "noesis" precisely to avoid necessarily being drawn into evoking familiar psychic episodes that may be picked out linguistically with terms such as 'seeing', 'believing', 'hoping' and so on. It is, I suggest, precisely for the same reason that the "neutrality modification" is introduced as a more general term than any skeptical doubting, putting into suspension, disbelieving, negating and so on, in Chapter Four § 109.

As we said above, Husserl does not concentrate on the noetic dimension of experience in this chapter but he does have some observations that are worth noting. He speaks of the experience "viewed from the noetic side" as containing certain "noeses" that are conditioned by "modes of attentiveness" (*Ideen* 184/213–14). In fact, at § 92, he says that he is concentrating on the intentional layer of perception "for simplicity" but recognizes that noeses have much more complex forms. Most of the focus from then on in the chapter is on "describing the perception in a noematic respect." In this regard he believes the analysis in the *Logical Investigations* had been too concentrated on the noetic side. As we shall see, various dimensions will be discovered in the intentional experience as analyzed under the *epoché*. The noetic moments in the experience will be distinguished from the "hyletic aspects" (*hyletische Momente*), for instance (see *Ideas* § 98). Husserl sought to clarify the meaning of noesis in an additional supplement collected in Husserl 1976. Thus, in Supplement 51 (written around 1923), he comments on his use of the phrase "noetical moments" or "noetic aspects" (*Ideen* 191/221)

> It was not until page 199 [*Ideen* 199/221] that it is said in passing that 'Noesis' means pretty much the 'complete concrete intentional experience' while 'emphasizing its specific noetic moments'. To noesis therefore also belong the hyletic moments in so far as they carry the functions of intentionality, experience meaning-bestowal [*Sinngebung*], help to constitute a concrete noematic sense. But it must be said earlier with appropriate solemnity. I myself came to waver, since earlier noetic and hyletic moments were distinguished. (Husserl 1976, p. 606)

There are a myriad of noeses—distinguishing the various shadings of the "act" part of the experiences–that can sit on top of one another, run parallel with one another, conflict with one another or modify each other in various ways. And much of this will be discussed in the following Chapter Four. However, already in Chapter Three, Husserl recognizes that memories can be accessed within memories (§ 92). One can remember from one memory through to an earlier memory which itself is founded on a perception. Many of the noeses have names in English and other languages, thus we can distinguish (although not perhaps very exactly) wondering, pondering, deliberating, mulling over, musing, ruminating, and so on. But Husserl also thinks he has identified new noetic phases and moments that have never before been identified (e.g. the neutrality modification).

The notion of what belongs precisely to the noetic is somewhat complex. It is clear that Husserl thinks that the hyletic moments belong to the noetic act rather than to the noema (which of course also contains intended sensuous properties)–and in fact that is consistent with what Brentano says, albeit confusingly, in his *Psychology from an Empirical Standpoint*, when he speaks of "seeing a color" as belonging to the "psychic act" rather than being one of the "physical phenomena". In the following Chapter Four Husserl will more clearly locate the hyletic moments (the 'stuff' moments, the sensed colors) in the noetic side of the experience, whereas the color attributed to the object is located in the noema:

> ... *everything hyletic* belongs in the concrete experience as a *really obtaining* integral part [*als reelles Bestandstück*] of it, while what 'displays' and 'profiles' itself in it as a manifold belongs, by contrast, to the noema. (*Ideen* 196/227)

But even these sensuous "stuffs", as Husserl inelegantly calls them, are animated or enlivened (*beseelt*) with noetic aspects even while the ego is not turned to them but to the intentional objects. These 'animating construals' belong to the really immanent aspect of the noesis. On the other hand the "profiles" or "shadings" (*Abschattungen*) belong to the object side or the noema. They are noematic aspects, indicating aspects of the intentional object.

How do we discover the essential laws that govern how these noeses intertwine? Husserl is very careful to disentangle essentially different acts that may be found together. Thus he is concerned not to allow a kind of fantasy representation to be admitted to the perceptual process. Perception must not be confused with any other kind of representation—otherwise it is representations all the way down—repeats an argument already put forward in *Logical Investigations* and in his 1907 lectures of *Thing and Space* (Husserl 1997). If a perceiving was composed of both a filled intuition of the presented side of the object along with an "empty intending" (*Leermeinen*) of the co-meant but sensuously empty or unfilled other sides of the object, and if this latter *Leermeinen* were interpreted as a fantasy, then we would never be able to grasp the essence of perceiving as such. Fantasy can, of course, become involved but this involves a new imposition onto the original perception, enabled by that perception and founded on it. Because fantasy in turn is considered as a modification of a perceiving, we cannot then explain perceiving as essentially involving a fantasy-component. So the only upshot is that we have to recognize within the act of perception, different entangled noeses—one that presents in sensuous fullness the front-side "profile" or "shading" (*Abschattung*) of the object, and another "re-presentation" or "envisaging" (*Vergegenwärtigung*) that is explicitly not a fantasy, imagining or picturing (which would have its own fantasy colors, etc.). Husserl speaks here explicitly of "modes of indeterminate suggestion and non-intuitive co-presence" (*Modi unbestimmter Andeutung und unanschaulicher Mitgegenwärtigung, Ideen* 183/212) that are wrapped up in the experience. These will later understood as the horizons which necessarily belong to any experience.

With regard to the intentional object of an experience, Husserl recognizes that there can be the same intended object shared across different perceivings, imaginings, etc., of the same thing. But in fact although one has the sense of the object as the same, the phenomenology is more complicated and "noematic correlates are ... essentially different for perception, phantasy, pictorial envisaging, remembering, and so forth" (*Ideen* 181/210). There is a unique and specific sense belonging to each act: "*sense of a perception*, the *sense of a fantasy*, the *sense of a memory*—and that we find as *necessarily pertaining to them in correlation to the relevant kinds of noetic experiences*" (*Ideen* 181/210). In this chapter, Husserl is not completely clear on the nature of the noema and the manner in which it relates to the identical ideal sense it contains or supports in some way. Husserl speaks of a "noematic core" (*Kern*), that guarantees that is the same object that is being experienced under different noeses. But there is also a "noetic core" (§ 92). The ego's focal ray (*Blickstrahl*) can penetrate several strata of noetic acts e. g. remembering an earlier act of remembering, but there is—Husserl always insists—something that unifies the experience as a whole.

In the previous chapter § 85, on the "sensuous *hyle*, intentive *morphe*", Husserl had made some remarks on the need for terminology and here the notion of "noesis" (German: *Noese* and 'noeses' in the plural) is introduced to replace words like "moments of consciousness", "awarenesses" (*Bewussheiten*) (*Ideen* 167/194). He writes:

> These noeses make up the specific character of *'nous' in the widest sense* of the word; leading us back, in terms of all its current actualized forms of life, to cogitations, and then to intentional experiences in general. Hence it encompasses everything that is (and essentially only what is) an *eidetic presupposition of the idea of a norm*. At the same time, it is not unwelcome that the word 'nous' calls to mind one of its pre-eminent meanings, namely precisely *'sense,'* although the 'affordance of sense' [*Sinngebung*] that is achieved in the inherent noetic aspects encompasses many sorts of things, and only as a foundation is it an 'affordance of sense' that is connected to the precise concept of sense. (*Ideen* 167/194)

This is in many ways peculiar—Husserl claims that the Greek *nous* (νοῦς) has a connection with 'sense' (*Sinn*) whereas it is more usually understood as 'mind' or 'intellect' and '*noein*' as 'understanding'. In fact, 'nous' or the 'noetic' is now put forward as a more accurate way of identifying the processes which Brentano somewhat misleadingly called 'psychic'. Husserl concludes by saying that "*the stream of phenomenological being* [*Der Strom der psychologischen Seins*] *has a material layer and a noetic layer* [*Schicht*]" (*Ideen* 168/196). He also acknowledges that he had earlier failed to distinguish these two strata clearly.

The noetic is returned to in Part III Chapter 3 in Section 88 where Husserl says that "every intentional experience is noetic thanks precisely to its inherent noetic aspects. It is its essence to contain in itself something like a "sense"... (*Ideen* 174/202). Something noetic is something oriented towards sense (in some meaning of sense: incuding the sensuous). Husserl is still retaining the language of "noetic aspects" or "moments" and he is suggesting they are best understood as "focal rays" or radiations of the ego. What is somewhat unfortunate is that the notion of noetic aspects is not analyzed in detail at this point. These noeses occur in strata at lower and higher levels. In fact, there is very little further about noesis in this chapter. Husserl is more interested in the components that can be found in the full concrete experience. Sometimes, however, he is interested in the purely noetic components and here especially the so-called "mental focus" (*geistiges Blick*) of the ego is singled out (see § 92).

Husserl is not very happy with mental focus being identified with "attention" since the term is vague in psychological discourse and what is phenomenologically pertinent has not been singled out. "We tend to compare attention with a light that illuminates things" (*mit einem erhellende Lichte*, *Ideen* 183/213), he complains. On the other hand, his own account does not seem to get away from this spotlight metaphor. Husserl speaks here of a "phenomenology of attention" (*Phänomenologie der Aufmerksamkeit*, § 92–also invoked earlier in the *Logical Investigations*) and notes that is one of the chief themes of modern psychology but claims that psychology has misunderstood it and not seen it as a "fundamental form of intentional modification". Husserl insists attention is a fundamental and irreducible form of intentionality distinct from other forms of intuition such as perception. It is not just a component within an existing act but rather an act of a new kind. Furthermore–and this is an important point–attention does not focus solely on the subjective contents of the act (e.g. becoming more aware of the perceiving) but can traverse across all aspects of the original act and its object. Furthermore, Husserl wants primarily to stress that there are specific "shifts in attention" (*attentionalen Wandlungen*, *Ideen* 182/210), not just in actual variations in attention but ideal possible variations. The nature of attention is complex, and there are different modifications possible in terms of the amount of attention being paid, right to the limit case of inattention where the perceived or remembered object is barely present, present in a dead kind of way that does not awaken anything.

Husserl is also aware that in the varying aspects of perceiving as my eyes linger on the object different aspects come into focus and others recede into the background although they do not disappear altogether (§ 92). There are "modes of actualization" (*Aktualitätmodi*) and corresponding "modes of inactualization" (*Modus der Inaktualität*) in a kind of 'dead consciousness'. At this point Husserl makes an interesting but undeveloped remark about the place of the ego in the act of attending. In attending there is a beaming or radiating out from the ego–this is not separate from the ego–the ego-ray is the ego itself radiating:

> The radiating is not separated from the ego, but instead itself is and remains the ego radiating (*Der Strahl trennt sich nicht vom Ich, sondern ist selbst und bleibt Ichstrahl*, *Ideen* 184/214)

Is this another eidetic truth? Husserl describes the ego as living in its acts, not as a content of experience (he agreed with Natorp here) but as the experience of a streaming, radiating, intending and suffering life (§ 92).

Husserl does not develop his phenomenology of attention here. He acknowledges that attention did receive a preliminary treatment in the *Logical Investigations*, especially in Second Logical Investigation § 22 and also in the Fifth Logical Investigation § 19.

In the Fifth Logical Investigation § 19 Husserl repudiates the claim that attention is a special act that picks out only the 'content' of the subjective act rather than being focused or absorbed in the object of the act. Husserl thinks attending is a new character of act. Revisiting the discussion of expression in the First Logical Investigation, he here gives the example of listening to a spoken expression. He says we say the words and attend to the meanings and we can of course attend to the sounds specifically in themselves but then the meaning is lost. This attending to the sounds is not actually a component act of the original listening to the meaning but a new intentional act with a new object: "*Attention is an emphatic function which belongs among acts*" (Husserl 2001b, p. 118). More or less the same view is articulated in *Ideas* Chapter Three: attention is a new and irreducible form of intentionality.

In Husserl first discussion of attention in the Second Logical Investigation § 22, entitled "Fundamental deficiencies in the phenomenological analysis of attention", Husserl distinguishes selective attention from abstraction in the course of criticizing traditional empiricist (Locke, Berkeley, Hume) accounts of abstraction as a selective focusing on part of the individual content of an experience. Here he criticizes the "Lockean prejudice" according to which attention picks out the mental contents of the experience but locates them in the subject so that seeing a green tree is interpreted as having a sensation of green:

> Unthinkingly one credits to *contents* everything which acts, in their straightforward reference, place in the *object;* its attributes, its colors, forms etc., are forthwith called 'contents' and actually interpreted as contents in the psychological sense, e.g. as sensations. (Husserl 2001a, p. 273)

He continues:

> Led astray by the seemingly obvious, one takes experienced contents to be the normal objects to which one pays attention. The concrete phenomenal thing is treated as a complex of contents, i.e. of attributes grown together in a single intuitive image. And it is then said of these attributes, taken as experienced mental contents, that their non-independence precludes their separation from the concretely complete image: they can only be noticed in the latter. How could such a theory of abstraction intelligibly account for the formation of abstract ideas of that class of attributive determinations which are indeed perceived, but which by their nature never are adequately perceived, which cannot be given in the form of a mental content? (Husserl 2001a, p. 273)

This is an important point. Attention (and a mistaken understanding of psychological reflection) has assumed that the intentional object is actually a collection or complex of psychic contents each of which can be focused on. This precisely misconstrues the intentional structure of the experience and the role of the hyletic stuff in portraying on conveying the sensuous properties of the object.

Let us now examine more closely Husserl's concept of noema as introduced in this chapter. That everything somehow has a kind of sense, that 'makes sense' to the subject or ego, is the fundamental intentional starting-point. Everything that is manifest in consciousness has some kind of coherent sense. Each *phase* of the experience also has a sense and here we have to think of sense in some sort of component feature, perhaps like phonemes in the constitution of languages. There is, moreover, a number of threads of unity running across the experiences. The object is experienced first and foremost as the same object given through different profiles and also apprehended in different noeses. They are all experiences *of the apple tree blossoming in the garden.* At the same time the noeses themselves are coordinated in a rigorous manner and 'crisscross' each other in very specific and determinately ordered ways. There are a number of noetic elements that come together and are united around a 'noetic core'. This is equally important as the 'noematic core' that guarantees the sameness of the object. The hyletic aspects belong to this noetic core but are different from the noetic aspects also in that core.[7]

Husserl is aware that the object has an identity in and through these manifestations. The hyletic data furthermore do not determine or anchor this identity. For example, I can talk to John on the phone [aural data] and see John on the street (without hearing him)–visual data. The visual and aural data are entirely different clusters of data–yet they are both *appearings of the same John.* Furthermore, John is not some ideal limit at the end of an infinite series of such experiences but present in each of them yet not in a static or immanentist manner. The hyletic data–although they do, for Husserl, anchor the intentional function, as Husserl says–at the same time underdetermine the intentional object. There can be no perception as a perception without hyletic sensory experiencings. That is what makes perception perception. Yet the perception of the intentional object as such is an achievement that goes well beyond and is essentially different from the experiencing of hyletic contents.

Husserl often says that noematic content or noema in a perceptual experience is "the perceived as perceived". He also calls it "the noematic correlate" or the "objective sense":

> We may notice by this means that, within the noema *in its entirety* (indeed, as we had announced at the outset), we have to sort out *essentially diverse layers* [wesentlich verschie-

---

[7] For the relation of the hyletic moments to the act quality of the experience, see the contribution of John J. Drummond in this volume.

dene Schichten] that group around a *central 'core,'* [*um einen zentralen 'Kern'*] around the pure *'objective sense'* (*um den puren 'gegenständlichen Sinn'*, Ideen 181/210)

The core is the purely objective 'sense'; the sense that remains the same, when we perceive, remember or think about the same object. This noematic core has to be stable across different noeses that take different stances or attitudes (perceiving, imagining, remembering) towards the intended object. But how could this core sense be grasped–is it 'John', as it were, in my example of speaking on the phone, or 'the blossoming apple tree'–abstracted from the fact that it is seen from this or that side? This discussion of the apple tree as such (*der Apferbaum schlechthin*) is already ambiguous. Husserl means the transcendent apple tree, the 'real' tree as it were. This tree has real properties including the property of combustability. The tree does not lose any 'nuance' of its meaning and the perceiving and liking remains perceiving and liking. In attending to this we describe perception in its noematic aspect.

The problem in this Section is to identify the noema distinction without postulating an internal object that is different from the transcendent actual object. Perception cannot involve a depicting or else there is an infinite regress–with depiction explained in terms of perception and perception assuming depiction, and so on. Husserl here is distinguishing the kind of intentional indwelling of the intentional object from the imaginative depicting of an object. Husserl distinguishes the noema from the sense in this chapter, although he does say repeatedly that the noema is a sense. The sense does not exhaust the "full noema" (*Ideen* § 90). Furthermore, the noema can be uncovered only in the phenomenological or transcendental attitude (the two are equated in this chapter), whereas senses can be found in linguistics, logic and so on.

Husserl's discussion of the noema is unclear in this chapter because he does not really relate it to the intended object. Noemata do not survive–as it were–the withdrawal of the noetic act that supports them and to which they are correlated. They can be abstracted out or separated out but in this case one is simply focusing on one pole of the correlation. Noemata are not the same as senses. Furthermore, it is not necessarily the case that all noemata are expressible in linguistic terms. The peculiar experience of the quality of light filtering through the trees on an autumn day can perhaps be captured in painting or photography or in perception and memory–it has an undoubted sense–but there is no reason to think this sense is expressible in any natural or even ideal language.[8] We might have to

---

[8] Smith and McIntyre in their study articulate the 'expressibility' thesis, namely, that every noematic *Sinn* is in principle expressible in language. Furthermore even John J. Drummond supports

make up new words or simply refer to "component noetic moment no. 1" or whatever. If that is what expressibility means then, of course, it is possible. But I really think Husserl was more concerned with intuitive identification—we should be able—in suitable reflection—to recognize the peculiar operation of component noetic moment no. 1 and also be able to identify the specific function it is performing.

Husserl goes on to say that this does not affect the sense of what is being manifested but only the mode of its manifestation. "Changes of illumination" (*Beleuchtungswechsel*) do not alter the sense. But is this right? I can—in a case of vision—imagine that my car, seen under the dappled light of a street light that is shining through a screen of leaves from a nearby tree, will have a dappled appearance. Do I neglect this mode of actualization of the phenomenon? Is that even what he is talking about? What Husserl says is as follows:

> Obviously, the modifications in the noema thereby are not anything like merely external annexes that come to something that remains identical. Instead, the concrete noemata vary through and through; it is a matter of necessary modes in the manner of givenness [*Modi der Gegebenheitsweise*] of something identical. (*Ideen* 184/213)

The noema is not the same as the sense, because the noema changes under different noetic forms of attending, whereas the sense, as something ideal, remains constant across different noetic forms. Husserl will later in the book speak of the core of the noema as a "determinable X".

Husserl is claiming that there are very specific forms of attention that seem to belong essentially to certain noetic moments. This might be considered to be another eidetic law:

> Rather it is apparent, viewed from the noetic side, that certain noeses, whether it be a matter of necessity or their specific possibility, are conditioned by modes of attention and, in particular, by positive attention in the paradigmatic sense. (*Ideen* 184/213–4)

Thus a decision-taking has as a definite mode of actuality. Husserl clarifies with an interesting list of position takings such as decisions, denials, valuations, and resolving-to-do scenarios that have a definite modality of attention attaching to them:

---

it in a qualified way (Drummond 1990, pp. 127–30). Why should that be? It depends on what we mean by 'expressibility'—it is certainly the case that specific noetic moments may have no names in natural language.

> Every instance of 'carrying out, implementing an act,' 'actually [*aktuell*] taking a position,' for example, 'carrying out, implementing' [*Vollzug*] the process of resolving a doubt, rejecting something, positing a subject and attributing a predicate to it, or carrying out the process of making an evaluation [*Wertung*] and an evaluation 'for the sake of someone else,' the evaluation of a choice, and so forth–all that presupposes focusing attention positively on that toward which the ego takes a position [*wozu das Ich Stellung nimmt*]. *Ideen* 184/214)

In other words, it belongs to the noetic side of the essences of conscious acts that there is a certain attentional focus [*Aufmerksamkeit*] on the matter being decided, denied, evaluated, proposed. There is also a manner in which that matter is presented, whether it is being doubted and affirmed, willed, and so on.

Husserl passes from the consideration of perception to other acts and, specifically, judgment. He clearly distinguishes between judging as a psychological process and judgment as an ideal act (§ 94), citing Bolzano, whom he believes has not made this fully clear even with his notion of "judgment in itself". Although Husserl praises Bolzano highly in the *Logical Investigations* and especially in his Draft Introduction to the Second Edition, in this chapter he claims that Bolzano did not see that the judgment in itself has to understood from two different sides–has two different senses–depending on whether it is the noetic or the noematic moment that is being specified. As a logician he was interested narrowly in the noematic aspect of judging and did not see that the judging itself also had a specific character.

> Bolzano never saw that *two* intrinsically possible interpretations lie at hand here, both of which would need to be designated as 'judgment in itself': the specific character of the experience of judgment (the *noetic* idea) and the *noematic* idea correlative to it. (*Ideen* 188n. 33/218 n. 1)

Bolzano was interested solely in the idea or ideal sense, the proposition, expressed in the judgment. But, as Husserl points out, focusing on this idea is not yet phenomenology, which involves a relation to a subject. For that reason, logic and mathematics are eidetic sciences but not yet phenomenology. The noema that is focused on in logic is the noema devoid of its noetic element. Whereas, for Husserl, what is important is the essential correlation between noesis and noema.

In § 94, Husserl analyzes the nature of the noema in judgments of the form "S is P". What is judged–what he calls here the "content of the judgment"–is the proposition or thought that S is P. In this sense, Husserl says the noema of the judgment is "the judgment", i.e. the content of the judgment rather than that which is judged about:

> The judged [*Geurteilte*] is not to be confused with what the judgment is made about [*Beurteilte*]. (*Ideen* 186/216)

But considered phenomenologically a judgment has both noetic and noematic components and these are essentially correlated. The manner of the act of judging (declarative, putative, possible, made evidently, asserted blindly, and so on) directly affects and modifies the judgment made (the judgment noema). Husserl says that the the full noema, the judgment, must be actually taken here in its full concreteness in which there is consciousness of it in the concrete judging. Husserl says across different kinds of judging of the same judgment content, the 'noematic "What"' has to be the same, this is the noematic core, the element that guarantees different kinds of judgment are *about the same matter*.

For simplicity he excludes the verbal features of judgment, the grammatical features of the sentence (analysed by Bertrand Russell and others) in order to focus on the essential structure of the judgment as such. Husserl thinks the phenomenological analysis of judgment is interested in something more than logic. Logic is not interested in the full noema of the judgement, the "noema in its full composition" (*Noema in seinem vollen Bestand, Ideen* 187/218), but only in a certain aspect of this judgment noema, its abstract ideal sense. The phenomenological approach is interested in the manner in which the judgment is given, the "how of givenness". As Husserl points out

> Consider a judgment 'S is P,' made on the basis of evidence, and 'the same' judgment, blindly made. The two judgments are noematically diverse but identical in terms of a core of sense [*Sinneskern*] that is alone determining for the formal logical consideration. (*Ideen* 188/218)

The noema—understood as the logical noema—does not stand alone; it is not 'self-standing':

> The same 'S is P,' as *noematic core*, can be the '*content*' of a certainty, of a surmising of it as possible, or of a supposing, and so forth. The 'S is P' does not stand alone in the noema; instead, insofar as it is thought there as content, it is something not self-standing [*Unselbständiges*]. (*Ideen* 189/219)

This is an important point. If the noema is not something "self-standing" or "independent" then it cannot be conceived of as an ideal mind-independent abstract object in the manner of a Fregean sense. Husserl does not say in this chapter that the noema is particular or universal, it is a kind of meaning but a meaning which includes reference to the subjective point of view. This makes it a very peculiar kind of entity.

Having discussed first straightforward perception and then judgment, paragraph 95 focuses on emotional acts and acts of willing. Husserl simply wants to make the point that the noesis/noema correlation applies here also but with a different essential structure. A new layer is added to an intentional experience when the element or moment of "valuing" is introduced. Not only do we value something (i.e. perform an act of valuing or appreciating, correspondingly the valued object appears as valued, as appreciated. We can simply say, it is a valuable object, or as Husserl says "it introduces valuableness as a new objective layer". The intended object has the property not only of being actually valued now by someone but as being valuable, although this needs a great deal of further analysis.

As the chapter concludes Husserl has brought to light the essential correlation between noesis and noema. He has introduced the new concept of noema which is meant to cover all that is involved in "the perceived as such", "the judged as such", and he has also begun to recognize how differences in the noetic bring about changes in the noema. Only hinted at in this chapter is the complex manner in which sense-contents (what Husserl calls the "hyletic" contents) are actually part of the noetic character of the act. The object intended is characterized primarily as transcendent. In order for different noetic acts to be anchored to the same intentional object there must be a common "noematic core". These are all discoveries on which the discussions in Chapter Four will build. Much more will be said about the concept of noema.

Bibliography

Bernet, Rudolf (1990): "Husserls Begriff des Noema". In: Ijsseling, Samuel (ed.), *Husserl-Ausgabe und Husserl-Forschung*. The Hague: Nijhoff, pp. 61–80.
Drummond, John (1990): *Husserlian Intentionality and Non-Foundational Realism: Noema and Object*. Dordrecht: Kluwer.
Drummond, John/Embree, Lester (eds.) (1992): *The Phenomenology of the Noema*. Dordrecht: Springer.
Føllesdal, Dagfinn (1990): "Noema and Meaning in Husserl". In: *Philosophy and Phenomenological Research* 50, pp. 263–271.
Geniusas, Saulius (2012): *The Origins of the Horizon in Husserl's Phenomenology*. Dordrecht: Springer.
Husserl, Edmund (1976): "Ideen zu einer reinen Phänomenologie und phänomenologischen Philosophie. Erstes Buch: Allgemeine Einführung in die reine Phänomenologie. Zweiter Halbband: Ergänzende Texte (1912–1929)". In: *Husserliana*. Vol. III/2. The Hague: Nijhoff.
Husserl, Edmund (1987): "Vorlesungen über Bedeutungslehre, Sommersemester 1908". In: *Husserliana* Vol. XXVI. The Hague: Nijhoff.

Husserl, Edmund (1997): "Thing and Space: Lectures of 1907". In: *Husserl Collected Works* Vol. VII. Dordrecht: Kluwer.
Husserl, Edmund (2001a): *Logical Investigations*. Vol. 1. London/New York: Routledge.
Husserl, Edmund (2001b): *Logical Investigations*. Vol. 2. London/New York: Routledge.
Husserl, Edmund (2005): "Wahrnehmung und Aufmerksamkeit: Texte aus dem Nachlass (1893–1912)". In: *Husserliana* Vol. XXXVIII. Dordrecht: Springer.
Husserl, Edmund (2008): "Introduction to Logic and the Theory of Knowledge 1906/07". In: *Husserl Collected Works* Vol. XIII. Dordrecht: Springer.
McIntyre, Ronald (1987): "Husserl and Frege". In: *Journal of Philosophy* 84, pp. 528–535.
Smith, David Woodruff/McIntyre, Ronald (eds.) (1982): *Husserl and Intentionality: A Study of Mind, Meaning, and Language*. Dordrecht/Boston: Reidel.
Sokolowski, Robert (1987): "Husserl and Frege". In: *Journal of Philosophy* 84, pp. 523–528.
Welton, Donn (1987): "Frege and Husserl on Sense". In: *Journal of Philosophy* 84, pp. 535–536.

Nicolas de Warren
Concepts without pedigree: The noema and neutrality modification

Section III, chapter 4, On the problems of noetic-noematic structures

> "*Everything* is difficult."
> - Edmund Husserl

1. Phenomenological pedagogy

"On the problems of noetic-noematic structures," the heading for a sweeping set of paragraphs 97–127 in *Ideen I*, represents a central discussion for the inception of pure phenomenology and phenomenological philosophy. As Husserl states in § 84, "intentionality is the basic theme of objective oriented phenomenology." As the unique subject-matter of phenomenological inquiry and the principle acquisition of its method of *epoché* and reduction, intentionality essentially characterizes the "absolute region" of pure consciousness and its field of phenomenological structures. Before we enter into the depth and details of the noetic-noematic structures under consideration in these paragraphs, we do well to remind ourselves of Husserl's over-arching enterprise and ambition. In the paragraph immediately preceding (§ 96, appropriately titled "transition to subsequent chapters") this turn to "the problems of noetic-noematic structures," we find yet another occasion where Husserl reminds his readers of the spectacle unfolding before their eyes within the dense progression of *Ideen I*.

Husserl writes: "Phenomenology presents itself in our exposition as a science *that is commencing.* Only the future can instruct us on how many of the results of the analyses attempted here are ultimately valid" (*Ideen* 193/224). This emphasis on phenomenology as a commencing science (*anfangende Wissenschaft*) was first announced in the opening statement of the Introduction to the *Ideen*. As Husserl there proclaims: "Pure phenomenology is an essentially new science, one that, by virtue of its very distinctiveness, lies far afield of natural thinking and consequently presses now, for the first time, for development" (*Ideen* 3/3). From these very first lines, the reader and would-be phenomenological thinker is invited to participate in an unheralded enterprise, the significance of which is deemed pressing for our times, yet without any initial transparency regarding the direction and object of this adventure. This invitation to pure phenomenology is in truth an initiation to an original manner of thinking and new form of seeing (Husserl speaks of developing a "new intellectual eye"), and as such struggles against the inertia and inhibition of "all our previous habits of thinking." There is something unnaturally demanding with Husserl's enterprise, the difficulty of which cannot be fully anticipated or measured from the beginning. This implication of a fundamental ignorance as phenomenology's necessary point of departure is repeatedly signaled at key junctures in Husserl's text (much as with § 96 noted above), and becomes only gradually lifted and transformed over the arduous course of *Ideen I*. Such is the blindness with which phenomenology must begin as a philosophical Odyssey that even *after* the presentation of its change in attitude, suspension of the natural thesis, and deployment of its method of reduction, we still cannot discern clearly the true object of phenomenological inquiry. As Husserl remarks at the beginning (§ 76) of the section "Universal Structures of Pure Consciousness," "we have learned how to employ the phenomenological attitude; we have removed a series of erroneous reservations regarding method; we have defended the legitimacy of an unadulterated description. The field of research lies open. But we still do not know *what* the *major themes* in it are, more specifically, *what basic directions for description are prescribed by the most universal, essential division of experiences*" (*Ideen* 138/161). All of this gives pause to any hurried conclusion or decision as to what phenomenology is actually after–a question that 50 years after its first breakthrough, as Merleau-Ponty famously wrote in the Introduction to his *Phenomenology of Perception*, still remained open, and no less so for us today one hundred years after the publication of *Ideen I*.

These "major themes" of phenomenological research enter into clearer visibility under the general heading and discussion of noetic-noematic structures in §§ 97–127. But even here, on the very threshold of this entry, Husserl once again cautions his intrepid readers. As he writes: "Our way of proceeding is that of someone on a research trip in an unknown part of the world, who carefully describes what presents itself to him on its untraveled paths, paths that will not always be the shortest" (*Ideen* 193/224). The pathway of the *Ideen I* towards pure phenomenology and phenomenological philosophy is a "journey of exploration in an unknown part of the world." This critical metaphor expresses an underlying attitude without which the *aspiration* of phenomenology is not intelligible. With this attitude in mind, *Ideen I* can be seen as the *avant-garde* for a philosophical, that is, phenomenological modernism–where it is less the military provenance of the term that resonates as it is the meaning of an exploration to an unknown world; less the prospective triumphalism of conquest and more the wonder of cautious discovery.

Husserl's method of *epoché* and reduction opens onto a "new world," yet contrary to an overly literal rendering of the term "world," the world thus disclosed through phenomenological reflection is neither an alternative world to the world of experience nor a part of the world somehow hidden since the beginning of time, nor a world beyond–a metaphysical world of reverie. It is rather the world reclaimed for philosophical inquiry, approached and *thought* differently from the radical standpoint of phenomenological reflection and its defining transcendental orientation. If the general thesis of the natural attitude, as Husserl proposes, has obscured and inhibited *the possibility* of phenomenological thinking, phenomenology must consequently be initially received as an *impossibility*, and its is largely against this impossibility that Husserl's own struggle with the method of phenomenology itself struggles. The natural attitude is an imprisoning naiveté; it is neither a form of stupidity nor a metaphysical illusion, but an ignorance of its own ignorance, a kind of original forgetting of the naturalness of its own attitude towards the world as "being," or at all given with a sense of being, for our knowledge, action, and values. In this ignorance there is anchored a power of seeing that we take for granted, on the basis of which the regimes of human knowledge are established. The suspension of the natural attitude is thus equivalent to a self-inflicted *blindness*, but also, a disruption of inherited (philosophical) ways of speaking–an issue explicitly addressed by Husserl in the penultimate paragraphs of his Introduction. Most significantly–and here resides the *philosophical* force of Husserl's thinking–the methodological tandem of *epoché* and reduction places us in a fundamental situation of unknowing: we are led into an unfamiliar land with an acute awareness of our own map's incompleteness. As Husserl wonderfully remarks: the book itself–*Ideen I*– is this opening onto a new land.

Despite the outward appearances of a settled system of thinking, we are dealing in fact with an inward movement of exploration and exercise of mapping, where the main geographical features of this new philosophical landscape are mountains and ravines of problems. With the progression of Husserl's discussion (Husserl reports to Edith Stein that he wrote the *Ideen* in six weeks as if in a trance), markers are placed with which to signal *future* work on problems here freshly formulated. As Husserl states with conviction, the aim of *Ideen I* is not to solve the main problems of phenomenology, but to delineate them, to work them out from obscurity (*herauszuarbeiten*) (*Ideen* 286/333). Husserl speaks against the prevailing *Ideenfeindschaft* in philosophy and understands his own phenomenology as the institution of new *Ideenfreundschaft*, not, however, in any Platonic sense, as friend of Platonism or Platonic ideas, but in the spirit of *l'ami du concept*.

As Deleuze and Guattari propose, the history of philosophy can be divided into three ages of the concept: the age of the encyclopedia, the age of the formation of professional commercialism, and the age of pedagogy. In each age, the relation between philosophy and thinking (concept) is configured differently. Husserl's thinking in *Ideen I*, and elsewhere, does not turn on producing a universal encyclopedia of concepts nor does it succumb to the formation of pseudo-professionalism, i.e., academic commercialism – arguably the pervasive malaise of *our* contemporary thought that Husserl already perceived during his time. As Husserl alerts his readers in the Introduction, "basic concepts in philosophy cannot be pinned down in definitions by means of fixed concepts" (*Ideen* 7/9). Husserl's task with *Ideen I* is in one sense more modest that the desire for an encyclopedia of concepts and yet in another sense more challenging. It is the task of developing *une pédagogie du concept*. In my own way, I propose to approach *Ideen I* as a pedagogical treatise and to think of phenomenology as a pedagogy for thinking. Having said this, I do not think that the *Ideen I* is a text that calls for commentary or paraphrase, which would merely produce either an encyclopedia or professionalism of the concept at the expense of true pedagogy. Inherent to phenomenology as pedagogy is the risk of losing one's way as well as obscurity, but equally, the promise of genuine discovery and transformation. Husserl himself concludes the section in *Ideen I* just before §§ 97–127 by speaking of his explorations as *Wanderungen*. I shall follow suit and wander.[1]

1. Phenomenological invention

The strangeness (*Andersartigkeit*) of Husserl's phenomenological adventure is directly proportional to the kind of objects that phenomenological reflection discovers within its field of "pure" experience. To speak in the idiom of Husserl's critical-metaphor, the strangeness of phenomenology is a function of the strangeness of the creatures it observes. In a crucial sense, Husserl's method of reduction undoes the methodological achievement of Kant's Copernican Revolution. For if for Kant, the object must be determined, or prescribed, by the method (experience must stand before the tribunal of reason), for Husserl, the method must follow the object – reason stands before the tribunal of experience, i.e., the principle of all principles, intuition as the legitimating source of reason itself. As Husserl expresses this idea: "Method is, indeed, not something that has

---

[1] My discussion will therefore not survey exhaustively the full cluster of problems discussed in these paragraphs.

been, or needs to be, brought into a domain from the outside" (*Ideen* 138/161). Yet, the kind of experience salient for Husserl's phenomenology of reason–Husserl's genuine ambition–is not the kind of experience commonly passed about as the object of phenomenology currently understood, by which is widely (mis-)understood "first person point of view," "what it is like to be-conscious," *qualia*, and the like.[2] As Husserl signals in the first paragraph of the Introduction, phenomenology takes an interest in "phenomena"–in experience–from an entirely different attitude. The *sense* (*Sinn*) of phenomena becomes transformed against the sense firmly entrenched and familiar to us from the natural sciences and psychology.

Only two features of this novel sense in which experience enters into phenomenological consideration can be highlighted here. Through-out *Ideen I*, Husserl is unambiguous that pure consciousness, the object of phenomenological inquiry, circumscribes the essential properties of the sphere of experience as such (*Wesenseigentümlichkeit der Erlebnissphäre überhaupt*). Husserl repeatedly defines the task of phenomenological analysis as a descriptive investigation of the *structures* of pure consciousness, by which Husserl specifically understands *eidetic structures*. This stress on the essential structures of consciousness must be borne in mind, especially as a safe-guard against the present vogue of conceiving phenomenology as an analysis of "first person point of view." The operative concept in this regard is the phenomenological understanding of consciousness as a manifold, indeed, as Husserl envisions, as an "infinite field" of "eidetic manifolds" and "apriori forms of consciousness" (§ 63). The descriptions and distinctions presented in *Ideen I* are the results of an implicit process of eidetic variation, which, presumably, Husserl himself has performed, and which, by his own admission, trace an unfinished trajectory into the future that invites us as readers to participate.

These structures of intentionality are moreover not *inert*. As Husserl remarks (§ 63), we cannot simply reach into the field of phenomenological experience and grab willy-nilly objects by the hand, as one would do with rocks, plants, and other objects lying in a field for the taking. In this respect, Husserl's own comparison with an explorer who comes upon an undiscovered land is misleading since the objects of phenomenological discovery are not simply already there (already constituted) awaiting to be unveiled. What characterizes the concres-

---

[2] In the draft of a letter to an unknown correspondent from 1917/1918, Husserl speaks of noble profession of phenomenology as an investigation into the origins of reason and as the "sworn enemy against all phrases, all stupid prejudices, all ambiguity, all confusing passions" (*der geschworene Feind aller Phrase, aller dumpfen Vorurtheile, aller Unklarheiten, aller sinnverwirrenden Leidenschaften*) (A I 39/11b, 12b).

cence of the objects of phenomenological inquiry is a complex dynamic of structuration as enlivened problematics, as problems with a life of their own. The veritable objects of phenomenological inquiry must be constituted through phenomenological reflection and yet such objects are not the mere figments of such acts of reflection. As we shall recognize, Husserl's concept of the noema exemplifies this challenging sense of how phenomenological reflection discloses its objects of investigation. We also encounter here a fundamental feature of Husserl's thinking, namely, its uncompromising dedication to working *on* problems and the sense in which phenomenological research is measured by the capacity to generate new problems, or lend new meaning to established problems. Husserl openly flaunts the risk of a spiraling proliferation of problems without end, thus giving the appearance of a baroque celebration of folds. Indeed, it may be said that Husserl creates a science based on the generation of problems that other philosophical systems or approaches cannot *afford*. Hence the impression, not entirely unfounded in light of its historical reception, of Husserl's thinking as either overly esoteric or intensely Scholastic.

Of all the strange conceptual creatures inhabiting the wild of Husserl's *Ideen I*, none is as controversial as the concept of *noema*. As Étienne Bimbenet has rightly observed: "Le noème est un objet directement philosophique. Il représente, de fait, l'une des grandes créations conceptuelles de Husserl." As with every conceptual invention in Husserl's thinking, "le noème n'est pas seulement un concept qui répond à un problème; il est philosophique également en ce qu'il *pose problème*" (Bimbenet 2012, p. 187). And as with other conceptual inventions, the noema emerged from a lengthy period gestation in Husserl's thinking extending back to the years after the original breakthrough of the *Logical Investigations* and its critique of Brentano's notion of intentional relation in the Fifth Investigation. The details of this complex development need not detain us here.[3] The idea of noematic sense firsts appears in Husserl's 1908 lectures on the theory of signification and finds its linguistic baptism with term "noema" in 1912.[4] Beyond *Ideen I*, Husserl continued to wrestle with his unruly creation, and often expressed his own dissatisfaction with its various formulations. As Husserl remarks in the manuscript "NOEMA und SINN": "Ich muss die Begriffe von Noesis und Noema neu gestalten."[5] The noema is an experimental concept in the making over which Husserl never gained complete mastery. Even the most cursory reading of "NOEMA und SINN," due to appear in the Husserliana edition *Studien*

---

[3] For an especially detailed account, see Lavigne 2005.
[4] See Husserl 1987 and Husserl 1976, p. 567.
[5] "I must fashion the concepts of noesis and noema anew." B III 12 IV/85a (1921).

zur Struktur des Bewußtseins, reveals a truly anarchic situation to fit together different pieces of a puzzle for which is lacking a fixed image.

If we survey the progression of *Ideen I* until "the problems of noetic-noematic structures" (§§ 97–127), we recognize a clear strategy: after the introduction and performance of the suspension and reduction in §§ 27–32, we are led to a preliminary description of basic structures of consciousness in §§ 33–46 where significantly Husserl does not *explicitly* speak of intentionality and, indeed, never invokes the terms noesis and noema. It is indeed crucial that the terminology of noesis and noema does not and strictly speaking *cannot* make its appearance in these paragraphs; such concepts still remain unintelligible without proper phenomenological *Bildung*. Instead, in this discussion of consciousness in which Husserl heuristically adopts the first-person point of view (and later abandoned in §§ 97–127), we are given a *preview* of the basic structures of pure consciousness without yet finding ourselves completely within a mature and abiding performance of the reduction. As Husserl observes, we have not yet fully accomplished the reduction even thought we have just learned it. These eidetic descriptions serve as anticipations of what can only truly be seen and grasped with the passage into an analysis of the "problems of noetic-noematic structures" in §§ 97–127. Only now, after a period of phenomenological apprenticeship spanning paragraphs §§ 27–62, do we finally gain access to the "universal structures of pure consciousness" *from within a genuinely transcendental reflection*, as developed in the Third Section of *Ideen I* (§§ 63–127), albeit only in a preliminary way.

2. The Noema and the transcendental

Husserl's central and celebrated thesis, taken over and transfigured from his mentor Franz Brentano, is less a solution for a problem than a problem for which a solution becomes freighted with ever increasing difficulty. As Husserl notes: "At first glance, it appears to be a matter of something self-evident: each consciousness is conscious of something, and the manners of consciousness are very different. But as we draw closer to it, the enormous difficulties became palpable to us" (*Ideen* 192/222). The center of these difficulties, as Husserl further specifies, is *not* what one might expect, namely, the commonplace view of attending to the "first person point of view" and what it is like to be-conscious. Instead, Husserl's critical attention is drawn to the manner of being of the noema–to how the sense-beholden character of objects appears in consciousness. In a word: how we experience objects as imbued with sense (*Sinn*). In the paragraphs preceding Husserl's turn to the "problems of noetic-noematic structures," a basic distinction between noesis and noema, as the structure of intentionality, was established, yet far from mastered. Mastering this distinction, as Husserl now affirms, carries the "greatest import for phenomenology" (*Ideen* 192/222), and it is with this import in mind that Husserl launches into a more detailed analysis of noesis-noema structures. Exploring these difficulties and, one might add, allowing oneself to become sensitive–open–for such difficulties–difficulties that are no at all obvious–marks however *one* path into phenomenology. As Husserl remarks, "there is no 'royal path' into phenomenology, and so, too, there is none into philosophy" (*Ideen* 193/223).

Husserl's pursuit of intentionality takes the form of an analysis of its noetic-noematic structures that have been methodologically opened for reflection through the suspension of the natural attitude and the reduction to the field of pure experience. The term "pure" marks a significant qualifier in Husserl's understanding of *how* consciousness, or, in other words, intentionality, makes its appearance within the scope of a phenomenological, that is, transcendental inquiry. Contrary to its Kantian meaning (the salient contrast for Husserl), where "pure" stands opposed to "empirical," "pure" in Husserl's understanding does not enforce a contrast with experience per se, but only with a certain form of experience that has not become modified through the proper means of phenomenological reflection. Indeed, the field of phenomena (Husserl's "new world") released through the method of reduction is emphatically a field of *experience*, albeit, a field of *pure experience*. I cannot here delve further into Husserl's method of reduction–treated elsewhere in this volume–and its singular accomplishment of revealing a field of pure experience. One reminder is nonetheless in order: as Husserl repeatedly states through-out *Ideen I*, the theme of phenomenological inquiry are the *structures of consciousness*, and these structures are made transparent–seen–through a process of eidetic variation, the fruits of which are presented in the form of Husserl's own discussion. The descriptive dimension of Husserlian phenomenology, often celebrated as its methodological signature, is likewise deployed as a description of essential distinctions and clarification of equivocations within concepts. Described are not individual experiences *per se*, the quality of having such experiences, or any introspective reporting. Instead, description operates in Husserl's thinking as a praxis of shaping conceptual distinctions that in turn render distinct, and thus articulate, structuring activities of consciousness, gathered under the principle heading of the problem of constitution.

The central distinction with which Husserl leads into his discussion of the noetic-noematic structures (in these paragraphs 97–127) is the distinction between real (*reell*) and intentional components–a distinction originally introduced in the Fifth Logical Investigation. In the present discussion, this distinction is situated within the context of perception: a paradigmatic form of consciousness due to its relative simple form vis-à-vis more complex, nested forms of consciousness (cognition, imagining, willing, etc.) as well as its foundational role for any experience. Husserl takes the example of perceiving a tree. The description appears straightforward: "we look out just now into the garden. In one, unified consciousness we observe this tree here, first standing still where it is, then appearing to be moved by the wind. All the while, it affords itself in quite different manners of appearance as we change our spatial position toward it [...]" (*Ideen* 194/225). Let me first note Husserl's attentiveness to the unified character of a perceptual consciousness of change. Features of how the tree appears are changing, not only due to shifts in spatial position ("stepping towards the window or merely altering the position of our hear or eyes"), but due as well to causal interactions of the tree with the world at large: wind blowing through the leaves. This implicit stress on variability in the tree's appearance (and which Husserl develops more fully in *Ideen II*) establishes one of the central issues pursued through the distinction between real (*reell*) and intentional components, namely, the distinction between appearance and object. As with Husserl's example, the object (the tree) is inseparable from its manifold ways of appearing, and such appearances are constantly liable to *different* forms of change, or modifications. As Husserl remarks: "the unity of *one* perception can contain in itself a great variety of modifications" (194/225). In the case of wind blowing through the leaves, a change in the appearance of the tree reflects a change in the object's causal relation with the world. With shifts in how the tree appears due to changes in spatial positioning of an observer, changes in appearances do not correlate to changes in the object. The tree does not become smaller as I walk away from it.

Husserl's own stress on the term "one" underlines the basic problem for which the analysis of intentionality is fashioned: the unity of objective experience as a manifold of modifications. This distinction between changes in the appearances of an object produced by the subject herself (her change in spatial position) and changes in the appearances of the object due to causal changes in the object itself (wind blowing leaves) are *equally* changes in the appearances of an object. Within the natural attitude, as Husserl contends, we would be inclined to introduce an *ontological* separation between, on the one hand, subjective experience ("mind") and, on the other, objective thing ("world"). For we would be inclined to regard the change of appearance caused by the wind as occurring *in* the object, irrespective of whether we are there standing as witness, and likewise conclude that changes in the appearance of the object were induced by a change in our own comportment points to a purely subjective dimension irrespective of the object. With the performance of the *epoché* and reduction, such a temptation to "ontologize" the distinction between appearance and object becomes inhibited. The reduction "de-ontologizes" the distinction between appearance and object spontaneously generated within the natural attitude. The distinction between appearance and object, once liberated from its ontological falsification, can be re-discovered as an integral spacing between the noema of the tree (the perceived-tree as such and such) as precisely *not* contained in consciousness and the noetic aspects (the act of perceiving, the quality of such an experiencing) as precisely contained in consciousness. The reduction discloses a genuinely transcendental sense of transcendence as the transcendence of *sense* (*Sinn*), the noematic sense, from an ontological construal of transcendence. As Husserl writes: "this noema with its 'tree' in quotation marks *is not contained in the perception as really inhering in it any more than the actual tree*" (*Ideen* 202/194). The noema must always be thought in quotation marks, that is, under the operator of the reduction: the tree as a unity of sense, its sense of being as a tree (with its colors, shape, etc.) is a transcendent object for consciousness (i.e., not contained in it) much as the actual tree is not in my mind. Is the actual tree therefore identical with the tree as noema ("full noema")–the unity of the tree as a unity of sense? This crucial question exceeds the framework of Husserl's *first* presentation of the noetic-noematic structure of intentionality in paragraphs 97–127. In fact, Husserl's presentation of the noema is distributed across two sections in *Ideen I:* §§ 88–108 and §§ 128–135. Only with the treatment of "The Noematic Sense and the Relation to the Object," and hence, only within the heading of a phenomenology of reason, is the entire sweep of Husserl's reflections on the noema, and hence on intentionality, complete.[6]

In the present context of discussion, the transcendent character of the noema is approached from the insight that it is not an inherent part of consciousness even though it appears within consciousness. The color of the tree's leaves, for example, is not qua color an inhering moment in the act of perceiving even though, as Husserl contends, there is nonetheless an "hyletic aspect" or "color-sensation." This sensing of color is not itself green. As we move around the tree or observe the tree at dawn or dusk, we perceive different shadings of green. These shadings belong to the tree itself as an unfolding continua of its appearances, or as we might say in a more contemporary idiom, as the continua of its variable *looks*. Yet, this example of color shades is not deployed by Husserl in the

---

6 This distribution of Husserl's treatment of the noema–and hence intentionality–reproduces within *Ideen I* the conceptual and argumentative relation between the Fifth and Sixth Logical Investigations.

context of a debate concerning the relation between concept and observation (intuition) and the question of non-conceptual perceptual content. One thinks, for example, of John McDowells' appeal to the example of color-shades against the argument for non-conceptual perceptual content in Gareth Evans. One phenomenon that attracts Evans' argument is the rich determinacy of fine-grained detail in perceptual experience. As he writes in *The Varieties of Reference:* "Do we really understand the proposal that we have as many color concepts as there are shades of color that we can sensibly determine?" (Evans 1982, p. 229). The example of shades leverages an argument for non-conceptual perceptual content by exemplifying the poverty of concepts, which must remain general and coarse, against the putative specification and fineness of intuitions. McDowell's retort in *Mind and World* hinges on his over-all suspicion against any form of the Myth of the Given, to which Evans (partly) succumbs by virtue of his espousal of an operative distinction between coarse-grained conceptual capacities and fine-grained perceptual discriminations.

McDowell's contestation of Evans' argument through his crafty appeal to the kind of conceptual capacity expressed linguistically in the phrase "that shade" shall not concern me here nor the modification in McDowell's considered view after *Mind and World*.[7] My point instead is to illustrate how Husserl's example of color shades is situated within a philosophical, that is, phenomenological context that is not geared towards providing a solution to the *Kantian* (or, in historically more correct, *Neo-Kantian*) problem of the relation between concept and intuition. That problem, in both its ontological implication and epistemological explication, rests tacitly on an unquestioned and unassuming adherence to the natural attitude. By contrast, the example of color shades within *Ideen I* delineates a different framing-device with which Husserl proposes a re-configuration of Kant's original problem. Rather operate with the paired concept and intuition, Husserl develops an alternative framework of noetic and noematic intentionality. The significance of this shift is registered through the problem that gradually takes shape with this initial description of the distinction between real and intentional dimensions: the constitution of an object as unity of a manifold. Shadings of color indicate that color must appear in a certain manner, namely, in a constantly changing continuum of appearances, but that these changing appearances must equally belong to a unity, namely, the unity of the object as such. As Husserl writes: "the shadings of colors belonging to any fixed color of a thing relate that color to as a continuous 'manifold' to a 'unity.'" (*Ideen* 195/227)

---

7 For McDowell's riff on the phrase "that shade," see McDowell 1994, pp. 56–57.

It is here, however, that Husserl proposes a fateful claim that might appear both unwarranted and unwise given his analysis thus far. He remarks that it is "absolutely indubitable that here 'unity' and 'manifold' belong to *totally different dimensions* and, of course, that *everything hyletic* belongs to the concrete experience of a *really obtaining*, integral part of it, while what 'displays' and 'profiles' itself in it as a manifold belongs, by contrast, to the *noema*" (*Ideen* 204/196). The talk of hyletic content and noema refers to Husserl's account of the functional relation between the objective features of an intentional object (the green of the leaves) and the non-intentional, lived experience (*erlebt*) of *sensing* the green of the leaves. As with every perceptual feature of an object, the green of the leaves is given, or appears, through profiles or adumbrations: the green is not apprehended *in toto* and at once. On Husserl's rather technical description, the noematic content (the green as perceived in the tree) is adumbrated through a continuous series of underlying hyletic moments: the color "green" remains identical across its fluctuating shades (due to changes in lighting conditions, due to wind, etc.). Husserl understands this functional relation in terms that harken back to the Fifth Logical Investigation (although in this early account, the noematic dimension remained absent): the non-intentional hyletic moments are "animated" by noetic acts of perception in view of the objective features of green. Importantly, these noetic elements (the act of perceiving along with its subtending hyletic moments) can only be described in view of their intentional object. Consciousness as such, and especially in its most intimate moment of sensing, cannot be described without recourse to its transcendent object. The difficulties that plague Husserl's account (presented earlier in § 85) shall not detain us here, however, since there is a larger and more evident difficulty that looms over this entire discussion.

This problem resides with Husserl's insistence that the noetic aspects and noematic features belong to "totally different dimensions." What could "totally different dimensions" mean in this phenomenological context? It should be clear from the foregoing that "totally different dimensions" cannot be taken *ontologically*, since it was precisely the aim of the suspension of the natural attitude to render inoperative any ontological dualism between mind and world. The Kantian separation between intuition and concept is bereft of traction within the terrain of pure experience. If the meaning of "different dimensions" cannot be understood ontologically, in what sense can and should it be understood?

On the one hand, this insistence on two "totally different dimensions" is meant to underscore the specificity of intentionality, namely, the non-inherence of the transcendent noema *in* consciousness, where the meaning of "in" is shorn from any spatial and/or ontological meaning. To speak in a contemporary idiom with which admittedly I shall *over-state* Husserl's insight, the "alterity" of the noema, its transcendent character, appears within the immanence of consciousness; consciousness, in this sense of its structuring form of intentionality, is an opening, or encounter, with the "alterity" of the world. The noema is irreducible and non-identical with the consciousness in which it shows itself. On the other hand, one begins to gain added clarity on the meaning and motivation for this insistence on "totally different dimensions" when Husserl repeats that the central problem here at issue is the complex juxtaposition of *different senses of unity and multiplicity*. For as Husserl explains, the unity of hyletic and noetic aspects is "totally different" from the unity of the moments within the noema. Once again, Husserl states clearly that his underlying problem is the constitution of unity and multiplicity, and in different senses. It is on this occasion that Husserl comes to speak explicitly about the meaning of "transcendental" within his thinking. He notes that the designation of the phenomenological reduction and the pure sphere of experience as "transcendental" allows for a recognition of "that wonderous process of having become conscious of something determinate or determinable–given in such and such a way, as something standing over against consciousness itself, something in principle different, irreal, transcendent–belongs, *as a matter of an immanent essential necessity*, to determinate ways in which those materials and forms are interwoven" (*Ideen* 196–197/228).

At least two thoughts are here important. The first is that the meaning of "different dimensions" must be taken in the sense of the distinct, yet necessarily related dimensions of "real, immanent consciousness" and "irreal, transcendent" as a relation between two forms of unity and multiplicity. The second thought is that this difference of dimensions is "carried within (*in sich trägt*) consciousness" or better: consciousness "is" this differentiation between dimensions. The difference with the world does not come from the outside, as it were, as a limitation or constraint brought onto consciousness externally. Instead, what is "wonderous" is precisely that consciousness envelops the world with its self-presence, with its consciousness, so as to allow the world to *appear* as what and how consciousness itself is not. To speak in the register of high metaphor: consciousness lends its light to the world such that the world itself, as other than consciousness, enters into its own appearance. If "appearance" has historically designated either a metaphysical illusion or a purely subjective apparition as set against the object itself (*das Ding an sich* in Kant, for example), in Husserl's usage, appearance is the proper designation for the transcendent character of the world (thought here under the aspect of the noema) as "in principle different" from consciousness *and yet* essentially related to its own ways of relating to the world.

For Husserl, this original distinction and "gegenüber" within immanence, within pure consciousness, reveals the "original source for the only conceivable solution to the profoundest problems of knowledge [*Erkenntnisprobleme*]" (*Ideen* 197/228). This invocation of *das Erkenntnisproblem* allows us to measure the distance between Husserl's "solution" of intentionality and the Kantian solution prevalent in Husserl's time (and still prevalent in various modified forms today). Contrary to Kant and Neo-Kantianism, the problem of knowledge does not turn for Husserl on demonstrating how certain a priori categories of the pure understanding (pure concepts) must necessarily be synthetized with a priori forms of pure intuition (space and time). It is not, in other words, the issue at play in the Transcendental Deduction in conjunction with the murky discussion of the schematism (the application of concepts to pure intuitions). Rather, the entire landscape of the problem of knowledge (expressed in general terms: "possibility of objectively valid knowledge of something transcendent") has been displaced, and this displacement critically depends on the performance of the *epoché* and the disclosure through the reduction of noematic unities of sense in their functional correlation to noetic acts. The reduction opens an investigation of the various "essential relations" (*Wesenbeziehungen*) between noetic and noematic dimensions. The noema designates *both* the objectivities of consciousness as such (the tree as such) *and* the forms of noematic sense, namely, the manner in which the object is given, its "noematic manner of being."

Let us take a moment to glance back at Kant's *Revolution in Denkart* in the form understood by the Neo-Kantianism of the Marburg School–the dominant representative of transcendental idealism for Husserl. Kant introduces a radically new philosophical conception of the relation between concept and object (*Begriff und Gegenstand*). For Kant, to know an object (*Erkennen*) depends on the synthesis of recognition in the concept (within the wider sweep of more rudimentary forms of synthesis). The manifold of intuition is thereby subsumed to a *rule*, or norm, and this rule operates synthetically as the principle of unification and objectification. Consciousness becomes itself shaped (given a determinate form) through this conceptual rule, and this rule thus provides unity for both the object of consciousness (as synthesis of manifold) *and* the consciousness of that object. Hence the supremely critical role ascribed by Kant to the transcendental apperception for the unity of experience as such. The concept is both a rule and the unity constituted (as Hermann Cohen speaks: *erzeugt*) through this rule. In this manner, the relation between object and concept is transformed into a synthetic unity. As Cassirer argued in *Substance and Function*, Kant's re-formulation of the problem of knowledge displaces an ontological conception of unity, as unity of substance, with a *functional* conception of unity: a synthetic unity as the possibility of an relation to an object. As Cassirer further argues, the metaphysical and ontological sense of the transcendent object is thus undermined. The *sense* of the object as transcendent, as belonging to an entirely different dimension, cannot be understood with either metaphysical (thing in itself) or ontological (as spatial outside, as substance existing in itself, etc.) notions. Knowledge and object do not stand in a spatial relation of inside and outside. The object of knowledge, its determinate meaning, is constituted through a determinate form as based on an a priori function of knowledge. Cassirer understands this revolutionary shift as a transformation in the very sense of "transcendence." As he argues in *Philosophy of Symbolic Forms* (Vol. III), the transcendence of meaning (*Bedeutungstranszendenz*) is not the same as ontic transcendence (*ontische Transzendenz*) such that the *Übergang im Sinn ist nicht Übergang im Sein*. The meaning of transcendental is thus inseparable from a critique of ontology, and the passage from the centrality of the question "what is it?" to the question "how it is given?" as a question of sense.

With this sketch in mind, this (Neo)-Kantian assessment of the problem of knowledge becomes significantly re-configured in Husserl's phenomenology, or better: integrated into his description of intentionality. It is thus that we can begin to clearly discern *how* Husserl's central theme of intentionality–the main theme of inquiry in *Ideen I*–attacks the question of knowledge (*Erkenntnis*) or, in other words, how intentionality is the source for a solution to this problem–as Husserl himself just indicated. For we have seen that, broadly speaking, Kant's central intuition consisted in the thought that objects of possible knowledge are determined in an a priori manner by determinate *functions* of knowledge, or concepts, and that the basic function of such concepts was the unification of a (sensible) manifold. For Husserl, this functional relation between concept and object is no longer deployed within a Kantian distinction between intuition and concept. Instead, as Husserl writes: "it is inherently part of the essence of the respective object [*Gegenstand*], objectively [*objektiv*] determined in this or that way, to be a noematic object precisely in perceptions of that descriptive type, and to be able to be so only in them, and so forth" (*Ideen* 197/228).

These "essential relations" within noetic and noematic structures of intentionality are the true objects of philosophical research–its terrain. In keeping with the general position of Neo-Kantianism, the *critical* enterprise of transcendental phenomenology is directed towards the a priori *forms, or ways, of knowledge:* the How (*das Wie*) of knowledge, not the What (*das Was*)–the latter is the proper domain of the natural sciences. This shift from "what" questions to "how" questions is accomplished in Husserl's case with the suspension of the natural attitude and the form of question that dominates the sense in which the question of knowledge is there raised. Coupled with the reduction, phenomenological reflection critically investigates the eidetic correlations between forms of knowing (noetic forms) and objects (noematic unities of sense) as determined in such and such a manner ("so und so bestimmt"). The a priori correlation is not a set of concepts in conjunction with forms of intuition (Kant) or certain a priori forms of cognition within any intuitions (Cohen); but instead, neither concepts nor intuitions, but a novel structure of noetic-noematic intentionality that cuts across, and thus undercuts, the Kantian distinction between intuition and concept. What further distinguishes Husserl's transcendental phenomenology from Neo-Kantianism is the claim, forcefully proclaimed, that phenomenology is the "genuine positivism," by which, of course, Husserl does not mean Comte's positivism or anything comparable to the positive natural sciences, but rather, that phenomenology does not a special and unique "object" or "domain," namely, the domain or object of pure consciousness as transcendental field of experience.

3. The anarchy of the noema

The noema is Husserl's phenomenological concept with which to pursue the lead problem of the transcendence of meaning (*Sinn*) as the transcendental clue for an understanding of the constitution of intelligible experience. Before we enter into the details of Husserl's discussion of the noema (in the context of the paragraphs currently under discussion), let us recall the original problem for which Husserl first developed his conception of intentionality in the *Logical Investigations* and the motivation for its further development into a full-fledged account of noetic and noematic structures.[8] In Husserl's trenchant critique of psychologism, its philosophical confusion rests not only on a conflation between two kinds of objects (the real, psychological states and ideal objects of logical and mathematics) but resides at a more instructive level as the obfuscation of a distinction between "sense" and "object." As Husserl argues, the proper formulation of a distinction between sense and object is inseparable from a proper clarification of consciousness in its structure of intentionality. On the one hand, sense (*Sinn*) is itself not an object in any straight-forward sense; it is the manner in which objects are given, or appear. On the other hand, objects–this tree in the yard, the number three, etc.–cannot be given without a determinate sense. Thus although there is no object where there is no sense, sense itself is not an object. Sense, moreover, at least on Husserl's account in the *Logical Investigations*, is "irreal," or, in other words, not to be conflated with the real objects or instances in which it appears. Sense itself is not something "existing" in

---

[8] By way of a reminder: the question of the relation between noema and object is the topic of Husserl's discussion in subsequent paragraphs and thus falls outside the scope of my present reflections).

the manner of an object. As an ideal species, sense is equally not a merely a semantic construct since sense can be given, or fulfilled, in intuitive acts of consciousness.

Although Husserl succeeds in drawing a distinction between sense and objects, his handling of the problem of sense in the *Logical Investigations* remained hampered by his construal of the relationship between sense and experience as a relation between species (ideal species of sense) and particular (actual) acts of intentional consciousness. As Krzysztof Michalski notes, the irreality of sense "cannot be explained with the aid of such concepts as 'essence' and 'individual,'" since this way of thinking "fails to do justice to its specific character, which prevents placing meaning either on the side of subjectivity or objectivity" (Michalski 1997, p. 32). This insight is crucial in two respects. Both set the course for the development of Husserl's thinking during the years leading from the *Logical Investigations* to *Ideen I*. A first consequence is the thought that sense is an intentional correlate of consciousness that is neither an inhering content in consciousness ("meaning is not in the head") nor an object in the form of a thing or entity. Sense is that in terms of which objects are given or experienced for consciousness as such and such, namely, as having such and such a sense. A second consequence is the related thought that the distinction between sense as an ideal species and its instantiation in particular acts of consciousness in the *Logical Investigations* (i.e., Husserl's notion of intentional essence) is framed by a conception of intentionality based on the schema of "apprehension–content of apprehension." This distinction further reflects a distinction between "generality" (type) and "individual" (token) that imposes an ontological form on the problem of sense. In response to problems engendered by his first breakthrough with the problem of sense and intentionality in the *Logical Investigations*, epistemological as well as ontological, Husserl arrives at the concept of noema as the irreducible dimension of sense that is neither subjective nor objective, and that, moreover, cannot be fitted into an opposition between "generality" and "individuality" (qua instantiation of a species).

The noema as such (always considered in correlation to corresponding noetic acts and underlying hyletic moments) is disclosed in reflection. In this regard, the noema as such (the tree as perceived) is not an object, as Husserl remarks, "logically speaking." The noema is not an object because it is non-self-sufficient and, in this sense, must borrow its manner of being (*Seinsweise des Noema*) from consciousness. Yet, on the other hand, as Husserl emphasizes, if the "being" of the noema resides in its *percipi*, namely, in reflection, this cannot and must not be taken in Berkeley's meaning since the noema is not an inhering moment in consciousness, *even that of* reflective consciousness. The strange status of the noema is diametrically opposed to Berkeley's Idealism, at least as understood by Husserl, where *esse est percipi*. On the contrary, *esse* is not *percipi* in the sense that the noema transcends the very act of reflection that reveals it, that "perceives it," even as the noema is not logically speaking an object: it does not subsist independently of perception (reflection). Although Husserl himself speaks of the "noema's manner of being," we stumble in fact upon a transcendental intrigue where the noema has the manner of not-being consciousness (its *esse* is not *percipi*) while also not-being an object *stricto sensu* since it does not enjoy any independent existence (i.e., not an object logically speaking). This liminal status of the noema is not to be understood as a "medium" or "intermediary" representation, or semantic entity, between consciousness and its object–a view that Husserl explicitly rejects.[9] The noema does not have an origin in the different regions of being nor can its sense be captured through traditional oppositions such as "real-ideal," "actual-possible," and "individual-generality." We are thus led to recognize what Jacques Derrida has astutely called the "anarchy of the noema." As Derrida notes, the noema is anarchic not only due to its lack of origin within a determinate region of being. It is anarchic in its disorderly movement, or differentiation, in traversing and crossing-out different regions of being (see Derrida 1978, 163). Husserl's passage from ontology to transcendental idealism passes through this discovery of the noema as ontologically anarchic, yet transcendentally indispensable.

Although Husserl argues that noetic acts (and hyletic content) and noemata do not relate to each other as mirror images, a strict correlation nonetheless obtains. As Husserl writes: "The noematic is the field of unities, the noetic that of the manifolds 'constituting' [them]. The consciousness that 'functionally' unifies the manifold, thereby constituting at once a unity *never* in fact shows identity, whereas the identity of an 'object' is given in the noematic correlate" (*Ideen* 207/199). The term "function" offers a further clue for grasping Husserl's originality with the "problem of knowledge" as centered on the transcendence of sense. I have already noted Cassirer's suggestive re-formulation of Kant's revolution as the passage from "substance" to "function."[10] An object of experience is constituted as the synthetic unity of manifold based on the functional operation of a concept, which provides the rule, or norm, on the basis of which an object can be recognized, i.e., identified. In Husserl's frame-work of intentionality, the tran-

---

9 B III, 12. This speaks directly against the so-called West Coast interpretation of the noema.
10 As Husserl writes in § 86: "Yet the *functional problems,* or those pertaining to the '*constitution of the objectivities of consciousness,*' are the greatest problems of all." The term function was a critical term in Carl Stumpf's thinking, but as Husserl remarks: "It should be noted that the terms in question here [*function and appearance*] have, in our presentations, a completely different meaning from their meaning for our esteemed researcher" (*Ideen* 171/199).

scendental function of Kant's synthesis of recognition becomes re-formulated entirely for what is immediately original in Husserl's account is that identity (recognition) is not located on the side of noetic consciousness, but on contrary placed within the noematic correlate. Moreover, and critically, the noematic sense is *not* a rule or "norm" (in the sense understood by Kant and subsequent Neo-Kantians–excluding, however, Cassirer) through which the object, as unity of a manifold, is produced or constructed. The diversity or manifold is placed on the side of noetic consciousness–the spread of adumbrations, shifting appearances and perspectives–whereas the identity is placed on the side of the noema. It is therefore not consciousness that unifies the manifold of givens into an object but the object that guides the manifold of "non-identical consciousness"–a consciousness that only itself gains unity by virtue of its intentional object.[11]

In this manner, Husserl quietly reverses Kant's celebrated Copernican Revolution without thereby returning to any kind of pre-Kantian position. For if, in Kant, the concept of the understanding provids the unity for the manifold of intuitive givens, for Husserl, on the contrary, the unity of consciousness and recognition of the object is situated within the noema, and precisely in terms of the transcendence of the noema as a non-inhering dimension within consciousness. The manifold that becomes united is the manifold of noetic moments. And yet, even though it is the noema that functions as the *pole* of identification, it is still consciousness, the noetic (objectifying) acts and their underlying hyletic moments, that *constitutes functionally* the unity in manifold of experience. Striking is how Husserl combines two seemingly opposing thoughts. On the one hand, the noematic sense-core provides the pole of identity that transcends and unities into one consciousness the appearance of an object as such and such.[12] The identity of the object, thought as the unity of a manifold is stamped, as it were, with the function of recognition (i.e., I perceive this tree as such and such; as a tree with leaves, etc.). On the other hand, although the identity of the object is imbued with a determinate sense, it is therefore not projected onto the object nor constructed through concepts (as would be the case for Neo-Kantians, despite obvious differences, such as Rickert and Cohen), even as it is the objectifying (noetic) acts of consciousness that *constitutes* the object in its givenness. We see clearly that what Husserl understands by constitution–

---

11 The implicit teleological structure of constitution and intentionality can here not be investigated.
12 Again: the relation between the noema and the object X is left here outside consideration since it is only treated in the second installment of Husserl's presentation of the noema in §§ 129–135.

an issue that evidently cannot be fully broached here–does not fit into any pre-established mold.

4. Noematic characterizations

Husserl's phenomenological account of the constitutive relation between unity and manifold does not exclusively rest on a description of the synthetic form of a continuous unfolding of noetic acts (e. g., successive moments of perceiving a tree) in view of its abiding (in terms of identity) noematic object (the tree as perceived). This functional interplay between noetic manifold and noematic unity of sense is manifest across different manners of presentations: perception, remembrance, imagining. With the visual perception of a tree, the tree appears in an original manner–in "flesh and blood"–while in the case of a remembrance of having perceived this very same tree yesterday, the tree appears as a memory (in which the original perception of the tree is re-activated and given again, as it were, but a distance).[13] In both instances, the tree–considered as a noematic unity of sense–is characterized respectively in a determinate manner: either as "perceivable" or as "memorable." Such characterizations belong to the noematic unity of sense, the "how" (*Wie*) of its appearance for consciousness. The object affords itself as a memory much as the same object can afford itself as a perceptual experience. The thought here is arguably not immediately illuminating, yet gains phenomenological traction when one comes to appreciate the subtly of Husserl's proposed distinction between the object of consciousness–the tree– and its inseparable manner of appearance, i.e., the manner in which the object appears or is given in consciousness. Husserl designates the "how" of an object's appearance as a form of characterization: the object's appearance is stamped, so to speak, with the character of "perceptibility" or "memorability." The finesse of this distinction resides with Husserl's insight that *how* objects appear to us, as either through perception, imagination, etc., is reflected within the character of the object's appearance itself. We might search for an analogy, for the sake of instruction, by thinking of how acts of remembrance are often displayed in films with scenes imbued with a hazy halo (and often cued with a corroborating musical signature). The fuzzy image and distilled colors that we perceive on the film-screen are meant to indicate a remembered episode. What we see–the objects of the remembrance–are visually characterized by fuzziness, etc., and such perceptible characterizations can be taken as somewhat analogous to Hus-

---

[13] For Husserl's account of remembrance, allow me to refer to my study De Warren 2009.

serl's thought that every form of experience (perception, imagination, etc.) is such that its objects are likewise characterized by the manner in which those objects enter into consciousness. Much as with any feature of the noema, such characterizations are not "inhering moments" in consciousness. As with the example of the visual depiction of memories in films, the character of "being-remembered" is seen in the appearance of the object itself: it is the image that is fuzzy, not our perception of it.

Husserl identifies another form of noematic characterizations, what he calls characterizations of being, or, in other words, characters of belief. With this second form of noematic characterization, Husserl has unquestionably proposed one of his more original, if under-stated, insights that has largely been overshadowed and, indeed, forgotten, in light of the greater fanfare paid to Husserl's description of the noetic-noematic structure of intentionality. Perceptual experience is continuously configured by beliefs regarding its objects: whether I take the tree to be there, whether I come to question whether the tree is moving, etc. Such beliefs, which determine the various ways in which acts of consciousness posit their objects (take their objects to be), correspond to noematic characterizations of belief, by which Husserl understands, that the object's appearance, or manner of giveness, is itself characterized by credulity or incredulity, or any kind of doxic modification. The object appears itself "to be questionable," "to be doubtful," etc., and these characterizations of belief can become modified over the course of experience: an object that appeared to be "certain" can now appear to me as "doubtful"–for example, when I recognize that something is not right about how objects in my room are arranged, or when something changes in the appearance of a statue that leads to me to question whether it is in fact an actual person. Objects are, in this manner, characterized by a venue of affordances for belief: the object affords this or that belief through the way in which it makes an impression on me, appears to be slightly off, etc. With this genial insight, Husserl has in single stroke "de-subjectified" belief from the merely subjective or psychological. Belief has been emancipated from the illusion immanence. Moreover, Husserl thus expands the critique of reason along the lines of the problem of sense (as argued above), where the transcendence of sense is inseparable the transcendence of belief. That things appear as *Sinnhaftig* is inseparable from that things appear as questionable, etc.–as imbued with characterizations and solicitations of belief and disbelief.

The perceptual world is a dynamic sprawl of beliefs structured by continuous negotiation between changes in my own acts of believing and affordances of the objects for credulity or incredulity. Objects motivate me to change or re-assess whether indeed what I see is truly there. As Husserl illustrates: "The thing itself 'suggests' that it is a human being. Then an opposite suggestion enters; it could be a tree moved [by the wind], one that appears, in the darkness of the woods, similar to a human being moving about. But now the 'weight' of one 'possibility' becomes considerably greater, and we decide for it, such that we definitively presume: 'In any case, it was a tree after all' " (*Ideen* 206/239 – 240).[14] Horror movies or everyday experiences of fright, offers here a range of examples for such a phenomenon. *Something* in how the object appears renders it "questionable," "probable," etc., that is, that motivates us to modify our own stance towards it's existence. One might hazard an extension of Husserl's basic insight into noematic characterizations to include w richer gamut of affordances, such as the affordances (or characterizations) of objects as imbued with values–and indeed Husserl in his ethical writings does at times experiment with the thought that values are perceived directly "in" objects, thus suggesting another form of noematic characterization in terms of values: the object's appearance is characterized as valuable, as beautiful, etc. In Husserl's lectures on passive synthesis, Husserl colorfully describes objects as speaking to consciousness, much as in Alice in Wonderland, as saying "turn me," "look at me more," etc.

Husserl's analysis of doxic characterizations–to return to Husserl's immediate discussion in *Ideen I*–has significant import for the issue of evidence, since on the account just presented, whether or not an object is questionable can be adjudicated by appeal to evidence, namely, to how in fact the object appears, or is given. Moreover, Husserl speaks suggestively of the "weight" of possibilities and motivations. The appearance of objects is itself weighs in this way or that, motivating conscious to take up different stances and explore different possibilities (is this truly the case? might this be the case? etc.). Experience becomes experience through a texture belief-modifications: the world is rendered in motion by possibilities and the weight of evidence that speaks for or against such possibilities, that motivates consciousness to re-assess its prior and entrenched convictions, and take up new stances ("position-takings") and attitudes.

With this notion of noematic-doxic characteristics, Husserls tacitly anchors modal categories of judgments within perceptual experience. The way in which objects appear to consciousness is already inscribed with various doxic modifications on the basis of which modal judgments can be established. Husserl situates his account of how judgments of denial and affirmation are inscribed within noematic characterizations–an analysis that becomes further developed in a genetic register with *Experience and Judgment*. With this analysis of negation and affirmation, Husserl effectively breaks the "logical prejudice,"

---

[14] Husserl would develop this kind description more powerfully in his lectures on passive synthesis.

namely, the historically entrenched view since Aristotle that negation and affirmation are operations of predicative judgments.[15] Husserl intimates how negation and affirmation at the level of judgments take shape in a more original manner within perceptual experience. As Husserl argues, these modal modifications play themselves out within intuitive presentations "without the participation of any sort of 'thinking' in the specific sense, without a 'concept' and predicative judgment" (*Ideen* 206/240). The negation of a state of affairs is described as "striking through" an earlier experience, for example, when my registering of movement in a statue "strikes through" my initial perceptual conviction that I was beholding a statue and not a person. The animation of the "statue" is visible evidence against my prior perceptual experience. With expressions such as "striking through," Husserl admits that he is "figuratively speaking," yet this figure of speech is well suited to capture the sense in which an appearance becomes "struck through" or "crossed-out" by another appearance. Given Husserl's argument that negation and affirmation are founded on noematic characterizations (modifications) that are not produced by or determinations of reflection, the "striking out" of one experience through another is a negation effected *in the world*. In an extremely suggestive example, Husserl observes: "Even the natural way of speaking, not misled by any psychological prejudices, provides a witness for us here, if we would still need one. Looking into the strereoscope, we say that this pyramid appearing in it is 'nothing,' is mere 'semblance.' What appears as such is the obvious subject of the predication, and we ascribe to it (a thing-noema that is, however, anything but a thing) what *we find as a character in it, precisely, this nothingness*" (*Ideen* 212/247). Husserl here undermines his earlier cautious remark concerning the *figurative* use of expressions such as "crossing out," for he now speaks of "seeing" nothingness, albeit as the determinate *character* of an object's manner of appearing. We see the negation in the appearing itself of the object. As Husserl writes: "Am erscheinenden Gegenstand als solchen erfassen wir die Negate," much as it is "on the appearing object itself" that we apprehend its questionability, doubtfulness or certainty, etc.

Noematic characterizations of belief are modifications: to question whether this tree is there presupposes a sense of "is there" that duly becomes modified, viz., into a questionable belief as to whether the tree is actually there. Husserl's claim is that there is something akin to a default condition of taking the world to be and therewith an anchoring certainty as the pre-condition for any and all doxic modifications. As Husserl himself remarks, there is something "extremely remarkable" here in play that requires an "expression of its own." Husserl

---

[15] For an examination of the logical prejudice, see Dahlstrom 2001.

speaks in this respect of an "original doxa" (*Urdoxa*) or "primary belief."[16] With this title, Husserl seeks to name a primal form of belief that cannot be equated with a certainty that could either be fundamentally broken or arrived at through a particular act of volition or conviction. What, however, does this straightforward consciousness of being–this anchoring sense *that something is*–reside in? Husserl's own indications in his extremely brief remarks are far from exhaustive or conclusive. What equally remains unexamined is the connection between this *Urdoxa* and the general thesis of the natural attitude, and which Husserl had earlier identified and suspended as the first moment in the development of phenomenology. Yet, as Husserl himself casually remarks, his discussion merely "sets forth and underscores a *group of problems*"–problems requiring further phenomenological exploration.

5. Neutrality modification

Husserl's examination of these groups of problems associated with noetic-noematic modifications brings consciousness into relief as a life of continuous engagement in the manifold ways in which the world presents itself as a texture of possibilities. Underlying these fluctuations of belief resides the ground of *Urdoxa*–an anchoring sense of "being," that something, and the world, *is*. Husserl now comes to identify what he calls a "supremely important" form of modification that occupies a place by itself, and which cannot be equated with other doxic characterizations and modifications. The modifications thus far assessed always adhered to a determinate object in the warp and weft of its appearance: this shadow that appears doubtful, etc. Husserl proposes to have uncovered yet another form modification–a *universal* modification of consciousness–and claims that this kind of modification "has never been set forth scientifically, and hence it has also not been terminologically pinned down [...] Even in ordinary language there is no unambiguous name for it" (*Ideen* 213/248). Once again, we witness the discovery of a concept without precedence or pedigree, thus further exemplifying the fruitfulness of Husserl's exploration of uncharted territory. Husserl's delineation of this new modification proceeds circumspectly. As Eugen Fink aptly observes: "Die 'zirkumskriptive' Aufweisung *Husserls* lässt zunächst eine verwirrende Fülle von Bedeutungen sehen, aus der das einheitliche Wesen der Neutralitätsmodifikation herauszugrenzen ist" (Fink 1966, p. 69). In-

---

[16] Merleau-Ponty will further explore this "extremely remarkable" original doxa with his notion of "perceptual faith" in *The Visible and the Invisible*.

deed, Husserl's descriptive strategy resembles an ever tightening circumscription that slowly progresses towards its quary by way of contrasts with other related forms of consciousness. Under the title of "neutrality modification" or "neutralized consciousness," Husserl seeks to identify a form of consciousness manifest in attitudes in which one leaves something open, inhibits any decision, and refrains from taking any stance. With such examples of a so-called neutralized consciousness, Husserl understands both the neutralization of an acts of consciousness, in which cases one might speak of the self-neutralization of consciousness, as well as the neutralization of the object of consciousness.[17] In the first instance, consciousness neutralizes its own act of positing, or belief: the object is presented to consciousness without any attached stance of belief. In the latter instance, the object is presented to consciousness in a neutralized manner, as neither "real" nor "unreal," as bereft, in other words, of any determinate doxic characterization. In both instances, as Eugen Fink does well to point out, neutralization is not identical with a lack of interest or modification of attention, as when I have lost all interest in an activity or object, or when for want to adequate sleep I "zone out" during class (Fink 1966, p. 70).

Yet, Husserl stresses that neutrality modification resembles doxic modifications in so far as a neutralized consciousness cancels or disempowers (*entkräftet*) doxic modalities. Unlike doxic modifications, however, the negating force of neutralized modification is "totally different from negation"–in the case of doxic negation has a "positive accomplishment of its own in what is negated, a non-being that is itself again being" (*Ideen* 213/247). As noted above with Husserl's own example, the "nothingness" or "negation" that clings to the appearance of the object, as when an experience "strikes out" another experience (e.g., the statue begins to move and I realize that the statue is in fact an actual person) is in turn posited as an object, precisely, as "not-being such and such." As Husserl writes: "we can also direct our focus at what has been crossed out as such, apprehending it, i.e., what has been *affixed with the [negation] stroke. It then stands there as a new 'object,'* and does so, to be sure, *in the simple doxic, original mode of 'being.'* The new attitude does not produce the new object in its being; even in 'implementing' the rejection, we are conscious that what is rejected has the character of being crossed out. But only in the new attitude does this character become a *predictable determination* of the noematic core-of sense" (*Ideen* 210/244). In an extremely compressed form, Husserl is here speaking to the question of non-veridical intentionality that had vexed Brentano and his

---

17 In the *Logical Investigations*, Husserl had already introduced the notion of "qualitative modification," namely, the neutralization of the qualitative, or thetic, act of consciousness.

cadre of students; but, it would require too much of a detour to examine in greater depth Husserl's own account.[18]

The salient point for our discussion consists in Husserl's suggestion that neutrality modification does not accomplish anything and does not cancel out an object: it does not posit an object as "non-being." In this remarkable manner, a neutralized consciousness is a consciousness bereft of *any* belief towards "being," and might be compared to an attitude of wonder and *Gelassenheit* in which an object is left to appear without any determinate noetic *or* noematic characterization. Neutralized consciousness is still in its own way an objectifying consciousness, and in this sense, remains "productive."[19] What is intriguing about this peculiar modification is that strictly speaking one cannot even speak of an *act* of consciousness, even if Husserl tacitly understands the possibility of neutralization (an eidetic possibility for any positional consciousness) as a supreme manifestation of freedom–the freedom that prefers *not to have a view in order to have view*. That freedom, however, comes upon consciousness not entirely though its own volition since Husserl explicitly separates neutrality modification from any volitional act [get]. And yet, even with the neutralization of the object, an object nonetheless still appears or is given to consciousne; but here again, we come up against the situation that strictly speaking the object appears without any determinate doxic characterization, as if were doxically characterless, as it were, with not even any character of "being." By the same token, the neutralized object does not appear as "irreal" or "non-being" since this would in turn impart a doxic characterization. The question of how exactly to understand this liminal sense of neutralized constitution, as not identical with "inactuality" (*Unwirklichkeit*) or "irreality"–the provenance of fiction and imagination, is very much open. Husserl equally guards against any possible conflation of neutralized consciousness with phantasy. The difficulty here, as Husserl recognizes, is that phantasy and neutralized consciousness are often entangled. Husserl argues that, on the one hand, phantasy is a form of neutralized consciousness, yet, on the other hand, it is "the *neutrality modification of the 'positing' re-presentation*, thus, of memory in the widest conceivable sense" (*Ideen* 225/215). Fink's proposal to understand neutrality modification as a constitution in the mode of "as if" (*im Modus des Als-ob*) meets the challenge half-way, or has it both ways, in rejecting any conflation between neutrality and *Unwirklich-*

---

[18] On this point see Benoist 2001.
[19] And thus contrary to Marcus Brainard's contention that neutrality modification is not productive in Brainard 2001, p. 160. See also Fink 1966, p. 69.

keit and yet in characterizing neutrality modification as "as-if" and "the semblance of constitution" (*Scheinkonstitution*) (Fink 1966, p. 69).

This entire discussion, despite its difficulties, touches on a central intuition in Husserl's thinking. A fundamental feature of rationality is the capacity for "positing" or "positional consciousness," by which Husserl understands broadly the capacity and indeed responsibility of taking a stance and staking a claim about how the world is. With different forms of positional consciousness, both negation and affirmation, beliefs and objects of belief, are subject to rational adjudication on the basis of the "principle of all principles," appeal to intuitive givenness. The universality of neutralized consciousness introduces, however, a "radical scission" within consciousness between positional and neutralized consciousness. Positional consciousness is always accompanied by the possibility of neutralization. With neutralized consciousness, however, as Husserl writes: "the question of reason and unreason makes no sense" for both the neutralized noeses as well as the neutralized noemata. We thus reach a form of consciousness that remains bound to the world–since objects are still given albeit in a neutralized manner and so importantly: not a loss of the world–and yet that occupies a "non-stance" or indifference beyond reason and unreason. Neutralized consciousness does not take a stance; it is an attitude that can neither be "correct" or "dismissed" as incorrect. It is an attitude beyond reproach that sees without judging.[20]

6. Concept without pedigree

Neutrality modification exemplifies Husserl's invention of a concept without historical pedigree. As Husserl remarks, the kind of modification designated under the heading of "neutrality modification" has "never been set forth scientifically." Along with noema, *Urdoxa*, and other concepts found within *Ideen I*, Husserl's "commencing science" (*anfangende Wissenschaft*) of transcendental phenomenology emerges as a constellation of such concepts, each of which would provided impetus for further developments and transformations within the phenomenological movement during the 20th-century. The reach of Husserl's thinking across the landscape of philosophy is directly proportional to the degree of its fruitful-

---

[20] This form of neutralized consciousness is not to be conflated with "assumptions" or "suppositions"–the theme of Alexis Meinong's *Über Annahmen*. For Husserl, assumptions involve a kind of positing whereas neutralized consciousness, as for example with experiences of "thinking to oneself," is an openness without prejudice and orientation of belief, without taking a stance for or against.

ness for *other* attempts to bring into visibility–to think–forms of consciousness that Husserl first discovered without fully mastering. Neutrality modification is a case in point. It is often said that what Husserl had in view with the notion of neutrality modification proves hard to solidify into a genuine philosophical acquisition and indeed Husserl's own circumspective description in §§ 109– 112 leaves much in the dark. As with so many of Husserl's phenomenological discoveries, one *senses* the draw of the concept without being able to discern clearly where its center of gravity resides. And perhaps like all great explorers, there is no discovery without an intangible sense for that something which draws us forth into discovery. If, as I have suggested through-out these pages, Husserl's thinking should be considered as a pedagogy for thinking, it makes eminent sense to conclude such wanderings with how other thinkers have learned from Husserl's *Ideen I*, and in this particular instance, from the concept of neutrality modification. Let me end, therefore, with two other beginnings, with two variations of Husserl's neutrality modification in Sartre and Lévinas, respectively: *nausea* and *insomnia*. My claim is decidedly *not* to say that these two phenomena are identical with each other nor identical with what Husserl himself spells out as neutrality modification. My point instead is to demonstrate how nausea in Sartre and insomnia in Lévinas can be regarded as variations of a basic phenomenological theme.

It is well known that Sartre wrote his novel *Nausea* during an intense period of engagement with Husserl's phenomenology while in Berlin in 1933–1934. As he reportedly once remarked, he worked on his seminal essay "The Transcendence of the Ego" in the morning and on his novel in the afternoon. "Nausea" is the general heading for a creeping existential malaise that afflicts Roquentin; it is significant that Sartre originally entitled his novel *Melancholia*, thus suggesting that the basic condition of nausea is intimately linked to the possible, or indeed, impossible achievement of a contemplative attitude. Antoine Roquentin's existential narrative of dis-integration culminates with on ontological epiphany in a park standing before a chestnut tree. Roquentin finds himself sitting on park-bench staring at the protruding roots of a chestnut tree sprawling under his feet. He comes to experience a breathless vision that reveals to him the meaning of "existence." Sartre's description of this experience progresses through various stages of dis-articulation. At first, Roquentin experiences a neutralization of positional consciousness in judgments, or cognition. Sentences such as, as Sartre's prose indicate, "the ocean *is* green" are unhinged from any comprehension. The meaning of "is" slowly dawns upon Roquentin through a suspension of language and the predicative judgment "S is p." Translated in Husserlian terms, the level of noematic sense as unity of noematic predicates–what can be determined and said of an object as such and such–is here neutralized. The world's appearance loses the supporting armature of appearances structured by noematic predicates and its correlates of belief, or doxic modifications. In a phenomenologically emphatic sense, the world fades to black. In Sartre's literary crafting, the essential structures of things becomes neutralized, leaving the remainder of unalloyed existence. As Roquentin expresses himself: "Or rather the root, the park gates, the bench, the sparse grass, all that had vanished: the diversity of things, their individuality, were only an appearance, a veneer. This veneer had melted, leaving soft, monstrous masses, all in disorder–naked, in a frightful, obscene nakedness" (Sartre 1964, p. 127). In keeping with the dual-directions of neutralization (neutralization of acts and neutralization of object), Roquentin's own consciousness becomes neutralized in the form of a pervasive de-personalization (much of Sartre's description resonates strongly with Cotard's Syndrome). Roquentin becomes incapable of action and remains frozen to the drain hole of his own dissolution. The complete neutralization of consciousness implicates as well a neutralization of any differentiation with the world. The world becomes unmoored from the stable and intelligible form of objectivities: no relations can be established ("posited"), no differentiation between actual and possible positing, and thus, in such an enveloping sense, nausea neutralizes rationality and rational order of the world. As Roquentin reports: "In vain I tried to *count* the chestnut trees, to *locate* them by their relationship to the Velleda, to compare the height with the height of the plane trees: each of them escaped the relationship in which I tried to enclose it, isolate itself, and overflowed" (Sartre 1964, p. 128). This transcendental collapse of any differentiation produces the apocalypse of intentionality: the noetic and noematic differentiation becomes neutralized at its root with the consequence that consciousness finds its immanence *in things* even as those things have dissolved away. As Roqeuntin remarks: "I *was* the root of the chestnut tree. Or rather I was entirely conscious of its existence."

The neutralization of consciousness entails a neutralization of positional consciousness and hence, as noted, the neutralization of *language* and the intelligibility of speech. For to speak about the world is essentially to stake (publically, that is, inter-subjectively) a position and posit something "as being such and such" about the world. It is thus with absolute consistency that Roquentin only comes to *name* what is revealed through his neutralized consciousness only after the experience itself. As he writes: "The word absurdity is coming to life under my pen; a little while ago, in the garden, I couldn't find it, but neither was I looking for it, I didn't need it: I thought without words, *on* things, *with* things" (Sartre 1964, p. 129). The experience can only be narrated afterwards as a writing of the disaster. Through this deferred act of writing, Sartre in this manner tacitly amalgamates an ontologically aggressive neutrality modification with the universality of a phenomenological *epoché*, but an *epoché* that does *not* (as with Husserl) lead into a new form of positing, namely, the positing of transcendental field of experience in reflective consciousness (and hence a certain philosophical writing). Instead, the neutralization modification of nausea has reached into and through the *epoché* in order to neutralize any possible moment of reduction *to* a new field of objects and knowledge (and hence new form of positings). The neutralized modification in extremis renders present the sheer facticity of the "there is"–the absurdity of existence in its contingency. This contingency of existence is not something towards which consciousness takes a stance, or posits; it is beyond reason and unreason, in other words, absurd.

I have argued that in Sartre's handling, neutralized modification becomes amalgamated with an existential *epoché*, yet the force of the neutralization forecloses any trajectory towards a phenomenological reduction in the manner proposed by Husserl. In Lévinas' phenomenological description of insomnia, we find yet another another variation on the neutrality modification in relation to the complex of *epoché* and reduction. Lévinas looks to insomnia as a phenomenological exemplification of a radicalized reduction to the sheer fact "that there is" (*il y a*). This reduction of beings to being, to the anonymity of existing, or being, without any differentiation and determination into beings, reflects a Sartrean conception of absurdity and the contingency of existence. Insomnia, for Lévinas, can be understood as a neutralized consciousness, yet what is particular about its modification is that it modifies drastically the implied self-positing of consciousness *for itself*. Consciousness exists in a neutralizing modification its own sense of "being," which Lévinas understands as the suspension of the constitutive difference for consciousness between wakefulness and sleep. To be awake is implicitly to be awake to oneself as conscious, and hence, to posit oneself as present, as self-present. To be asleep is a modification of being-awake, yet a modification that preserves in a modified form the self-positing of my existence since upon waking up I still know myself to be the person who has just slept. As Lévinas remarks, "consciousness is the power to sleep" (Lévinas 1987, p. 51). Through this neutralization of consciousness as for itself, subjectivity is thrust into a condition beyond sleep and wakefulness revealing the impersonality and horror of existence. Insomnia is time out of joint: consciousness is transfixed to an unremorseful and ceaseless present with neither beginning nor end.[21] Consciousness is no longer "for itself" but abandoned as "without-self," beyond its own reason and unreason for being itself.

---

21 The structure of inner time-consciousness becomes itself neutralized.

Bibliography

Benoist, Jocelyn (2001): *Représentations sans objet: aux origines de la phénoménologie et de la philosophie analytique.* Paris: PUF.
Bimbenet, Étienne (2012): "La double théorie du noème: sur le perspectivisme husserlien". In: Grandjean, Antoine/Perreau, Laurent (eds.): *Husserl. La science des phénomènes.* Paris: CNRS Éditions, pp. 187–211.
Brainard, Marcus (2002): *Belief and its Neutralization: Husserl's System of Phenomenology in Ideas I.* Albany: SUNY Press.
Dahlstrom, Daniel (2001): *Heidegger's Concept of Truth.* Cambridge: Cambridge University Press.
De Warren, Nicolas (2009): *Husserl and the Promise of Time.* Cambridge: Cambridge University Press.
Derrida, Jacques (1978): "'Genesis and Structure' and Phenomenology." In Derrida, Jacques: Writing and Difference. Chicago: University of Chicago Press, pp. 154–168.
Fink, Eugen (1966): *Studien zur Phänomenologie 1930–1939.* The Hague: Nijhoff.
Evans, Gareth (1982): *The Varieties of Reference.* Oxford: Clarendon Press
Husserl, Edmund (1917/1918): Manuscript A I 39. Preserved at the Husserl Archive in Leuven.
Husserl, Edmund (1921), Manuscript B III 12 IV. Preserved at the Husserl Archive in Leuven.
Husserl, Edmund (1976): *Ideen zu einer reinen Phänomenologie und phänomenologischen Philosophie. Erstes Buch: Allgemeine Einführung in die reine Phänomenologie. Zweiter Halbband: Ergänzende Texte (1912–1929).* Husserliana. Vol. III/2. The Hague: Nijhoff.
Husserl, Edmund (1987): *Vorlesungen über Bedeutungslehre, Sommersemester 1908.* Husserliana Vol. XXVI. The Hague: Nijhoff.
Lavigne, Jean-François (2005): *Husserl et la naissance de la phenomenology.* Paris: PUF.
Lévinas, Emmanuel (1987): *Time and the Other.* Pittsburgh: Duquesne University Press.
McDowell, John (1994): *Mind and World.* Cambridge, MA: Harvard University Press.
Krzysztof, Michalski (1997): *Logic and Time. An Essay on Husserl's Theory of Meaning.* Dordrecht: Kluwer.
Sartre, Jean-Paul (1964): *Nausea.* New York: New Directions.

John J. Drummond
The Doctrine of the noema and the theory of reason

Section IV, chapter 1, The noematic sense and the relation to the object

Husserl discusses the noema in detail in three successive chapters, but the discussion in Chapter One of Part Four is distinctive. In the two previous chapters, Husserl has discussed the noema as the correlate of the noesis. His attention has been centered on the intentional correlation wherein the noema is considered in its relation to the noesis and as a mode of presentation of the intended object to the experiencing subject. In the present chapter, however, his attention turns to the relation of the noema, and especially of the noematic sense, to the intended object itself.

This shift in Husserl's attention is a direct consequence of his concern in Part Four to develop a theory of reason. The shift in attention from the relation of the noema to the noesis to the relation of the noema to the intended object serves as the transition from Husserl's consideration of intentional structures to his consideration of reason. What must be accounted for in the transition is the character of fulfilled intentions that present the object directly and "intuitively," in a broad sense of "intuition." Once this is accomplished, Husserl can lay out a theory of reason that is rooted in his special notion of evidence. But to account for fulfilled intentions, Husserl must clarify the relation of the noema or intentional object to the intended object itself.

The framework for my discussion is set by a remark Husserl makes at the beginning of § 90 in the previous chapter, shortly after introducing the notion of the noema:

> Like perception, *every* intentional experience has its 'intentional object,' i.e., its objective sense–precisely what makes up the fundamental component [*Grundstück*] of intentionality. In other words, to have a sense [of something] or 'to have something in mind' [literally, 'to have something in the sense' (*im Sinne zu haben*)–JJD] is the basic character of all consciousness that for that reason is not only any experience at all but a 'noetic' experience, one having a sense. (*Ideen* 177–78/206)

More specifically, I want to focus on the apparent equivalence of the expressions "to have a sense [of something]" and "to have something in the sense." This equivalence becomes important in Husserl's discussion of the relation between the noema and the intended object in the first chapter of Part Four. We find not exactly a reformulation but a similar idea expressed when Husserl in § 128 sets the problem for this chapter:

> [T]he phenomenological problem of the relation of consciousness to an objectivity has, above all, its noematic side. The noema in itself has a relation to an object and, to be sure, via the noema's own 'sense.' If we ask how the 'sense' belonging to consciousness comes to the 'object,' i.e., its own [object], and how that object can be 'the same' in manifold acts with very diverse noematic content, and if we ask how we see this in the sense, we find that new structures present themselves, structures whose extraordinary meaning is patent. (*Ideen* 255/296 – 97)

In viewing the noema in its relation to the noesis, Husserl's earlier discussions examine the noema in the context of a distinction between the real and intentional content of experience. The analysis of intentional content in *Ideas I*, however, revises substantially the analysis presented in the *Logical Investigations* of 1900 – 1901. There Husserl's analysis of intentional content revolved around the notions of quality and matter and avoided all talk of the intentional object, since Husserl, still committed to a kind of descriptive psychology, allowed only the really inherent (*reell*) contents of an experience to be brought into the analysis. The quality and matter, however, could not be merely really inherent contents; otherwise the resulting analysis would be psychologistic. So Husserl appealed to an intentional essence to secure the ideal character of the meanings found in experience. The quality of the experience, on this account, tokened an experience-type, and the matter of the experience instantiated a meaning-species. The experience's reference to the object, whether existent or non-existent, was realized via the reference of the instantiated meaning-species.

In the *Investigations* Husserl had characterized the matter of the experience as follows:

> *The matter is the moment in the act that first confers the relation to an object, and with such complete definiteness that by this matter is set not only the object in general that is meant but also the manner in which it is meant.* The matter—we can say still more clearly—is the peculiar moment in the phenomenological content of the act that determines as what the act grasps the objectivity, what properties, forms, relations it attributes to it. It is in the matter of the act that the object of the act counts as this object and no other. It is the *sense of the objective apprehension*. (Husserl 1970, p. 589, translation modified; Husserl 1984, pp. 429 – 30)

This view of intentionality evokes comparisons with contemporary views that characterize mental events or states as a combination of a representational content and a psychological mode (cf. Searle 1983; Crane 2001; Crane 2013). The contemporary view can be developed in such a way as to avoid the problem of non-existent objects by arguing that intentionality is not a relation but merely the having of representational content. Tim Crane, for example, argues that representations are ways of representing things (cf. Crane 2013, p. 97), and the content of a representation is "the way the object of a representation is represented" (Crane 2013, p. 99). This claim commits one to the existence of representational content but not to the existence of the object represented. The intentional object is merely the object as represented in and by the representational content. Hence, Crane argues, there are non-existent intentional objects, but this does not entail that there is more in the world than what physically exists. It does entail that, for Crane, the notion of representation and, by extension, the notion of an intentional object are basic notions (cf. Crane 2013, p. 93). It also entails that intentionality is not "in general" a relation (cf. Crane 2001, p. 26; Crane 2004, p. 225), although certain kinds of mental events, e. g., perceptions, do involve a real relation to an object (cf. Crane 2013, p. 90).

Ideas I, however, revises the earlier notion of intentional content in favor of a clearly correlational view of intentionality. The act-quality remains what it was, but Husserl in § 129 now identifies a noematic correlate for that act-quality, which he calls the "being characteristics" or "posited characters" or "thetic characteristics" that attach to the sense of an experienced object. Act-matter, by contrast, is fully assimilated to the noematic side of the correlation: "the 'matter' [...] corresponds now to the 'noematic core'." (*Ideen* 257/298) The German here reads: "Offenbar enstpricht nun die 'Materie' [...] dem 'noematischen Kern." In this context, I understand the expression "enspricht dem noematischen Kern" to have the sense "equates to the noematic core." I do so because, while Husserl continues to refer to the qualitative characters of acts (perceptual, memorial, etc.) as correlated with posited and thetic characteristics, in neither this text nor later texts does he employ a noetic sense of "matter" to refer to a really inherent moment of the act that instantiates a meaning-species and is the "sense of the objective apprehension" or to indicate a correlation between an act-matter and the noematic core.

Husserl in § 129 also summarizes the earlier analyses of the noema as intentional content, recalling in particular the distinction between the "noematic core" and the posited and thetic characteristics. The two together make up the full noema. What is important to Husserl at the moment is that the noematic core can remain the same in the variation of the experience's quality and being- and belief-modalities (although, it is also true that this variation can be reversed and the noematic core can vary as the quality and being- and belief-characteristics vary). Husserl then introduces a new moment into the noema. In a sentence apparently important enough (or perhaps disconnected enough!) to be a full paragraph, Husserl says: "Each noema has a '*content*,' namely, its 'sense,' and refers through the sense to 'its' *object*." (*Ideen* 256/297) What does he mean by this claim?

Husserl, as we have seen, previously and seemingly equated the expressions "having a sense" and "having something in the sense." That equation suggests some kind of internal identity of the sense (the intentional content) and the object in the sense. The present quotation, however, seems to separate them in its suggestion that reference to the object is achieved "through" the sense. This in turn might be thought to suggest that the intentional and intended objects are ontologically distinct entities, a distinction that would lend credence a mediator-theory of the noema. There are two importantly different variations of the mediator theory. The first is Dagfinn Føllesdal's interpretation of the noema as an ideal meaning-species instantiated in the act or, alternatively, as a type tokened in the act (cf. Føllesdal 1969; 1990). The second is Smith and McIntyre's interpretation of the noema as an abstract particular that is the correlate of the experience such that the experience is said to "entertain" a noema (with its noematic sense) that, in turn, prescribes the intended object (cf. Smith and McIntyre 1984, p. 143).

Føllesdal's interpretation is motivated, first, by the early Husserlian accounts of meaning and intentionality in the first edition of the *Logical Investigations* with their doctrine of the instantiation of semantic and intentional essences and, second, by the similarities of this view to Frege's notion of sense and its referential relation to an object. Føllesdal argues that noemata are abstract intensional entities as follows:

(1) Husserl characterizes the noema as a *Sinn* (rather than an object) (cf. Føllesdal 1969, p. 681; Føllesdal 1990, pp. 268–69);
(2) the noema is a mode of presentation of the object and is not, therefore, the concrete, intended objectivity itself (cf. Føllesdal 1969, pp. 682, 684; Føllesdal 1990, pp. 266–67, 269–70); and
(3) some intentional acts have no existent object to which they are directed, but they do have an intentional object or sense.

Since all experiences are intentional and have an intentional object even when the experiences are not aimed at an existent thing, experiences of non-existents must have their noematic content independent of the intended object. Thus, Føllesdal concludes: "The noema is like a Peircean type, which is instantiated in various individual acts. These acts are characterized by a pattern of determinations whose common structure is the noema" (Føllesdal 1990, p. 271). An experience, in other words, refers to its intended object insofar as it correlates with a noema that tokens a noema-type understood as an abstract, intensional entity.

The experience presents and refers to its object by virtue of the noema-token (cf. Føllesdal 1969, p. 682; Føllesdal 1990, p. 266).

Smith and McIntyre, on the other hand, undertake their interpretation in the light of discussions of the noema in *Ideen I*. They recognize that the Husserl of *Ideen I* has abandoned the notion that the real content of the act instantiates an intentional essence in favor of speaking of the correlation between real and intentional content, i.e., between noesis and noema (cf. Smith and McIntyre 1984, pp. 120–21). On this basis and unlike Føllesdal, they argue that the noema is an abstract particular rather than a species or type (cf. Smith and McIntyre 1984, pp. 121–24), but, like Føllesdal, they view the noema as an intensional entity mediating the relation between the experience and its intended objectivity. The noema, for Smith and McIntyre, is a particular because (i) all the properties making up the object belong in a suitably modified way to the noema as their mode of presentation and (ii) qua particular the noema can present particular intended objects. The noema is abstract, on the other hand, because it is a sense rather than a worldly object, and, as such, it does not have spatio-temporal determinations (cf. Smith and McIntyre 1984, pp. 123–24).

But this view raises problems of its own. This sense of "abstract particular" does not provide a basis for distinguishing, say, perceptual noemata from intended ideal objects, such as geometric figures. These ideal figures do not in and of themselves exist in space and time, nor does an object such as a melody (as opposed to its performances). How, then, is the noema with its ontological status as an abstract mediating, intensional entity to be distinguished from the ontological status of an abstract, ideal object that is the object of an intention?

Moreover, on both Føllesdal's and Smith and McIntyre's understandings of the noema, the experience is intentional by virtue of having a noema, i.e., an intentional object. It is the noema as intensional entity which in the first instance refers us to the object, and the act refers because it has an intensional entity as its intentional content. But Husserl insists that intentionality belongs primarily to the noesis and only secondarily to the noema, whose intentionality is a function of the horizons introduced therein by the temporal structure of experience. I shall return to this point below; for the present, however, we can say that Føllesdal's and Smith and McIntyre's accounts fail as accounts of Husserl's view of intentionality insofar as they transform the fundamental datum of the intentionality of conscious experience into something no longer fundamental. Intentionality belongs first and foremost to individual experiences, but these mediator-theories make the intentionality of experience a function of the prior referentiality of an intensional entity. They thereby transform the intentionality of acts into the different (semantic) relation of the intensionality of sense (cf. Drummond 1992, pp. 99–100; cf. Crane 2001, p. 8).

Finally, this insertion of an intensional entity into Husserl's theory of intentionality transforms a two-place relation between an experience and its object into a three-place relation between the experience, an intentional object (= intensional entity), and an intended object. This, however, involves a misunderstanding of the phenomenological reduction. The reduction neither discloses new entities–heretofore, not experienced–as mediating our relation to objects nor introduces a reductionism that explains intended objects by appeals to ontologically distinct intentional objects. The reduction instead changes the attitude in which we consider the objects of our experience such that we focus on them precisely as objects of our experience having a certain significance for us. In this way, we refocus our attention from the object (in its significance for us) to the significance (of the object) for us. This is not to find a new entity but to reorient our relation to the object.

There is enough that is correct in Føllesdal's and Smith and McIntyre's interpretations to give plausibility to their readings of Husserl. It is true, for example, that all intentional experiences have a noema as their correlate, that the noema is or has a *Sinn*, that the noema is a mode of presentation, and that some acts intend objects that do not exist. All these features of intentionality seemingly point to the noema as an entity of some sort that is ontologically distinct from the intended object. Moreover, Husserl seems to admit this when he claims in a famous (or infamous) text that we predicate different kinds of properties to intended objects and noemata. I quote the paragraph in full:

> It is clear that all *these* descriptive assertions, despite being able to sound like assertions of actuality, have undergone a *radical* modification of their sense, just as what is described itself, although presenting itself as 'exactly the same,' is nonetheless something radically different, by virtue of altering its operation sign, so to speak, to invert it. 'In' the reduced perception (in the phenomenologically pure experience), belonging indelibly to its essence, we find the perceived as such, something that we need to express as 'material thing,' 'plant,' 'tree,' 'blossoming,' and so forth. The *quotation marks* are obviously significant; they express that change in the operation sign, i.e., the corresponding radical modification of the meaning of the words. *The tree simply*, the thing in nature, is anything but[1] this *perceived-tree as such* that belongs, as the sense of the perception, to the perception and does so inseparably. The tree itself can burn up, dissolve into its chemical elements, and so forth.

---

[1] The German reads "nicht weniger als." While this can be read as "nothing less than" and in this context can mean "the tree simply is the perceived-tree as such, nothing less," it can also be read idiomatically as an intensified negation and mean "the tree simply is anything but the perceived-tree as such." Kersten and Dahlstrom adopt the former reading. However, the context, especially the immediately following sentences, suggests the latter reading, which was adopted by Boyce Gibson. I think the Boyce Gibson reading correct (even though it complicates the argument I wish to make!); hence, I have modified the Dahlstrom translation here.

The sense, however, – the sense of *this* perception, something necessarily inherent to its essence – cannot burn up; it has no chemical elements, no forces, no real properties. (*Ideen* 176–77, translation modified/205)

This text, I believe, is exceptional in the strength of its separation of the noema from the intended object. The point that it makes about the categorial differences between natural ascriptions of predicates to objects and the phenomenological ascriptions of predicates to senses can be maintained without asserting an *ontological* difference between the intended and intentional objects. The tree as perceived in this perception remains for our *reflective* consideration *as a sense* even when the perception is no longer occurring or the tree no longer exists. One does not predicate of the perceived object as perceived, i.e., the perceptual appearance of the object upon which we reflect philosophically, what one predicates of the perceived object itself that we experience straightforwardly. As Husserl puts it in § 130, expressions that characterize the noema, such as "as perceived" or "intuitively clear," are excluded from the descriptions of the intended object. "They pertain," he says, "to another dimension of descriptions, not to the objective something *of which* one is conscious but to the *way one is conscious of it*." (*Ideen* 258/300). That is true in natural speech as much as it is in phenomenological speech. There is no contradiction in saying "The wall is uniformly white" and "The wall as perceived does not appear as uniformly white; it appears mostly white with patches of light gray." We predicate ontological categories of the intended object; we predicate logical or phenomenological predicates to the object considered within the phenomenological reflection as perceived. In both instances, however, we refer to one and the same object.

Another objection to the proposal that there is a reflective differentiation but no ontological distinction between the intentional and intended objects is that it fails to take into account Husserl's claim that "while objects simply (understood in an unmodified sense) stand under fundamentally diverse supreme genera, all the senses of objects and all noemas whatsoever, however diverse they may otherwise be, intrinsically belong to one sole supreme genus."[2] (*Ideen* 254/295–96) If, the objection goes, intended objects belong to multiple species and intentional objects (noemata) belong to only one, then intended objects and intentional objects cannot be the same. The response to this objection is similar to the response to the previous objection. The object of an intending experience can be considered in two ways: straightforwardly as an entity having a certain significance for me or reflectively such that I focus on the significance that entity has for me. Straightforwardly considered objects belong to multiple genera,

---

[2] Walter Hopp (Boston University) pressed this objection during the conference presentation.

but the meanings on which I focus reflectively all belong to the single genus of meaning. This does not conflict with the idea that there is no ontological difference between the object as meant and the object whose meaning in reflection becomes the theme of my consideration.

Just as Husserl accepted the equivalence of the expressions "to have a sense [of something]" and "to have something in the sense," he now accepts, at least provisionally, the equivalence of two other expressions: "relation to something objective" and "consciousness of something." But he draws the line at accepting both expressions as referring to a relation between the noesis and "the full noema as its intentional and full 'what.'" (*Ideen* 257/299) Husserl's point, I take it, is that the full noema that corresponds to what he previously called the matter of the act along with the being-characteristics that are the correlate of the belief-modalities of the act is something different, in some sense of "different," from the object *simpliciter*–the something–that is the object of the intention. The sense of the object that is the noematic core presents the object in a particular manner, with certain properties, relations, categorial forms, under a certain description or conception, and so forth. The object is never given *simpliciter*. It is given as an identity in a manifold of noemata understood as "full Whats." The intended object *simpliciter* is not identical to the object as given in a determinate manner and with a certain being-characteristic.

Despite these texts in § 129, Husserl nevertheless rejects the view that the object is something *ontologically* distinct from the noema. To say that the noema is the object as given in a determinate manner is to say, at least in part, that the noema is at the very least the object of the intention. Hence, Husserl draws the conclusion that talk of the object *simpliciter* of the intention–the object to which the experience is related, the something of which we are conscious–refers to "an *innermost* inherent aspect of the noema." (*Ideen* 257/299) "It is," Husserl says, "not the just designated core itself but instead something that, so to speak, makes up the necessary central point of the core and functions as 'bearer' of the noematic properties specifically pertaining to it, namely, the noematically modified properties of 'what is meant as such.'" (*Ideen* 257–58/299)

In summary, then, Husserl distinguishes three moments in the noema: the thetic characteristic (the noematic correlate of the act-quality), the noematic sense (the assimilation of act-matter into the newly conceived intentional content), and the determinable X (the "innermost moment" of the noema). Husserl uses the image of a core to distinguish the noematic sense from the full noema (the union of noematic sense and thetic character). To get to that core, however, we have to work through the outer covering of thetic and being-characteristics and disclose the core lying within. In a similar manner, Husserl now identifies an innermost moment that is the core of the core, an innermost moment that we disclose only by working through the core (the noematic sense) to uncover the determinable X lying *within* it (cf. *Ideen* 261/303). Hence, Husserl can characterize the noema as both (1) that *in* which we find the identical object itself and (2) that *through* which the act intends an object. The language of "through" does not posit an instrumental entity ontologically distinct from the intended object. The noema is not a mediating entity that takes us through *and beyond* the sense to the object. We instead go "through" the noematic sense by penetrating it and finding its "innermost moment," the objective something to which the act is directed.

The intended objectivity just as it is intended is, therefore, "contained" within the noema, it belongs to the intentional content. The determinable X is that object considered formally, apart from its determinations. As such, it is capable of providing a principle of identity by virtue of which a variety of noematic phases or concrete noemata, all intending the same object in different manners, can truly be said to intend an identical object. In § 131 Husserl is emphatic about this. Again, I quote most of a long paragraph:

> The predicates [belonging to the noematic sense–JJD], however, are predicates of 'something,' and this 'something' also co-belongs, and obviously inseparably, to the core in question. It is the central point of unity […]. It is the point of connection or 'bearer' of the predicates but in no way a unity of them in the sense in which just any sort of complex, any sort of combination of predicates might be named a unity. It [this central point of unity–JJD] should be distinguished from them [the predicates], but not placed alongside them and not separated from them, just as, conversely, they are themselves *its* predicates, unthinkable without it and yet distinguishable from it. We may say that, in the continuous or synthetic progression of consciousness, one is always conscious of the intentional object [*Objekt*] but that in the same progression it again and again 'affords' itself 'differently'; it is '*the same*,' only it is given in different predicates, with a different determination of its content; 'it' shows itself only from diverse sides in the course of which the predicates that had remained undetermined would come to be determined in detail; or 'the' object [*Objekt*] remained unaltered in this stretch of givenness, but now 'it,' the identical [entity], changes, becoming more beautiful through this change, forfeiting some utility, and so forth. If this is continually understood as a *noematic description* of what is respectively meant as such, and if this description is given in a fully adequate way (as is always possible), the identical, intentional 'object' [*Gegenstand*] quite evidently differs from the shifting and variable 'predicates.' It distinguishes itself *as a central, inherent noematic aspect:* '*what stands opposite us*' [*Gegenstand*], the '*object*' [*Objekt*], the '*identical* [entity],' 'the determinable subject of its possible predicates,'–*the pure X in abstraction from all predicates*–, and it is distinct *from* these predicates or, more precisely, from the predicate-noemas. (*Ideen* 259–60/301–302)

There are three points of interest in this passage:

1. The language mixes the ontological and the logical. The determinable X is both the (ontological) "bearer" of predicates (better, attributes) and the (logical) subject of predicates.
2. The determinable X unifies the predicates but is not a unity of them. The object, in other words, is no mere sum of properties.
3. The determinable X as the "identical" also unifies the multiplicity of presentations or noematic senses directed to the same object "in the continuous or synthetic progression of consciousness" in which the sense of the object becomes differently–and more fully–determined.

The distinction between the core and the determinable X allows Husserl to say that the object is presented *in* the noema or sense. Furthermore, Husserl's account reveals how the noema is both the sense (the intended object considered insofar as it is significant for us) and the intended object itself (just as it is intended in the act, i.e., with just that significance for us).

The notion of the determinable X is Husserl's way of securing the identity of the intended object in a manifold of differing appearances within the confines of the purely static account of *Ideas I*. It is misleading, however, insofar as "the identical" and the X appear as purely formal notions. It is only when we take into account the temporality of our experience and the flow of noematic phases and of concrete experiences that we can adequately understand Husserl's claim that "*the determinable Xs of the united senses* come *to coincide with one another and with the X of the entire sense of the respective unity of* sense" (*Ideen* 261/303–304). If we consider a temporally extended perception, each phase of the perception has its noematic correlate with the threefold structure of thetic characteristic, noematic sense, and determinable X. The perception as a whole also has its noematic correlate; we can call it the concrete noema as opposed to the noematic phase. The concrete noema has the same threefold structure. The determinable X of the concrete noema is the identical object as perceived in the flow of perceptual phases. Each noematic phase introduces new moments of sense insofar as it provides new appearances and new determinations. The introduction of temporality, in other words, reveals that the notions of the identical and of the X are not purely formal; they are dynamic concepts imprisoned by *Ideas I* in the straightjacket of a static analysis. Outside the limits of a purely static analysis, the determinability of the X is the object's capacity to come to a more complete–and, in some cases, more precise–determination in the course of a temporally extended experience (cf., e.g., Husserl 1966, 5; 20–22; Husserl 1973/1997, § 27). The determinable X, therefore, is both a formal and a teleological characterization of the identical object.

This leaves open the question of how the multiple noematic phases and the multiple concrete noemata are related to the identical object that is given in and through each of them. Aron Gurwitsch provides a detailed account of the relation between the noema and the intended object. Generalizing the Gestalt account of sensory organization, he conceives the relation between the intended object and the multiplicity of noematic phases and concrete noemata as a whole-part relation. The intended object just is the whole made up of the noematic parts that do or could present the thing from different sides and different perspectives.

Using perception as his example, Gurwitsch notes that the perceived thing, when presented from a certain side or under a certain aspect, is presented as a whole by virtue of the horizons of what is directly perceived. The intended object, in other words, is ideally presented in perception with its full empirical significance, even though it is actually presented only in a finite set of noemata. Gurwitsch provides multiple statements of this view (cf. Gurwitsch 1964, pp. 184; 223; 227; Gurwitsch 1966, p. 132),[3] but perhaps the clearest indication of both the strength and weakness of his view appears in the following text:

> There remains the task of defining the relationship between the perceptual noema and the thing perceived. While actually appearing in a determinate manner of adumbrational presentation, the thing is capable of appearing in other manners. It actually so appears in the course of the perceptual process, when, e.g., we walk around the thing and, in general, perceive it under various conditions of different sorts. In the course of that process, the thing is perceived as identically the same, presenting itself from different sides, under varying aspects, in a variety of orientations. The thing cannot be perceived except in one or the other manner of adumbrational presentation. It is nothing besides, or in addition to, the multiplicity of those presentations through all of which it appears in its identity. Consequently, the thing perceived proves to be the group, more precisely put, the systematically organized totality of adumbrational presentations. (Gurwitsch 1974, pp. 236–37)

Gurwitsch is correct to stress that the intended thing is identically the same in the different perceptions or perceptual phases. Nevertheless, there is a difficulty with his position. Gurwitsch argues from the fact that the object is nothing over and above its noematic phases to the conclusion that it is a whole of noematic parts. Thus, he claims that the object "appears in its identity" through "all" its presentations. Gurwitsch understands this "all" collectively. The object appears in the whole of these presentations because the partial presentations are functionally connected to one another such that any given noematic presentation

---

[3] Although I am citing texts dealing with the perceptual noema and the perceived object, Gurwitsch generalizes this account to other kinds of experience, including higher-order acts such as judgment; cf. Drummond (1990, pp. 73–74). I shall therefore consider these texts indicative of Gurwitsch's general position.

calls forth horizontally the whole series of presentations. Hence, he can conclude that the identical object–"the thing perceived" in the text above–is a totality of presentations.

Given the essential inadequacy in the evidencing of objects, however, we can never experience this totality; it is an "idea in the sense of Kant" (Gurwitsch 1964, p. 227). The perceived thing as a real existent is, according to Gurwitsch, "the very idea of an infinite system or continuum of appearances all realized in actual sense-experience" (Gurwitsch 1964, p 227). Since we cannot experience the infinite system of appearances, we never, on this view, actually experience the object; we experience only some of its presentations. Gurwitsch, in short, reduces the perceived thing itself to its presentations and thereby confuses the categories of sense and object (cf. Drummond 1990, §§ 16 – 17). Gurwitsch's position transforms Husserl's view into a kind of phenomenalism, not, to be sure, the phenomenalism of the empiricists but a kind of "phenomenological phenomenalism" (cf. Drummond 1980, pp. 9 – 21; Drummond 1990, pp. 95 – 99) that reduces the intended object to the infinite whole of its possible noematic presentations. It is certainly correct that the *complete presentation* of objects is an idea in the Kantian sense. It does not follow from this, however, that the presented, identical *object* itself is an idea in the Kantian sense.

How, then, are we to understand the relation between the noematic presentations and the intended thing? Contra Gurwitsch, we must understand the "all" distributively rather than collectively. The object is the identity presenting itself in each noematic moment and in each set of noematic moments rather than, as Gurwitsch claims, the whole of noematic moments. The identical object, although not ontologically distinct from the noemata (its modes of presentation), is not reducible to any single noema or to any set, including the whole set, of noemata.

The X as the identical (rather than as a mere substrate of properties) can be understood only against the background of the manifold in which the continuity of or relation among the noematic components displays the object as having the identity characteristic of the type of object it is. The noematic sense, as a moment of the full noema, refers to the identical, intended object not simply by virtue of its relation to the determinable X within it, but by virtue of its horizonal connections with the manifold of noemata presenting that same object. If we think, for example, of a material thing in space as perceived in vision, we can see certain patterns of continuity and overlapping in the perceptual appearances motivated by different bodily activities involved in the perceiving. Since these different appearances are horizontally intended in any perceptual phase, we intend the patterned multiplicity of phenomenal changes in any perceptual phase and recognize the self-transforming identity within the manifold. Similarly, if we think of an empirical concept, we can see certain patterns of similarity in our experience of the objects that underlie the formation of the concept, and we are thereby able to comprehend the species as the identity in the manifold of its instances. The presence of such patterns underlies our grasp of objects as identical. Reference goes *through* the noematic sense of a particular phase of consciousness to the "identical" *within* it by virtue of its horizontal connections with the manifold of noemata presenting one and the same object. It is in this way that the object is presented both *in* and *through* the (noematic) sense.

Having developed an account of sense and its relation to the object, Husserl is now in a position to connect his doctrine of the noema to the account of reason in two ways. First, one of the manifolds in which the identical object is experienced is the manifold formed by the experience that emptily intends an object and the experience that fulfills that empty intending. Husserl hints at this relation in § 132 when he says:

> Being dimly conscious of something and being conscious of that same thing in a clear way are, with respect to their noematic concreteness, very different, just as the entire experiences are. But nothing stands in the way of the determinate content in the former case being absolutely identical with that in the latter case. (*Ideen* 262/304)

Here Husserl's idea is that we have a more or less empty experience in which the meant is not clearly present to mind contrasted with the full (and fulfilling) experience in which the same object with the same determinations is clearly present. By clarity Husserl means direct presence to an attentive mind, and this is the nature of fulfillment in which we grasp the truth and the truthfulness of our experience. The identity of the object, in other words, manifests itself in the tendency toward fulfillment that we find in conscious life, and, in this, we once again see the X as a teleological notion. This teleological sense of reason, in its ordering toward truth, is the fundamental sense of reason. Reason in this sense is evidence, the having of the object in an experience which directly and intuitively presents the object as it is. Husserl devotes the next, penultimate chapter of *Ideas I* to this notion of reason.

The second way in which this discussion of the noema and object connects to the theory of reason is in its identification of the determinable X/noematic predicate structure within the noematic sense. This underlies the possibility of developing what Husserl calls "*the idea of a systematic and universal doctrine of the forms of senses* (meanings)" (*Ideen* 264/306)–a formal *apophansis*. This involves, first, a pure logical grammar that identifies the forms of judgments, both simple and complex. These forms are subject to modal modifications, and the notion of form is thereby enlarged, and it is further enlarged by considering the forms of judgment appropriate to the axiological and practical spheres of reason.

The distinction between the attitude in which we focus straightforwardly on intended objects and the attitude in which we reflect on intentional objects (i.e., the intended object just as intended with particular properties, relations, and categorial forms) provides the basis upon which Husserl can gesture toward formal ontology, a science correlative with formal *apophansis*. Here Husserl points to a systematic and universal doctrine of the forms of objects (cf. *Ideen* 268/311–12), but he does not develop the idea. Nevertheless, this discussion in § 135 points back to the *Logical Investigations* and forward to *Formal and Transcendental Logic* and their discussions of the correlation between formal logic and formal ontology.

A pure logical *apophansis* also involves, at a second level, an analysis of the possible forms for combining judgments into argumentative structures. This notion of reason as *reasoning* occupies Husserl's attention in the final chapter of the work. The notions of reason as *reasoning* and reason as *evidence* are inseparable, for the construction of sound arguments in a process of reasoning requires that we start with what is known to be true, with reason as *evidencing*.

References

Crane, Tim (2001): *Elements of Mind*. Oxford: Oxford University Press.
Crane, Tim (2013): *The Objects of Thought*. Oxford: Oxford University Press.
Drummond, John J. (1980): "A Critique of Gurwitsch's 'Phenomenological Phenomenalism'". In: *The Southern Journal of Philosophy* 18, pp. 9–21.
Drummond, John J. (1990): *Husserlian Intentionality and Non-Foundational Realism: Noema and Object*. Dordrecht: Kluwer Academic Publishers.
Drummond, John J. (1992): "An Abstract Consideration: De-Ontologizing the Noema". In: John Drummond/Lester Embree (Eds.): *The Phenomenology of the Noema*. Dordrecht: Kluwer Academic Publishers, , pp. 89–109.
Føllesdal, Dagfinn (1969): "Husserl's Notion of the Noema". In: *The Journal of Philosophy* 66, pp. 680–87.
Føllesdal, Dagfinn (1990) (Supplement). "Noema and Meaning in Husserl". In: *Philosophy and Phenomenological Research* 50, pp. 263–71.
Gurwitsch, Aron (1964): *The Field of Consciousness*. Pittsburgh: Duquesne University Press.
Gurwitsch, Aron (1966): "Contribution to the Phenomenological Theory of Perception". In: Gurwitsch, Aron: *Studies in Phenomenology and Psychology*. Evanston, Ill.: Northwestern University Press, pp. 332–49.
Gurwitsch, Aron (1974): "Husserl's Theory of the Intentionality of Consciousness in Historical Perspective". In: Embree, Lester (Ed.): *Phenomenology and the Theory of Science.*. Evanston, Ill.: Northwestern University Press, pp. 210–40.

Husserl, Edmund (1966): *"Analysen zur passiven Synthesis: Aus Vorlesungs- und Forschungsmanuskripten 1918–1926"*. In: Husserliana. Vol. XI. The Hague: Nijhoff.
Husserl, Edmund (1970): *Logical Investigations*. Trans. Findlay, J. N.. London: Routledge and Kegan Paul.
Husserl, Edmund (1973): *"Ding und Raum: Vorlesungen 1907"*. In: Husserliana. Vol. XVI. The Hague: Nijhoff.
Husserl, Edmund (1984): *"Logische Untersuchungen. Zweiter Band, Erster Teil: Untersuchungen zur Phänomenologie and Theorie der Erkenntnis."* In: Husserliana. Vol. XIX/1. The Hague: Nijhoff.
Husserl, Edmund (1997). *Thing and Space. Lectures of 1907*. Trans. Rojcewicz, Richard. Dordrecht: Kluwer Academic Publishers.
Searle, John (1983): *Intentionality: An Essay in the Philosophy of Mind*. Cambridge: Cambridge University Press.
Smith, David W./McIntyre, Ronald (1984): *Husserl and Intentionality: A Study of Mind, Meaning, and Language*. Dordrecht: Reidel Publishing.

Daniel O. Dahlstrom
Reason and experience: The project of a phenomenology of reason

Section IV, chapter 2, Phenomenology of reason

In keeping with the aim of the present volume, the following paper provides a sketch of the major topics, together with commentary on the salient moves made by Husserl, in the penultimate chapter of *Ideas I*. The chapter's basic theme is the phenomenology of reason. In the chapter Husserl outlines a project of investigating rational consciousness and determining its possibility, ideally and essentially, by way of discerning and describing its various manifestations. Since Husserl characterizes the fundamental form of rational consciousness, as noted below, as a kind of intuitive discernment, what is investigated and the manner in which it is investigated coincide in this respect. In other words, the phenomenology of reason exemplified by this chapter is inherently reflexive, a rational account of rationality. After highlighting the distinctiveness of Husserl's concept of reason in relation to some of his prominent predecessors, I go over what he considers the essential distinctions and tasks of a phenomenology of reason, before returning to its aim. In the course of these considerations, I flag a problem and conclude with a gloss of what I take to be the crucial and undeniably valuable insight underlying it.

1. Reason

Reason for modern German philosophers, as for many medieval philosophers, has been associated principally with inference. Following a tradition that hearkens back to the first three books of Aristotle's *Organon*, Immanuel Kant divided logic into theories of concepts, judgments, and inferences (*Begriffs-, Urteils- und Schlusslehre*, respectively). A different cognitive capacity corresponds to each of these theories or doctrines. Concepts are the work of understanding, judgments that of the power of judgment, and syllogistic inferences that of reason (*Vernunft*) (cf. Kant 1968, pp. 197–198). To be sure, Kant does not restrict the term "inference" to rational inferences, i.e., full-blown syllogisms. In his logic lectures, he distinguishes the immediate inferences made by the understanding and the inferences of induction and analogy made by the power of judgment from the mediated inferences, i.e., the syllogisms that are the work of reason. But it is exclusively the work of reason to recognize the necessity of a proposition on the basis of its subsumption under a given universal rule. Evidence of this way of construing reason can be found in the structure of the Transcendental Logic in Kant's *Critique of Pure Reason*. Whereas the transcendental analytic contained analyses of the pure concepts of the understanding and the fundamental principles of the transcendental power of judgment, the transcendental dialectic examined the ideas generated by pure reason's distinctive capacity to make inferences, where the ideas correspond to something like a fulfillment of the complete set of conditions for particular inferences. Thus, Kant distinguishes reason as a strictly logical cognitive faculty and a transcendental one, where the latter can lead to the overreaching peculiar to speculative metaphysics but can also serve a sound regulative function (cf. Kant 1930, B364 ff, B378–389). However, in both instances, reason is first and last something we do. Any constraints are self-imposed and it is, in a matter of speaking, at arm's length from the world we experience and our sensory access to it.

Though there are some notable exceptions, many nineteenth century German philosophical approaches to theoretical reason echo Kant's account along these lines (cf., e. g., Sigwart 1831, p. 33; Herbart 1834, p. 69; Lotze 1843, p. 18). The opening paragraph of Husserl's "Phenomenology of Reason," (Chapter Two of the final section of *Ideas*) signals a decisive break with this tradition. For Husserl, reason is a matter of demonstrating (*ausweisen*), but not in the sense of an inference. Instead it is demonstrating in the etymological sense of the original Latin word, i. e., showing that something is the case, thus closely corresponding to the German term, that may be variously translated as "pointing out," "identifying," "showing what is in question." For example, at Passport control, the agent asks, "Ihren Ausweis, bitte," requesting a form of identification that shows who you are, i. e., the document or papers that, together with a photo, identify you for him. Once he sees the papers and gives you a second look, he has evidence of who you are. The agent does not infer that you are the same person who is portrayed in the picture; he sees it. That is to say, he detects at least a sufficient likeness between the mien in the photo and your mien as you stand in front of him. He takes the detection to demonstrate, i. e., to be sufficient evidence, that you are the person identified in your passport; he is satisfied that it identifies you with the person pictured and named in the passport. Detecting that likeness is a form of rational consciousness on his part.[1]

---

[1] One might argue that the officer in charge of inspecting passports infers from the likeness that you are the same person as pictured in the passport. However, if the argument is not to fall prey to the myth of the given, the likeness must coincide with some relevant proposition, e. g., "The face in the photo looks sufficiently like the face of the person before me." After all, inference, strictly speaking, is a relation between propositions alone. Still, even on this interpretation, the

In that same opening paragraph Husserl adds that being rationally demonstrable or identifiable correlates with being true and being actual, an addition that hearkens back to the principle of all principles and his insistence upon being the true positivist. Reason, truth, and actuality are equivalent in some sense or, at least, there is a kind of metonymy among his uses of the corresponding terms.

> If one speaks rationally–whatever one then says of the objects–what is meant as well as what is said must be capable thereby of being *'justified,' 'demonstrated,'* directly *'seen'* or, *in a mediated way, 'discerned.'* In the logical sphere, the sphere of assertion, *'being true'* or *'being actual'* and *'being rationally demonstrable'* stand intrinsically in correlation [with one another–D.O.D.]. (*Ideen* 270/314)

While Husserl's approach to reason breaks, as noted above, with the Kantian tradition, it has notable affinities with Hegel's account of reason. Hegel places his account of reason within the *Encyclopedia* version of the *Phenomenology of Spirit*, characterizing it as "the truth existing in and for itself... the identity of the subjectivity of the concept and its objectivity and universality" (Hegel 1970, §§ 437–438, p. 228). Similarly, in the same context, he notes that "only if the true content becomes objective for me, does my intellect acquire, in a concrete sense, the significance of reason" (Hegel 1970, §§ 437–438, p. 228).[2]

2. Three essential distinctions

In the penultimate chapter of *Ideas I* Husserl elaborates his phenomenology of reason by making three essential distinctions.

The *first essential distinction* is the contrast between rational consciousness in its most fundamental form and other forms of rational consciousness, i.e., the difference between seeing or perceiving something in an originary way and not seeing it in quite this way. Thus, for example, perceiving a tree contrasts with remembering it, reading a sentence with comprehension contrasts with reciting it from memory. So, too, discerning the necessity of a mathematical equation contrasts with recalling that necessity. At the most fundamental level, rational consciousness or rationality takes the form of grasping something in an immediate

---

likeness itself is not inferred any more than its requisite coincidence with the relevant proposition is. Instead both that likeness and that coincidence are matters of insight, intuitive discernment, the fundamental form of rational consciousness.

2 "Erst wenn mir der *wahrhafte* Inhalt gegenständlich wird, erhält meine Intelligenz in *konkretem* Sinne die Bedeutung der *Vernunft*." (Hegel 1970, §§ 437–438, p. 228)

way; hence, the ocular metaphor that is as old as Plato and Aristotle. As the examples suggest, rational consciousness, so construed, extends from sensory perception and reading with comprehension to discerning some necessity or essential feature. What differs is not the sense that can be abstracted from the experiences (the *abstractum*), since it is the same (i.e., the tree posited in memory and in perception, the equation's necessity, whether discerned or merely recalled). The difference pertains instead to how that sense is concretely experienced (the *concretum* in which it is more or less filled out). In every experience there is a positing and a posited, a noetic and a noematic dimension, but they are rational when and only when they are based upon a sense that has been filled out or filled in, affording something in an originary manner. Other manners of positing, e.g., via memory or imagination, are not by any means to be discounted, but they lack the prerogative ground of legitimacy that is inherent to rational positing, to rational insight alone, namely, the prerogative of an originary givenness.

The *second essential distinction* is the distinction between perceiving an individual and discerning an essence. The perception of an individual landscape, for example, certainly warrants the perceiver's assertion of its presence to her. In other words, it provides assertoric evidence. But this perception and evidence are essentially different, respectively, from the discernment of the essential character or truth of a mathematical equation and the apodicticity of the evidence for it.

At this point, a caveat is in order, regarding a difference in the uses of "evidence" and the German *Evidenz*. The term "evidence" in English is often used to designate an indication or even substantiation of some state of affairs that is the subject of a hypothesis or hunch. In other words, while relative to an intentionality, evidence is something that English speakers attribute to facts in relation to other facts (e.g., "The finding of a flammable at the site provides some prima facie evidence of arson"). By contrast, Husserl uses the term "evidence" to designate different forms of rational consciousness, as indicated in the presently flagged distinction between assertoric and apodictic evidence. After noting that "evidence" and "insight/discernment" are usually synonyms, Husserl signals the need to depart from this normal use and to employ "evidence" in a generic sense, encompassing both "assertoric seeing and apodictic discerning" (*Ideen* 274/318).[3]

---

[3] This distinction between the generic sense of *Evidenz* (in effect, a word of art) and the normal, restricted sense that overlaps with insight suggests a parallel with Heffernan's differentiation of Husserl's talk of "the relativity of evidence in the loose sense" and "the absolute ideal of evidence in the strict sense"; see Heffernan 1983, pp. 68–69; 165.

The *third essential distinction* also concerns evidence, namely, the contrast between inadequate and adequate forms of evidence. The evidence is inadequate where the perception is necessarily one-sided and indeterminate in a variety of ways. Real things, Husserl maintains, can in principle only appear in this way.

> A real thing, a being having such a sense in an isolated appearance, can in principle only appear '*inadequately.*' It is essentially connected with this, that *no rational positing resting upon such an appearance (that affords things inadequately) can be 'definitive,'* that nothing of the sort can be 'incontrovertible,' [...] (*Ideen* 275/319).

So, just as rational consciousness can be merely assertoric or apodictic, it can also be inadequate or adequate.

In sum, there are three distinctions essential to rational consciousness, each of which concerns different possible ways of being conscious of something rationally, i.e., different forms of evidence (in Husserl's generic sense of the term). With the respect to its rational character, our consciousness of something–or, alternatively, the evidence attaching to it–can be

(1) either originary or non-originary
(2) either assertoric or apodictic (pure, impure)
(3) either adequate or inadequate.

To see the different possible combinations of these disjunctives, consider:
A. my discernment of the necessity of the law of non-contradiction,
B. my perception of my current weight, and
C. my memory of my weight when I was 21.

A–or, equivalently, the evidence of A (*genitivus subjectivus*)–is presumably (1) originary, (2) apodictic, and (3) adequate, while B is (1) originary, (2) assertoric, and (3) inadequate. By contrast, C is (1) non-originary, (2) assertoric, and (3) inadequate. The evidence for my identity with the person portrayed in the photo in my passport is presumably like the evidence for B, i.e., originary, assertoric, and less than adequate (since the evidence is the detection of an empirical likeness).

3. The tasks of the phenomenology of reason: differentiating levels, kinds, and degrees of evidence

This penultimate chapter of *Ideas I* is highly programmatic. A substantial part of it consists in identifying the tasks of a phenomenology of reason and flagging the studies required to accomplish these tasks. Three tasks may be considered paramount, namely, determining the essential possibilities of evidence of coherence, confirmation, and corroboration. Alternatively, keeping in mind that evidence applies to the sort of rational consciousness involved, the phenomenology of reason is faced with the responsibility of determining the essential possibilities of coherent, confirmatory, and corroborative forms of rational consciousness.

3.1 Evidential coherence

In the case of real things, i.e., those consciousness-transcending realities that can only appear in an inherently inadequate way, the phenomenology of reason is set with the task of studying "the diverse cases prefigured a priori in this sphere" (*Ideen* 275/319). Accomplishing this task requires study of
  (a) essential possibilities of coherence and incoherence in the course of appearances (that is to say, the possibilities of something affording itself in the same way and in different, even conflicting ways);
  (b) the different weights and counterweights of the motivating force of what is posited accordingly, ranging from progressive reinforcement to doubt or even cancellation of what originally afforded itself and was thus posited;
  (c) what in the sense, as the relevant *material of the positing*, essentially determines the alterations in the characters of the positing;
  (d) *the essence of every kind of unmediated act of reason*, noetically and noematically (e. g., memory, like perception, is unmediated, though lacking the latter's originary evidential character);
  (e) the kind of senses or posits for each region and category, the kind of consciousness affording those senses, and the basic type of originary evidence inherent to it.

To see what Husserl might mean by the first four of these items, consider the example of a pattern of wallpaper partially covered up by a piece of furniture next to the wall. It is essentially possible for the pattern to continue in the same way or in different ways, but it is essentially impossible for the pattern to be devoid of some color. If I look behind successive pieces of furniture and continue to find the same pattern, the motivating force for positing the same pattern increases accordingly. The material of the positing that determines any alterations is the wallpaper pattern. Of course, this example can only provide inadequate evidence, however it be augmented. It is, nonetheless, prefigured a priori that the only possible evidence (rational consciousness) is inadequate. In general, the sort of possible evidence (e.g., its adequacy, inadequacy and capacity of augmentation or diminution) is prefigured a priori. Thus, the perfect sort of evidence appropriate to essential relations is not appropriate to other spheres, and to demand it of them is, Husserl declares, "absurd" (*Ideen* 276/321).

The task of differentiating the sort of evidence involved is not limited to straightforward beliefs or theoretical judgments; it concerns every thetic sphere (every sphere of positing). To be sure, Husserl makes the claim that all doxic modalities (modalities of belief, e.g., conjecture, supposition, doubt) refer back to original doxa and all original beliefs refer back to "originary and ultimately perfect evidence," i.e., "its *original reason* or, better, to the 'truth.'" (*Ideen* 277/322) Nevertheless, he notes that "evidence" is by no means a name "merely for instances of reason of the sort found in the sphere of belief (or even only in the sphere of the predicative judgment)" (*Ideen* 278/323). In the spheres of emotion and willing, there are positings and questions of their evidence as well. Paralleling "theoretical" or "*doxological truth*" (evidence) are instances of "*axiological and practical truth or evidence.*" (*Ideen* 278/323) It is a task for the phenomenology of reason to investigate not only the latter sorts of evidence, but also their relation to the former.

3.2 Evidential confirmation and identification

A further task for a phenomenology of reason is the study of the combinations of theses that coincide in some respect. Not least among these combinations are those "that must be produced *between acts with the same sense and posit, but differing rational value*" (*Ideen* 279/324), where what is posited in one act confirms, verifies, or identifies what is posited in another. The possibilities of such verification are prefigured by the essence of the respective positings and posits. Such possibilities are not purely logical but instead "motivated in a definite way by what the posit contains in itself, depending upon how fully it is given" (*Ideen*

279–280/325). I cannot see the underside of the chair I am sitting on, but the sense that it is a chair motivates me to look for four legs, not ten, and to expect that sense to be fulfilled in a variety of ways (e. g., I expect the legs to be at least some distance from on another and to be equidistant from one another). As a result, this perception of the chair is able to pass over seamlessly into perceptions of the legs themselves that are prefigured by the sense of the chair and that fill out that sense accordingly.

These first two tasks of a phenomenology of reason, determining the essence of evidential coherence and confirmation, coincide with what Husserl subsequently calls "the problem of constitution." (*Ideen* 302/351) I cite the following paragraph in full, despite its length, because in it Husserl spells out the concrete steps that he envisions as a means of accomplishing these tasks and, in the process, moving closer to a solution to the problem of constitution as a problem for rational consciousness.

> What it comes downs [sic!] to here in particular is studying systematically the continuous unifications of identity and the synthetic identifications in all domains, in terms of their phenomenological constitution. The first thing that one needs to do is become familiar with the inner construction of the intentional experiences in terms of all the universal structures, the parallelism of these structures, the layers in the noema, such as sense, subject of sense, thetic characters, fullness. Once one has done this, then what matters is making completely clear not simply how act-combinations with those structures take place but rather how they are combined into the unity of *one* act. In particular, what matters is how identifying unifications are possible, how here and there the determinable X comes to coincide with various determinations, how the determinations of sense and their empty places (that is to say here, their inherent aspects of indeterminacy) behave thereby, and, likewise, how we make clear, and achieve analytic insight into, the instances of fullness and, with them, the forms of corroboration, demonstration, and advancing knowledge in lower and higher levels of consciousness. (*Ideen* 288–289/335–336)

After familiarizing ourselves with all the structures inherent to the intentional experiences in question, the next step is to make clear how combinations of acts with those structures are able to come to constitute one act, yielding instances of degrees of fullness or, in other words, instances of confirmation and corroboration.

In some cases, to be sure, the evidence is imperfect. In some cases of memory, for example, the path prescribed cannot terminate in some *corresponding* originary evidence. Moreover, there are cases where discerning the possibility coincides with discerning the actuality of what is thereby posited, and cases where it does not. Cases of the first sort include cases of envisaging an essence's perfect fulfillment; that is to say, the envisaging is equivalent to fulfillment–or at least all the fulfillment available to us. By contrast, only actual experience and not merely running through possibilities demonstrates the existence of natural events that are posited.

3.3 Evidential corroboration

The discussion of the problem of constitution has already led us to the topic of evidential corroboration. While the original source of all legitimacy consists in the immediate, originary evidence of what is posited, the rational value of a positing can draw on or be derived from such sources in different ways. Husserl considers two general cases: first, cases where the rational positing is immediate but corroborated by the originary evidence and, second, cases where the rational positing is mediated, i.e., where it is derived since it has no evidence in itself (cf. *Ideen* 281–282/326–328).

The main example for the first case is memory. Memory is an immediate, yet non-evident rational positing, that can be more or less corroborated by connecting it to other memories and, if possible, to current perceptions. While memory remains intrinsically inadequate in a certain way, the more closely connected it is with other memories, the more evidence it enjoys. (Here we see, once again, the importance of evidential coherence.) If, however, the connection with current perception is made, its evidence casts a positive, corroborating light on the memory. (Here the connection with some form of evidential confirmation yields some evidential corroboration.)

After describing memory as one way of drawing on originary evidence, Husserl turns to the other way, namely, the cases of derived, mediated evidence. He sets the phenomenology of reason with the task of studying the general and specific essential cases of reason in every kind of mediated demonstration. That includes tracing the diverse principles of demonstration back to their phenomenological origins and making them intelligible on the basis of those origins (regardless of the immanence or transcendence of the kinds of objects involved and the adequacy or inadequacy of how they afford themselves).

4. The aim of a phenomenology of reason and a problem registered

Following this summary of the tasks and studies that make up a phenomenology of reason, Husserl sums up its aim, namely, "the universal clarification of the essential correlations that combine the *idea of what truly is* with the ideas of truth, reason, and consciousness" (*Ideen* 283/329). A basic insight at work here is the equivalence between an object, as it truly is, and its capability of being given completely, in every respect, and so posited.

> To each object 'that truly is,' there corresponds in principle (in the a priori [sense] of an unconditioned, essential universality) the *idea of a possible consciousness* in which the object itself can be apprehended *in an originary* and thereby *perfectly adequate manner*. (Husserl 2014, 283/329).

Categories of objects and categories of construing objects are accordingly correlative, and the perfect or imperfect ways of construing the objects are essentially prefigured in the essence of the respective category of construal. If the manner of construal is imperfect, then the manner of perfecting it is essentially prefigured as well. Each category of object, Husserl adds, is a universal essence that must, in principle, be capable of being given adequately. When it is given adequately, it prescribes a rule for the way that objects falling under it might be brought to "an adequate, originary givenness, according to the object's sense and manner of givenness" (*Ideen* 284/330).

Prima facie, Husserl acknowledges, these remarks seem to contradict his earlier observation that "a real thing can in principle only appear '*inadequately*'" (*Ideen* 275; 284/319; 331). He notes that the observation was made, however, with the qualification "*in an isolated experience*," (*Ideen* 284/331) thus leaving open the possibility for an open-ended progression in the determination of the object. Thus, "*the perfect givenness is prefigured as an 'idea*' (in the Kantian sense) [...] an a priori determined *continuum of appearances* with diverse but determinate dimensions, dominated by a fixed, essential legitimacy" (*Ideen* 285/331). Every side of this continuum, Husserl adds, is infinite yet co-ordinated, leading to a continuously coherent connection of the appearances of some determinable object, given as one and the same throughout the process, allowing it to be determined "more specifically" but "never as something else." To be sure, we can only have an *idea* of this continuum and the perfect givenness exemplified by it, but such an idea is, Husserl submits, patently discernible, a matter of insight. In this way Husserl innovatively appropriates Kant's understanding of the regulative use of ideas.

With this conception of ideas in hand, Husserl returns to the analysis of the essence of "truly being." "Truly being" is equivalent to "being given adequately" in one of two senses: either (a) in the sense of what is given finitely as an isolated experience or its noematic correlate, or (b) in the sense of what is given infinitely in the form of an idea. In the former sense (a), being is immanent being, e. g., the experience itself with its contents. In the latter sense (b), it is transcendent being, and what is adequately given is not something objective itself, but the idea of its sense and "epistemic essence," containing an a priori rule for the conformity of endless, inadequate experiences to that sense. Hearkening back to the regulative function that Kant assigns to ideas of reason, Husserl characterizes the idea of the adequate givenness of a thing as "an idea in the Kantian sense."

The latter idea is, I have to admit, rather puzzling, perhaps because Husserl is short on examples, on the derivation and scope of the ideas, and on the meaning of "a priori" in this connection. To be sure, there is a positive insight here. Without doubt there are multiple sorts of prefigurings of things in the form of ideas (or something like ideas) that are at work in our experience, holding things and the experiences together, enabling experiences to be continuous and discontinuous on multiple levels. Whether or not infinities are pre-figured, there is also every reason to think that, in relation to the relevant idea, any particular experience is enshrouded in indeterminacies and indefinite features. On both these scores, Husserl has ingeniously captured essential aspects of the phenomenology of experience. However, none of these aspects entails anything like an a priori idea. Husserl does refer to his subsequent discussion of the ideas of *res extensa*, *res temporalis*, and *res materialis* but it is far from clear how this help matters, since any specification of these ideas would seem to replicate contentious conceptions of space, time, and material existence.

To be sure, Husserl adds that, on the basis of past experience and the a priori rule for infinite but law-governed, inadequate experiences, we cannot foretell unequivocally how the further course of experience will play out. It remains a task for "the phenomenology of specifically experiential reason, and, in particular, for the phenomenology of reason in physics, psychology, and natural science in general," to search for the ontological and noetic rules pertaining to those empirical sciences, and to trace them back to their "phenomenological sources" (*Ideen* 286/331). It is for this new layer of research, he adds, to determine how experience may be of further assistance here. But if experience can be of assistance, why characterize the ideas as a priori?

With these last qualifications no doubt in mind, Mohanty reads Husserl as claiming that, the idea can be "contradicted by a discordant experience" and that, "despite the role of the Idea, the being of all empirical realities remains presumptive." (Mohanty 2008, p. 394) Mohanty's reading strikes me as correct as a view of the matter, but I am less sure of it as a faithful interpretation of Husserl's views. There are two reasons for my hesitation. First, in the very passages cited by Mohanty, Husserl does not, and perhaps on pain of contradiction, cannot claim that the ideas are refuted by experience. Second, Husserl insists that, while endless possibilities lie open, they are precisely possibilities "pre-figured" a priori. So there are clear constraints placed upon experience by reason, constraints that allegedly follow from the a priori idea of the adequate givenness of the things experienced.

No doubt Husserl thinks that something like eidetic variation will do some of the heavy lifting here. Yet however we arrive at them, the relation between the possibilities prefigured by them and actual experience remains in need of clarification. The following remark, made by Husserl in this context, illustrates this outstanding issue.

> The system of rules of geometry determines in an absolutely fixed manner all possible forms of motion that could supplement the instance of motion observed here and now, but it does not single out any single, actual course of motion of something actually moving. (*Ideen* 286/332)

On a certain reading, the remark seems even disingenuous since the single, actual course of motion cannot be other than one of the possibilities specified by geometry. But how do we know that the relevant geometrical idea of space or spatial being is essentially universal?

5. Conclusion: Husserl's crucial insight

But let me end on a positive note. Crucial to Husserl's project of a phenomenology of reason is his insight that motivated, pre-figured possibilities are inherent to every thesis, i.e., to every positing and thus to every posit or sense. Reconfirming the old insight that possibility is more basic than actuality, this insight provides the wedge for extending the scope of reason across every sort of experience and consciousness. While never identical to actual experience, the possibilities pre-figured by the sense posited are precisely rational possibilities, i.e., the possibilities of congruence and incongruence with that sense and, ultimately, the possibilities of verification and falsification. Thus, evidential coherence, confirmation, and corroboration as well as their opposites are means of rational demonstration, enabled by the crucial insight that pre-figured possibilities are inherent to every thesis and positing. This insight also provides a means of explaining both the degree of continuity and discontinuity of experience, while also underscoring the fully sensible yet pre-judicial character of experiences, (even where the foregoing posit is itself a judgment).[4] Indeed, in a powerful, rudimentary

---

4 In a certain respect, every identity contains a difference but the congruence and thus the continuities secure a continuity that makes discontinuity possible in turn.

fashion this insight explains why, as Heidegger puts it, we are always ahead of ourselves.

6. Bibliography

Heffernan, George (1983): *Bedeutung und Evidenz bei Edmund Husserl*. Bonn: Bouvier.
Hegel, Georg Wilhelm Friedrich (1970): "Enzyklopädie der philosophischen Wissenschaften". In: Eva Moldenhauer/Karl Markus Michel (Red.): *Werke*. Vol. 10. Frankfurt am Main: Suhrkamp.
Herbart, Johann Friedrich (1834): *Lehrbuch zur Psychologie*. Königsberg: Unzer.
Kant, Immanuel (1930): *Kritik der reinen Vernunft*. Berlin: Meiner.
Kant, Immanuel (1968): "Anthropologie in pragmatischer Hinsicht". In: *Kants Werke*. Vol. VII. Berlin: de Gruyter.
Lotze, Herrmann (1843): *Logik*. Leipzig: Weidman.
Mohanty, Jitendra Nath (2008): *The Philosophy of Edmund Husserl: A Historical Development*. New Haven/London: Yale University Press.
Sigwart, Heinrich Christoph Wilhelm (1831): *Vermischte philosophische Abhandlungen*. Tübingen: Laup.

Sonja Rinofner-Kreidl
Husserl's analogical and teleological conception of reason

Section IV, chapter 3, Levels of universality of the problems of a theory of reason

The first book of Husserl's *Ideas*, as has been noted recently, "had a cold reception and was marked since its publication by a general misunderstanding that distanced him [sic] from generations of phenomenologists." (Lerner 2013, p. 415) It is reasonable to assume that for a wider audience Husserl's teleological theory of reason largely contributed to this misunderstanding. Even those later phenomenologists who started off to explain Husserl's relating ideas clearly recognized the need for defense and correction.¹ I take it that, notwithstanding the difficulties of presenting Husserl's teleology of reason in a convincing manner, it is among the most important and illuminating parts of his phenomenology. The final steps of unfolding this theory of reason can be found in §§ 146–153 of *Ideas I*.²

What does Husserl aim at in these sections? What does he offer in terms of an ultimate rationalization of his project? At this point, the reader certainly expects the author to once again demonstrate and explain his grip on the guiding ideas of his phenomenological investigation. Under the title of a theory of reason Husserl indeed picks up the thread. Referring to the rich and detailed inquiries into the noetic-noematic structures, which have been unfolded in the previous chapters, he now turns towards a more general and encompassing view. Accordingly, the third chapter of part IV is entitled "Levels of Universality of the Problems of the Theory of Reason" (*Allgemeinheitsstufen der vernunfttheoretischen Problematik*). In a certain sense this title promises too much. What Husserl ac-

---

1 Cf. Bernet (1979, p. 119): "*Edmund Husserl's* phenomenology is essentially dominated by teleological concepts. [...] This extensive use of teleological concepts is encountered with bewilderment or an ironical reaction of a Nietzschean variety on the part of most contemporary thinkers. They consider Husserl to be a belated representative of an outdated rationalism, and his teleologically determined theories appear, at best, as the expression of a naïve faith. One of the objectives of the following considerations concerning the *teleological constitution of cognitive life* is to contribute to a revision of this widespread misunderstanding."
2 For the sake of brevity, I shall mostly use "Ideas" when referring to the first book of Husserl's *Ideas*. In contexts where it might be misleading to do so because I also dwell on the second book of *Ideas*, I shall use "Ideas I" or add "the first book" or "the second book."

tually does is to outline his idea of a phenomenological theory of reason by drawing attention to *some* ramifications and implications that are inherent in those problems of constitution that have been dealt with up to this point. Contrary to what the title may suggest, there is no complete and comprehensive presentation of all different levels of universality a phenomenological-constitutive analysis comprises. Nor is there any systematic approach to address them with a view to an explicit and fully spelled out consideration of the general features of a phenomenological theory of reason. Doing so would require, among others, to resume the discussion of the principle of intuition, the different types of evidence, the different types of reduction and so on. Of course, Husserl's intention is not to merely summarize what has been elaborated in the previous parts. He rather aims at offering a convincing outlook on how the preceding investigations could be comprehended (and indeed should be comprehended) in the light of the idea that reason functions in a unitary fashion.

Given this to be the general purpose of the concluding part, the key notions lying beneath Husserl's presentation of his idea of reason, as I shall argue in the following, are *foundation, stratification analysis (Schichtenanalyse), analogy of reason* and *teleology of reason.* These notions are at work in a more or less explicit and prominent manner in §§ 146–153. Especially the notion of a teleologically operating reason, at first sight, might seem controversial and contestable. However, here as in other places we should keep in mind that Husserl requests us to retain our usual philosophical and, in particular, metaphysical understanding of such well-entrenched philosophical notions.[3] Accordingly, talking about "teleology" in the present context exclusively refers to the immanent structure of consciousness. (Or: to the functions of pure reason as it appears in the wake of effectuating the phenomenological reduction.) Its basic manifestation is the structure of intentionality which implies a direction towards fulfillment and, in all variants of different types of acts, a tendency towards clarification, elucidation and experiential saturation. A so-conceived teleological structure of human consciousness represents a phenomenological-descriptive task. More complicated variants of Husserl's teleological-evidential notion of reason refer to the a priori possibility of objectifying whatever the accomplishments of different types of acts into theoretical positings, thereby making explicit a hitherto

---

[3] When addressing the idea of a teleology of reason here, we should remember what Husserl notes as the result of the phenomenological reduction at the beginning of § 50: "In this way, common sense talk about being is reversed." (*Ideas*, p. 90/106). See also § 76 where Husserl talks about "*an operation sign that transforms the value of what follows it*" (*Ideas*, p. 136) or, in the German original, about a "*umwertende[n] Vorzeichenänderung*", (Husserl 1976, p. 159). For further comments see Rinofner-Kreidl (2000, pp. 694 ff.).

tacit claim for truth. Paradigmatically, this refers to perceptual judgments that are based on perceptual experiences. At another level, a corresponding turn towards making explicit a previously hidden though arguably clearly present reason-imbued structure is effectuated when, for instance, value judgments follow value-ceptions.

Contrary to the teleological conception of reason as roughly indicated above, the *analogy of reason*, which Husserl frequently refers to in the decade before publishing his *Ideas* (cf. Husserl 1988, pp. 3–69), takes a second-order point of view. The teleological notion of reason focuses on the immanent structure and dynamics of intentional acts and noematic contents with a view to an abstract, that is, materially unspecified relation of intention and fulfillment. The analogy of reason addresses the question of how this structure and dynamics presents itself as spread out over a given diversity of act-types and correspondingly differentiated ("concretized") noematic configurations, respectively. In the former case we are concerned with a tendency of unification that is implied in each and every intentional act insofar as it is embedded in a horizon of a variety of motivated steps representing and realizing a gradually progressing exploration which aims at, so to say, appropriating the objects at issue in an ever more distinct way. Under the title of an "analogy of reason" Husserl, too, raises the issue of unification although in this case the primary focus does not lie with intentional relations and intentional objects as they present themselves from a merely formal point of view. It rather shifts towards a materialization or concretization of consciousness with regard to both noeses and noematic contents: how should we conceive of consciousness's unity in terms of reason-based intentional activities given that it presents itself as a variety of different types of noeses (i.e., intentional acts) and correlating noemata? The analogy of reason comprises at least the following theses (cf. Husserl 1988, pp. 58–69, 340–348).

(1) Not only acts pertaining to the sphere of theoretical reason but also emotional and conative acts (i.e., acts of willing) claim for rightfulness. On condition that we are referring to so-called "positional consciousness" Husserl takes it that all and every noeses are susceptible to the difference between right and wrong accomplishments.[4] The scope of authorizing evidence covers the whole range of different types of acts although the precise meaning of "fulfillment" and "being directed towards an object"

---

4 Cf. *Ideen* 290–291/337–338: "The fact that positional consciousness with its thetic characters can be characterized in the most general sense as a 'supposing' [*Vermeinen*] and that, as such, it necessarily stands under reason's opposition of validity and invalidity ...." Cf. Husserl (1988, p. 280).

or the concrete processes involved in attaining fulfillment may differ (cf. Husserl 1988, p. 343 146]).

(2) Irrespective of its occurring in whatever theoretical, axiological or practical context, every noesis can be objectified in terms of a corresponding judgment although it need not be so objectified. As to the latter, it should be noted that it is a peculiar and very important aspect of Husserl's theory of reason that it leaves room for and indeed claims to regain primordial experiences that lack objectification in terms of corresponding judgmental expressions.[5] Yet, nonetheless, every non-doxic positing harbors, at least implicitly, "something 'logical'" (*Ideen* 234/27) and should be considered *potentially objectifying*.[6]

(3) With regard to all these (predicative and pre-predicative, reflective and pre-reflective) manifestations of theoretical, axiological and practical reason it is possible to attain a priori knowledge. On the one hand, the latter refers to the immanent constitution of the relating *founded* types of acts and noematic correlates. On the other hand, it refers to formal rules that govern judgments and conclusions in the respective field of concern (formal apophansis, formal axiology, formal practice). Yet even if we agree with Husserl that the rationality of emotional and voli-

---

[5] Cf. Gillan (1972, p. 527): "The idea of reason thereby gains a concrete meaning. To the ideality of meaning is joined the necessity of intuitive fulfillment as the foundation of a discourse motivated by the presence of true being. Rationality rests for Husserl, then, only partially upon logic; in its full significance it is an opening up to a discourse that lives within the primordial consciousness of things."

[6] Cf. *Ideen* 234/272: "... all acts in general–including acts of emotion and acts of willing–are 'objectifying,' [i.e.,] 'constituting' objects originally; they are necessary sources of diverse regions of being and, with this, also sources of the relevant ontologies. [...] Every consciousness of an act, not doxically implemented, is in this way *potentially* objectifying; *the doxic cogito alone implements an actual [aktuell] act of objectification.*" As an important corollary to this, one should bear in mind that with regard to higher-order objects there is a difference between turning towards *the immediately present object* of a non-objectifying act (e. g. a valued object) and seizing on its *full intentional correlate* (e. g. a specific value) which requires an objectifying turn. Cf. *Ideen* 65/76: "…'being turned toward a subject matter in the sense of valuing it' does not mean 'having' the value '*as an object*' in the particular sense of an apprehended object, such as we must have it in order to apply predicates to it–and so, too, in all logical acts that refer to it." Here, it is interesting to compare Kersten's former translation: "… 'being *turned valuingly* to a thing' does not signify already '*having*' the value '*as object*' in the particular sense of the seized-upon object such as we must have it in order to predicate about it; …" Husserl (1983, p. 77; cf. Husserl 1989, §§ 4–6). For a more detailed account of this two-tiered constitution involved in evaluative experiences see Rinofner-Kreidl (2013).

tion acts rests with their expressibility,⁷ this does not mean that it is only when axiological and practical experiences are *actually* expressed in judgments that they are undergone and understood as sense-conveying.

Given that (1)-(3) hold, we should be ready to acknowledge a *qualified* predominance of theoretical reason which, according to Husserl, lies with (a) the important role of objectifying acts with regard to higher-order non-objectifying acts, and (b) the possibility of objectification relating to all accomplishments of reason. With regard to (b) Husserl's ideas of a teleological and an analogical structure of reason coincide: objectifying acts, in some specific sense, turn implicit positings into explicit ones.⁸ The above-mentioned similarities between the different spheres of theoretical, axiological and practical reason notwithstanding, there also must be substantial differences. Otherwise the analogy of reason collapsed into simple identity. If "teleology" implied an unqualified, that is, all-embracing, and therefore unbalanced predominance of theoretical reason Husserl had to concede that the teleological character of reason undermines the analogy of reason. (It is true from trivial reasons that if we agreed upon using the term "reason," without exception, only with regard to objectifying acts or judgments in particular we had to give up any talk about a parallelism of *different* functions of reason.) A so-conceived hegemony of theoretical reason, however, must not be read into Husserl's conception. The presumption that his teleology of reason might be incompatible with his analogical considerations regarding different functions or "sorts" of reason does not suggest itself if we do not overstate or

---

7 According to a currently discussed variety of metaethical theories, arguing along these lines amounts to acknowledging a cognitivist position. The latter takes moral claims to express beliefs and argues in favor of the truth-aptness of moral beliefs.
8 Cf., e.g., Husserl (1988, p. 63–64): "It is the task of reason in its logical function to point out, state and determine, that is, to objectify in a precise sense. Reason in its axiological function is, so to speak, *hidden to itself*. It only becomes manifest by virtue of a knowledge that is based on emotional and conative acts (*Gemütsakte*, SR). However, knowledge does not invent anything; it merely makes explicit what in a certain way is already present. If emotivity (*Gemüt*) itself were not a domain of intentional experiences (*Vermeinungen*, SR), it would not already, by itself, though in the manner of emotional and conative acts (*Gemüt*, SR) make decisions, toss its vote, knowledge could not find anything like values and value contents. In this case, knowledge would only find blind experiences like, for example, sensations of red and blue. A mere sensation, a mere living-through of sensous data does not intend anything; yet an approval (*Gefallen*, SR) does intend, a wishing intends and so on. Intending does not always amount to judging (in the usual sense) which is a mode of believingly holding-for-something (glaubend Für-etwas-Halten, SR). However, intending is analogous to judging." See Husserl (1988, p. 68). This and all other translations from Husserl 1988 and Husserl 2012 are mine. For giving them the final touch I'd like to thank Andrea Staiti.

misinterpret the analogy of reason. Abstaining from too strong an interpretation means that we should not assume that, for instance, all and every formal mode of reasoning that works within the field of theoretical reason must be transferable (without modification) to the domain of axiological and practical reason and *vice versa*. One of Husserl's examples dwelling on the relating *identity cum difference* is the axiological law of excluded fourth (*Gesetz des ausgeschlossenen Vierten*, cf. Husserl 1988, § 11) that parallels but does not coincide with the law of the excluded middle whose validity is uncontested in the domain of theoretical reason given that we stick to the scope of traditional logic.[9] It is due to the peculiar material constitution of the axiological sphere that besides the positive ("S is p") and the negative thesis ("S is not p") the additional option of value neutrality (*adiaphoron*) must be taken into account. As should be clear from this example, we must take care not to overstate the analogy of reason or, correspondingly, not to underestimate the differences lying in the very nature of the types of noetic-noematic complexities at issue.

According to the above presentation of Husserl's relating views, the analogy of reason and its teleological character overlap and support each other. On careful consideration, the relation turns out to be more complicated. Given that "teleology of reason," on some conditions, can also be interpreted in terms of a predominance of practical reason, as often has been assumed at least with regard to Husserl's later ethical works, the allegedly clear relation between an analogous and a teleological functioning of reason becomes confused. Should we assume that Husserl, in his last period, abandoned the previously acknowledged supremacy (*Allherrschaft*) of logical, that is, theoretical reason (cf. Husserl 1988, pp. 57, 261, 285) which he plainly confirms in his *Ideas?* Yet how could this be reconciled with Husserl's rational analysis of the intentional complexity of higher-order acts?[10] In particular, could we really continue understanding human

---

9 Cf. Husserl (1988, p. 83): "Hence these are essential differences between the domain of theoretical truth and the domain of (so to speak) axiological truth, axiological validity. They manifest themselves in different ways, especially insofar as the domain of axiological truth lacks an equivalent of the law of excluded middle, according to which there is no third option beyond yes and no. Reversely and contrary to the sphere of axiological truth, there is no neutrality in the sphere of theoretical truth. In other words: any conceivable (vorstellbare, SR) matter is objectively determined with regard to being or non-being; yet it is not true that any matter susceptible to evaluation (wertbare, SR) is determined with regard to being positively valued and being negatively valued (positiv Wertsein und Unwertsein, SR)."
10 Recently, a corollary issue has been dealt with by Henning Peucker (2014): Should we assume that the later Husserl abandoned the foundation model with regard to acts of willing? Given that we follow this assumption, can we still refer to a unified conception of will in Husserl's work? In this vein, Peucker's considerations, systematically viewed, focus on some "local"

reason as a unity of different functions if we abandoned Husserl's idea of a predominance of theoretical reason? Addressing these questions would go far beyond the present task of commenting on Husserl's theory of reason in his *Ideas*. However, I shall offer some sketchy ideas on how to approach these further complications at the end of this paper (cf. Rinofner-Kreidl 2013, esp. pp. 74– 80, and Rinofner-Kreidl 2014b).

In order to grasp and set off sharply the novel and philosophically exciting theory of reason, rather outlined and announced than actually elaborated in §§ 146–153, I finally abandonned the plan to give a detailed section by section comment on the text. Instead, I shall proceed as follows. In a first step, I shall highlight the crucial role of unity within the framework of a phenomenological constitution analysis dealing with different types and complexities of objects. In this part, the notions of foundation and stratification analysis will be elucidated by referring to § 152 which addresses these issues in an appropriate though inchoate manner (1.). Secondly, I shall argue that for phenomenologists it is equally crucial to raise the issue of a higher-order unity referring not to different types and realms of objectivities but to the very functions of reason itself which enable us to recognize objects of diverse kinds and to notice the relations holding between them. In this part, I shall try to shed some further light on Husserl's conception of reason, according to both wording and spirit of the text, by delving into the analogical and teleological structure of reason. In doing so, I shall pick out and scrutinize a passage from § 148 which clearly indicates the pertaining problems (2.). The selected parts from § 148 and § 152 raise key issues of part IV, chapter three. In a concentrated manner, they highlight and illustrate Husserl's philosophical intentions in bringing to a close his *Ideas*. The gist of my relating comments will be to offer evidence that speaks in favor of a thoroughly unifying view on human reason according to a transcendental-phenomenological analysis. In this connection, it is arguable that Husserl indeed follows a distinctive and promising account of reason when engaging in the overall project of his *Ideas*. My discussion of this account focuses on the following questions.

Section 1: What does "foundation" mean according to Husserl's usage? What does the relating conception accomplish in terms of a descriptively rich and differentiated constitution analysis referring to different regions of objects? How is

---

effects of Husserl's transition from static to genetic phenomenology. Certainly, this transition, among others, is of crucial importance with regard to assessing the relation between theoretical and practical functions of reason. Although *Ideas I* operates within the framework of a static phenomenology, even excluding the primitive level of time-constitution, it nonetheless harbors conceptual and descriptive elements (e.g. the notion of horizon) that give rise to a much more dynamic conception of consciousness than can be found in the *Logical Investigations*.

the originally ontological conception of foundation, which Husserl transfers into the noetic-noematic correlative investigations of his *Ideas*,[11] connected with the methodological issue of a stratification analysis? Does the notion of foundation play a crucial role for justifying Husserl's thesis of an analogy of reason?

Section 2: What are the "[d]eep and important problems of the phenomenology of reason" (*Ideen* 295/343) that, according to Husserl, are implied in his thesis of a parallelism or analogy between logic, axiology and ethics? How are logical (theoretical), axiological and practical reason related to each other? What does it mean in this connection to refer to an interwovenness of various regions of objects and, correspondingly, various "configurations of consciousness that constitute the originary givenness of every sort of objectiveness" (*Ideen* 305/355)? How (if at all) is the analogy of reason interrelated with the teleological structure of reason? Why does it make sense to offer considerations dealing with these issues as final keystone of Husserl's *Ideas*?

As indicated above, the present comment follows an integrative and synthetic path. Its prevailing interest is to figure out the unity of Husserl's investigations. For this purpose, it leaves aside a considerable amount of details that can be found in §§ 146–153. Presenting Husserl's line of reasoning in these sections in a more fine-grained way certainly allows for better understanding the title of chapter three: "Levels of Universality of the Problems of the Theory of Reason." On the one hand, this title refers to the differences between formal and regional ontologies which are owing to varying degrees of abstraction. (A purely formal analysis requires total emptiness of material content.) On the other hand, the title addresses different levels of constitution according to the stratification analysis as applied within *one* specific region (e. g. the region of physical things). In the sequence of §§ 146–153 Husserl accomplishes what he announced earlier when he noted that the hitherto presented results of a phenomenological investigation would not yet have touched on "the essential ramifications of the problems, and their connections with formal and regional ontologies" (*Ideen* 290/337). The relating ramifications, as far as the analogical structure of logical, axiological and practical reason is concerned, are dealt with in § 147. Subsequently, Husserl goes into the connections with formal (§ 148) and regional ontologies (§§ 149–152).

---

[11] Cf. *Ideen* 304/354: "Very difficult problems adhere to the *way the various regions are interwoven*. They condition interweavings in the configurations of consciousness that are constitutive."

1.

Among those issues that immediately suggest themselves when glancing over Husserl's line of reasoning in part IV, chapter three of his *Ideas* is the very basic insight that the idea of unity, which crystallizes as against various types of manifolds, is of crucial importance. It is operative at different levels of a variety of constitution processes and structures. When Husserl talks about the problem of constitution his first and foremost concern is with objects or (more or less complex) objectivities. This accurately reflects itself in the formulation of the so-called transcendental clue (transl. F. Kersten) or transcendental guide (transl. D. Dahlstrom) of the constitution of things:[12] "*How are the noeses and noemas inherent to the unity of the intuitively presenting consciousness of the thing to be described systematically?*" (*Ideen* 300/349)[13]

With regard to this and other levels and issues of constitution the functional achievement of unity is indispensable in order to experience a non-casually structured reality. The latter comprises different types of entities that can be reliably distinguished and re-identified over time–notwithstanding a more or less radical change of particular features or properties which may occur in course of time. Encountering the world as it is given to us means being aware of a manifold of appearances whose lawful organization is guided by the idea of unitary and identical objects. Following Husserl's basic insight into "the *thoroughgoing* trenchancy of the fundamental correlation between noesis and noema" (*Ideen* 181/211),[14] those manifolds of appearances can be understood in terms of both a specific noematic diversity and a pertaining noetic multiplicity. Moreover, depending on the varying complexity of the constituted objects, the unity involved consists in a hierarchical structure of several distinguishable sub-unities that, taken as a functional whole, bring to appearance a more or less complex objectivity. One of the examples Husserl gives in order to illustrate this sort of complexity refers to the fact that in analyzing the constitution of physical things

---

12 Cf. *Ideen*, § 86 ("The functional problems").
13 Kersten's translation explicitly refers to the *physical* thing: "*How are we to describe systematically the noeses and noemas belonging to the unity of the intuitively objectivating consciousness of the physical thing?*" Husserl (1983, p. 360).
14 Cf. Husserl (1973, p. 211): "…versichern wir uns zugleich der *durchgängigen* Geltung der fundamentalen Korrelation zwischen Noesis und Noema." See also *Ideen* 86/100 – 101, 243/282 – 283, 305/355.

we can distinguish between the thing as *res temporalis, res extensa* and *res materialis* (cf. *Ideen* 299/348).[15]

In everyday perception and perception-based judgments on physical things *res temporalis, res extensa* and *res materialis* are not and could not be encountered separately. They are not even vaguely discerned. Rather, there is always the full-blown thing equipped with a certain amount of qualities or properties. It is only on occasion of the intentional analysis that we recognize the transcendence of the perceived things as being constituted in consciousness (cf. *Ideen*, § 52) and that we distinguish different layers of meaning constitution when inquiring into those complex processes that ultimately result in the constitution of physical things. It is only within this framework, which requires a specific methodical attitude on part of the analyzing subject, that we realize the a priori truth of the assertion that every possible *res materialis* is founded upon a *res extensa* and a *res temporalis*. Yet referring to a *res extensa, res temporalis* and *res materialis* is owing to the artifical attitude of an intentional analysis. Given that there are objectivities that are far more complex than physical things it should be clear that taking account of Husserl's conceptions of foundation and stratification analysis is absolutely vital for a phenomenological investigation.

For the first time, Husserl introduced the term "foundation" in the third investigation of the second volume of his *Logical Investigations*. "Foundation" designates a relation of dependence between a and b according to which a is founded in b if it is based on b and if a's existence necessarily presupposes b's existence. Foundation can be realized in terms of a one-sided or a mutual dependence of different moments. Distinguishing dependent and independent parts within an overall pertaining whole is a groundbreaking step in the development of Husserl's intentional analysis. Without bearing in mind mereological relations it is impossible to correctly understand what Husserl means when he talks about different strata of intentional experiences (i.e., noetic-noematic correlations), either at different or at the same levels of constitution. According to the introduction of the notion of foundation in the *Logical Investigations*, referring to such strata must not be mixed up with referring to separable entities. Entering a phenomenological investigation we must take care that attending to conceptual distinctions and descriptively distinguishable aspects of noetic-noematic complexities, on the one hand, and attending to entities whose ontological sep-

---

[15] Whereas in the final chapter of *Ideas I* Husserl confines himself to a rather scarce presentation of these different aspects or layers that are involved in the constitution of physical things, an extensive analysis can be found in the second book of his *Ideas*. Cf. Husserl (1989, §§ 9–10 and §§ 12–18).

arability and independence is taken for granted, on the other hand, are two different tasks that must be strictly kept apart. Only the first one is a phenomenological task. Phenomenology proper, as Husserl argues in his *Ideas*, is not concerned with straightforward ontological inquiries (cf. *Ideen* 308–309/359). Mereological statements call for some kind of abstract attitude that has to be cultivated in order to effectuate an intentional analysis. This attitude consists in the ability to focus on different aspects or strata of complex intentional wholes and relating constitution processes without thereby losing out of sight the dependent status of the aspects and strata at issue.[16] A stratification analysis, which is understood along these lines, represents the methodological equivalent to the thesis that foundational relations make up the eidetic structure of human consciousness. It is therefore not surprising that the notion of foundation is of crucial interest too when it comes to think about the so-called analogy of reason. I shall take up this issue in the next section. At this juncture, it may suffice to say that if Husserl rightly holds that human consciousness, with regard to the entire range and diversity of its different types of intentional correlations, vastly manifests relations of foundation this represents strong evidence in favor of his thesis of an analogy of reason. The relating evidential support refers to the fact that consciousness shows an overall rational, that is, unifying structure which runs through all of its concrete manifestations and therefore "crosses the borders" of the widely acknowledged distinction between theoretical, axiological and practical reason.[17] However, it falls within the scope of theoretical reason to analyze foundation relations.

---

16 For an overall interpretation of Husserl's idea of phenomenology, as laid down in his *Logical Investigations*, from a mereological point of view which convincingly shows its consistency, versatility and descriptive fruitfulness see Sokolowski (1968).

17 From the above, it should be clear that Husserl's analogy of reason does not exclusively refer to those formal rules of deductive as well as inductive and abductive reasoning that can be applied with regard to different domains of objects. Husserl indeed aims at showing a parallelism between formal apophantics, formal axiology and formal practice. Yet logical procedures as such neither capture the *specifically* rational structure of evaluative and volitional experiences because doing so requires taking into account the peculiar complexity and constitution of the objects at issue. Nor do logical procedures bring to light the peculiar character of Husserl's phenomenological brand of epistemic intuitionism whose first and foremost purpose is to defend the justifying force of evidential giveness with regard to different types of objects. Hence Husserl's analogy of reason cannot be explained by pointing to the universality of logics because of the latter's disregard of material contents, different types of objects and so forth. Contrary to pure logics, the idea of foundation allows for differences in terms of varying degress of complexities on part of the objects referred to. Foundation does not function in an altogether identical but analogous way with regard to the domains of theoretical, axiological, and practical reason.

In § 152 of *Ideas* Husserl resumes his reference to relations of foundation which both occur within the realm of theoretical reason and across the distinction between theoretical, axiological and practical reason (though it quickly turns out that "across the distinction" calls for careful explanation). For the first case, we may think about psychical realities that are founded in physical realities. For the second case, we may consider value objects that are founded in natural objects. In each case the important point is that whenever relations of foundation are involved we are faced with objectivities of a higher-order which are not reducible to lower-order objects or materials. It is therefore not surprising that the notion of foundation plays a pivotal role in Husserl's refutation of psychologism or, on a larger scale, in his refutation of naturalism. This is due to the fact that the conception of foundation allows for an appropriately fine-grained description of complex objects without denying what Husserl later on, for instance in § 8 of his *Experience and Judgement,* calls "the (indirect) naturalization" of the mind[18] or, in other contexts, its "secondary naturalization." Relating to this, Husserl argues that although higher-order objects like works of art or value objects ("goods") cannot be reduced to natural objects like physical objects or psychical occurrences they nonetheless are anchored in the natural world in a sound and explicable way. This anchorage is rendered possible by the fact that higher-order objects necessarily include specific relations of foundation which characterize them as complex entities involving some basic stratum according to which they participate in the natural world. The relating stratum occurs as a dependent part that, by definition, is bound up with a more comprehensive whole whose existence is required for the stratum to exist as well. Consequently, the relevant whole is anchored in the natural environment or is interpreted as part of it because it includes this dependent part which is the ontic correlate of either a simple representation or a judgement. However, owing to its integration into the encompassing whole, which cannot be reduced to a natural fact (i.e., a physical or psychical occurrence), the dependent part is transformed and therefore does not represent a "natural fact." To put it in Husserl's terminology: a representation or a judgment that functions *as a dependent part of,* for instance, *an evaluative act* must be distinguished from a representation or judgment that appears *as an independent act of its own.* Though the latter clearly represents a theoretical function of reason, the former does not. Recognizing this to be so does not undermine the idea that the conception of founda-

---

[18] Cf. Husserl (1989, p. 36); Husserl (1952, p. 33): "Men and animals are *spatially localized*; and even what is psychic about them, at least in virtue of its essential foundedness in the Bodily, partakes of the spatial order." Cf. Husserl (1952, pp. 29–33, 201–211, 228–247, 275–288); Husserl (1989, pp. 32–33, 211–222, 239–259, 288–301).

tion, which pinpoints the rational structure of objects pertaining to different regional ontologies, is an essential part of Husserl's analogy of reason. An analogous functioning of foundation allows for differences with regard to various domains of objects. Yet differences in terms of varying hierarchies and complexities of constitutive order do not result in "crossing border" entities that represented an add-on ontological nature (e.g. a work of art as a physical thing plus some additional aesthetic properties or a person as a physical thing plus some psychical and spiritual properties).

Given that encountering objects of these kinds is part of our everday life, it seems appropriate to ask what it means to deny such add-on entities. A contrafactual consideration may help to figure this out. The ontic correlate of the representation or judgment, that is, an object or state of affairs would come to appearance as a full-fledged natural object if the relating dependent part were transformed into an independently existing act. As long as such a *functional change* does not take place the "natural" layer remains bound up within the complex higher-order act. Among others, this means that the natural as component of a higher-order object and the natural as positing of an independent object must not be naively conceived as identical. Disregarding the transformative power of higher-order acts with regard to their dependent parts results in (nonintentionally) endorsing a thoroughly misguided idea of foundation (cf. Drummond 2004; Rinofner-Kreidl 2013). Accordingly, it might seem near at hand to argue that a founded unity consists of a basic stratum of natural properties and a pick-a-back stratum of non-natural predicates. Whereas the latter view seems to fit descriptions of supervenience, it does not fit Husserl's conception of foundation and higher-order acts, respectively (cf. Rinofner-Kreidl 2015a). The pick-a-back conception encourages another serious misconception: it suggests that foundation yields complexity in terms of bringing forth objects that belong to *different* ontological regions (see the above-mentioned examples: works of art and persons). Yet this view is clearly excluded by what Husserl explains in the first part of his *Ideas* when introducing the idea of eidetic knowledge.[19] In later parts, nonetheless, he himself nourishes the misconception due to his unclear or equivocal wording.[20] As argued above, in the relevant cases the natural stratum is integrated into higher-order noematic complexities

---

19 Cf. *Ideen*, § 16. My thanks go to Claudio Majolino for reinforcing this crucial point with his straightforward statement on how important it is to stick to a rigid definition of region within the whole context of *Ideas I*.
20 See e.g. *Ideas I*, § 152, where Husserl, with a view to higher-order objects like value objects, explicitly addresses "the *way the various regions are interwoven*", Ideen 304/354. See Husserl (1976, p. 354): "*Verflochtenheit der verschiedenen Regionen.*"

(with corresponding noetic multiplicities). The relating whole is unified in accordance to the overall and dominating character of the complex act at issue. As such a unified whole it does not (and cannot) represent a multi-regional entity. This view is warranted when Husserl refers to an *archontic* positing.[21]

The comprehensive, unified noematic whole that is constituted by means of higher-order acts, due to the peculiar character of relations of foundation explained above, cannot be reduced to any of its (dependent) parts. Consequently, it cannot be described as representing *nothing else than* a natural entity. Referring to i) the "natural" stratum contained in the complex whole, and ii) the non-reducibility of the whole to its dependent parts, the anchorage at issue, that is, the naturalization of the relevant higher-order object should be dubbed "indirect" or "secondary". Based on Husserl's conception of foundation, it therefore can be argued that indeed the lowest level, that is, "material reality ultimately underlies all other realities, and, as a result, the *phenomenology of material nature* enjoys *a pre-eminent position* without question." (*Ideen* 305/354–355) Yet, notwithstanding this pre-eminent role of a phenomenology of material nature we can also insist that the founded unities are "unities of a *new kind*. As the intuition of the essence teaches, what is new that is constituted with them can never be reduced to mere sums of other realities" (*Ideen* 305/355). Here, the pivotal role of the idea of foundation in Husserl's *Ideas* becomes evident: failing to correctly grasp this idea and its unifying functioning with regard to consciousness one risks to ignore that a transcendental-phenomenological investigation marks off both from an unmotivated and seemingly arbitrary ontological abundance (in terms of, for instance, value Platonism) and the opposite extreme of a reductionist naturalism. As should be clear from the above, Husserl's sophisticated phenomenological description gives credit to neither of these positions. A phenomenological analysis uncompromisingly withholds any attempt to interpret the results of its intentional analysis in terms of straightforward metaphysical findings, either Platonist or nominalist.

In his *Ideas* Husserl acts as if the readers were familiar with the conception of foundation as introduced in his *Logical Investigations*. In the final sections he utilizes it without taking account of the above-mentioned subtleties and without

---

[21] Cf. *Ideen* 232/269: "It is essentially inherent to each intentional experience, whatever else may be found in its concrete composition, to have at least one, but as a rule several 'theses,' 'characters of positing' that are bound up with the manner of founding. Among these several positings, one is then necessarily, so to speak, the *archon*, unifying all the others in itself and dominating them throughout."

indeed offering any further explanation of this basic and systematically far-reaching conception.²²

> These [intersubjective, human or animal, SR] communities, although essentially founded in mental realities that are themselves founded in physical realities, prove to be new *kinds of objects of a higher order.* It is generally apparent that there are various kinds of objects that defy any psychologistic and naturalistic re-interpretation. Examples of these include every kind of *object of value* and *practical object*, as well as all the concrete creations of culture that determine our current life as hard actualities, such as, for example, *state, law, custom, church*, and so forth, All these sorts of objectiveness must be described, just as they are given, in terms of the basic kinds of them and in their successive orders, and *the problems of constitution* for them must be posed and solved.
>   It is quite evident that their constitution also leads back to the constitution of the sorts of things in space and to that of subjects with minds. They [the kinds of higher order objects just mentioned] are founded precisely on such realities. As the lowest level, material reality ultimately underlies all other realities, and, as a result, the *phenomenology of material nature* enjoys *a pre-eminent position* without question. But viewed without prejudice and led back phenomenologically to their sources, the founded unities are just that, i.e., they are founded unities and unities of a *new kind*. As the intuition of the essence teaches, what is new that is constituted with them can never be reduced to mere sums of other realities. Thus, *every distinctive type of such actualities* in fact *brings* with it *its own constitutive phenomenology* and, along with this, a *new concrete doctrine of reason*. The task is everywhere the same, as far as the principle is concerned. What matters is making known, at every level and layer, the complete system of the configurations of consciousness that constitute the originary givenness of every sort of objectiveness, and, by this means, making intelligible the equivalent in consciousness to the kind of 'actuality' in question. (*Ideen* 304–305/354–355)

The above considerations can be summarized by holding that, as far as the issue of unity is part of the constitution of objects it is crucial to take note of the problem of complexity which materializes in different ways depending on the type of object involved: there are different layers, that is, levels and strata of meaning constitution with regard to one and the same type of object involving different unities (e.g. in case of the constitution of a physical thing). Yet there are also other types of objects whose constitution involves a more complicated structure. This holds, for instance, with a view to the constitution of value objects which are higher-order (founded) objects that cannot be reduced to their respective layers of "naturalness."

---

22 Part of this explanation is the above-mentioned fact that the stratification analysis is the required methodological equivalent to Husserl's thesis that all rational connection, that is, all unification, that can be found in consciousness is due to relations of foundation. Cf. Husserl (2001b, p. 36; 1984a, p. 283).

2.

Now let us go beyond those problems of unity that are involved in the different levels and strata of object constitution. Dealing with the notion of unity within a philosophical framework can be expected to show a self-referential dimension, too. The latter addresses the question of how we could describe and justify the unity of reason amidst its different modes of functioning. Within the framework of transcendental phenomenology, unity of reason should be spelled out in terms of possible manifestations of a variety of different forms of consciousness whose internal connectedness does not require harking back to some kind of additional unificatory activity or meta-unity. Rather, it is accounted for by the interweaving of these very forms themselves. Since these forms or functions reflect the accessibility of a given reality, parceled out in different regions of objects, the phenomenological description of how the different functions of reason work (in terms of a priori structured possibilities of givenness) can simultaneously be elaborated in the shape of formal and regional ontologies. With a view to Husserl's correlation thesis, we may even say: the unity-of-reason issue responds to a problem of complexity and multiplicity on part of the noematic structures. Husserl indicates this tight connection when he maintains in § 152 that the problems involved in the mode of interweaving of various regions of objects "condition interweavings in the configurations of consciousness that are constitutive" (*Ideen* 304/354).[23] Understanding what this exactly means is of utmost importance for approaching Husserl's line of reasoning in the final sections of his *Ideas*.

As to Husserl's considerations, one objection that seems near at hand is that the analogy of reason does not offer a suitable tool for coping with the issues of complexity and unity because it notoriously overstrains the latter and therefore downgrades the former. Taking seriously Husserl's thesis of an analogous functioning of reason therefore seems to level down the distinction between theoretical, axiological and practical reason. Actually, it has been advanced as an (allegedly) effective objection to the analogy of reason that it disregards essential differences by unduly subordinating the spheres of axiological and practical reason to the sphere of theoretical reason and thereby intellectualizing ethical concerns (cf. Melle 1990; Schuhmann 1991). In the following, I shall argue that denying this suspicion and defending the peculiar character of the different

---

[23] See the German original, Husserl (1976, p. 354): "Sehr schwierige Probleme haften an der *Verflochtenheit der verschiedenen Regionen*. Sie bedingen Verflechtungen in den konstituierenden Bewusstseinsgestaltungen."

functions of reason and pertaining regions of objects, according to Husserl's suggestions in the last part of his *Ideas*, cannot be warranted by stipulating conceptual distinctions, that is, by defining the concepts of theoretical, axiological and practical reason in a merely top down fashion. What rather is required, according to the analogy of reason, is that we show the concrete interweaving of the different functions of reason as they manifest themselves in different regions of objects. This includes figuring out the variable relations between a cognizing subject and the domain-specific results of reason's activity. It is with a view to these descriptive tasks that one must see to avoid overstraining Husserl's analogy of reason in terms of an unqualified supremacy of theoretical reason. Given that it is possible to defend Husserl's analogical consideration as against the objection of an unwarranted predominance of theoretical reason in what precise sense should we then consider this thesis to be interrelated with a teleology of reason as inchoately traced out in the final part of Husserl's *Ideas*? Relating to this, my primary concern will be to show that the *prima facie* predominance of theoretical reason that is conspicuous with regard to the analogy of reason actually does not exclude considering an alternating predominance of different functions of reason.

§ 148 ("Rational-theoretical problems of formal ontology") of Husserl's *Ideas* ends with the following consideration:

> One notices *that, in these considerations, the concept of 'formal ontology' has been expanded.* Values, the kinds of object pertaining to practice, arrange themselves under the formal heading 'object,' 'something in general.' From the standpoint of the universal analytic ontology, they are materially determined objects; the 'formal' ontologies of the latter, i.e., the ontologies of values and of the kinds of objects pertaining to practice, are material disciplines. On the other hand, there are analogies grounded in the parallelism of thetic genera (belief or, better, a modality of believing, valuing, willing) and the syntheses and synthetic formations specifically attributed to them. These analogies have a force of their own and, indeed, one so efficacious that Kant directly designates as 'analytic' the relation of willing the end [Zweck] and willing the means[24] (thereby, of course, confusing analogy with identity). The genuinely analytic [character] that pertains to the predicative synthesis of the doxa may not be confused with the formal analogue that is related to the syntheses of emotive and volitional suppositions. Deep and important problems of the phenomenology of reason are attached to the radical clarification of these analogies and parallels. (*Ideen* 295/343)

What Husserl says at the beginning of this passage meets well with what has been explained above with regard to the notion of foundation. Given that it is

---

[24] Cf. Kant (1964, A417): "Whoever wills the end, wills [...] also the means which are indispensably necessary and in his power. So far as willing is concerned, this proposition is analytic [...]."

possible to point out relations of foundation in diverse regions of objects, it suggests itself to extend the notion of formal ontology in terms of including all these other inquiries into the rational structure of different types of objects. Yet doing so may unintentionally promote misconceptions concerning the scope or strength of the relevant accomplishments of theoretical reason. It may suggest that the analogous functioning of theoretical, axiological and practical reason actually results in reducing the other forms of reason to the achievements of theoretical reason. We would then end up with identity instead of an analogous structure. This is what Husserl, focusing on the issue of the means/end relation, thinks Kant must be accused of. With the following, I do not intend to open up a wide-ranging Husserl versus Kant debate. Rather, I am interested in finding out what it tells us about Husserl's conception of reason that he feels urged to protest against Kant's above-stated (alleged or real) misconception. I shall argue that, in a nutshell, the above quotation contains some very important and peculiar aspects of Husserl's theory of reason. In order to approach these aspects it is suitable to take a closer look at Husserl's above criticism of Kant. At first glance, this criticism is surprising because, on the one hand, it is presented in an incidental way without any further explanation following. Yet, on the other hand, Husserl's reply spreads an air of vigor and certainty so that the reader gets the impression that Husserl wants to point out an essential difference between his own conception of reason and Kant's. What does it mean when Husserl complains about Kant's (alleged) confusion of analogy and identity in the present context? Can we really expect that digging into this rather "local" or narrow-focused disagreement on what at first sight looks like a minor detail of an ethical theory could give us some decisive clues with regard to Husserl's theory of reason? In order to answer these questions we, first of all, have to make sure what Kant refers to in the relevant context.

In the second part of his *Groundwork of the Metaphysic of Morals* Kant distinguishes the moral law, that is, the moral (categorical) imperative, from different types of hypothetical imperatives. The latter either refer to optimizing the relation of means and ends (imperatives of skill) or they refer to a given aim of happiness or well-being (imperatives of prudence). Hypothetical imperatives, in general, are characterized by the fact that they become effective only on condition of some pre-given purpose (and a corresponding intention). Relating to this purpose an action can be dubbed "prudent" or "skillful." For example, with regard to imperatives of skill, we should say: "Here there is absolutely no question about the rationality or goodness of the end, but only about what must be done to attain it." (Kant 1964, A415) A few lines after this remark we enter the precise context of the statement Husserl refers to:

> The question now arises 'How are all these imperatives possible?' This question does not ask how we can conceive the execution of an action commanded by the imperative, but merely how we can conceive the necessitation of the will expressed by the imperative in setting us a task. How an imperative of skill is possible requires no special discussion. Who wills the end, wills (so far as reason has decisive influence on his actions) also the means which are indispensably necessary and in his power. So far as willing is concerned, this proposition is analytic: for in my willing of an object as an effect there is already conceived the causality of myself as an acting cause–that is, the use of means; and from the concept of willing an end the imperative merely extracts the concept of actions necessary to this end. (Synthetic propositions are required in order to determine the means to a proposed end, but these are concerned, not with the reason for performing the act of will, but with the cause which produces the object.) That in order to divide a line into two equal parts on a sure principle I must from its ends describe two intersecting arcs–this is admittedly taught by mathematics only in synthetic propositions; but when I know that the aforesaid effect can be produced only by such an action, the proposition 'If I fully will the effect, I also will the action required for it' is analytic; for it is one and the same thing to conceive something as an effect possible in a certain way through me and to conceive myself as acting in the same way with respect to it. (Kant 1964, A417)

Kant talks about different ways a human will can be determined according to different types of imperatives. The theoretical interest lying beneath this consideration is to offer a clear-cut distinction between different types of imperatives. Doing so is meant to clarify the specific conceptual requirements an imperative must meet in order to qualify as a principle of moral, that is, as a categorically commanding principle. Clearly, Kant's statement on the analyticity of the means/end relation is meant to be the outcome of a reflection on the "pure" notions of means and ends. Now, what is wrong with Kant's statement? I take it that Husserl (had he offered some further explanation here) would have responded in the following way. Supposed that we agree upon starting with conceptual demarcations nothing is wrong. However, arguing like this *within the above-sketched context* amounts to giving priority to theoretical reason within the realm of practical reason in an inappropriate way. It is not at all clear that here, judging on purely conceptual relations and thereby tacitly skipping the whole range of possible practical problems or practical situations does make sense. From a phenomenological point of view, proceeding like this indicates a thoroughly problematic grip on the practical sphere.[25]

To be sure, the means/end relation can be conceived as analytic–from the point of view of theoretical reason. Yet it cannot be conceived like that from the point of view of practical reason which is the relevant framework in the pres-

---

[25] Here, Husserl might even talk about a *metabasis eis allo genos*, thereby taking up a line of reasoning that goes back to his *Prolegomena of a Pure Logic*. Cf. Husserl (2001a, § 2).

ent context. Practically viewed, we are exclusively interested in ends that could be chosen by someone in accordance with their preferential realization. To be sure, one may consider the means/end relation analytic on condition that one arbitrarily decides to take into account only pure conceptual relations and pure concepts which are devoid of any content and comparative weight. As soon as we abandon this abstract attitude of a purely theoretical analysis it is, however, clear that every possible end is embedded in more or less extended systems of ends. Accordingly, the means that are recognized as necessary for realizing certain ends, too, are embedded within the horizon of possible ends. Otherwise, one had to argue that it would always be irrational to dispense with realizing a specific end due to one's assessment that the necessary means are strongly problematic or even totally inadmissible from a moral point of view. In many cases, arguing in this way strongly opposes our moral common sense.[26]

While Kant's statement strictly adheres to analyzing what the pure concept of willing something implies, Husserl's line of reasoning runs as follows. Willing something always means willing something within a given practical context whose structure, among others, is determined by the following issues: alternative possible ends; assessments of those harming effects that can be expected to occur on occasion of utilizing certain (necessary) means; losses of missed opportunities for realizing alternative ends if the realization of a certain end will be preferred on given constraints, and so on. In other words: On dilemma and nondilemma conditions of possible practical situations we cannot consent to the idea that willing an end and willing the necessary means to this end are connected by way of mere analyticity. Husserl's objection to Kant's statement is warranted given that we are interested in possible decisions and possible actions *that could be effectuated on real world conditions*. The latter do not only include a variety of types of situations and a variety of possible systems of ends. These conditions also include reference to an agent whose capabilities must not be considered unlimited. Taking account of the relevant limitations, again, amounts to denying a predominantly theoretical stance within the realm of practical reason. According to Husserl, we can enter discussion of these limitations by focusing on the notion of practical possibility as introduced in his early lectures on ethics and value theory.

Moral agents are bound to running through typical situations and thereby acquiring the requisite skills for perceiving, deciding and acting. Their moral identity does not tend towards a pure and impartial view from nowhere. It rather

---

[26] Relating practical conflicts, among others, comprise so-called "rescue torture," terror bombing, or double effect theorizing in case of high-risk pregnancies or indirect euthanasia.

hinges on acknowledging certain systems of ends and corresponding hierarchies of values lying beneath them. As Husserl argues both in his early and late ethics although in connection with markedly different lines of reasoning and thematic as well as methodical priorities (cf. Husserl 1988 and 2004), it is necessary to consider an agent's actual commitment to specific ends.[27] Equally, it is necessary to consider that different individual agents show different abilities of realizing specific ends and of realizing the importance of those systems of ends that are brought into play by specific (types_of) situations. The notion of practical possibility indicates that talk about possible ends for acting has to take account of these individual differences (cf. Husserl 1988, p. 149).[28] It therefore indicates a thorough-going difference between the functioning of theoretical and practical reason. As to the latter, it is impossible to disregard the particularity of different situations which can be classified according to different types. It is equally impossible to ignore how the subject is committed to the relevant (types of) situation(s), that is, whether and how she is committed to specific systems of ends and values. Consequently, how the agent feels engaged in situations of the relevant type and how she grasps these situations as meaningful within her own personal history is part of what we may call "the practical horizon." It therefore is part of the volitional and axiological problems and phenomena a phenomenologically orientated ethicist is expected to describe and analyze. Relating to this, we may explain Husserl's position as follows: confusing analogy with identity with regard to the above-cited disagreement on analyticity means to misidentify the relevant phenomena and their intentional horizons. What Husserl has in mind when criticizing Kant in § 148 is not restricted to rejecting an undue concern for purely conceptual reflections. It can be developped further.

The immediate ("naïve") practical interest, which manifests itself in a given situation, does not dwell on the distinction between hypothetical imperatives and categorical imperatives. This distinction rather is owing to a specific theoretical approach. Moral agents are used to (tacitly) acknowledge the complex affordances of practical situations. Giving priority to the distinction between hypo-

---

27 To be sure, within the framework of Husserl's axiology it is the notion of *practical possibility* (or *practical sphere*) that reminds us of such a pre-given commitment. Here, the practical issues of (self-)commitment do not yet play a pivotal role. On the contrary, the investigation revolves round figuring out a modified categorial imperative. The latter, when scrutinized more carefully, turns out to be hypothetical. Cf. Rinofner-Kreidl (2010).
28 Nota bene: formulating the relating contraints on occasion of a phenomenological investigation does not mean to refer to empirical persons and empirical circumstances. It rather amounts to making explicit a constraint that is inherent in the sphere of willing and reasonable choice because it belongs to the pertaining eidos. See Husserl (1988, pp. 248–249).

thetical and categorical imperatives we impute a predominantly theoretical view within a genuinely practical realm. In doing so, we indicate that we have distanced ourselves from the "density" of concrete practical situations. On condition that moral agents cannot be addressed without considering their embeddedness in various histories of moral experience and various practical situations, "safely" embarking on hypothetical imperatives, as defined by Kant (i.e., imperatives of prudence or skill), does not present itself as a relevant option in terms of real possibility. Whatever concrete situations one may imagine there is none that, on principle, could exclude challenging given ends.[29] In real-life situations it is always possible that conditions emerge according to which previously unproblematic ends turn into non-starters. In such situations the agent does not act (and does not reflect on her acting) as if her practical sphere were closed. Yet this "as if" idealization determines Husserl's own previous investigations dealing with formal axiology and formal practice. The purpose of these investigations, which is to make explicit the immanent rationality of evaluative and volitional acts, strongly favors a static approach (i.e., the assumption of closure). Contrary to this, the perspective on the interweaving of theoretical, axiological and practical reason vaguely sketched at the end of *Ideas I* offers a dynamic view which announces Husserl's ethical considerations in the 1920s. In a certain sense, these considerations approach a virtue ethicist's view–at least insofar as the agent's overall striving for self-perfection then clearly comes to the fore. From this point of view, analyzing how an agent with a given set of preferences and with a view to artificially isolated situations had to think, decide and act in order to behave in a rational way does not appear any more as primarily relevant task of an ethical theory. However, as Husserl's thoughts on the notion of practical possibility in his lectures on ethics and value theory 1908–1914 indicate, there is a tendency of going beyond any such idealizing preferential analysis in his earlier writings. From the point of view of *Ideas I*, given that the above reading is correct, we should hold that what is at stake in possible practical situations (though this may be more or less obtrusive depending on the prevailing circumstances) is the totality of an agent's practical concerns.[30] In his early ax-

---

[29] Of course, endorsing this thesis would be doomed to failure beforehand if one did not presuppose the agent's freedom, that is, her ability of redefining and going beyond given situations. Though Husserl does not claim to offer any proof in favor of this thesis he does not question it either. However, elaborating proofs on behalf of whatever metaphysical thesis goes beyond his phenomenological tasks.

[30] According to the above, Husserl scholars may ponder the exegetical thesis that the teleology of reason as sketched in §§ 146–153 of *Ideas I* can help to further elucidate or explain the transition from Husserl's early ethical writings to his late ethics (though he, as far as I can see, did

iological investigations Husserl, accordingly, argues that phenomenologically describing the "natural" striving of practical agents is directed towards a categorical imperative. Yet this imperative, as conceived in Husserl's early lectures on ethics and value theory is determined in a thoroughly non-Kantian way, that is, as the solution of the problem how to sum up partial value contributions (*Wertsummation*).[31] What does that mean with a view to the conflict between Husserl and Kant in § 148? Though Husserl himself occasionally considers the analyticity of the means/end relation (cf. Husserl 1988, p. 350) he ultimately gives priority to demanding a categorical imperative which, so to say, swallows up all subordinated considerations concerning a purely conceptually determined (analytic) relation of means and ends.[32]

---

not pretend that his early formal axiology and formal practice represent a full-fledged ethical theory). In my view, it is inappropriate and entirely unsatisfying to consider this transition as a more or less incomprehensible leap from a special brand of preferential utilitarianism to an ethics of love. Undoubtedly, there are important differences. However, I take it that a suitable interpretation of the analogy of reason allows for recognizing the compatibility of Husserl's considerations in his early and late period. (Note that compatibility does not require that their primary philosophical interests and projects coincide.)

31 In his late ethical writings Husserl re-addresses the categorical imperative by appropriating it in an "individualizing" manner. Both the early and the late account are problematic although from different reasons. Here, I cannot dwell on the relating exegetical and systematic problems. Cf. Melle (1992; 2002); Drummond (2010); Rinofner-Kreidl (2010).

32 At this juncture, it is suitable to take note of a parallel line of reasoning on part of two Kant scholars. The first one stems from Jean Hampton. When trying to make sense of Kant's analyticity statement discussed above she argues that (contrary to a widespread opinion) explaining the bindingness of a hypothetical imperative is no easier than explaining the bindingness of the categorical imperative. As Hampton sets out the notion of reason as an objective authority lies beneath both of them. Hypothetical imperatives therefore depend upon an antecedent categorical imperative. "Theorizing about the nature of instrumental reason also requires taking a stand on the nature of the good, which means, paradoxically, that any theory of instrumental reason can't be ‚instrumental' after all." (Hampton 1998, p. 166) See Hampton 1998, pp. 130–135 and pp. 161–166. The second critique can be found in Christine Korsgaard's famous essay on "The Normativity of Instrumental Reason" (cf. Korsgaard 2008, pp. 27–68) whose core ideas (pp. 47–64) and outcome corroborate and refine Hampton's considerations. Korsgaard elaborates in a detailed manner why the instrumental principle cannot stand alone and why it indeed "is not a principle of practical reason that is separable from the categorical imperative: rather, it picks out an *aspect* of the categorical imperative: the fact that the laws of our will must be practical laws, laws that constitute us as agents by rendering us efficacious." (Korsgaard 2008, p. 68) Roughly sketched, Hampton and Korsgaard the objection of a predominantly theoretical understanding of reason that, according to Husserl, comes to the fore in Kant's account of hypothetical imperatives. Or, to be more precise; Hampton and Korsgaard convincingly argue that the very nature of practical reason, if appropriately explained in accordance with the systematic unity of Kant's philosophy, requires denying the separability of a hypothetical imperative which *Kant himself*

"And as to the ways and means, the end does not justify the means but it gives credit to them. Suppose that the means get into a rightful discredit it requires sensibly appraising the relation between credit and discredit in order to figure out whether the means are still admissible. A lesser evil may possibly lose significance in the face of a superior good. These and other insights can be drawn from the established formal laws in an unconditionally valid and purely formal manner. Now, what matters with regard to the consideration of those things that practically ought to be done, that is, the particular practical good that has been stated as valid [des jeweiligen thetisch gültigen praktischen Gutes, SR] is this: within the overall sphere of the possibly attainable the agent or the subject who ponders her end finds a great variety of goods, adiaphora, and evils that she could realize. All evils and adiaphora ought to be avoided unless they either increase the value of those goods with which they are bound up or function as means to attain higher goods." (Husserl 1988, p. 351)[33]

Let us summarize the above considerations on Husserl's critical reference to Kant in § 148. Given that the factors, which Husserl considers as determining a practical situation in his lectures on ethics and value theory 1908–1914 (i.e., systems of ends, systems of means, practical possibility) have been grasped correctly, it seems clear that within the horizon of the so-called analogy of reason there are considerable differences between the functioning of theoretical and the functioning of practical reason. On the one hand, the findings of formal axiology and formal practice strengthen the demands of theoretical reason within the practical field and, consequently, corroborate the analogy of reason. On the other hand, there are considerable differences left that must be taken into account. Failing to do justice to these differences due to a theoretically biased approach to practical issues is the main objection Husserl raises against Kant in § 148. To be sure, this is a tentative reconstruction of Husserl's objection based on what he extensively elaborates at other places, especially in his early lectures on ethics and value theory. In the present chapter of *Ideas* he keeps silent as to the precise intention and background of his critique. As we have seen above, the relevant point of departure for Husserl, as far as the realm of practical reason is concerned, is not the purity of concepts as if doing conceptual analysis would be a purpose of its own. For phenomenologists, who first and foremost are interest-

---

erroneously suggests when uttering the analyticity statement at issue. Although Husserl's theory of reason and his notion of a categorical imperative in particular differ from Kant's there is an obvious grain of truth (or: a proper philosophical 'instinct') in Husserl' critique of Kant's analyticity statement. As I tried to make clear above, doing justice to Husserl's idea of a practically functioning reason we must also go beyond a merely logically conceived relation between means and ends in favor of considering the practical (moral) agent as subject of a possible plurality of ends, that is, as subject of reasonable practical commitments.
33 Cf. Husserl (1988, §6).

ed in grasping the phenomena in exactly the way they are given ("so wie sie gegeben sind"), the crucial points rather are: what is the relevant unity in terms of an agent's 'naïve' turning towards the objects that can be given in a certain region?[34] What sorts of intentional interweaving should be acknowledged on part of the noema in case that specific types of noeses are realized?

At this juncture, it is illuminating to compare what Husserl, in connection with his exemplary reference to the region of physical things, indicates in §§ 149–151 as general task of a phenomenological-descriptive analysis. As we know, this analysis must be done at all levels of constitution and according to all aspects of all types of objects. Establishing a stratification analysis of this sort requires distinguishing different systems of manifolds and pertaining formations of relative unities that are effective at different levels of constitution.[35] Given that constitution is understood in this way, that is, as a concatenation of relative unities occurring at different levels, we are faced with the following problem: we can either assume that picking out specific unities from the relating hierarchies of relative unities is a matter of arbitrary theoretical decision. Or we assume that there are specific unities that force themselves upon us as ultimately relevant and guiding unities which represent manifestations of an inner teleological structure of human consciousness. Compared to such self-disclosing ultimate unities, all other relative unities that, in course of the relating intentional analyses, are located at some intermediary level of constitution must be considered abstract unities. They rightly can be designated "abstract" because they would not come to appearance at all if we did not inquire into the relating intentional structures, thereby taking an artificial reflective attitude. Yet in order to grasp the guiding unities of a phenomenological investigation it is necessary to take account of the full variety of "natural" experiences that we undergo previous to and independent of our theoretical and specifically philosophical attitudes. Husserl's paradigmatic case in the final sections of his *Ideas*, which he considers transferable to other types and regions of objects, is the constitution of physical things. Here, the relevant unity is the material thing presenting itself as temporally and spatially located. Compared to this unity, the unities of *res ex-*

---

34 Note that "turning towards" does not imply seizing upon the object. See above fn. 6.
35 Hence Husserl notes that *"the problem of constitution* clearly means [...] nothing other than that the series of appearances, regulated and *necessarily* belonging together to the unity of what appears, can be intuitively examined and theoretically grasped [...]. It means, too, that the series of appearances are analyzable and describable in their *eidetic* uniqueness and that the *law-governed achievement of the correlation between what appears in a determinate way as a unity and the determinate infinite manifolds of appearances* is something that can be fully discerned, and, hence, that any enigma can be stripped away." (*Ideen* 302/351)

tensa and *res temporalis* represent merely theoretically relevant intermediate levels of thing constitution.

> These investigations are essentially determined by the various levels and layers of the thing's constitution, in the framework of the consciousness experiencing [erfahrend] things in an originary way. Each level and each layer in the level are characterized by the fact that each constitutes a unity of its own, that is, for its part, a necessary intermediate member of the thing's full constitution (Ideen 302–303/352). [36]

It is useful to compare the present issue with the above-sketched debate on whether the means/end relation should be considered analytic on certain conditions. Doing so, similarities *and* differences with regard to theoretical and practical functions of reason come to the fore. What are the relevant similarities? Both with regard to physical things and practical objects there is a penetrable rational structure of intentionality. In both cases, it is suitable to distinguish different levels of constitution and different complexities involved. Nonetheless, there are important differences. As to physical things, we may say that so far as we can discern different levels of constitution it does make sense to refer to necessary intermediate members as indicated above. In this and other cases, reference to intermediate members depends on what is recognized as ultimate unity. The latter appears as the "meaning" and overall object, that is, the *full intentional correlate* of the pertaining noesis (cf. *Ideen*, § 117). Relating to those peculiar practical objects referred to above, that is, the noematic correlates of specifically qualified imperatives, it is either the rational fashioning of a given means/end relation or the reasonable (morally admissible) choice of possible ends that functions as ultimate unity. However, what might easily be identified as an intermediate member of a practical object's full constitution (i.e., a hypothetical imperative) resists integration into an overall and ultimate unity. Correspondingly, it does not merely represent a subordinate level of constitution. Hypothetical and categorical imperatives, stated noematically, do not synthesize

---

[36] Here, one should recall that the conception of foundation reflects the idea that the formation of unity is the all-pervading task and function of consciousness. In order to understand the complex forms of constitution connected with this function it is necessary to analyze unification processes in terms of the distinction between different part-whole relations. Doing so while permanently keeping in mind the difference between naive experience and reflectively discriminating aspects of consciousness results in the thesis of a two-tiered process of value-constitution (see above fn. 6). In this connection, it is of vital importance not to lose sight of the original guiding clue of this whole investigation, that is, the obejct's unity as it presents itself in our pre-theoretical ("naïve") experience. (In the present context, this is an evaluative experience directed towards some specific good.)

into one and the same object. In this case, the "object" is what should be done in a given situation, that is, the object is an "ought to x" whose validity cannot be considered both relative and irrelative to certain circumstances. The practical type of object addressed here, that is, a normative state of affair which presents itself as a specifically characterized "ought-to-be-done," differs from the objects theoretical reason deals with. Practical objects cannot be identified (determined) unless taking into account a certain "material" relation between subject and object.[37] To some extent, my self-understanding as a practical agent determines what system of ends I recognize as appropriately responding to a given situation, including different (hypothetical or categorical) modes of ought-validity. This includes reference to future states, namely a more or less distinct idea concerning the person I would like to become. There is no equivalent to this specifically practical engagement of the subject as far as the perception and knowledge of physical things as a function of theoretical reason is concerned. The well-known fact that possible objects of perception and knowledge are selected and attended to according to some presently prevailing practical interest does not annihilate the above-stated distinction between theoretical and practical reason.[38] It rather indicates that the interweaving of different functions of reason takes place at different levels of constitution and involves various points of view. Distinguishing theoretical and practical functions of reason therefore should not be considered an ontological endeavor.[39] It does not introduce a clear-cut partitioning of reality according to which we were faced with either overall theoretical or overall practical objects. Rather, it addresses different levels and strata of constitution, different aspects that can be discerned with regard

---

[37] A material component even comes into play when Husserl, in his lectures on ethics and value theory from 1914, introduces the principle of contradiction with a view to the axiological sphere: "Provided that we are faced with the same value material and the same motivation we can state that if positive evaluation is reasonable negative evaluation will be unreasonable and vice versa. Correspondingly, in case of identical presuppositions of evaluating (value premises) opposed values, which stand in contradiction to each other and show the same content, exclude each other. For instance, if the same content 'S is p' presents itself as agreeable and non-agreeable. It would be unreasonable or an axiological contradiction to be pleased with the fact that S is p and, on the same motivational conditions, grieve over the fact that S is p." (Husserl 1988, p. 81)

[38] Cf. Cairns (2013, p. 260): "Every act [...] which is an act of the ego, a cogito, includes a volitional element. But the goal of some acts is knowledge, a grasping and 'possessing' of the object as it is 'in person'."

[39] Doing so is still wide-spread in recent philosophical discussions on related topics, for instance the fact/value-dichotomy. The latter often has been presented as if the crucial point would be how to possibly give queer entities like values a place in our scientific world view. A Husserlian approach radically challenges this picture. Cf. Rinofner-Kreidl 2014d.

to complex objectivities and different attitudes that can be taken towards objects.

The above considerations may help to clarify a statement that can be found in § 145 of *Ideas* whose precise meaning is not accessible without further ado. There, Husserl holds that it is a matter of a theory of reason to distinguish physical objects, values and practical objects and to ask for the correlating constitutive structures of consciousness. Why should we consider the relating distinction as involving a *theory* of reason–instead of, for instance, considering it as a matter of a more or less arbitrarily chosen *descriptive* perspective? Husserl's reply should insist that the relating distinction calls for a theory of reason because it involves reference to different types of objects which are not only distinct in terms of their concrete experiential content ("matter") but above all distinct as to formal aspects. For instance, they may be either simple, non-founded objects or founded objects, and in the latter case either founded in a simple or multiple way. Any talk about a theory of reason presupposes the distinction of form and content. Elaborating a theory of reason, according to Husserl, means to figure out eidetic differences regarding the constitution of objects, thereby taking into account different types of objects and different levels of constitution, including the interweaving of different functions of reason that are involved in the formation of the objects at issue. Therefore, it should be stressed that describing objectivities ("objectivenesses") in a determinate manner presupposes a determinate idea of reason. Insisting upon the tight connection between describing given phenomena, on the one hand, and endorsing a theory of reason, on the other hand, is a distinctive mark of Husserl's (and other brands of) transcendental phenomenology.[40] The relevant task is to understand human reason, both according to its unity and its different functions or manifestations, by inquiring into given forms of objectivities. This is the general drive behind Husserl's objection to Kant's statement concerning the analyticity of the means/end relation. The deeper ground of Husserl's critique is that what Kant's statement (*pars pro toto*) exemplifies is a non-phenomenological attitude according to which the notion of reason and its relevant specifications are introduced in an abstract or top down fashion. Contrary to this, Husserl's idea, as documented in the final part of his *Ideas*, is that elaborating a theory of reason requires strongly focusing

---

[40] For matters of convenience, we may designate the nexus of descriptive and constructive tasks as *AID*-structure of transcendental phenomenology, cf. Rinofner-Kreidl (2014a). Doing so calls for explaining how the methodically crucial moments of *Attitude*, *Intuition*, and *Description* mutually require each other and how reference to the AID-structure enables us to refute a well-known objection, which refers to a "myth of the given", by pointing out the sophisticated brand of intuitionism that lies beneath Husserl's transcendental phenomenology.

on the concrete manifestations of human reason. This exactly reflects Husserl's critique with regard to the above-sketched issue of analyticity. Kant's relating confusion of analogy with identity, according to Husserl, results from a failure to consider the interlacing of different functions of reason and their various achievements at different levels of constitution.[41] Therefore, Kant is accused of propelling a theory of reason that represents a top down construction that is far more interested in clear-cut conceptual distinctions than in phenomenological accuracy.

Presenting a well-balanced view on the similarities *and* the differences between logical, axiological and practical reason must be considered part of Husserl's theory of reason. In particular, this is required in order to defend the analogy of reason. There is, however, another problem we did not touch hitherto. On various occasions one is puzzled by a certain wavering in Husserl's presentation of the analogy of reason. There are many contexts in which talk about the ubiquitous predominance of logical reason clearly prevails (cf., e.g., Husserl 1988, pp. 3–69; 274–292). On other occasions, especially in his later works, Husserl seems to be more concerned with appropriately discerning how theoretical as well as practical interests come to bear with regard to specific achievements of human consciousness than to talk about the primacy of theoretical reason or practical reason in general and in an abstract manner (cf. e.g., Husserl 1973, § 14, §§ 17–20, § 48). In general, he does not seem to be much troubled by the fact that our relating views tend to vary according to changes of contexts and corresponding shifts of attitudes. It seems indeed appropriate to associate the natural attitude with a predominance of practical interests and the phenomenological attitude with a predominance of theoretical interests. However, doing phenomenological-descriptive work, again, gives raise to a more differentiated view. For instance, there are different meanings of "practical interest" that should be distinguished according to different levels and layers of meaning constitution.[42] In what follows, I take it that the systematic problem lying beneath

---

[41] From the point of view of Husserl's constitution analysis in his *Ideas*, considering means/end relations as analytic is based upon a rigorous distinction between a theory of pure forms of posita (*reine Formenlehre der Sätze*) and a formal theory of validity (*formale Geltungslehre*) which, among others, is addressed in § 147. In the former context ends are only relevant insofar as corresponding posita are possible in terms of the formal possibility of the relating syntheses. On the contrary, with regard to a formal theory of validity (which one may have in mind when distinguishing different types of imperatives) ends must be considered as possible practical goods.

[42] Take, for instance, the practical interest that (i) manifests itself when something arouses our attention and sets going a process of perception; (ii) is efficacious in drives and inclinations, habitual ways of acting and similar "unconscious" modes of behavior; (iii) is realized in choosing

Husserl's allegedly problematic wavering with regard to the primacy of particular functions of reason is the very manner in which the analogy of reason and the teleology of reason are intertwined.

What, at first glance, may appear as a wavering actually results from the unproblematic fact that we can consider the overall achievements and different functions of reason from different points of view and in compliance with different attitudes. In order to shed some light on the problems at issue, I propose to consider some ideas which Husserl elaborates in lecture courses held several years after the first edition of his *Ideas*, in 1919/1920. The relevant lectures, which have been published recently as vol. IX of *Husserliana Materialien* (cf. Husserl 2012), are entitled as follows: *Apriorische Wertelehre und Ethik*, *Soziale Ethik* and *Teleologie*. In the present context I confine myself to offer a short and tentative interpretation of a (seemingly) enigmatic utterance that is part of the first of these lectures (cf. Husserl 2012, pp. 51–59).

In Husserl's lecture course on *Apriorische Wertelehre und Ethik from 1919/20* we find the following remark which turns out to be fruitful with regard to understanding the interweaving of different functions of reason called upon in the final part of *Ideas:*

> "Both the highest eidetic forms of reason and their three correlating notions of truth, that is, logical truth, axiological truth, and practical truth and the objective (i.e., object-related) being in general, value-being in general, and the being of all those things that ought to be realized in general (gesolltes Sein, SR) stand in this peculiar relation of coordination and yet mutual encompassing though this needs to be interpreted with due caution." (Husserl 2012, p. 156)

How can we make sense of this? At first sight, Husserl's remark is quite perplexing. "Coordination" and "embracement" refer to different types of order which do not seem to be compatible. Coordinated elements or theories are related as equally independent (and presumably equally strong) at one and the same level. "Embracement" indicates a mereological relation to the effect that there is a whole containing something as its part, the latter being subordinated or integrated in a more encompassing reality. Relations of this sort, that is, relations of one-sided dependence, necessarily exclude reversibility: whatever functions as embracing cannot function as embraced. Wholes and parts (by definition) do not allow for interchanging functions given that the elements involved remain

---

certain ends for acting; (iv) lies beneath when someone intentionally strives for moral self-perfection, either in terms of specific virtues like benevolence or courage or in terms of a general concern for cultivating one's capability of rational self-determination and reason's responsiveness (see below in the text).

unchanged. Accordingly, the term "mutual embracement" calls for explanation. Mutuality implies reversibility. However, in the present case, "mutuality" cannot mean that a and b mutually embrace each other *with regard to one and the same aspect*. On this condition, it could not be true that the relating elements mutually embrace each other while simultaneously being coordinated to each other. This is owing to the (eidetic) fact that coordination requires not being partially identical or being separated from each other, respectively. Given that these considerations are on the right track, how then should we interpret Husserl's above statement?

Mutual embracement is compatible with coordination if and only if we either refer to (complexes of) elements that change in course of time or to varying aspects (questions and so on) according to which the relation at issue is considered. Correspondingly, we can understand Husserl's statement as follows. Logical, axiological, and practical truth and, correspondingly, logical, axiological, and practical reality are coordinated to each other as far as reason actually functions in an analogous manner. They, however, mutually embrace each other in terms of an alternating predominance of theoretical, axiological or practical reason which amounts to a mutual embracement in course of time. In the present context, mutual embracement is possible on condition that the achievements and functions of reason can be acknowledged from different points of view. The mutual embracement which is at stake here can, among others, be explained with regard to four paradigmatic situations of changing point of views:

A) According to the difference between natural attitude and phenomenological attitude
    i) Considering the functions and achievements of reason from the "external" point of view of the natural attitude, one has to acknowledge a primacy of practical reason. In this context, practical reason embodies our pre-theoretical ("natural") practical interests which are bound up with Husserl's so-called *general thesis* of the natural attitude (cf. *Ideen*, § 30). Hence practical reason is effective insofar as it is relevant and useful with a view to concrete (and presently urging) decisions and actions. Heading for the realization of certain ends is founded upon their positive appraisal. Practical reason therefore presupposes the achievements of axiological reason although the latter mostly remain hidden in contexts of everyday decision-making and acting.
    ii) If we consider the functions and achievements of reason from the "internal" point of view of the phenomenological attitude, we have to acknowledge a predominance of theoretical reason which is due to the fact that in all and every sphere of intentional constitution (logical, axiological or practical) it is a genuine theoretical accomplishment to

make sure of the difference between right and wrong as something that matters in a universal sense and that enables us to set up a claim for objectivity–although the ideas of objectivity and/or the modes of approaching it may differ to some extent. (See Husserl's reference to "objectification" with regard to logical, axiological and practical objects and the pertaining judgments.)

B) According to the difference between a static and a dynamic (intentional-genetic) approach

On condition that the phenomenological reduction has been effectuated we may discern the following options:

i) We are faced with a primacy of theoretical reason in terms of the just-mentioned claim for truth and objectivity as far as this claim is reflectively endorsed ("objectified"). This primacy appears according to a static analysis of intentional constitution.

ii) A primacy of practical reason takes place within the framework of an intentional-genetic ("dynamic") investigation. In this context, practical reason assumes a different meaning as compared with the various manifestations of pre-theoretical practical interest. Now we deal with a second-order practical interest whose formation involves pure reflective activities. Being practically interested in this sense means to strive for the truth with regard to the functions of theoretical, axiological and practical reason and to acknowledge this specific interest as a personal commitment. Doing so, the subject explicitly incorporates a corresponding striving into her self-conception which, again, is based on previously recognizing the positive value of the related end. (Here, it seems fit to call to mind Husserl's hints towards an existential meaning of truth in his *Crisis*.) At this higher-order level, the subject cannot take for granted whatever concrete ideas or ideals may be present to her under the heading of a "practical interest." Every possible practical interest has to be acquired, tested, acknowledged–or as Husserl presumably preferred to say: "durchgearbeitet." This includes making explicit one's commitment to leading one's life according to the ideal of reflection whose realization is acknowledged as a preeminent positive value. Again, the axiological sphere, in a certain sense, remains subordinated to the practical sphere: though a clear and resolute stance towards some particular values is included and presupposed when living a practically interested life as defined above, the attention exclusively rests with the latter. There is no separate attention to the axiological demands that are implied in realizing this specific practical interest. (In other words: the axiological concern is itself guided by the practical interest which is brought forth by means of it. It is not theoretically motivated.) At the second-order level, which is at stake here, being practically interested means to have an explicit stake in the realization of reason–according to all its manifestations and for the sake of itself. What comes to light here is a second-order willing that is not directed to whatever concrete objects or states of affairs whose existence may appear desirable. Rather, I am practically interested insofar as I am willing myself as a reasonably willing subject. Here, reasonably acting is equivalent to acting in an authentic way: an agent who achieves authentic reason lives her life "aus vollkommener Vernunft" (Husserl 2013, p. 180), that is, "is rational in the full sense" (Drummond 2010, p. 443). In this very peculiar sense, it is appropriate to consider an "ethical" transformation of reason and a theory of reason, respectively.

While option A) refers to the overall methodical framework of Husserl's *Ideas* (and other works of transcendental phenomenology) and while option B) enlarges the issue of an analogical and teleological theory of reason by going beyond the limits of a static phenomenology (as represented, among others, in the *Ideas*), the idea of a mutual embracement of theoretical, axiological and practical reason can also be elucidated by more narrowly focusing on §§ 146–153. Relating to this, we may add two further options.

C) According to the difference between lower and higher levels of constitution
Based on Husserl's conception of foundation and stratification analysis mutual embracement can be spelled out as follows:
  i) Claiming that the logical laws are universally valid means that they hold for every possible something, according to the purely formal idea of an object. Hence logic embraces all higher-order founded objectivities too. Among these are axiological and practical objects.
  ii) Every actually or possibly existing object can be positively, negatively or neutrally (*adiaphoron*) evaluated. In this sense axiological reason is universal. It also includes the sphere of logic and practical reason.
  iii) Axiological objects as well as theoretical objects of different sorts can function as ends of willing and striving. Sciences, theories and similar positings can be considered as practical objects. In this sense practical reason embraces axiological and theoretical reason.[43]

---

[43] Note that the idea of mutual embracement, as understood along these lines, does not interfere with the essential nature of the different spheres of reason which does not suffer any change. Cf. Husserl (2012, p. 156): "A logical law covers a law of evaluation logically only insofar as the latter is a law and not insofar as it deals with values. For the axiology as such is about

D) According to the difference between eidetic (pure) possibility and actual manifestation
  i) As long as we refer to the level of abstract designations and positings (formal logic, formal axiology, formal practice) these three spheres are coordinated to each other. Yet as soon as we consider concrete manifestations of possible objects and corresponding acts, a mutual embracement in terms of options A)–C) takes place.

We need not expect the above distinctions to exhaust all possible variants of changing points of views with an accordingly alternating predominance of theoretical or practical reason. However, making explicit the options stated above should improve our understanding of what Husserl means when he argues that a phenomenological theory of reason has to take note of the peculiar interweavings of different types of objects and, accordingly, of different functions of reason. I take it that digging into the issues sketched-above is part of what Husserl has in mind when, at the end of § 148, he states: "Deep and important problems of the phenomenology of reason are attached to the radical clarification of these analogies and parallels." (*Ideen* 295/343)

As far as the idea of a teleology of reason is elaborated in the final part of Husserl's *Ideas,* the following clarification seems appropriate. The multifarious unity, which results from reason's activities and the relating noematic correlates, represents an immanent or rational unity. The relating tendency towards unification is owing to the immanent nature of consciousness. This should be clear with a view to the relation of intention and fulfilment which operates as basic teleological principle.[44] Owing to the diversity of objects that can occur as objects of

---

values and laws of value, not about laws of truth and being in general. The same holds the other way round: a law of value does not cover a logical law axiologically as if a logical law dealt with a statement about values within the logical sphere. This is because logic does not at all deal with values; the notion of value does not appear in it, generally speaking. But truth, after all, is also valued and can be subsumed under predicates of value. As soon as this is the case and as soon as we judge upon this [evaluative interpretation of truth, SR] we find ourselves within the sphere of scientifically relevant values." (Husserl 1912, p. 156, this passage put in brackets in the German original, SR)

44 Cf. *Ideen* 291/338: "Without the concepts of sense, posit, filled out posit (epistemic essence in the manner of speaking of the *Logical Investigations*), there is no way at all of approaching the radical formulation of any problem pertaining to a theory of reason." Since the relation of intention and fulfilment also has been introduced as a determining factor with regard to Husserl's understanding of the analogy of reason, it should be clear that the latter is committed to the peculiar brand of teleology of reason that Husserl advances in his *Ideas*. On the other hand, he should also be ready to argue that the teleological consideration includes reference to the

possible experience and owing to the succession of constitutive levels and the dynamics of the process of constitution, which gradually brings to light manifestations of hidden reason, the teleological core principle of intention and fulfilment unfolds into a corresponding variety of forms. In this vein, the teleological character of pure consciousness brings to bear dynamic aspects of meaning-constitution within the framework of a static phenomenology that does abstain from inquiring into the processes of time-constitution, original association, and so on. These dynamic aspects, moreover, reflect themselves on part of the experiencing subject. From a teleological and multi-level constitutive perspective, the relating descriptions clearly go beyond the well-known abstract determination of the pure ego as a merely formal implication of the structure of intentionality.[45] Husserl describes the latter, among others, as a "process of having in focus, of having the mind's eye on something, inherent to the *essence* of the cogito, of the act as such" (*Ideen* 64/75). In German, the relating process is called the "Blickstrahl," that is, the radiating focus of the pure ego (cf. *Ideen* 105/123). Contrary to such merely formal characterizations, there is a correlation holding between the gradually progressing thing-constitution, on the one hand, and the experiential "enrichment" of the perceiving and embodied subject, on the other hand.[46] As to the latter it should be stressed that the teleologically structured perceptual process is always realized kinaesthetically (cf. Husserl 1997).

It is crucial to note that adhering to a teleological consideration as part of transcendental phenomenology, instead of dealing with a teleological metaphysics, we dwell on a strictly immanent or rational unification tendency (cf. Husserl 2013, pp. 137–263). Relating to this, one further and final demarcation is required. The teleological considerations at issue do not depend on a normative transformation of Husserl's transcendental-phenomenological theory of pure

---

analogy of reason insofar as the former is not meant to talk about a purely formally characterized "thin" notion of consciousness. It rather dwells on a structurally rich and, correspondingly, experientially saturated consciousness which, among others, comprises objectifying acts as well as diverse types of non-objectifying acts. (See, for instance, the opening statement of § 147.)
45 Cf. *Ideen*, § 80. Furthermore, cf. *Ideen* 60/70–71: "[...] it is necessary to characterize the *unity of consciousness* that is required *purely by what is proper to the cogitationes* and, necessarily required, such that they cannot be without this unity."
46 Cf. *Ideen* 304/354: "The *thing* is not something isolated opposite the experiencing subject, as has already become obvious from the indications [...] about the intersubjective constitution of the 'objective' world of things. But now this experiencing subject itself is constituted, in the experience [...], as real, as *human* or *animal*, just as the *intersubjective communities* are constituted as animal communities." As to the intersubjective constitution of things cf. Husserl (1989, pp. 82–95); Husserl (1952, pp. 77–90).

consciousness.[47] Accordingly, it would be totally ill-conceived to refer to these considerations as presenting a guideline for how to accurately make use of one's reason in terms of looking for unification at different levels of conscious activities. The teleology of reason as presented in the final sections of *Ideas I* does not amount to such a normative transformation or "technical" extension that transcends the theory of pure reason. It rather is an original and specific part of this theory which, among others, comprises an intentional analysis of those types of human experiences (i.e., non-objectifying acts) that are usually designated as "normative," for instance, aesthetic, moral or religious experiences. In other words: Husserl's teleology of reason operates within the limits of an eidetic analysis of possible forms of human experience. It shows how reason's activities, at different levels of constitution, tend towards a maximum of explicitness, a maximum of fulfilment (in accordance with the respective kind of intended objects), and a maximum of self-illumination, that is, reflective clarification with regard to the workings of reason. Practicing a teleological inquiry thereby helps to render visible the complex structure of meaning-constitution that is involved in the multifarious manifestations of intentionality. The primary task of phenomenologists is to explain (i.e., accurately describe) how different types of unity can be effective at different levels of constitution by synthesizing different types of manifolds. Yet what does it mean to argue that manifolds of different types of conscious content are organized according to necessary relations that hold from a priori reason? As Husserl makes clear in the final part of his *Ideas* it does not do to merely understand pure (i.e., phenomenologically reduced) consciousness as a complex whole containing manifolds of manifolds whose organization follows a priori laws referring to different types of contents or objects. Rather, it is necessary to go beyond such an abstract account of consciousness. Phenomenologists are expected to show how precisely the interplay between diversity and unity manifests itself with regard to *concrete* types of noeses and noemata. It is this specific attitude towards a philosophical treatment of the manifold/unity issue that is distinctive of Husserl's theory of reason as compared to other traditional philosophical conceptions of reason.[48]

---

47 In his *Logical Investigations* Husserl designated such a normative transformation of a pure theoretical conception (pure logic) a "Kunstlehre des richtigen Vernunftgebrauchs (technology of correct reasoning)." Cf. Husserl 2001a, §§ 13–16.

48 I would like to express my cordial thanks to John Drummond whose critique of my attempt to make sense of Husserl's analogy forced me to get much more deeply involved in the problems at issue. It goes without saying that the author alone is responsible for any obscurities that may have remained. My thanks also go to Rudolf Bernet and Philipp Berghofer for carefully reading and commenting on the penultimate draft of the manuscript.

References

Edmund Husserl

(1952): "Ideen zu einer reinen Phänomenologie und phänomenologischen Philosophie. Zweites Buch: Phänomenologische Untersuchungen zur Konstitution". In: *Husserliana*. Vol. IV. The Hague: Martinus Nijhoff.
(1973): *Experience and Judgment. Investigations in a Genealogy of Logic*. Revised and ed. by Landgrebe, Ludwig. Trans. Churchill, James S./Ameriks, Karl. Introduction by Churchill, James S. Afterword byEley, Lothar. Evanston: Northwestern University Press.
(1983): *Ideas Pertaining to a Pure Phenomenology and to a Phenomenological Philosophy. First Book: General Introduction to a Pure Phenomenology*. Trans. Kersten, Fred. The Hague/Boston/Lancaster: Kluwer Academic Publishers.
(1984a): "Logische Untersuchungen. 2. Bd., 1. Teil: Untersuchungen zur Phänomenologie und Theorie der Erkenntnis". In: *Husserliana*. Vol. XIX, 1. The Hague: Nijhoff.
(1988): "Vorlesungen über Ethik und Wertlehre 1908–1914". In: *Husserliana*. Vol. XXVIII. Dordrecht/Boston/London: Kluwer Academic Publishers.
(1989): *Ideas Pertaining to a Pure Phenomenology and to a Phenomenological Philosophy. Second Book: Studies in the Phenomenology of Constitution*. Trans. Rojcewicz, Richard/Schuwer, André. Dordrecht/Boston/London: Kluwer Academic Publishers.
(1997): *Thing and Space. Lectures of 1907*. Trans. Rojcewicz, Richard. Dordrech/Boston/London: Kluwer Academic Publishers.
(2001a): *Logical Investigations, Volume 1*. Trans. Findlay, J. N. from the Second German edition of Logische Untersuchungen. Preface by Dummett, Michael. Ed. with a new Introd. by Moran, Dermot. London/New York: Routledge.
(2001b): *Logical Investigations, Volume 2*. Trans. Findlay, J. N. from the Second German edition of Logische Untersuchungen. Ed. by Moran, Dermot. London/New York: Routledge.
(2004): "Einleitung in die Ethik. Vorlesungen Sommersemester 1920 und 1924". In: *Husserliana*. Vol XXXVII. Dordrecht/Boston/London: Kluwer Academic Publishers.
(2012): "Einleitung in die Philosophie. Vorlesungen 1916–1920". In: *Husserliana Materialien*. Vol. IX. Dordrecht: Springer.
(2013): "Grenzprobleme der Phänomenologie. Analysen des Unbewusstseins und der Instinkte. Metaphysik. Späte Ethik (Texte aus dem Nachlass 1908–1937)". In: *Husserliana*. Vol. XLVII. Dordrecht: Springer.

Others

Bernet, Rudolf (1979): "Perception as a Teleological Process of Cognition". In: Tymieniecka, Anna-Teresa (Ed.): *Analecta Husserliana* Vol. IX: *The Teleologies in Husserlian Phenomenology. The Irreducible Element in Man*. Part III: *'Telos' as the Pivotal Factor of Contextual Phenomenology*. Dordrecht, Boston, London: D. Reidel Publishing Company, pp. 119–132.

Cairns, Dorion (2013): *The Philosophy of Edmund Husserl*. Embree, Lester (Ed.). Dordrecht/Heidelberg/New York/London: Springer.
Drummond, John (2004): "Cognitive Impenetrability' and the Complex Intentionality of the Emotions". In: *Journal of Consciousness Studies* 11. No. 10–11, pp. 109–126.
Drummond, John (2010): "Self-Responsibility and *Eudaimonia*". In: Ierna, Carlo/Jacobs, Hanna/Mattens, Filip (Eds.): *Philosophy, Phenomenology, Sciences. Essays in Commemoration of Edmund Husserl*. Dordrecht/Heidelberg/London/New York: Springer, pp. 441–460.
Gillan, Garth (1972): "The Noematics of Reason". In: *Philosophy and Phenomenological Research* 32. No. 4, pp. 524–530.
Hampton, Jean (1998): *The Authority of Reason*. Healey, Richard (Ed.). Cambridge: Cambridge University Press.
Kant, Immanuel (1964): *Groundwork of the Metaphysic of Morals*. Trans. and analysed by Paton, Herbert J. New York: Harper & Row.
Korsgaard, Christine M. (2008) *The Constitution of Agency. Essays on Practical Reason and Moral Psychology*. Oxford/New York: Oxford University Press.
Lerner, Rosemary R. P. (2013): "*Ideas I* Confronting Its Critics". In: Embree, Lester/Nenon, Thomas (Eds.): *Husserl's Ideen*. Dordrecht, Heidelberg, New York. London: Springer, pp. 415–431.
Melle, Ullrich (1990): "Objektivierende und nicht-objektivierende Akte". In: Ijsseling, Samuel (Ed.): *Husserl-Ausgabe und Husserl-Forschung*. Dordrecht, Boston, London: Kluwer Academic Publishers, pp. 35–49.
Melle, Ullrich (1992): "Husserls Phänomenologie des Willens". In: *Tijdschrift voor Filosofie* 54. No. 2, pp. 280–304.
Melle, Ullrich (2002): "Edmund Husserl: From Reason to Love". In: Drummond, John/Embree, Lester (Eds.): *Phenomenological Approaches to Moral Philosophy: A Handbook*. Dordrecht: Kluwer Academic Publishers, pp. 229–248.
Peucker, Henning (2014): "Hat Husserl eine konsistente Theorie des Willens? Das Willensbewusstsein in der statischen und der genetischen Phänomenologie". In: *Husserl Studies* (forthcoming).
Rinofner-Kreidl, Sonja (2000): *Edmund Husserl. Zeitlichkeit und Intentionalität*. Freiburg, München: Karl Alber Verlag.
Rinofner-Kreidl, Sonja (2010): "Husserl's Categorical Imperative and his Related Critique of Kant". In: Vandevelde, Pol/Luft, Sebastian (Eds.): *Epistemology, Archeology, Ethics: Current Investigations of Husserl's Corpus*. London/New York: Continuum Press, pp. 188–210.
Rinofner-Kreidl, Sonja (2013): "Husserls Fundierungsmodell als Grundlage einer intentionalen Wertungsanalyse". In: *Metodo. International Studies in Phenomenology and Philosophy* 1. No. 2, pp. 59–82.
Rinofner-Kreidl, Sonja (2014a): "Phenomenological Intuitionism and Its Psychiatric Impact". In: Fuchs, Thomas/Breyer, Thiemo/Mundt, Christoph (Eds.): *Karl Jaspers' Philosophy and Psychopathology*. New York: Springer, pp. 33–60.
Rinofner-Kreidl, Sonja (2014b): "Gebrauchsdinge und wissenschaftliche Gegenstände, phänomenologische Wertungsanalyse und Wertfreiheitsthese". In: Därmann, Iris (Ed.): *Kraft der Dinge. Phänomenologische Skizzen*. Munich: Wilhelm Fink, pp. 193–208.

Rinofner-Kreidl, Sonja (2015a): "Mereological Foundation vs. Supervenience? On How to Phenomenologically Tie Up Moral Experience and Metaethical Theorizing". In: *Metodo. International Studies in Phenomenology and Philosophy* (Special Issue on Supervenience, Fall, forthcoming).

Rinofner-Kreidl, Sonja (2015b): "Disenchanting the Fact / Value Dichotomy: A Critique of Felix Kaufmann's Views on Value and Social Reality". In: Salice, Alessio/Schmid, Hans Bernhard (Eds.): Social Reality: The Phenomenological Approach. Dordrecht: Springer (forthcoming)

Schuhmann, Karl (1991): "Probleme der Husserlschen Wertlehre". In: *Philosophisches Jahrbuch* 98, pp. 106–113.

Sokolowski, Robert (1968): "The Logic of Parts and Wholes in Husserl's *Investigations*". In: *Philosophy and Phenomenological Research* 28. No. 4, pp. 537–553.

Further recommended readings

Brainard, Marcus (2002): *Belief and Its Neutralization: Husserl's System of Phenomenology in Ideas I*. Albany: State University of New York Press.

Crowell, Steven (2001): *Husserl, Heidegger, and the Space of Meaning*. Evanston, Il.: Northwestern University Press.

Crowell, Steven (2006): "Husserlian Phenomenology". In: Dreyfus, Hubert L./Wrathall, Mark A. (Eds.): *A Companion to Phenomenology and Existentialism*. London: Blackwell Publishing, pp. 9–30.

Crowell, Steven (2010): "Husserl's Subjectivism: The 'thoroughly peculiar "forms"' of Consciousness and the Philosophy of Mind". In: Ierna, Carlo/Jacobs, Hanna/Mattens, Filip (Eds.): *Philosophy, Phenomenology, Sciences. Essays in Commemoration of Edmund Husserl*. Dordrecht, Heidelberg, London, New York: Springer, pp. 363–389.

Crowell, Steven (2012): "Transcendental Phenomenology and the Seductions of Naturalism: Subjectivity, Consciousness, and Meaning". In: Zahavi, Dan (Ed.): *The Oxford Handbook of Contemporary Phenomenology*. Oxford: Oxford University Press, pp. 25–47.

Drummond, John (1990): *Husserlian Intentionality and Non-Foundational Realism. Noema and Object*. Dordrecht/Boston/London: Kluwer Academic Publishers.

Drummond, John (1992): "An Abstract Consideration: De-Ontologizing the Noema". In: Drummond, John J./Embree, Lester (Eds.): *The Phenomenology of the Noema*. Dordrecht, Boston and London, pp. 89–109.

Drummond, John J. (2005): "The Structure of Intentionality". In: Bernet, Rudolf/Welton, Donn/Zavota, Gina (Eds.): *Edmund Husserl. Critical Assessments of Leading Philosophers. Vol. III: The Nexus of Phenomena: Intentionality, Perception and Temporality*. New York: Routledge, pp. 31–60.

Drummond, John (2012): "Intentionality without Representationalism". In: Zahavi, Dan (Ed.): *The Oxford Handbook of Contemporary Phenomenology*. Oxford: Oxford University Press, pp. 115–133.

Embree, Lester (1996): "Advances regarding Evaluation and Action in Husserl's Ideas II". In: Nenon, Thomas/Embree, Lester (Eds.): *Issues in Husserl's Ideas II*. Dordrecht/Boston/London: Kluwer Academic Publishers, pp. 173–198.

Embree, Lester/Nenon, Thomas (Eds.) (2013): *Husserl's Ideen*. Dordrecht/Heidelberg/New York/London: Springer.
Klockenbusch, Reinald (1989): *Husserl und Cohn. Widerspruch, Reflexion und Telos in Phänomenologie und Dialektik*. Dordrecht/Boston/London: Kluwer Academic Publishers.
Levin, David Michael (1970): *Reason and Evidence in Husserl's Phenomenology*. Evanston, Northern University Press.
Mohanty, Jitendra Nath (1985): *The Possibility of Transcendental Philosophy*. Dordrecht/Boston/Lancaster: Martinus Nijhoff Publishers.
Mohanty, Jitendra Nath (1997): *Phenomenology between Essentialism and Transcendental Philosophy*. Evanstaon, Il: Northwestern University Press.
Mohanty, Jitendra Nath (1999): *Logic, Truth and the Modalities from a phenomenological Perspective*. Dordrecht/Boston/London: Kluwer Academic Publishers.
Moran, Dermot (2001): *Introduction to Phenomenology*. London: Routledge.
Nenon, Thomas (2005): "Husserls antirationalistische Bestimmung der Vernunft". In: *Acta Universitatis Palackianae Olomoucensis. Philosophica* VI, pp. 237–247.
Rinofner-Kreidl, Sonja (2012): "Moral Philosophy". In: Overgaard, Søren/Luft, Sebastian (Eds.): *The Routledge Companion to Phenomenology*. Routledge: London, pp. 417–428.
Sokolowski, Robert (1974): *Husserlian Meditations and How Words Present Things*. Evanston, Il.: Northwestern University Press.
Sokolowski, Robert (2000): *Introduction to Phenomenology*. Cambridge: Cambridge University Press.
Soffer, Gail (1991): *Husserl and the Question of Relativism*. Dordrecht: Kluwer Academic Publishers.
Welton, Donn (2000): *The Other Husserl: The Horizons of Transcendental Phenomenology*. Bloomington: Indiana University Press.
Zahavi, Dan (1999): *Self-Awareness and Alterity: A Phenomenological Investigation*. Evanstan, Il.: Northwestern University Press.
Zahavi, Dan (2003): *Husserl's Phenomenology*. Stanford: Stanford University Press.
Zahavi, Dan (Ed.) (2012): *The Oxford Handbook of Contemporary Phenomenology*. Oxford: Oxford University Press

Appendix

Ben Martin
A Map of the noesis-noema correlation

At the end of the third chapter of the third part of *Ideas I*, Husserl describes phenomenology as follows:

> Our way of proceeding is that of someone on a research trip in an unknown part of the world, who carefully describes what presents itself to him on its untraveled paths, paths that will not always be the shortest. He is rightly filled with the sure consciousness of asserting what *had to* be asserted according to the time and circumstances, and what, because it is a faithful expression of what was seen, retains its value ever after–even if new research will demand new descriptions with many sorts of improvements (*Ideen* 193/224).

Inspired by this image, I have sought to draw a map of the phenomenological territory uncovered by Husserl in *Ideas I*. I have attempted to do this for a number of reasons. First, for anyone taking his or her first steps into the world of Husserl's phenomenology in general and into *Ideas I* in particular, some kind of road-map would be extremely helpful. Second, beyond its pedagogical function, a map could prove useful in clarifying the relations among the wealth of concepts which Husserl employs. Putting things down on a two-dimensional sheet of paper forces one to grapple with the relations among concepts in a new way. Finally, Husserl himself suggests this very image: of mapping the paths through an unexplored territory.

At the same time, this undertaking brings with it some important caveats. First, any such map must remain open to further development. Husserl himself says as much, as cited above. Second, and more importantly, no map of concepts can be allowed to undermine the essential method of phenomenology, i.e. of proceeding from what is given clearly in intuition. Even though phenomenology, as a science, seeks to pin down the meanings of its terms scientifically and to provide us with descriptions of consciousness "sub specie aeterni," the science of phenomenology must remain rooted in the intuitively given (see *Ideen* 193/224; § 66).[1] This is its principle, the principle of all principles (see *Ideen* § 24). Therefore, with regard to our map of concepts, we will take Husserl's advice concerning all phenomenological investigations: "In the same spirit, we want, in what follows, to be faithful expositors of the phenomenological formations and to pre-

---

[1] Whether this may ever amount to a 'geometry of experiences' Husserl leaves an open question. Cf. *Ideen* § 72–75.

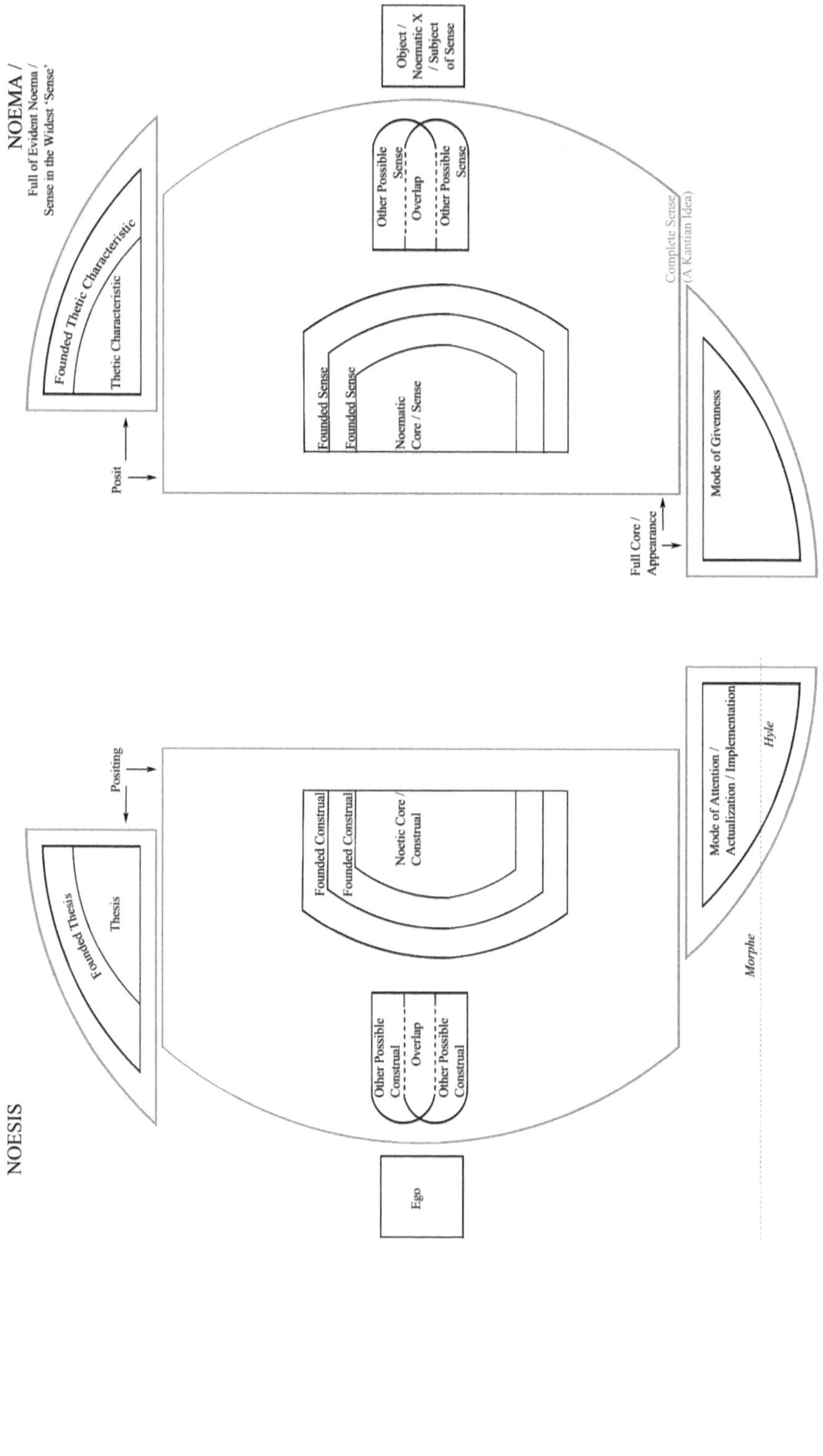

330 — Ben Martin

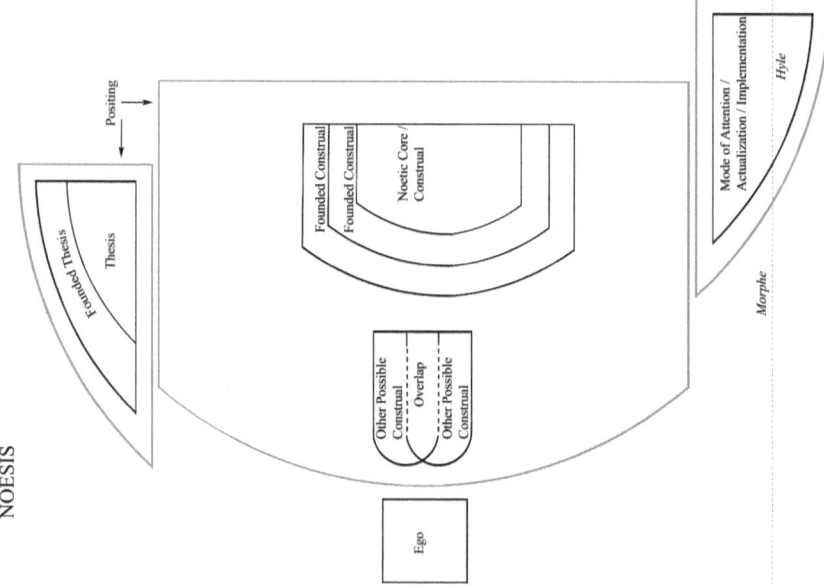

Fig. 1: A map of the noesis-noema correlation

serve, moreover, the habitus of inner freedom even opposite our descriptions" (*Ideen* 193/224).²

Now we may proceed to the map. I would like to address four parts: first, some of the symmetries of the map; second, some of the details of its construction; third, the disambiguation of some common terms; and finally, a brief note on the tripartite structure that we discover in Husserl's descriptions of consciousness. We begin with symmetry because it is the chief purpose of the map to demonstrate the correlations between the components of noesis and noema. The noesis and its parts lie on the left, and the noema and its parts lie on the right. Many of the correlations are immediately obvious: the thesis is matched with the thetic characteristic, the positing with its posit, a number of construals with their corresponding senses. In addition to these, there are two less obvious symmetries, each of which deserves a moment of consideration.

First, the map associates mode of attention/actualization/implementation with mode of givenness. Husserl discusses these in section ninety-two of *Ideas I*. When he addresses the "series of ideally possible shifts [of attention] that presuppose a noetic core and [other noetic moments,]" he writes, "these shifts do not alter the pertinent noematic achievements, and yet they display variations of the *entire* experience" (*Ideen* 182/211–212). He clarifies further: "these modifications ... modify [the] manner of appearance [of what appears] ... [its] manner of givenness" (*Ideen* 183–4/213). This means that, as attention shifts, different parts of an object are brought to intuitive fullness, while, barring disappointments, the sense of the object remains constant. Thus Husserl himself correlates attention and intuitive fulfillment of sense.³

Second, the ego and the noematic x stand opposite one another, outside the areas of construals and senses. The boundaries of the latter area come from Husserl's conception of a 'complete sense' or a 'complete core,' i.e. "the manifolds of every possible 'subjective manner of appearance,' in which [an object] can be constituted noematically as identical" (*Ideen* 267/310). He calls this complete determination a Kantian idea. The area of possible construals corresponds to this. The ego is placed in a box behind this area in order to show that it is not a really

---

2 This habitus of freedom seems to be both one of the most valuable characteristics of the phenomenological method and one of the characteristics which makes Husserl's phenomenology so difficult to follow. Because phenomenology proceeds by faithful description of the phenomena of consciousness, its basic terms and concepts must continuously undergo change and enrichment: thus the need for both a road-map and its accompanying caveats.

3 While mode of attention and mode of givenness are distinguished as parts of noesis and noema, respectively, the division of the two all but disappears in Husserl's treatment of evidence. For this reason, these are the corresponding parts placed closest on the map.

obtaining component of the noesis. Of the pure ego, Husserl writes, "*In no sense can it count as a really obtaining piece of*...experiences themselves *or an inherent aspect of them*"; rather, it is a "not constituted...*transcendence in immanence*" (*Ideen* 105/123).

On the noematic side, Husserl's x plays a similar role. It is the subject behind, distinct from, and presupposed by all "shifting and variable 'predicates' [or senses]" (*Ideen* 260/302). Yet he also calls this "*a central, inherent noematic aspect: 'what stands opposite us'*" (*Ideen* 260/302). This suggests that the noematic x does correspond to the ego, but the relationship is possibly asymmetric: the x belongs among the "layers in the noema[:] sense, subject of sense [or noematic x], thetic characters, [and] fullness," while the ego does not belong among the really obtaining components of the noesis (*Ideen* 288–289/335).

Next, let us examine a few details of the map's construction. First, the nested construals on the right side of the noesis represent a series of implemented, founded construals. Husserl calls the corresponding series of founded senses on the noematic side the object's "*entire What*," i.e. the whole, many-layered sense through which the object is given (*Ideen* 186/216). The construals on the left represent other possible construals, and so other possible senses also appear on the noematic right. These construals and senses also overlap, due perhaps to confusion. Certainly construals and their corresponding senses may empirically run together in any individual consciousness, but Husserl notes that careful attention to the regions of being to which an object belongs reveals the *ideal* possibility of "meshing and partial overlap," exemplified in the way the region of 'soul' is founded upon the region of 'material thing' (*Ideen* 32/38).[4]

Second, the mode of attention/actualization/implementation is associated with *hyle*; the two are placed in the same shape. According to Husserl, "[hyletic] data are animated by '*construals*' ... and in this process of being animated, they perform the '*exhibiting function*' or, better, in unison with that animation they make up what we call the 'appearing of' color, shape, and so forth" (*Ideen* 73/

---

[4] With regard to the map, one may ask: why is one set of construals and senses nested while the other set overlaps without such nesting? Let's take, for example, my apprehension of a fellow classmate. In the personalistic attitude, I attend to the physical features of his face in order to constitute the further senses of his facial expression and the thoughts and feelings this reveals empathetically. In the naturalistic attitude, I attend to the same physical features of his face but instead constitute further naturalistic, rather than personalistic, senses. Thus, these two possible experiences of my fellow classmate share certain basic construals, but because they arise in different attitudes and therefore constitute unrelated further senses, they may be said to overlap, but they are not nested within one another. Senses constituted in a single attitude, on the other hand, may more likely be said to be nested within one another.

86). While construals play a central role in the appearances of objects, by endowing them with their senses, the *hyle* in particular makes possible intuitive givenness of objects and provides the matter to which the ego's attention may turn. Therefore, we find that our concept of attention is inseparable from our concept of *hyle*. This comes with a caveat: Husserl claims that "*the sensual [layer] has nothing of intentionality in itself*" (*Ideen* 165/192). Thus, *hyle* does not share in the intentional character of attention. But, as long as we make a note of this–and indicate its distinction from the rest of the noesis–nothing prevents us from linking these two aspects of the noesis. For this reason, mode of attention/actualization/implementation and *hyle* have been placed together on the map.

Third, the concept of *morphe* has been associated with the rest of the noesis. In § 85, Husserl describes *morphe* as the affordance of sense. He writes, "intentional experiences stand there as unities *through the affordance of sense* ([but] in a quite expanded sense)" (*Ideen* 166/193 my italics). Thus, Husserl does not identify *morphe* with construal, which is responsible for sense more narrowly understood; rather, both 'affordance of sense' and *morphe* refer to all of the noesis that is not *hyle*. Though the distinction of *morphe* and *hyle* is a traditional one in epistemology, its minor appearance on the map indicates the degree to which Husserl surpasses it with regard to the complexity of his analyses.

Fourth, full core/appearance has no correlate on the side of the noesis. This happens simply because Husserl does not attend to the combination of noetic core and attention in his later analyses in *Ideas I*.

Finally, the map affords us with an opportunity to examine Husserl's sometimes confusing usage of the terms 'core,' 'fullness,' and 'sense.' For the most part, Husserl uses the word 'core' to refer to the noematic *core*, in contradistinction to the thetic characteristics. However, even this simple use is difficult to grasp from a first reading of *Ideas I*, and for the following reason. While Husserl treats the doxic modalities and their corresponding ontic modalities extensively, the significance of the 'thesis' is only grasped through an appreciation of the entire set of analogous series of doxic, axiological, and practical modalities. These represent a very important portion of the formal region and the *mathesis universalis*, and their categories are essential to the life of consciousness; they become especially relevant in their connections to attitudes and to the life-world. But they do not appear on the scene until late in *Ideas I*. Furthermore, because Husserl does not expand much beyond the belief characteristics in *Ideas I*, one might mistake the thetic components of noesis and noema as a relatively thin dimension of consciousness. This would undermine Husserl's notion of a 'core' of sense, against which to distinguish the thetic characteristics, in every intentional experience. Therefore, it is worth noting the meaning of 'core' in the 'noematic core,' i.e. the sense, as distinguished from the thetic characteristics. For these reasons, the noematic core is identified with sense and is placed at the center of the noema.

Husserl also makes use of the notion of a 'full noematic core.' He calls the full core "precisely the full concreteness of the relevant noematic component ... the *sense in the mode of its fullness*" (*Ideen* 262/304–305). This is straightforward. Whenever Husserl uses the term 'fullness' he refers to intuitive fulfillment, i.e. evidence. The full noematic core remains a noematic core because it does not include the thetic characteristics. Further, Husserl uses the phrase 'full noema' to refer to "*the entire What ... that is judged* and taken ... with the [thetic] *characterization*, [and] in the *manner of givenness* in which there is *consciousness of it* in the experience" (*Ideen* 186/216–217). In other words, the full noema includes the thetic characteristics; the sense, in all its layers; and its intuitive fulfillment: it is the full noematic core plus the thetic characteristics. These concepts must be distinguished with care, because Husserl also calls the full noema "the 'sense' (understood *in the widest way*)" (*Ideen* 186/217). Because Husserl has already employed the phrases 'full noema' and, elsewhere, "evident posit," this widest understanding of sense need not be used often, in order to avoid confusion (see *Ideen* 234/271–272).

Corresponding to the noematic core is the 'noetic core.' This phrase appears only once in *Ideas I*. Husserl writes that "shifts [in attention] ... presuppose both a noetic core and generically different inherent [noetic] aspects" (*Ideen* 182/211–212). Just as Husserl identifies noematic core with sense, it follows that the noetic core is what he has named the construal. Furthermore, just as the noematic core is distinguished from the thetic characteristic, so too should the noetic core be distinguished from 'generically different inherent noetic aspects,' which, because these differ from attention, appear to be the noetic theses.

In addition to the noetic and noematic cores, Husserl also writes of a 'core of attention' and a 'core of insight, or evidence.' In § 92, he describes the core of attention as "the *entire* noematic content"; this content, he writes, is "characterized [according to a certain mode of] attention [and is not] preserved over against any modifications of attention" (*Ideen* 184/213). Unfortunately this appears to be an ambiguous phrase: what counts as noematic *content*? As indicated, it is determined, at least in part, by the mode of attention. At this point in *Ideas I*, Husserl has not yet introduced the doxic modalities, so by 'entire noematic content' he may here refer only to the sense and the mode of givenness of an object. If this is the case, then the 'core of attention' may be identified with the 'full noematic core,' since it includes both sense and its fulfillment, and this continues to exclude from the 'core' any thetic components. If not, it is difficult to tell what justifies Husserl's use of the notion of a 'core.'

Husserl may also employ this understanding of core when he writes the following: "A thing is necessarily given in mere '*manners of appearance*,' and necessarily is thereby a *core of* '*what is actually displayed*,' surrounded, in keeping with the respective construal of it, by a *horizon of [both]* '*what is co-given*,' *but not genuinely*, and a more or less vague *indeterminacy*" (*Ideen* 77/91). Here Husserl describes the 'core of what is actually displayed' in terms of an object's mode of givenness accompanied by the horizons determined by its sense; this appears to be exactly what he calls the 'full core.'

Husserl describes the core of evidence as the "*unity of rational positing with what essentially motivates it*" (*Ideen* 272/316). Thus it is the unity of the posit and its fulfillment, or, in other words, the full noema. Because thetic characteristics influence what counts as evidence for a posit, this 'rational' core is no longer a core because it excludes thetic components of the noema.[5] Instead, such a core is perhaps a core because it excludes any unmotivated givenness; it pertains only to intuitive fulfillment rationally sought. Thus this notion of a core differs from the above notions because it concerns Husserl's concept of reason, as opposed to his more basic phenomenological descriptions of the components of conscious acts.

Finally, we may step back and appreciate a striking quality, revealed by the map, of Husserl's description of consciousness: its simplicity. Each side (noesis and noema) has three main components, and under these few, broad headings fall nearly all of Husserl's descriptions of the phenomenon of consciousness. First, the central component: the noetic core and its corresponding noematic core. Construals constitute the modes of intuition and kinds of attention: perception, recollection, anticipation, phantasy, empathy, depiction, and designation; and their accompanying noematic horizons: typical; temporal, e.g. retentional, protentional, recollective, anticipatory; spatial; and thematic, e.g. internal, external. These act-components may envelope one another as well as other noetic moments; their corresponding senses and themes exhibit the same layering.

Second, there are the noetic theses and their corresponding noematic characteristics. The noetic theses apply to any noetic core or other noetic moment on any level of constitution. They include the original doxa, the various doxic modalities, the emotive and volitional correlates of these, as well as the neutralizations of them all. Applying theses to theses allows for more complex modalities,

---

[5] Thetic characteristics influence what counts as evidence when, e.g., they characterize a sense as really possible, so that fulfillment should be sought through imagination, or as presently real, so that fulfillment might be sought through perception.

such as denial, affirmation, and assumption. Finally, all theses may be transformed into some modification of an original doxic thesis.

Last is attention and its consequent mode of givenness. The ego's focus may pass through any number of layers of noetic moments, either directly or reflectively. These modes range from full apprehension to unnoticed background intuition, with a further mode of simple inattentiveness. Corresponding to these are the various noematic modes of givenness with their respective degrees of clarity.

Although *Ideas I* does not include Husserl's most developed thoughts on time, association, attitude, intellect, interest, and other topics, these main divisions of the aspects of consciousness provide a useful map for approaching much of his phenomenological project. Centered upon his key insight into the noetic-noematic structures of consciousness and the corresponding components of each, Husserl sketches out for his readers and students in *Ideas I* many of his most important concepts and many areas of research for the whole movement of phenomenology. Merely mapping these concepts of phenomenology is not yet *doing* phenomenology, just as mapping a newly discovered land differs from the discovering and the experiencing of that land. Hopefully, however, this paper has rendered a valuable cartographic service for all of those future explorers who seek entrance to the long hidden territory of phenomenology.

Authors

Dan Dahlstrom: Professor of Philosophy, Boston University (USA).
James Dodd: Associate Professor of Philosophy, The New School for Social Research (USA).
Nicolas De Warren: Research Professor of Philosophy, Husserl Archive, Katholieke Universiteit Leuven (Belgium).
John Drummond: Robert Southwell, S.J. Distinguished Professor in the Humanities and Professor of Philosophy, Fordham University (USA).
Robert Hanna: Co-Director Contemporary Kantian Philosophy Project, University of Luxembourg (Luxembourg).
Burt Hopkins: Professor of Philosophy, Seattle University (USA).
Hanne Jacobs: Assistant Professor of Philosophy, Loyola University Chicago (USA).
Sebastian Luft: Professor of Philosophy, Marquette University (USA).
Claudio Majolino: F. Fillon Professor in Philosophy of Language, Université Lille 3 (France).
Ben Martin: Doctoral Candidate, Loyola University Chicago (USA).
Dermot Moran: Professor of Philosophy, University College Dublin (Ireland).
Sonja Rinofner-Kreidl: Professor of Philosophy, Karl-Franzens-Universität Graz (Austria).
Andrea Staiti: Associate Professor of Philosophy, Boston College (USA).
Dan Zahavi: Professor of Philosophy and Director of Center for Subjectivity Research, University of Copenhagen (Denmark).

Index

Act
- emotional   223, 289
- evaluative   14, 297f., 308
- intentional   99–105, 114, 200–202, 217, 260, 289
- volitional   14; 250; 308; 335
Adorno, Th. W.   134, 149
Alighieri, Dante   75f.
Aristotle   6, 37, 39, 49, 247, 273, 276
Armstrong, David Malet   27
Attention   73, 78, 84, 88, 101f., 185f., 195, 202, 208–221, 249, 315f., 331–336
Attitude
- dogmatic   64–66, 144f.
- natural   8f.; 54–55; 69–71, 73, 76–78, 83f., 86–90, 97, 104, 108f., 112, 115, 134–139, 144f., 149, 153, 159, 161, 197f., 198, 203, 208–211, 227, 232–236, 239, 248, 315, 317
- naturalistic   54f., 64, 113f., 332f.
- personalistic   113f., 332f.
- phenomenological   9, 33f., 70f., 86, 109, 144f., 188, 198, 208, 210, 226, 315, 317
- philosophical   65, 144f., 311
- propositional   21
- psychological   18f., 198
Avenarius, Richard   71–73, 77
Averchi, Michele   5

Belief
- Hume on   79–81
- and holding for real   4, 25, 56, 81, 209, 211
- and positionality   90, 251
- and the general thesis   77–84, 91, 248
- as moment of experience   24, 81, 83f., 84, 90, 245, 253, 259, 264, 279, 303
- neutralization of   249–251
- suspension of   88, 91, 137, 188, 226–227
Benoist, Jocelyn   250
Berkeley, George   217, 241
Bernet, Rudolf   113, 199, 287, 322
Beyer, Christian   178–181
Bimbenet, étienne   230

Boehm, Rudolf   142
Boltzman, Ludwig   107
Bolzano, Bernhard   16, 204, 221
Brainard, Marcus   97, 250
Brentano, Franz   17, 27, 49, 79, 99–101, 107, 197, 203, 208, 213, 215, 230f., 249
Brough, John   27

Cairns, Dorion   4, 313
Carnap, Rudolf   73, 196
Carruthers, Peter   179, 181
Cartwright, Richard   21
Cassirer, Ernst   1, 238f., 242f.
Chapman, Andrew   53, 62
Chisholm, Roderick   18f.
Cicero, Marcus Tullius   69
Consciousness
- as absolute   3, 120f., 125–129, 141f., 160, 181, 189, 225
- as a tag-end of the world   137
- as *fundamentum inconcussum*   127, 129f., 160
- as immanence   106f., 108–111, 129, 143f., 208, 237, 253
- as *residuum*   137
- higher-order theories of   27, 178f., 181
- phenomenology as science of   2, 95, 97, 108, 119, 133f., 137, 139, 142f., 151–155
- philosophical significance of   8, 10, 15–16, 65f., 119, 121, 126, 190
- pre-reflective vs. reflective   123, 178, 181, 185f.
- pure   96, 107f., 114, 119–122, 128–129, 134–139, 141–143, 151–155, 159, 162, 189, 225, 229, 231, 237, 240, 321
Correlation
- of consciousness and world   23, 184
- of experience and object   22, 114, 124, 151, 321
- noetic-noematic   18, 195, 200, 203, 212, 219, 221–223, 238f., 241–243, 257, 259, 261, 295–297, 302, 311f., 329–331, 333
Crane, Tim   11, 19–23, 25, 258f., 261
Crowell, Steven   54

Dahlstrom, Daniel O. 10, 13, 120, 159, 247, 262, 273, 295
Derrida, Jacques 3, 14, 242
De Santis, Daniele 120
Descartes, Rene 86–89, 106, 127, 135, 137, 139, 159–161, 163
de Warren, Nicolas 3, 7, 84, 225, 244
Dilthey, Wilhelm 77, 138
Dodd, James 159
Doubt
– Cartesian doubt vs. epoché 86–89, 135, 139, 159 f.
– and skepticism 58, 89, 212
– as modification of perception 62, 85, 210, 245, 247 f., 279
Dretske, Fred 17
Dreyfus, Hubert 3
Drummond, John J. 3, 13, 18, 25, 27–29, 99, 102, 110 f., 114, 200, 202, 218 f., 257, 261, 267 f., 299, 309, 319, 322

Ego
– psychological 101–103
– pure 96, 126, 135, 139–141, 145–148, 202 f., 321, 332
– as Kantian regulative idea 140, 147
– as „radiating center" of acts 140, 202, 215 f., 321
Elsenhans, Theodore 2
Emotions
– emotive vs. conative acts 29, 289, 291 f.
– philosophy of 27–29
Empathy 29, 113, 183 f., 335
Epoché
– phenomenological 69–70, 89–91, 95, 114, 134, 198, 211 f., 254
– psychological vs. universal 91, 210
– and reflection 90 f.
– as act of freedom 86
Essence
– exact vs. morphological 174 f., 203
– formal vs. material 7, 35 f., 46, 48
– intentional vs. epistemic 200, 283, 320 f.
– knowledge of 51, 63 f., 171
– pure essence or *eidos* 42–45
Evans, Gareth 235

Evidence (*Evidenz*)
– adequate vs. inadequate 277
– and types of clarification (*Verdeutlichung vs. Klärung*) 166
– and reason 269 f.
– assertoric vs. apodictic 276 f.
– as confirmation 279–281, 284
Experience
– and *cogito* 73, 198
– intentional (*intentionales Erlebnis*) 20, 102, 108, 195, 197, 199, 201 f., 206., 212 f., 215, 222, 257, 262, 280, 291, 296, 333

Fantasy
– and eidetics 44, 170, 203
– and fictional objects 25
– and neutrality 225, 250
– as non-positional consciousness 82
– as vital element of phenomenology 170–172
– free 203
Farges, Julien 89
Ferrarin, Alfredo 6
Fichte, Johann Gottlob 82
Fink, Eugen 97, 149, 248–251
Fodor, Jerry 17
Føllesdal, Dagfin 3, 17–19, 21 f., 202, 260–262
Frank, Manfred 11, 178 f.
Frege, Gottlob 204, 260

Genuisas, Saulius 74
Genus/species
– and region 35 f., 47, 115, 311
– generalization/specification 43
– highest genus 40, 43, 45, 46–49, 115, 173
– lowest difference 36, 40, 45, 47
– subordination vs. subsumption 43 f.
Geometry
– and phenomenology 173, 175, 329 f.
– as material eidetic science 62, 64, 142, 171, 173
Gérard, Vincent 6
Gloy, Karen 178
God 16, 80, 127 f., 136, 141 f.

Gurwitsch, Aron 267 f.
Gyllenhammer, Paul 29

Hanna, Robert 51, 53 f., 62
Heffernan, George 276
Hegel, Georg Friedrich Wilhelm 145, 151, 275
Heidegger, Martin 2 f., 13 f., 28, 33, 48 f., 54, 77, 106, 127, 152, 187, 190, 285
Held, Klaus 11, 62, 85, 136, 141, 179, 316
Herbart, Johann Friedrich 79, 274
Hermberg, Kevin 29
Hopkins, Burt C. 89, 119, 129
Hopp, Walter 111, 263
Horizon
– and perceptual experience 23 – 26, 73 – 75, 125, 203, 206, 210 f., 214, 261, 267 – 269, 335
– as non-inferential 74
Hume, David 79 – 81, 217
Hyle
– and morphé 133, 203, 215
– as sensuous stuff 187, 197, 212 f., 218, 223, 234, 236 f., 241 – 243, 332 f.

Idealism
– Platonic 60 – 62
– psychologistic 58 – 60
– subjective 109, 241 f.
– transcendental 2, 13, 54, 66, 83 f., 142, 151, 189, 199, 238
Idea
– in the Kantian sense 140, 147, 174, 268, 282 f., 331
Ideation 43 f.
Imagination see Fantasy
Individual (*Individuum*)
– and *concreta* 35 f., 47 – 49
– and individuation 34 f., 38 f.
– and *tode ti* 35 – 40, 42
– as the primary object (*Urgegenstand*) 45, 48 f.
Intentionality
– as essential feature of consciousness 16, 98, 107 f., 197, 206
– evaluative and volitional 14

– as the main theme of phenomenology 15, 187, 225, 239, 322
– and minding 23
– and noesis/noema 240 – 245, 261 f.
– and perception 106
– non-ontological approach to 19
– vs. intensionality 18 f., 261
Intersubjectivity 14 f., 29, 321 f.

Jacobs, Hanne 91, 95, 113, 189
James, William 28, 98, 159
Judgment
– existential 82, 86
– theory of 4 f., 24, 79

Kant, Immanuel 4 f., 52, 66, 70, 75, 79 – 81, 83, 139, 141, 143, 145, 151, 155, 228, 235, 237 – 240, 242 f., 268, 273 f., 282 f., 303 – 310, 314 f.
Kern, Iso 134
Kinaesthesis 76, 321
Klein, Jacob 11, 129
Korsgaard, Christine 28, 186, 309
Kortooms, Toine 87
Kriegel, Uriah 27
Külpe, Oswald 107
Kusch, Martin 53

Landgrebe, Ludwig 86, 159
Lavigne, Jean-François 83, 97, 230
Lerner, Rose Mary 287
Lévinas, Emmanuel 3, 252, 254
Locke, John 27, 217
Logic
– and the reduction 87, 135 f., 142, 149, 232
– formal 142 f., 222, 270, 320
– pure 136, 142, 149 – 151, 269, 322 f.
– transcendental 151, 274
Lotze, Herrmann 274
Luft, Sebastian 83, 95, 133 f., 136, 146, 149, 151, 197, 210

MacDonald, Paul 90
Maier, Heinrich 2
Majolino, Claudio 1, 6, 33, 39, 49, 99, 112, 120, 299
Marion, Jean-Luc 127, 161

Martin, Ben   329
Martin, Wayne   80
Marx, Karl   120
McDowell, John   151, 235
McIntyre, Ronald   3, 16–19, 21f., 202, 219, 260–262
Meaning
– and intension   18f.
– and logic   40
– as species   17, 258–260
– as transcendent *Sinn*   18, 128, 202, 215, 231, 234, 240, 245, 257, 260, 262
– bestowal of   213
Meinong, Alexius   17, 251
Merleau-Ponty Maurice   13, 27f., 183, 226, 248
Messer, August   2
Metaphysics   3, 54, 56, 60, 62, 77, 99, 127, 129, 140, 142, 145–148, 161, 274, 321
Method
– analytic   18
– Cartesian   88f.
– in the sciences   1, 58, 105, 152
– empirical   52, 152
– inductive vs. deductive   1, 173
– phenomenological   14, 87, 91, 95f., 98, 107, 109–112, 123, 133–137, 155, 159–168, 175, 177, 182f., 190, 195–197, 203, 225–228, 232, 296, 319, 329, 331f.
Michalski, Krzysztof   241
Mill, John Stuart   1
Modification
– attentional   84, 185, 208, 216
– doxic   84, 245–250, 253, 279, 333–336
– intentional (perceptual)   88, 152, 170–171, 214, 216
– neutrality   9, 212f., 248–254
– reflection as   90, 123f., 183, 212
Mohanty, Jitendra N.   3, 39, 283
Moran, Dermot   53, 77, 195

Natorp, Paul   2, 140f., 146–148, 216
Naturalism
– and scientism   64, 66
– and skepticism   56, 58, 65
– empiricist   57, 63–66
– Husserl's critique of   16f., 53–57, 126, 129f., 298, 300
– positivist   15, 57, 64–66, 275
– scientific   53, 57f., 63–66
– as worldview   121
Nenon, Thomas   6
Neo-Kantianism   1f., 123, 138, 235, 238–240, 243
Neutrality   3, 9, 212f., 248–254, 292
Noema/noematic
– and noesis   18, 114, 133, 187, 195–197, 200, 203, 206, 212–214
– as abstract   202, 222, 260f.
– as intensional entity   260–262
– core   203, 214, 218–219, 222f., 249, 259, 264, 333–335
– full   219, 222, 234, 259, 264, 268, 334f.
– modifications   248
– sense   207, 213, 230, 234, 238, 243, 252, 257, 260, 264–266, 268f.
Normativity
– categorical   51–53
– Korsgaard on   28, 309f.
– transcendental-phenomenological (TP)   53–64, 66

Object
– as determinable X   220, 264–266, 268
– noema and   257–270
Ontology
– formal   6f., 33–37, 270, 303f.
– fundamental   48, 187
– material   6f., 95, 142
– meta-regional   7
– headless   33, 48

Patocka, Jan   159
Perception
– and belief   80f.
– and values   75
– as original consciousness   81, 167, 216, 219
– outer vs. inner   5, 178, 180
– veridical vs. illusory   24, 62, 90, 104, 111
Peucker, Henning   292
Phenomenology
– eidetic   145, 153

– constitutive 8, 301
– pure 95, 97 f., 108 f., 114 f., 119 – 124, 225 f.
– transcendental 8, 15, 48 f., 97 f., 108, 115, 129 f., 153, 189, 198, 239 f., 314, 321
Planck, Max 107
Plato 33, 129 f., 149, 276
Pradelle, Dominique 5 f.
Proudhon, Pierre-Joseph 120
Psychology
– and phenomenology 1 f., 8, 95 – 99, 109, 153
– as empirical science 55, 95, 161
– behaviorist 17
– phenomenological 8 f., 153
– psychologism 1 f., 17, 53, 59, 144, 240, 298
– rational 100, 102, 143
– reconstructive 141, 146, 148
– without a soul 99 f.

Quine, Willard van Orman 17, 33, 48

Rang, Bernhard 15, 26, 107, 169, 171, 246, 289, 297, 305, 336
Reason
– and fulfillment 5, 29, 288 – 290, 335
– axiological 290, 317, 319
– Husserl's theory of 5 f., 15, 257, 269, 287 f., 290, 293 f., 304, 310 f., 314, 315, 319 f., 321
– practical 290 f., 293 f., 297 f., 302, 306 – 310, 313, 315 – 320
– theoretical 5, 274, 289, 291 f., 297, 302 – 305, 310, 313, 315, 317, 328 f.
Reduction
– eidetic 198
– phenomenological 9, 22, 86, 133 f., 159, 189, 197 – 198, 204, 206, 237, 254, 262, 288, 318
– transcendental 8, 134
Reflection
– and pre-refective self-awareness 26 f., 123, 178, 181, 184 – 186
– as self-fission 186
– critique of 182 – 185

– phenomenological 163, 165, 168, 188, 190, 203, 208, 227 – 228, 230, 232, 239, 263, 121 – 125
– psychological 95 – 98, 100 – 104, 108, 113, 115, 120 f.
Region
– and ontology 3, 6, 35 f., 47 f., 115, 142, 294, 299, 302
– and *Urgegenständlichkeit* 6, 35
– material vs. formal 6 f., 333
– primordial 49
Rickert, Heinrich 2, 77, 243
Ricœur, Paul 70 f., 78 f, 81
Rinofner-Kreidl, Sonja 6, 102, 287 f., 290, 293, 299, 307, 309, 313 f.
Romano, Claude 86, 88
Rosenthal, David 27

Sartre, Jean-Paul 3, 13, 27 f., 178, 184, 252 – 254
Scheler, Max 28
Schuhmann, Karl 4 f., 13, 102, 133, 302
Science(s)
– human vs. natural 1, 77, 136 – 139, 229, 283
– phenomenology as a rigorous 2, 133, 155
Scotus, Duns 39
Searle, John 19 f., 22, 258
Sigwart, Heinrich Christoph Wilhelm 274
Simmel, Georg 77
Smith, David Woodruff 3, 16 – 19, 21 f., 27, 33, 202, 219, 260 – 262
Soffer, Gail 107
Sokolowski, Robert 3, 202, 297
Soldinger, Emanuele 71, 73
Sommer, Manfred 71, 73
Sowa, Rochus 42, 95, 152
Staiti, Andrea 1, 69, 86 f., 91, 291
Stein, Edith 6, 227
Steinmann, Gustav 2
Ströker, Elisabeth 91, 95, 97
Stumpf, Carl 107, 203, 242
Suarez, Francisco 34

Teleology
– and intentionality 29, 266, 269, 288

– and reason   29, 287–289, 291–294, 303, 308 f., 316, 319–323
– in nature   141
Time-consciousness   85, 140, 180 f., 203, 254 f.
Trizio, Emiliano   120
Tugendhat, Ernst   178
Turnbull, Colin   168
Twardowski, Kasimir   17

Validity
– absolute   149–150
– logical   52, 56, 292
– as subject matter of philosophy   1
– reality as   87, 109, 138, 184, 189

Vienna Circle   53 f., 57, 196
von Herrmann, Wilhelm   177, 190

Welton, Donn   3, 150, 202
World
– as experienced   72, 75–77, 83, 88, 137, 151
– as immune to doubt   78, 85
– historical   9
– life   9, 55, 77
– natural concept of the   9, 77
Wundt, Wilhelm   107

Zahavi, Dan   3, 95, 110, 142, 177 f., 183, 185, 190

www.ingramcontent.com/pod-product-compliance
Lightning Source LLC
Chambersburg PA
CBHW051207300426
44116CB00006B/455